Hugh Callan

Wanderings on Wheel and on Foot through Europe

Hugh Callan

Wanderings on Wheel and on Foot through Europe

ISBN/EAN: 9783744662345

Printed in Europe, USA, Canada, Australia, Japan

Cover: Foto ©Andreas Hilbeck / pixelio.de

More available books at **www.hansebooks.com**

WANDERINGS:

ON WHEEL AND ON FOOT THROUGH EUROPE.

LONDON:
PRINTED BY GILBERT AND RIVINGTON, LIMITED,
ST. JOHN'S HOUSE, CLERKENWELL ROAD.

WANDERINGS

ON WHEEL AND ON FOOT

THROUGH EUROPE

BY

HUGH CALLAN, M.A.

> "Though sluggards deem it but a foolish chase.
> And marvel men should quit their easy chair,
> The toilsome way, and long, long league to trace,
> Oh! there is sweetness in the mountain air,
> And life, that bloated Ease can never hope to share.
>
> — BYRON

LONDON
SAMPSON LOW, MARSTON, SEARLE, & RIVINGTON
St. Dunstan's House
FETTER LANE, FLEET STREET, E.C.
1887

[All rights reserved]

PREFACE.

IT is fast becoming a settled conviction with us moderns, the heirs of ingenious contrivances for rapid communication, that, if we would really know each other as we exist in various countries, we must, after all, take to the simple crural contrivance that nature has given us.

When the exalted ones of olden times wished to learn for themselves what life was, they left their seats of state and mingled among the people in some simple guise. We think more of Odysseus that he came home as a beggar-man, and of Caliph Haroun Alraschid that he went about as a merchant. King Alfred as minstrel in the Danish camp, Cœur de Lion as the Black Knight in "Ivanhoe," James V. of Scotland as Snowdon's Knight or "Gudeman of Ballengeigh," appear to us as truer men than in their royal robes. Rail and steamboat are *our* seats of state, which we do well to leave at times.

The surest and best mode of seeing the world and its ways is to travel on foot: and whether our aim be geography, ethnology, poetry, or philanthropy, no better mode can be found. Goldsmith, Rousseau, Wordsworth are standard examples of its benefits.

But there is another mode nowadays, which rids us of the slowness and monotony of walking, yet keeps us to the lanes and highways and among the people—and that is cycling. No elaborate administration nor formidable escort is needed for the cycle: *solus cum solo* a man may wander at will, wherever there is a passable road. Nor are there wanting shrewd men who look upon cycling as the best cosmopolitanizer yet discovered. Frontier lines are disappearing before it; the youth of all countries are being brought together and united in a common spirit of manly sport and a desire to visit all lands where men have thought and wrought or still live and work. Around the cycle class and race may well be forgotten in the thought: "*Homo sum: humani nihil a me alienum puto.*"

It is from a belief that this book may do something towards furthering a more general taste for the kind of travel that is its subject that it is now given to the public. It is an attempt to describe places, things, and persons, as they appear to one who seeks to enter into their spirit. Its objects will be gained, if, while it amuses, it enlightens, on the subject of foreign parts and foreign ways, those who cannot afford to witness them for themselves; and if, by the information it gives as to the facility, cheapness, and advantages of such travel, many are stimulated to go and do likewise.

CONTENTS.

Part I.

ON WHEEL DOWN EUROPE FROM THE GERMAN OCEAN TO THE ÆGEAN SEA.

CHAP.		PAGE
I.	Setting out—The passage from Leith to Hamburg	1
II.	Hamburg to Berlin—Reflections on Prussian character and customs	2
III.	In Berlin	8
IV.	On the road to Dresden, and in Dresden	12
V.	Saxon Switzerland—Lost in the mountain forests	17
VI.	From the Erz Mountains to Prague, and in Prague	20
VII.	Lower Bohemia—Some nice receptions	25
VIII.	A dangerous ride and fall	28
IX.	Austria proper—Vienna	31
X.	Along the Danube into Hungary—Austrian imperial unity	35
XI.	On the track of Stevens—Hungarian picturesque variety	38
XII.	Buda-Pest—Hungarian aspirations	42
XIII.	Incidents on the road along the Danube below Buda-Pest	46
XIV.	Through Sclavonia and "the military-frontier"	50
XV.	Semlin and Belgrade—Servian people and politics	54
XVI.	Scenes in Servia	59
XVII.	Servian scenery—"New Servia"	64
XVIII.	Sore treatment at the Turco-Servian frontier	68
XIX.	Receptions in Turkey	71
XX.	Difficulties of travelling in Lower Turkey—In custody	76
XXI.	"Speed the parting guest"—First sight of the Ægean	80
XXII.	An estimate of Eastern life	83
XXIII.	In Salonica	89
XXIV.	On the isle-spangled Ægean	93
XXV.	At Volo	98
XXVI.	From Volo to the Piræus	102

CHAP.		PAGE
XXVII.	The Piræus	105
XXVIII.	A trip to Ægina	109
XXIX.	Modern Greek spirit—A contrast with the past .	112
XXX.	A pilgrimage under difficulties to Marathon . .	116
XXXI.	Corinth—The earthquake	118
XXXII.	Scenes about Patras	123
XXXIII.	Home again	126

Part II.

ON WHEEL UP THE RHINE VALLEY, FROM AMSTERDAM TO GENEVA, AND BACK BY ANTWERP.

I.	From Carlisle to Hull	128
II.	Arrival in Holland	131
III.	Along the paved Dutch roads	135
IV.	Over the Dutch border into Rhenish Prussia . .	139
V.	Through the "Black country" of Germany . .	141
VI.	Beyond the smoke into the regions of art and romance .	143
VII.	Where every rock has its *ruin*, and every ruin its legend	147
VIII.	By the "links" of the Rhine	154
IX.	From Heidelberg to Strassburg	159
X.	Farewell to the Rhine	164
XI.	Into sight of the snowy Alps	167
XII.	From Berne to Geneva in twelve hours—A lively run .	172
XIII.	Northwards—"*Spectat ad septentriones*" . .	178
XIV.	From the Juras into Alsace-Lorraine . . .	183
XV.	The last stage homewards	189

Part III.

"ON THE TRAMP" IN FRANCE AND BELGIUM.

I.	To Newhaven—My life in Paris	191
II.	On the road to Brussels	193
III.	Sleeping in the fields	196
IV.	Scenes by the way—A strange lodging . . .	199
V.	Across the Belgian border—Working my passage .	203

WANDERINGS: ON WHEEL AND ON FOOT THROUGH EUROPE.

Part I.

ON WHEEL DOWN EUROPE FROM THE GERMAN OCEAN TO THE ÆGEAN SEA.

CHAPTER I.

SETTING OUT.

ON the 3rd of July, 1886, I rode from Glasgow round by Falkirk to Leith.

After a three hours' visit to the Exhibition at Edinburgh, we (my bicycle and I) got berthed on board the steamer for Hamburg.

If any one wants to see the mean and ludicrous side of humanity, let him be ready and able to mix with all classes. He will then see how those who are most servile to their superiors are those who abuse most and tyrannize most over their fancied inferiors. When I first came on board I thought of going second class; accordingly my wheel and I were treated, chiefly by the stewards, with cold neglect and ill-disguised contempt. But on my deciding that three nights passed on bare boards would not be a fit preparative to a long ride, and so taking out my cabin passage, lo! all was changed. The official superciliousness became obsequiousness; neglect became servility, for no passenger was served with more attention than I was: so, to show my appreciation, I rewarded all their efforts by *not* giving the customary tip.

WANDERINGS:

CHAPTER II.

HAMBURG TO BERLIN—REFLECTIONS ON PRUSSIAN CHARACTER AND CUSTOMS.

IT was early in the morning of the 6th when we got free of the ship at Hamburg. The money-changers' offices were not yet open : so I mounted my steel steed to have a run round the greatest commercial city of the Continent and have a look at its far-famed suburbs. When I reached the bridge at the inner lake (Binnen-Alster) the boats and steamers were already busy bringing in the people to business. Not thinking that the Aussen-Alster lake would extend beyond a mile at the outset, I set off to ride round it. But at each turn another stretch of water came in sight, other gardens and wooded walks, and rich tastefully built villas, each embowered in its little forest of verdure and blooming flowers. The romantic beauty and naturalness of these suburbs, including the Zoological Gardens, made me forget that I had made a *détour* of nearly ten miles, instead of one or two as I intended. After an admiring visit to St. Michael's and St. Nicholas' spires—two of the finest and tallest in Europe—I made for the high road to Berlin. But, as usual in cities, it was no light task to find that : people know the road to the next town or village, but to such a far-away place as Berlin only the more knowing few can direct you. However, to him who would be a wanderer, the difficulty often is how to get really "wandered": his instinct usually keeps him in the right direction, even when the pretended knowing, but really ignorant ones, would send him on the wrong.

It did not augur well for either speed or comfort, that the first three miles of the road were of cobble stones. The usual consolation in such a case is the pavement: but here that was impracticable, for the uniform of the military-police, omnipresent in Germany, glanced through the trees at every turn. At length relief came in the shape of a splendid road-surface with scarcely a hill. Already, however, the universal fault of foreign roads, and of too many British ones, began to show itself. The macadamization has originally been well enough laid, but sand and gravel have been most used since then, with the inevitable result that in dry weather the surface becomes a long bed of sand, and in wet, a mud bank. For nearly all the 180 miles to Berlin, the road passing through the great northern sandy plain, has been at first splendidly laid; but the fault mentioned has caused an accumulation all along of from one to three inches of dust. That and the long gradual ascent—there is about 100 miles of a constant rise—make the journey annoying; nor do the long stretches of ungainly cobbles near and through the numerous villages tend to lessen the annoyance. I do not see why a hard stone road could not be kept up throughout, and in the end prove cheaper, cheaper for both man and beast.

The first evening saw me quartered in the lovely town of Ludwigslust. Its church and stately palace with its galleries of treasures in art, and its exquisitely kept gardens and grounds, much delighted me. One young man would have me off to present myself to some Glasgow ladies residing there and often to be found in the park. After some difficulty I explained that our stiffer customs would not allow of such a step on my part. It is always a matter of wonder to foreigners why British people do not seek one another's company when abroad; they do not see that we are more self-contained, and thereby stronger-minded than they are. I remember once in Brest playing at billiards in a room where were also three Englishmen; all the time the barmaid kept calling out to us, "Messieurs, you are countrymen!" but, to her expressed disgust, we paid no heed. Another time in Brittany, a Londoner and I faced each other for hours in the train, until a Frenchman, not being able to stand it any longer, took the trouble to introduce us. I am afraid the story told of the Frenchman who declined to save another man from drowning because they had not been introduced, ought rather to be told of an Englishman.

Next day, at a village, I had an interesting talk with a country wight, who had spent some years in the United States, and come back again to his native parish. He thinks that no one is better off out there than they are here at home, if only the home government would tax less heavily. From every one it is the same story, "We are too heavily taxed to keep up the military and the empire;" and everywhere there are signs of want and discontent. One meets here almost as many tramps and beggars and poverty-stricken families as in Britain, only in Germany they are certainly better clad, owing probably to the milder climate. In time, no doubt, the imperial system may and should work right. But, in view of an increasing population, we in Britain are more securely constituted, even socially, than they can ever be in Germany under their present system. One great benefit it has produced, I grant, namely, it has welded together the divided states, and, by creating common laws, common coinage, and a common customs union (*Zollverein*), has made travelling and commerce immensely easier. But, as matters stand at present, the people of the various minor states take pains to impress upon you their distinction one from another, and from the Prussians especially. Even in Prussia they look regretfully back to the old free times when each state bore only its own burdens. In Berlin, where there is also the heavy municipal taxation, I have heard householders declare that it would have been a finer thing for them if, instead of Frederick William and Bismarck going to Paris, Napoleon III. had come and realized the cry à *Berlin*. They say they never were so well off as when under the first Napoleonic rule. Vivid recollections still linger among the people of that terrible struggle with the French. They remember its privations, its horrors and its cruelties; they remember the long trainfuls of dark-skinned Algerian prisoners packed in open trucks, divided man from man only by frozen snow, some sitting with open, stony eyes, stiff and stark in death, some, when lifted out, falling helpless or dead on the ground; they remember the train-loads of gold bars from France, which were to bring them peace and plenty, but which brought them only increased taxation; and they ask what has become of these.

The Prussians are a fine people on the whole, and deserve to succeed. They are kindly and frank, manly and spirited. Though they are often harsh in aspect and address, and stolidly haughty in their bearing, yet they show little or nothing of that in their private intercourse with you. The surpassing activity they show in every part of their public life, in education and manufacture, in agriculture and in military training, is more than enough to cover all the blemishes of custom and character that still appear to an observant foreigner and remind him of the Goths. In nothing better than in the life of the youth can the superiority of Prussia over other continental nations be seen. The boys and girls get liberty to play, and are not afraid to use it. I have sometimes seen here what can scarcely be seen outside of Britain—a regular stand-up school fight. There is certainly life among the rising generation of Prussians. Sometimes out from a village a boy has run along by my wheel for upwards of a mile, just for sport—that true British word. All this spirit has come from, or at least, has been deepened by the war successes. The poor, defenceless bicyclist has real cause to curse inwardly this superabundance of spirit, for too often it is exercised in tormenting him. But he must remember that mischief-making, especially among the youth, is a strong sign of a rising or successful nation.

A good way to prevent success from making people over-weeningly cruel, is to have them use a code of courtesy towards one another, and towards strangers, as, for instance, was done when chivalry prevented feudalism from degenerating into the tyranny of barbarous force. Now, there is much of this courtesy practised by the Prussians. While they do not carry their politeness into petty formalities, nor set it over themselves in the way the French do, as a thing outside of them, to which all must conform, they observe a much larger set of polite forms than we do in Britain. It is a fault if you enter or leave a beer-shop or restaurant without saying "Good-day," or uttering some similar greeting, and those inside are expected to answer you. This custom is all very good in principle, but irksome to the individual. In practice it comes to this: as the response is seldom forthcoming, the person entering looks as if he were muttering some charm against evil, and leaving, he looks as if he were saying, "I've had enough of you;" or, if you happen to be seated near the door and think it uncivil-like not to respond, then, what between answering incomers and outgoers, you will speak more than you will eat and drink. Every one who passes you on the road raises his hat or greets you in some way. One morning I saw a pretty sight illustrative of this: a score of little girls going to school met me on the road, and each was holding up the skirt of the dress of the one that went before her. The leader of the string said *Tag*, and courtesied as she said it. The others in succession did the same. The courtesy passed over them like a wave, and their *Tag* sounded so like the Scotch *tak* (take), as much as to say, "Come down and take a kiss," that my heart warmed to them, and I was about to realize the fancy, when the school bell rang, and the poetic string broke into twenty pieces.

Much more interest than I expected was excited by the appearance of me and my wheel. It was quite evident, from the number and nature of the questions put to me by the people who crowded around, and from the frequent shying of the horses, that cyclists did not wear the roads much there. Now I had been told (by Germans) that cyclists swarmed about Berlin and the roads leading to it; but in all Prussia I did not pass a single wheelman on the road. Of course there are cyclists and cycling clubs, but they are evidently afraid to wear out their machines or themselves, and so are not *Radfahrer* (wheelfarers) except in name. But even with only a little sport-spirit, what a difference it makes in an ordinary German young fellow! In the small town of Kyritz, the local club president sang out to me as I passed his window, took me into his house, and entertained me. Then we mended a wound in the wheel tyre, in which process I sliced off the top of my middle finger with a penknife which is at present, having been bartered for bread, undergoing penal servitude for life among the hands of the unspeakable Turk, no doubt in atonement for its treacherous assault on my person. How this president came by the British name of Richard Adams is a puzzle to me, as it is to him. Thinking that his might be an analogous case to that of the immortal Kant (which name is still found in Glasgow and other parts of Scotland), whose grandfather was Scotch, we tried to uncover the past; but, as there seemed no hope of a solution till we were verging rather near the original Adam, we gave it up. He sent one of the club members to escort me a bit on my way. The young man he gave me showed in every essential the spirit of a Briton. We set off in grand style—he with jacket off and knee-bands loosed, and I fully dressed and with about 12 lbs. of baggage in my pockets and in the knapsack behind. But a stiff headwind and a dusty road soon made him show his true skin, for instead of coming ten kilometres, as he had said he would, he stopped at five.

However, the Germans have made a good start, and I can see enough in the rising generation to make me wish to prophesy that before very long they will throw off still more their national phlegm and sluggishness, and strive to excel in all active, manly sports. The schoolboys asked me more questions about riding than all others did put together. Not only so, but when they learned I was English, they would ask me in English. I do not say that they succeeded in their linguistic attempts, but I do say that one would have to search long and late before he found an English schoolboy who would even have the courage to air the little German he might know.

CHAPTER III.

IN BERLIN.

EARLY on the morning of the 8th, I got into Berlin. After the soft roads it was a great delight to get on to the hard, wide, well paved streets, where one can go at full speed without any risk of a collision or a stop. But before I reached the Hamburger Thor, I was pulled off and informed that riding in the city was forbidden. Well, I never! But there is no use in grumbling, any more than there is in arguing. Submit, submit; it is the imperial decree: and no society of Germans have yet learned to question that, even though in this instance, as in many more, it is destitute of liberty and of common sense. Why, I know of no other city in Europe wherein cycling could be pursued with greater comfort and with less danger to traffic. The streets are wide and straight, and all the principal ones are paved with asphalt, and so long that you can often ride one or two miles without once turning a corner. Indeed, when I looked away down the two and a half miles of Friedrichstrasse, the temptation became too strong. Braving officialdom, and at the same time trying to evade it, I did not actually mount, but with one foot on the step and the other on a pedal, I pushed my way along as far as Belle Allianz Platz. The police evidently were at a loss what to make of that new style of propulsion, and in their doubt let me pass unchecked.

As long as you do not outwardly transgress their many laws and byelaws, the soldier-police are fine fellows towards you (they have some splendid men amongst them), but transgress these ever so little and they become a most uncompromising set of petty tyrants. Never was there a people so police-ridden and so much in terror of the police as the Prussians now-a-days. I was resting against the brim of a fountain in the Lustgarten, wondering how much of the wealth and decoration around me there in the Palace, Museums, Cathedral and Arsenal, was due to the French gold, when a policeman disturbed my reverie by driving me rudely from the place. If he took me for a Socialist, then I forgive him. But this and similar interference leads me to think that there is less individual liberty in Berlin than in Paris, little enough as there is there. Berlin is a fine city, no doubt : but it is too regularly built, too much planned-out for my taste. The Thiergarten was the only place that surprised and pleased me. However, this opinion may not go for much, as a Scotchman is proverbially ill to please. Let then the case of the Thiergarten stand as a rebuke to those who would maintain that he is never pleased. They say that much of the war-indemnity has gone to beautify the city ; but a simpler explanation of its expenditure has been suggested to me, namely, Berlin is always "on the Spree" and is year by year getting farther on it. In connection with this growth, it is an ominous fact that, although the city is spreading, the population in 1881 was over 61,000 less than in 1878. Is this a result of the military oppression?

The militaryism in Berlin and in all the towns within fifty miles of it is appalling. Everywhere are soldiers of every rank and arm parading about, off or on duty ; everywhere regiments on the march—foot, horse, and artillery : everywhere the clang of arms and blare of trumpets. Truly it is an iron rule. But if all be true that I heard clandestinely discussed (politics in Germany is a contraband topic) about the terrible losses on the German side, about them having lost in killed and wounded greatly more than the French, then the Prussians have need to keep up this iron rule and have reason to dread another conflict with France. Yet, as I watched several regiments of horse defile into barracks from morning drill, all covered with sweat and dust as they were; I could not but doubt if ever France could succeed in any " war of revenge " that may yet be. In all France I have not seen soldiers half the match of those stalwart, hardy, country-bred horsemen. For the sake of France I hope Prussia has not many more like them. In several villages I passed through, it was a mathematical treat to watch the infantry drilling in the market-place or on the green. Large bodies of men worked together through the various movements with the precision and speed of machinery. A sense of strength and solidity arose from the sight, as if a finished machine, perfect in all its parts, were before you.

But it is a wonder to me that such a military people have not better horses, or, rather, do not treat better those they have. Even their war-horses might claim kinship to Rozinante, for like her, they are almost " *tantum pellis et ossa.*" Although the land is all nearly level, yet it takes two horses to pull a vehicle that in Britain would only take one. Nothing could show more clearly the degenerate state of horses there than this almost universal yoking of them in pairs. Their draught-horses are about the skinniest, most ready-to-drop-like wretches conceivable. Though they tell me there is a branch in Berlin of the Cruelty Prevention Society, it surely cannot have force enough for any good. The first thing it should do is to cause the authorities to remove the asphalt from Friedrichstrasse, Leipzigerstrasse and Wilhelmstrasse, or at least to make it coarser, like what it is in London. Until that is done, it must remain a constant source of pain to every humane person to watch the struggles of the horses to keep their feet as they are lashed along the slippery streets. In summer time the watering-cart contrives to make matters worse, and then it is a case of horses falling every fifty yards. It puzzles me how the people can endure such sights. It was with a sense of relief that I read an eloquent newspaper leader condemning similar inhumanity towards horses, and ending up with the appeal, "*Ihr gute Leute, habt Erbarmen!*" (Good people, have pity.)

If ever the Prussians are to be the greatest nation, they must first alter or abridge their drinking customs. From early to late all classes keep on their potations. It is all the more dangerous that nobody thinks it ever injurious. The beer certainly helps to make the men heavy and big, but it also keeps them brutish, to be which is their natural tendency. I think there is no place in Europe where the beershops are so noisy. Everybody talks as loud as he can, and all together. A Prussian country beershop is the nearest approach possible to Pandemonium. Now, the result of all this drinking is quite apparent: corporeal inflation begins in most cases as soon as a man passes thirty. When in such a state, men have little wish to be active; and were it not for the present iron military rule, the nation, I believe, would lapse into sluggish indolence. They are themselves quite alive to the ugliness and the danger arising from their universal drinking habits. In their *Ulk* (like our *Fun*) there was a sketch of a common type of German obesity. A very disgustingly fat man is leaning over a trough, into which also a very fat pig is poking its nose. Two little boys are playing in the back of the yard One says, " Yonder's my father." Says the other, " Which ? "

CHAPTER IV.

ON THE ROAD TO DRESDEN, AND IN DRESDEN.

WHAT a pity we do not plant more fruit-trees by the roadsides in Britain! Some philanthropist has in this a practical opening for his zeal. For thirty miles the Dresden road is lined with cherry-trees, as are most roads of Central Europe. I helped myself to the fruit as I rode along. Better would it have been for me if I had not; for when I had done over sixty miles, the region of my stomach and liver had become hard as stone, and was causing me acute pain at every motion. So we crawled along through the thick mud which the rain had formed, till at twilight we got into a small inn. Some of the children and I slept in a large room, evidently used also as a dancing-hall, for it had an orchestral stand. But it was long past midnight before I closed my eyes, for guests whom the storm had driven in came noisily about the room to see and discuss the machine and the man who was "sure to be murdered by the barbarous Turks." Next morning, suffering an agony of pain, I staggered into Sonnenwalde. A pleasant name and a pleasant spot is Sonnenwalde (Sunnywoods); but the incessant rain all the time of my sojourn there belied the name. Much against my will, as it is against my custom, I here consulted the doctor, who is family physician to some Count that has his chateau hard by—I never think of inquiring the names of German counts and princes; one would need to engage a private compartment in one's memory for that alone. After a deluge of German technical medical twaddle, I made out that a cherry stone had lodged itself comfortably in my *Bauchfell*, and that a long period of absolute rest could alone remove it and prevent it from proving fatal. He would give me no sanction to continue my journey, but ordered me back home. However, he "reckoned without his host," and ignored the recuperative power of a Briton's constitution. For three days, therefore, I was a prisoner and limited to a vegetarian diet. I was not to stir, I was not to study. What was I to do? In my despair, as many a great man has done, I took to verse. Yes; I made a stanza, and sent it home to a friend. Yet, strange to say, it did not please me, for I could find neither solace in the sentiment nor merit in the work. It was pure torture thus to lie shelved in a sleepy German village, forced to keep company with stupid boors and drivelling old men, who would sit all day long in the *Gasthaus* smoking foul-smelling tobacco out of dirty long pipes, grinning at the poorest of jokes and pestering me with the insanest of questions. Still, what with watching the swallows and the pigeons busy on the belfry and roof of the modest church across the way, what with admiring the silvery speech and graceful ways of the landlord's blue-eyed, fair-haired daughter, and hobbling now and then next door to have a chat with the apothecary, the time went smoothly by.

When at last I set out again, it seemed as if some fate were still resolved that I should not do my tour. For the heavy rains of the previous days had made mud of the sandy roads, and to crown all, I took what I conceived to be a short road to Dresden, but which turned out to be only a forest track. However, I kept on, sometimes riding, oftener pushing, over endless plains of sand many inches deep, and through dark, broad forests of fir and oak. No wonder the Prussians are fair and sandy-haired, being born and bred amid such sand! All day long it rained thick and heavy, not the moderate-sized rain we get usually at home, but great heavy drops, each about enough to wet a square inch, and thousands of them coming down close together. Still I kept on, wet in every part to the skin, the water making channels for itself down between my clothes and my skin and gushing out at the points of my shoes. My very watch was flooded in my pocket, and declined to go farther. Not a creature was abroad. So, after crossing into Saxony, I could scarcely believe my eyes when I saw the unmistakable tracks of a bicycle. By-and-by, a figure ahead loomed through the mist and the driving rain; for all the world it looked like Sancho Panza seated on his donkey. It was a heavy, thick-set, burly-bearded German slowly plodding along on an old rusty "Kangaroo." The rain and wind had plainly put him out of humour, for all I could get out of him was something about *Hundewetter*, and that I should never get to Dresden that day. If I had told him my final destination and that I was British, ay, British "to the backbone," for my machine is a "*British* Challenge," he might have believed I could get to Timbuctoo that day if only my mind were bent thereon. As it was, however, my mind was not bent on getting even to Dresden; and what little resolve I had was sadly shaken by the sight of peasants crowding in doorways, laughing and jeering at me as a madcap to keep the road in such a deluge. At length the terrible weather and approaching darkness cowed me at Grossenhain. Here the hostess of the Rothes Haus, pitying my saturated condition, made me doff my wet clothes and don a suit of her son's, who was away at College. Then she placed me snugly in the family's own dining-room, and I assumed for the nonce the place to which my borrowed feathers entitled me. Much had been told me of the hospitality and *Freundlichkeit* of the Saxons. I, for one, have no fault to find on that score. They are, to my liking, the most genuine race in all Germany. It may be said that this liking arises from prejudice because the Saxons settled in Britain: well, I am glad they and not another German race came. It was in Saxony that Luther and the first heroes of the great Reformation fought the battle of religious freedom. Moreover, the Erse blood that is in me still cherishes a secret antipathy towards the Sassenach who robbed my Irish forefathers of their ancestral domains. Therefore my liking should be just.

After faring sumptuously on roasted pigeon and *omelette sucrée*, I smoked my pipe and drank my beer, while the two daughters of the house did their best to entertain me in conversation, now in French, now in German. We discussed the social economy of the various nations, the merits of the French dramatists, and the mysteries of Goethe, and altogether spent a merry and profitable evening. The mother was a tall, stately person, as like a genuine English lady as ever I saw a foreign woman; and the daughters took after the mother.

As next day it was still raging a perfect storm, I left my steed behind, and, armed with a borrowed umbrella, went by rail to Dresden. There are few cities with such beautiful scenery around it as Dresden. The long succession of green, wooded hills circling around it, most of them exquisitely built on with chalets and villas and chateaux, the heaths and groves, the mountains and valleys, and the grand Elbe coursing between, all combined with the domes and spires of the rich city, make a most romantic and enchanting spectacle. But withal, how poor would the place be without the noble museums, palaces and churches, with all their inestimable treasures of art, called into being by the fostering spirit of centuries of royalty! How poor would man's social life still be had all men all along the ages possessed the much-belauded equality of socialism! We may reckon that in such a case there would be little either of art, science or comfort now in the world. Under such a stinted *régime* where would be the Royal museums and libraries, the St. Pauls', the St. Peters', the Louvres, the Versailles, the Windsors, the Westminsters?

"Allow not nature more than nature needs,
Man's life's as poor as beast's."

Of course, my time in Dresden was passed mostly in the picture galleries, lost, as I was, in admiration and reverence before many noble paintings, but, "let me whisper in your lug," also sick tired of the endless array of crosses, nails and scars, blood and gashes that form the theme of most. In the greater irregularity and picturesqueness of Dresden than of Berlin, and in the more interesting appearance of the people, I strove to forget that I was still in a region subject to the bark and bite of Bismarck; but various sights and sounds, and chiefly the word *Kamerun* (the German form of Camaroons) startled me back to the ugly truth. It is amusing to observe how much, how absurdly much, the Germans make of this Camaroons affair. In Berlin thay have built of stone a panorama (save the word! for all it comprehends) of *Deutschen Colonien*, chiefly of *Kamerun;* and thousands flock to gaze lovingly and proudly upon it. There is a drink advertised and sold all over Germany called *Kamerun-Liqueur;* there are *Kamerun* confections, *Kamerun* tobacco, *Kamerun* match-boxes, *Kamerun* handkerchiefs, and even *Kamerun* hats. Really I did not know that the natives were so far civilized, or so luxurious as to possess sweets and hats. One would fancy it were some second India, instead of a miserable little patch of a corner got by fraud and massacre. But this massacre the Germans call a *battle*, and in every little town you are thus invited to enter some show of it: "This way, ladies and gentlemen, this way to the great *Kamerun-Schlacht!*"

CHAPTER V.

SAXON SWITZERLAND—LOST IN THE MOUNTAIN FORESTS.

ON the 14th I took regretful leave of my amiable hostesses of the Rothes Haus at Grossenhain. For twenty miles the road was like a ploughed field, but beyond Dresden, as far as Königstein, it was as pretty a spell of hard road as could be desired. At Pirna the road seemed to end in an abrupt mountainous ridge; but it wound up the steep face of the cliff commanding the town and topped by the fortress of Sonnenstein, now used as a lunatic asylum. Really this is an admirable and unselfish arrangement for catching the German fools before they escape into Austrian territory: and no more appropriate retreat could be discovered for those frequent cases of lunacy in which the head lies uneasy under the weight of fancied royal crowns. After a long pull up the steep, we got on to a long plateau. Here was a grand sight on every side—a long sweep of horizon, the Elbe, dotted with boats, rushing on its course between high red and yellow cliffs crowned with red-tiled houses and lordly castles, and then the majestic rock and fortress of Königstein as it towers frowningly, and seems to challenge its taller neighbour Lilienstein across the deep Elbe valley far below, a thousand feet and more. Down, down, down went the road here, so long and so steep that I began to tremble for my neck, if I had had time even for trembling; then along lovely banks by the riverside, as fine to my eyes as the Rhine, till it swerved abruptly southward, up by a tumbling, roaring stream. The overhanging rocks, the fir and pine trees waving and sighing overhead, the smell of the timber, the startled wild birds screaming through the air, the mountain flowers, and chief of all the "bluebell," took my thoughts and my heart with them back to the hills and dales of "bonnie Scotland." After I had ridden, upwards, ever upwards, for miles, a woodman advised me to change my course. It was then late in the afternoon, and rain was threatening. He said I ought to stay overnight at the inn in Schneeberg, a few yards farther up. But my energy for the day was not yet anything like expended; so I did not take his advice. There are three classes of men whose advice it is unsafe to reject: a sailor's on the sea, a shepherd's on the hill, and a woodman's in the woods. Ah me! I found it so this time. But I gained thereby an additional store of "that sad wisdom which folly breeds." Very soon I had to dismount and push my wheel up the rugged, stony, narrow mountain wood-road (*Waldweg*), and for ten miles I could not mount again.

When about a thousand feet up, I looked back through a gap in the forest, and the most gorgeous scene I ever beheld lay stretched before me. The peaks of the Erzgebirge, mountains and valleys, one behind another, all thickly clothed with forests, lay far and wide, all aglow with the full glory of the setting sun. Here and there a patch of yellow grain, or a wreath of smoke ascending, showed signs of human presence. But for these, the solitude would have been oppressive. Above me, in solitary grandeur, a thousand feet and more precipitously, rose a peak of crags (the Höhe Schneeberg, 2275 ft.), inclosed, as in a picture, by a rainbow superbly vivid. My way lay right round them and over their shoulder. Darkness came on apace and found me wandering in those awful woods. Thunder rolled among the hills, and lightning gleams, shooting across the sky, revealed the terrible magnificence of the place. By-and-by the road broke into two paths; up one I pushed, but it became so steep, so narrow, and so deep with sand that I retreated and followed the other. Desperately I pushed on through the foot-deep sand, till the sweat coursed down my body, though the wind was keen and chill. Over stagnant pools, loose rocks, and fallen timber we scrambled many a weary length till again the road parted into three. Sick at heart, I threw myself down among the soft prickly shrubs that lined the path, and thought with "the wandering poor Fitz James":—

"Some mossy bank my couch must be,
Some rustling oak my canopy."

Then as I felt how much harder would be my couch than his, and as my senses were leaving me, the cry of a wild animal struck my ear. I had heard that wolves were not unknown in the mountainous parts of Austria, and all the stories of belated travellers being devoured, darted with startling vividness through my brain. I lit a match, and read half-past ten on my watch. What was that dull glitter not far ahead? It was not wolves, but the wire fence that divides two great empires. On a rough stone near it I deciphered, by my fingers, on one side the word SACHSEN (Saxony), on the other BOEHMEN (Bohemia). The fence was about ten feet high, and in a tumble-down condition; the gate, through which I passed, a child could open. Surely no frontier could be crossed with less bother, as far as the actual barrier is concerned, than this between Germany and Austria. But my troubles were by no means yet at an end. For many miles I laboured on until ready to drop. Had it not been for the sight of a wooden cross raised over a mound, I should, after all, have succumbed to sleep and fatigue, and lain down. But the thought that some poor victim of the wolves lay buried there, and the fear lest I should become another such, inspired me with new strength to push on. At last a faint light glimmered away down in a valley. After passing through another high wire fence, we were at the light. It shone from the first house of a village; but, as it was now after midnight, the people would not admit us. The door of a house farther down being open, in went my wheel and I, only to be rejected again. The honest folks appeared not to fancy the look of my poor steed; and it unfortunately could not speak up for its own harmless character: it was the first of its kind ever to pass that way. Only after begging for admission through the whole straggling hamlet, waiting sometimes ten minutes before my knocks were answered, did I find a family bold enough or kind-hearted enough to give me shelter from the rain that was now coming down in floods. The house was a sort of inn or eating-house for woodmen and sawyers, and the village was Maxdorf. The housewife was up late, busy firing the week's batch of brown loaves, else I might have had to lie outside all night. The nice warm loaf I chose from the great oven, and the jug of coffee and milk they gave me brought eloquence to my tongue, as I told my adventure to the wondering household. That night, though I slept on a hard bare couch, I did not hear the "voices of the forest" in the tumultuous chorus of wind and rain.

CHAPTER VI.

FROM THE ERZ MOUNTAINS TO PRAGUE, AND IN PRAGUE.

WHEN daylight came, I got initiated into the mysteries of Austrian money, and, at the first lull in the storm, ventured forth. The road now ran very steeply down, so much so, that great patience and tact were needed to keep the machine from running off with itself and me behind it holding it back. Had it been a raft, we might quickly have glided down, so deep and full were the watercourses on the road. We reached the Elbe at Bodenbach, where the cataracts were roaring and foaming, and the rain pouring in torrents. We crossed the chain bridge to the pleasant town of Tetschen, where is Count Thun's fortified chateau with its beautiful gardens. Then what terribly rutty, narrow roads, what crossing of bridges and ferries till beyond Aussig! Much annoyance and delay arose from the narrowness of the roads in this part. Every quarter of a mile a waggon and team of oxen would block up the way, or it might be a herd of swine, many hundreds in number and consolidated through fear into one dense pack, that would compel me to dismount and stand by till they passed. Aussig, as the birthplace of the painter Raphael Mengs, I had hoped to find an old-world town; but the coal-dust from its traffic has begrimed its streets and houses so as to obliterate whatever poetry and romance it ever had. Being a firm believer in the moulding influence of early surroundings, I continued looking for some beautiful or striking object which might have first stirred the soul of the painter. With joy I discovered such in the picturesque cones of the Mittelgebirge, the chief of which is Donnersberg (2670 ft. high), studding all the horizon to the south. Here every spot holds memories of historical struggles or sufferings, some endured for dominion, as in the Thirty Years' War and the Seven Years' War, some for conscience, as in the brave but ineffectual Hussite war. All that day it was hard work to "prick the sides of my intent," for time after time, overwhelmed with recollections from history and fiction (Rienzi, "the last of the tribunes," was imprisoned near here), I dismounted to lie on some conspicuous bank and let my mind revel in images of the dead past when those hills and valleys before me were ablaze with the pageantries of chivalry and the pomp of war. But, once arrived on the solid highway at Lobositz, opportunity to look around disclosed to me some of the grandest, most romantic scenery in Europe. All the thirty miles through Schlan on to Prague it is up steep hill after steep hill and down again, with scarcely a level break at all: and all the way on every side stretch out long glorious views of rich, undulating country, bedecked with green and yellow fields, and castle-crowned peaks glowing in the sun, with villages of red-roofed houses environed with woods clustering beneath. The roads about here are tantalizingly numerous, and free of any milestones or signposts to direct the wayfarer; and it is astonishing how little the people (even less than in Germany proper) know of the various roads, and distances, and even of the nature of the country. Time after time they have grossly deceived me. At Lobochowitz on the Eger, out of a crowd of loungers in the market-place I could get no definite information about the best road to Prague. So I left them disputing about it in their own Bohemian, and took the road that pleased myself. Half-way up the steep side of a wooded ridge, a young man, whom I saw "to be somebody" from the way the passing waggoners saluted him, accosted me. He was a student of law at Prague, but home for the vacations. On learning that I hailed from Britain, he was all eagerness to have me spend the night with him at his father's farm. Not prevailing on me in German, he tried what effect the sounds of my native English would have upon me. His ridiculous mistakes had the effect of putting me into the best of humour. There is something intensely more amusing in an educated foreigner's attempts at English—in his tendency to meaningless or mysterious high-sounding phrases, —than there is in a common person's. He too gave me wrong notions about the nature of the roads. He said the road to

Prague was level, and so many kilometres; whereas it turned out to be nothing but an unbroken succession of long steep ups and downs, and twice the distance he had said it was. This shows one great harm railways have caused. People now-a-days do not know the roads and lie of the land as their fathers did; and on the Continent they have not yet learned, as we in Britain have, to counteract this harm by an extensive practice of cycling. The ridge on which our conference took place was the first of the Lobocher Gründe, an extensive series of ravines that run parallel for many miles, and look like some colossal field ploughed up into furrows by some colossal plough.

Certainly this was the land of Bohemia, and no mistake. Besides the beautiful variety of the country, the people are most interesting in manner and costumes. Real live Bohemians wander about the streets and highways, laden like pack-mules with pots and pans, and skirling their hideous bagpipes. One can see he is not among real Germans, for the people are mostly darker, softer-looking, yet handsomer far than, say, the Prussians. They are much poorer here too; if one may judge from tatters and rags, they are very poor. Men and women may be seen at any time of the day, either in street or field, playing for money on bagpipes or barrel-organs. Many gangs of harvesters have an old man or woman turning away at some last-century musical instrument, while they are cheerily busy at their work. The people are either eminently conservative or eminently abject in social and political affairs; generation after generation lives on in its old state, careless or ignorant of what goes on elsewhere: everything is old and strange and backward. So too they cling to their old Bohemian or Czech language, and see no reason to learn German. The traveller who relies on his German to take him through Bohemia will suffer for his error. Almost nobody, even of the well-dressed classes, speaks German in the country districts. On to even over the boundary of Austria proper, their Boehmisch is the ruling language.

If Mr. Browning could have seen me passing through the villages, he might have composed from the scene some second Pied Piper of Hamelin. Oxen and donkeys, goats and geese would start away in fright at the sight of me; dogs, small and big, in dozens, girls and boys in crowds would rush out of doors - and after me wildly :—

"And, like fowls in a farmyard when barley is scattering,
Out came the children running.
All the little boys and girls,
With rosy cheeks and flaxen curls
And sparkling eyes and teeth like pearls,
Tripping and skipping, ran merrily after
The wonderful *cycle* with shouting and laughter."

When we descended at night-fall into the busy town of Schlan, we were simply mobbed by big boys and girls. Nobody could understand me, and I could not read the shop signs written in Bohemian. From street to street we moved along seeking for lodgings, but always greeted with a shake of the head or a chorus of laughter. Annoyed by this reception, and by the cries and jeers of the surging crowd about me, I did a risky thing. For the first time, I produced my revolver (unloaded). Although this act kept them at a respectable distance, my ears were assailed by a perfect howl of execrations, which luckily I did not understand. At last a gentleman, comprehending my situation, conducted me to a good hotel, where the waiters spoke German.

The roads for thirty miles around Prague, north and south, were the best I had yet ridden; though hilly, their surface is hard and kept in excellent condition. Prague itself is probably the most remarkably situated city in Europe. From every side the roads to it run steep down through deep ravines, past imposing and venerable buildings, to where the river Moldau runs its lovely course under beautiful bridges, through the ancient, hallowed city; and all around the heights are decked with gardens and towers and castles and palaces. Truly to the student of archæology and the lover of history this is a spot where he may live in fulness of joy. The venerable Hradschin, the Burg, the Stern, the spacious Abbey of Strahow, the Cathedral, the Capuchin Monastery, the University (the oldest in Germany), are all clothed in a halo of deep historical interest. Turn where you may, you find memories of Huss and Jerome, the noble champions and martyrs of religious purity and freedom, and of Ziska, the blind warrior—memories embodied in names, in books, in pictures, and in monuments. But around the ancient Karlsbrücke the interest is deepest. It is 1742 ft. long, and stands on sixteen arches, and has an old watchtower at either end; it is richly loaded with statues and figures and groups of saints—a perfect epic poem in stone. Here perished for his faithfulness St. John Nepomuc, the patron saint of the Bohemians, who come in thousands to this bridge, as devotees to his shrine. Here the heads of murdered Protestant nobles rotted for ten years, in grim row on the tower. Here the townsfolk repelled the Swedes, and later on the Prussians, and here the students in 1848 fought their best for liberty. Yet to me a still more hallowed spot is that old neglected churchyard near the river's bend. It is said to date as far back as the dispersion after the destruction of Jerusalem. Here, amid hovels of poverty and mouldering walls, lie many generations of those who still "looked for the salvation of Israel." Here, overgrown with moss and creeping plants and alder-trees, thousands of hoary, time-worn stones proclaim in the sacred Hebrew, and by the emblems of the tribes, such as a pitcher for Levi, and two hands for Aaron, how the remnants of God's ancient people had lived and toiled and worshipped here with face and thoughts still Zionward. Gloomy and melancholy, it is a fit abode for the dead of that noble but deluded race,—

> " Round about whose home
> The glory that blushed and bloomed
> Is but a dim-remembered story
> Of the old time entombed."

Cycling within the city is forbidden; this I soon found out. But when once through the South gate, it seemed to me folly "to keep a dog and yet bark myself;" but before we got halfway up the hill a soldier-policeman took me in charge for riding within the city limits. The officer to whom he took me, wished to fine me, maintaining I was a Prussian and did it in contempt for Bohemian law. However, on my pleading ignorance that the city extended so far out, and on producing my English credentials, they acquitted me, "with an admonition." It is remarkable how tradition preserves likings and dislikings. The name Prussian, as one connected with the havoc wrought by Frederick the Great and other warrior-monarchs, is in especial ill-favour down here; the name English, associated with Wickliffe, whose disciples Huss and Jerome were, and with the '48 revolution, and other ties of sympathy, is a *sesame* to the good graces of the people about here. Strange it is that, while almost everywhere the people adore England, the government in politics thwart and abuse her to the utmost of their power.

CHAPTER VII.

LOWER BOHEMIA—SOME NICE RECEPTIONS.

AT Dnespek, near Beneschau, the charming hills and dales, the dread of another drenching, and above all the laughing eyes of two damsels looking on me from an upper window of a sort of grotesque union of butcher shop and tavern, induced me to call a halt. Imagine my disgust when, instead of the rustic beauties, only a dirty boy was within to welcome and wait on me. Before the sun rose in the morning, I had "shaken the dust off my shoes" (there was nobody else to do it), and gladly left the scene of my discomfiture. Next evening at Neuhaus, charmingly situated on a long hill surrounded by many broad lakes and long tracts of forest land, I had another strange reception. After winding our way through narrow lanes and between high walls, we passed under the ancient gateway and tower, and found the main street thronged with festive crowds arrayed in all the varieties of true Bohemian fashion. To escape from these, I entered what appeared to be a *Gasthof* (hotel), but what was only a *Wirthshaus* (public-house). Vines spread their fresh greenness over the front and clustered thick about the windows where inside bloomed luxuriant geraniums and fuchsias. The person who answered my call was a hard-faced, hard-voiced woman "of a certain age." She said she could easily make me as good a bed for the night as any in the town. The phrase "make a bed," sounded suspicious: nevertheless I agreed. The chief object in the *Gaststube*—the only public-room visible in the house—was a frightfully old man. He sat muffled-up close in by a stove, and smoked, or rather tried to smoke, a long wooden pipe, the bowl of which rested on the floor. Each recurring puff took two or more minutes to draw, and during the interval all was perfect silence and passiveness, and he sat there, with the firelight playing on his wrinkled, time-eaten face, a picture as of old age mummified. Yes, "he was old, old, old, and his heart was older still." For as often as his pipe went out, he would utter a sort of discord between a squeal and a grunt, in which all the petulance and peevishness and discontent of a lifetime seemed seeking for vent. By-and-by in dropped some neatly-dressed women and sat gossipping, and sipping some strong stuff with the landlady. Meanwhile customers came and went, until, tired with listening to the uncouth sounds of their language and with trying to read their native newspapers, I asked to be shown to bed. To my dismay, the buxom hostess placed chairs and benches together in a corner, brought pillows and blankets, then smilingly motioned to me that the bed was made. Well, here was a pretty go, to undress before that staring array of females, and get into bed over high-backed chairs, exposed to the view of the crowded street! My custom, when abroad, in order to avoid rising from bed with more life on me than when I entered it, is to sleep shirtless: but, no, thank you, not that night.

Just as there is a great change for the better from the bare flat monotonous land of Prussia to the wooded hills and broad lakes that abound here, so is there, too, from the bare, barn-like churches of Protestant Prussia to the neat, well-adorned churches of Catholic Bohemia. It appears that according as is the land so are the religion and religious structures of a people. This perhaps is the reason why Protestantism, the plainer form of religion, obtains most in colder, barrener climes, while Roman Catholicism, with its showier service, still holds on in the richer and warmer.

Of all days in the week, Sunday shows the people and their life to best advantage. Nothing could be more charmingly picturesque than the gipsy-like natives of Bohemia as they flock well-dressed to church or stand together in groups after service before they scatter to amuse themselves each in his or her own way. The women dress in keeping with the richness and beauty of the landscape: their dresses are tastefully, not gaudily, checked with blue and red, or blue and yellow spots or stripes, and over their heads they throw fine-wrought shawls of the most variegated hues and patterns. Their Sunday finery makes them wondrous bold: while on a week day they will scarcely dare to look at you, on Sunday they lavish on you their most ravishing smiles.

The milestones were now few and far between; and when they did come they were not " like angels' visits," for, the figures on them never indicating to what town they were directing, nor whether they were kilometres or *Stunden* or *Meilen*, they proved a riddle which I at last gave up trying to solve. With all my heart I pity the poor devout cyclist who would pass by here. Every furlong or two stands a wayside cross or a crucifix cell. If he dismounts at each, and does his devotions, he will have precious hard work, and may finish a pilgrimage, say, to Rome, at the end of his life, provided he gets the standard three-score years and ten. Why, in the name of decency and common sense, not convert all these crosses and crucifix cells into much-needed mile-posts, to the enduring comfort of the traveller? I fancy that thereby blessings would openly be pronounced that at present sound most sinfully like muttered curses.

CHAPTER VIII.

A DANGEROUS RIDE AND FALL.

WHAT makes the Austrians keep gutters crossing their highways in great big ridges on every hill? Surely they could find some easier and safer method of draining hills than this absurd and ugly practice. Accidents occasionally happen, they say, even with carriages, when they are being driven rapidly downhill. As for the unwary bicyclist who came on to their roads first by night, he would be likely never to ride any more. Such, indeed, was almost my fate.

At the top of one fearful hill I hesitated whether to dismount or risk the descent. Recurring every twenty yards was one of those confounded ridges, higher than usual, because the hill was exceptionally steep, and more water ran down it, requiring bigger gutters—I call them gutters for want of a better name. All the way up, the road was dotted with people who had come out of the church at the foot. But the element of danger involved in riding down a steep hill always has a strong attraction for me. When at last I thought it best to dismount, it was too late; we were going at too great a speed to admit of that being safely done: safer to go on, I thought. The brake had seen too much service already to be effectual on such a declivity, and I had foolishly neglected to replace it before starting on this tour. Over the first ridge we bounded some inches clear of the ground, then on over others, till the bound became half a foot. Half-way down the hill two boys were driving a string of cows attached together, as is the common custom in those countries, by chains round their necks. My shouts of warning and my bell served only to terrify the brutes and make them block the way. When we were only some feet from being up with them—they at the side and we in the middle of the road—they turned tail, and to keep clear of them I at once drew round the machine's head towards the other side. But the boys now lashed them back up the hill, and only another rapid jerk of the handle-bar towards the side they were first on saved me from a bad fall among them. Up till now the brake, worn and loose as it was, had moderated the downward pace. But just at that moment, before the machine's head was again straight downhill, we came on another ridge; the shock proved too strong: the brake shifted off the tire, and left us flying at the rate of twenty-five miles an hour down the hill. As we dashed over each ridge, it was first, in order to throw my weight on the hind wheel and so prevent a header, lie back with my head as near as possible towards the backbone, then forward swiftly to hold on desperately and keep the wheel upright when we had crashed down again from the bound. At each ridge I despaired of life. Still the steep and the pace are increasing; and now the last ridge is in view, and cruelly big it is. The turn round the church is here, and the slope appears still to go on; if I am not sharp and cool enough, *de me actum erit.* Not a sound hitherto had broken from the people on the hill, but as we banged on to the ridge, a confused cry reached me as of warning or terror. All I was conscious of was that both wheel and I now rose high off the ground—as much as three feet, the eye-witnesses declared, and the ridge alone was more than a foot high, though sloping—and the crash when we met the ground shook every spoke and rib and bone as if it would break them. Before my confused sight, not two yards off round the turn stood some children, all unconscious of the coming danger. As quick as thought, and at the same second, I turned the handle more directly towards the hedge on the right than the bend in the road was taking us. Then before I was aware, the machine dived into a deep dry ditch which I had not observed, rebounded many yards itself down the road, and pitched me forward some ten feet into the bushes. Then as soon as my dazed senses and throbbing temples let me think at all, I realized that our mad steeplechase, ending in my first serious fall, was over.

The bicycle backbone was buckled fast to the front wheel, one spoke was broken, one pedal bent. That was all. What a deliverance ! An hour or two in a blacksmith's and all was right again; well, nearly right. Two other spokes broke at the "cap," farther on in my tour. Passing some mounted peasants on my way that night to Horn, I asked how far it was, and, looking back for the answer, suddenly found myself on the ground among the stones. The M.I.P. knapsack had loosened and shifted by the fall, and had now jammed in between backbone and wheel. Such are the pleasant vicissitudes of a reckless wheeler's life. This ludicrous incident and the peals of derisive laughter that greeted my ears recalled to me Lucian's story of the man in the street accepting an invitation to dinner from a man at a window : " I'll be there without fail, trust me," said he, when a tile from the roof sent his soul to Styx, amid the inextinguishable laughter of "the grim ferryman, Charon," who was then on a holiday visit to the upper world.

CHAPTER IX.

AUSTRIA PROPER—VIENNA.

THE wheel is considerably in vogue in Austria proper. The first genuine bicyclist that passed me on this tour was near Gmünd, just beyond the Bohemian boundary; and he had warned me of road ridges and some dangerous hills. The local printer's son in Horn is a spirited young bicyclist, and a lively companion into the bargain. He and some other fellows had been having a day's run of about forty kilometres in all, and were celebrating their victorious return by a carousal at the *Goldene Krone*. Heroes as they were, they made fun of my folly in wearing such heavy clothes and dragging half-a-dozen kilogrammes of baggage behind me. On being quietly informed that the heavy knapsack had the effect of converting my ordinary bicycle into a "safety," and that most of the places on my route, especially in Turkey (the word Turkey was an eye-opener to them), had no railway station, they began to think that after all "there was method in my madness." They listened breathlessly to the story of my race down the big hill; then they set the town gunsmith to straighten what parts of my bicycle still were bent. Next morning we were a merry party in the printer's garden. Herr Printer, his Frau, his sons, and his soft-eyed, tender-voiced daughters were breakfasting in a sunny, vine-trellised bower. The Frau was delighted to try her French with me; and between compliments in French from her, and toasts all round in German, I was like to believe myself a hero. Then they relegated me to the care of a smart boy of twelve or fourteen years, who insisted on accompanying me as far as ten kilometres. He chatted all the way, pointed out and described the 12th century Benedictine Abbey of Altenburg and the spacious old castle of Rosenburg, with its tournament-ground and galleries, but boy-like had most to say about the ditch he first rode into, and the spot where he ran over a goose for which he was fined three guldens.

We hear not a little about the grand uses Prussia and Austria and France are going to make of the bicycle. The wonder to me is where they are going to get reliable bicyclists. One thing is sure, they will never excel in the sport either in Prussia or Austria, nor ever succeed in establishing a bicycling military corps till they mend their roads; or if they do succeed, there will be, as at present, bicyclists, but who do not bicycle. The roads have been, or look as if they had been, invariably well made at first, but now are so bad that usually only a narrow sidepath is rideable. From Stockerau, for example, fifteen miles on to Vienna, stretches a broad straight road, running between lofty, fine old poplars. So far thanks to Maria Theresa; but degenerate descendants have left it the most shockingly wretched road that could disgrace a country. It is one long *Stein-und-Staub Bett* (stone and dust bed), as a roadman fitly baptized it. The only rideable parts of it are five or six deep, half-foot wide ruts, between each of which are ridges of loose metal. To budge from the rut means a fall, or a tearing out of the tire.

It is remarkable how races get mixed on the Continent compared with the conservativism in that respect in the British Isles. I once knew a hairdresser named Victor Palvado, whose nationality was a mystery. His father was half a Spaniard, half a Frenchman by blood, and born in Switzerland; his mother was, as far as he knew, a Belgian; and he himself was born in Rotterdam: puzzle, what was he? He for one did not know; so in despair he emigrated to Brazil. A similar heterogeneous compound in the person of a little energetic gentleman made up to me in Meissau. His name was Hirsch, indicating a German origin; his mother was Belgian, he was born or brought up in Paris, and had spent his life mostly in Austria, where, I believe, he has married: puzzle, what are his children? One thing he himself certainly is, a regular battery of kinetic energy. He is the inventor and exporter of what is known in Britain as "moss-litter." He is the projector of a great canal to be cut between Vienna, Prague and the Elbe, and so, joining the Danube to the Elbe, form a waterway from the Black Sea to the German Ocean. Here's success to you then, Herr—I beg your pardon, I mean Monsieur—Hirsch!

It was early on an afternoon when we put up at Floridsdorf and engaged a bed for the night. Then learning that the city was four miles off, a distance I had not calculated on, I took the steam tram thither. So this is the Kaiserstadt, the city of the Emperors, the city of Maria Theresa, the city replete with memories of the glorious names of Haydn, Schubert, Mozart, and Beethoven. O the Past, the noble Past, the terrible Past, would that we could live thee and see thee all over again! What internecine struggles and momentous events in Europe's history has this spot witnessed since seven centuries ago the Scottish Benedictines came to its Schottenhof till now when I, their countryman, an unknown wanderer, with an unromantic modern contrivance, but filled with that life-hunger that is the sad heirloom of the Scot, am mingling in its crowds!

Truly it was beautiful as I saw it at night—the moon rising over the trees, bathing in its rich yellow light the stately buildings and bridges, and glittering with an old-world light on the spires and on the Danube, that great enchanting feature, as it rolls its current in eddies along between its walled and wooded banks.

It was past midnight when I reached my hotel and found all closed and dark. After half an hour's knocking and listening, the old porter was heard within fumbling with his keys and muttering to himself about young scamps disturbing decent folks from their sleep. Nor did his muttering cease on the promise of some kreutzers; it merely changed its drift to the effect that it was his due to get that in any case. So when he had secured the gate again, and left me to grope upstairs in the dark and enter the first bedroom I found (which luckily did not contain an occupant, as was the case much to my horror at another hotel), I heard him hobbling down the courtyard still muttering and mumbling away.

Vienna, having a finer natural situation than Paris, may yet be the finest city in the world, especially when the trees in the Stuben and Park Rings and other streets have grown up and shut out that offensive regularity, that too evident striving after effect, that is so prominent in continental cities. No doubt there is some fine variety in the Innerstadt; yet even there the fault is too much newness. It is a relief, amid so much that is new, to linger among the courts of the old Hofburg, wherein for so many centuries the destinies of Europe were planned.

Although the people here are not so gay and *entêté* as in Paris they are gayer far than in Berlin. Quite a number of indigenous foibles can be remarked here: for example, Vienna is the home of lap-dog culture. These pets get as much care from the ladies as the children get, if not more. A Viennese lady—as the story goes—may repose peacefully on her couch all through distressful choruses from the nursery, but at the first yelp of her idol up starts her ladyship. In one family, at breakfast, I was immensely tickled to hear the lady of the house thus greet her canine pet : " Good morning, Toto ; and had you sweet little darling dreams ? Come to your own dear mammy, and give me a kiss ! "

CHAPTER X.

ALONG THE DANUBE INTO HUNGARY—AUSTRIAN IMPERIAL UNITY.

THE Austrian militaryism pleased me by its scarcity, but displeased me in the quality of what I did see of it. Several thousand soldiers, with their blue caps and coats and dirty white trousers, passed me on the march. They were very bronzed, and evidently much drilled ; but they were small ; their faces were not intelligent; their step was not firm ; they were poor compared with the Prussians.

I wonder why the children, even big boys and girls, called after me so much. It must surely be that their wonder was greatly excited when they first saw a bicycle, and, having learned its name, though they still do not understand how it works, they give vent to their feelings of wonder and perplexity, in the uncouth cries of " *Velochipéd! Velochipéd!* " caught up as we pass along till the whole street resounds. In Bohemia they had called after me " *Hokay! Hokay!* " which had no meaning to my mind—except that perhaps they saw some resemblance in my get-up with the knapsack behind to the Italians that parade our streets selling ice-creams ! When Mr. Thos. Stevens heard the Hungarians shout " *Alien! Alien!* " he thought they were nicknaming him for a foreigner, whereas they were merely wishing him "a pleasant journey."

At Fischament, where we arrived in company with some waggoners we had joined, all of us as white as millers with the thick dust of the roads, the handsome hostess betrayed towards me no small regard. She wondered how such a young man should go into such wild places so far from home. " Oh ! " I said, "*das Herz ist immer jung und froh*, and can make its home anywhere." Whereupon she laughed merrily, "*Gewiss, das Herz ist jung*," and went about her duties, warbling snatches of songs, of which I could catch a line now and then, such as,—

> "Ich sass und spann vor meiner Thür,
> Da kam ein junger Mann zu mir." [1]

To all appearance she was a widow; and, were it not that I fear to incur the accusation, so often made against the men by the fair ones, that we imagine every woman in love with us, I should say she was "setting her cap at me" with a vengeance.

One of the waggoners, who was fond of boasting that he knew every foot of the country for fifty miles around, positively alarmed me by his description of it. "No, no, *mein lieber Herr*, you know not where you are going; *das Ungarland ist nicht das Oesterland:*" and he emphasized his speech with the favourite oath "*Um die Burg!*"

Of all strange oaths the Austrian oaths are the strangest. The above one means, "By the Castle!" that is, the old Hofburg at Vienna. But it is used out of veneration, not detestation like the similar one in vogue in the Emerald Isle, or this other one, "The curse of Cromwell and the crows be on you!" Another queer one with which they spice their speech is "*O crucifix!*" Alas! the cross once so revered has degenerated into a common oath! But it is ever thus. No man, no people, can be wholly religious or wholly anything. Life is composite. When anything, even religion, is made too common, it becomes degraded; and generations of reformers will hardly raise it up again. Although at every yard crosses and chapels abounded along my route, I saw only one devout group, and that was composed of an old woman and a little girl kneeling before a wayside cross.

In Austria they gave me frightsome accounts of the roads and the people of Hungary. "If you have a revolver, you must load it," they said, "for you are going among savages and robbers." The Hungarians, again, declare their own country safe and civilized, but warn you against Servia. Then in Servia, it is Turkey that is the barbarian, and in Turkey it is Greece. The

---

[1] "As I sat before my door and span,
    There came to me a nice young man."

black sheep is always beyond the border. So often indeed was the loading of my revolver insisted on, that at last I struck up a scale of my own for the various countries, which scale greatly amused and flattered the Austrians : one chamber loaded for Hungary—none for Austria—two for Servia and three for Turkey and Greece.

Now it is really curious how the peoples of Eastern Europe distrust and malign each other. The weakness of the Austrian empire is this want of sympathy between its component peoples. The Bohemians and Hungarians heartily hate the Austrians, calling them proud and tyrannical ; the Austrians despise them as *Pöbel-haüfe*—mere rabble-crowds. None but he who travels among them all, in the way I did, can realize how little unity there is. The majority of the soldiers know no German (except the words of command); and what with Bohemian, Hungarian, Sclavonian, Servian, and German, when drafted into regiments in an army, they will not understand each other. What a rabble ! What a Babel with which to make war against an army of one race and one speech ! Now I know why the Prussians beat them in 1866. Yet, though they are aware of the danger of this division, neither on the part of the chief state nor of the subordinate states will they amalgamate more closely. Ask an Austrian proper if he knows Bohemian or Hungarian, and you get for answer a surprised " *Gott behüte !*" In Buda-Pest I advocated a common speech (German) for the whole Austrian empire, and the company of Hungarian students, merchants, and editors, among whom I was, cried out, " *O Gott bewahre !* "

All this district is romantic and historic, worthy of the place it holds in the Niebelungen-Lied, the cradle-song of the Teutonic race. Hainburg, with its old towers and walls and rock-built ruins, confronts Theben's lofty towers across the river, and together they guard the entrance to *Hungarland*. For thus the people delight to term their country when speaking of it in German ; but however euphonious it may be to them, it sounds ominous to English ears.

CHAPTER XI.

ON THE TRACK OF STEVENS—HUNGARIAN PICTURESQUE VARIETY.

AFTER a run of about thirty miles from this picturesque spot, over heath and sand, I put up at the same hotel and slept in the same bed as Stevens had done the year before. So said Mr. Thallmayer, the professor in the agricultural college there, who was brought to me by the landlord of the *Bierhalle*, where I first went in, as soon as he learned I was English. It was aggravating when, fatigued and parched with thirst, I asked for coffee, to be answered by way of serving me, "*Was für ein Landsmann Sind Sie?*" (What is your country?) I did not satisfy them, however, till they brought me the coffee. Then they told me they had thought I was Italian and wished to get the professor over to have a chat with me. Once in his house, all my care was forgot at the sight of tea and soda-scones, which his kind English wife set before us. The room was dark when we entered, and the lady and her friends present at first mistook me for Stevens, till I began to laugh and joke, when one of them exclaimed that Mr. Stevens had surely grown merrier than he used to be. Stevens spent an evening with them, but was very quiet and reserved. He could speak no language but English; but he carried a book of words and phrases which he showed to the people when he wanted anything. How awkward! He must have paid double and had twice as much trouble as I had in procuring eatables and lodgings, and in asking the way. In one place I know the landlord put him in to sleep among the cows and horses, because he took him for a vagabond. People do have queer notions of a cyclist in those countries, and the more so if you cannot speak to them.

Everywhere, from high and low, came to me the same question, "*Es ist vielleicht eine Wette?*" (Is it a bet?) They cannot conceive how it can be for pleasure solely or for pure love of knowledge.

From Wieselburg to Buda-Pest the road, though not uniformly good, has usually a hard side-path. Often for miles at a stretch this side-path is the only rideable part of the road. Elevated as it is a foot or two above the road level and having on the outside a slope varying from five to twenty feet, one must guide most carefully and firmly, lest the wheel catch the sand on one side or go towards the ditch on the other. A mile of this work is as tiring as three on an ordinary road. Often there are long bits of deep sand, with not one square inch of hard ground from grass to grass, from left side to right. Hard work it is to drive or push a bicycle here. What then could the vaunted tricycle do on such a road?

But if the road is difficult, the country is glorious, enchanting. First there are the Schütts, Lesser and Greater,—mud-banks encircled by the Danube and containing a hundred villages and more and at the eastern corner the famous Gibraltar-like Komorn. Then comes Raab, the Roman Arabona, with its Feuerthurm (fire-tower), its palace and cathedral, all belonging to the Dark Ages. Then come the extensive fortifications of Komörn, the Roman Komaronium, as seen more clearly in the Magyar (Hungarian) form of the word, Komarom. This is a terrible country for confusion of names; in one or two towns people actually sent me farther on to find these very towns— they did not recognize their own towns by the names (German) given on the maps! One amusing instance of this occurred when I was inquiring at a village about a place called Tata. The first person asked was a pretty peasant maid, who first blushed, then shook her head, then laughed at me as I repeated the name with emphasis. In high dudgeon at her making a fool of me before the people about us, I started off bawling out Tata with a big interrogation mark after it in my voice to everybody I saw. But the more I bawled the more they roared laughing, till it dawned on me through my rage that I was giving what the simple folks thought a farcical or ironical rendering of the colloquialism for "Farewell"! The secret of the affair was that the Magyar for Tata is Totis.

Komorn bristles with arms and soldiers. At the Danube baths (where the current washed away the fifth nose-skin that sun and weather had given me since the start) more than a third of the bathers were officers. The Church has ever been eager to be near to the Sword; and accordingly here not far down the river from Komorn lies Gran, the seat of the Primate of Hungary. The beautiful palace of the Prince-Archbishop, and the costly cathedral rising on a hill in the vale with its huge dome eighty-five feet in diameter, are out-standing sights amid the fine Danube scenery. Not far off is the ruined castle of Vissegrad, the scene of one of those romance traditions that hallow the Danube banks. From as early as the 11th century it was a royal abode; but now, of all its former glory shorn, it is only a ragged keep with two walls running down to a ruined tower on the river's brink. Here dwelt in magnificence the famous Matthias Corvinus, and here at eventide he crossed the river to meet his simple peasant love, and wander with her along the Danube shore. But one day the fatal news was told her that her lover was her King; and in the madness of a hopeless love she drowned herself in the sight of his towers. And still the herdsman in that lonely place sees her spirit fluttering in white robes across the grass-grown courts, and sounds of wailing echo from the walls as if still her heart were breaking.

Fit home for romance is the country here. Along the river run the roads shaded by deep green acacia trees; strange birds flit from hill to hill; thousands of cattle lie on the banks or bathe in the water. Bank and stream are white with ducks and geese, which rose in fright as the wheel approached, and after circling over the hill above my head, went flap, flap, splash, splash, through the water or the air, across to islands on the river, while the hills resounded with their piercing cries.

Most amusing it is to note the various ways in which animals regarded my appearance. Two little boys in a donkey-cart met me. The donkey cocked his ears, and looked amused. Then he suddenly took a thought, bolted into the wide ditch, and up into a field, down which he cut till the ploughed ruts stopped him. Had not a tree kept up the wheel when they crossed the ditch all would have been upset. Another little chap stood laughing in the middle of the road, holding two horses by a halter; but he changed his tune when they plunged and made off dragging him on the ground between them.

Hungary is indeed the land of variety. Costumes, manners, scenery, are here in Protean forms. The houses are low-built, but high-roofed, with pillared porticoes all round them, and great wide courts; mosque-like churches tower above them: all pure white-washed. Not to speak of the herdsmen and herdboys who wear great white skin coats and broad-rimmed hats as good as a tent, nor of the women in one place whose style of dress shows brown legs in front as far as the thigh, and behind as far as the ham of the knee, what with half-naked forms, wide trousers, coloured blouses and head-gear, it is an enlivening picture. Donkeys yoked together drive cheerily by; geese in scores hiss and cackle by the way; pigs in droves of hundreds grunt and scamper about the fields and the sloughs; great white sleepy-eyed oxen, with horns measuring four to five feet from tip to tip, pull waggons lazily along. And over all the sun is staring with his fierce eye of fiery heat. He begins in the morning to operate on your left ear; at noon he is painting your front; then he touches up your right ear; and finally roasts and boils your back till evening drives him from his persecution.

The peasants here are not only picturesque, they are polite. The boys take off their caps—no small task considering the size of some of them—and greet me. At every meeting hats are touched or doffed to me. All want to recognize and be recognized. It is like the progress of a favourite statesman through an admiring crowd. Whether they are working in the harvest-fields, or lying in groups under the trees, men and women, boys and girls, eating or sleeping, they must all rouse themselves and call out as we pass. If I take no notice of them, they whistle and yell and halloo to make me look at them. As this happened so repeatedly, I sometimes never even looked; and so strong is the human instinct against being ignored, that they kept on shouting till we were half-a-mile away.

CHAPTER XII.

BUDA-PEST—HUNGARIAN ASPIRATIONS.

My reception in Buda was characteristic of the country. A number of gentlemen had gathered round me at a street-fountain where I was slaking my thirst so copiously as to attract attention. Bit by bit they learned what I was and what journey I was doing. Meanwhile a great crowd of respectable quiet folks had encircled us. All on a sudden the crowd parted, and a *constabler* with drawn sword rushed in, and in excited tones ordered me *fort!* Amid a long rattle of merry laughter at the policeman's officiousness, while he himself joined in the laugh against himself, I remounted my gallant steed.

This free-and-easy treatment of the police—so different from the cringeing attitude of the Prussian people toward their police—was manifested all through my sojourn in the Hungarian capital. I was allowed to sit or stand where I chose, and do what I chose without undue disturbance on the part of the guardians of the peace. Indeed I made as free and felt as free as in Britain, where, almost alone of the countries I have seen, the police know when *not* to interfere.

Nowhere, I think, are the English more admired, loved and respected than in Hungary. They remember England's aid and sympathy in '48; and they hate the Russians with undying hate. Among many instances, here is one. A bright, dashing young fellow escorted me to a good moderate hotel; but, on learning I was British, and a student moreover, he insisted on my sharing his lodgings for a day. And very hospitably he entertained me. We passed the evening in a private Hungarian family. The son was a law-student like my friend; the eldest daughter was affianced to a Hussar lieutenant. They danced their national *Csárdás* (*Chardanz*); the daughters played duets on the grand-piano; I sang some Scotch and Irish plaintive melodies that brought the tears to their eyes, while the lieutenant tenderly kissed the hand of his betrothed. Next day that young student devoted himself entirely to me. He was full of enlightened enthusiasm for literature, art, and public life. He never tired describing to me the various historical monuments and localities:—the Krönungshütel, around which the newly-crowned king must ride and brandish the sword of St. Stephen towards every part of the land—the Bruckbad and Kaiserbad which the Turks changed from a monastery and an archbishop's palace into baths—the Turkish mosque on the hill, with its grave of Shikh-Gül-Baba, the "Father of Roses." Then with pride—which he said I could share in, for the maker was a Scotchman called Clark—he brought me to the Suspension Bridge, the first built in the world, it being 1250 ft. long, 50 ft. above the water, and supported by pillars 150 ft. in height. We visited the gorgeous bath-houses of the famed Margaret's Isle, roamed among the trees and myriad roses, and listened to the splash of the *Heilthermen* waters as they fell over the cascade into the Danube. He was a near approach to my idea of "a proper man"—alive to all the varying moods and phases of nature, yet able to talk about and act firmly in practical affairs. The same man who pathetically related to me the romance of the *Margarethen Insel*, and brought graphically before my mind's eye the domination of the Turks and the struggles against them, and who got into raptures over the sunset view of the lofty palace and fortress, Buda's veteran citadel of twenty sieges, on the Blocksberg and the vine-clad heights where his countrymen had striven to the death against Turks and Austrians, was also quite in his element in bringing down, with the musket, eggs dancing on jets of water, in helping to raise a fallen horse, and in checking the rapacity of a landlord. The latter feat was exhibited at the hotel he took me to the first night. After taking a room for me, he countermanded it on deciding to take me to his own rooms. But the landlord fumed at this, and demanded the night's charge. This my friend maintained he had no legal claim to; and when ostler, waiters, landlady and landlord combined to retain my wheel as guarantee, he promptly brought in a gendarme to clinch his argument. On my voluntarily paying the charge, and the landlord returning half of it, the student exclaimed, "Oh no; the whole or none; a point is a point: you have taken money that does not belong to you against the law, and the law will remember that you have." Such determined fighting on the part of private citizens about the sanctity of the law I had not expected to witness out of Britain.

Buda-Pest is a marvellously fine city, and bids fair to outrival many a greater. Its site is superb, its public buildings antique, yet palatial in their size and beauty. Andrassy Strasse, in point of length, variety and beauty, is second only to Edina's Princes Street. One thing that greatly enlivens the town, is the universal habit of depicting on the walls outside what the shops contain. This is most useful as well as ornamental. Coffee-pots, sausages, meal-bags, rolls and butter, candles and oil-cans, hats and collars and shirts, and all the various paraphernalia of modern life are realistically painted outside.

Truly they now grow fine men in Hungary, noble, manly and enthusiastic, as indeed becomes the countrymen of Louis Kossuth. The people are rich and well-dressed, lively, yet sober-minded. They are very enthusiastic and very patriotic. Unlike what it is in Germany, politics is here the great theme, and freely discussed. Especially are they eager to know about Ireland and England. While they adore England, they sympathize with Ireland. As for themselves, they wish to be *Keine Deutscher* (no Germans); and they bitterly complain that the *Times* and *Standard* correspondents reside in Vienna, not in Pesth, so that the British public get Austrian not Hungarian views of Hungarian life and politics. One of their ablest poets read to me in public a tirade of his against "that dirty rag of black and yellow" (the Austrian ensign). If they are not to have full independence, at least, they say, they will fight to have the control of their own revenues and army in time of peace: and since they are the greater part of the empire, surely they should have some adequate share in its fame and profit. As it is, whenever the empire gains any profit or renown, although Hungary may have done most to secure such, no credit is given to Hungary, but "Austria, Austria did it all." This complaint of theirs is the same outcry against centralization that we are justly hearing so much about in the provinces of Britain. "We are rich, we are strong, we are educated," said a Hungarian editor to me, "and time will give us our due." Would that the Irish could say as much for themselves!

There was warmth in the grasp, and pathos in the words of my friends when we parted, and their farewell words rang in my ears for many a day : " *Adieu, adieu, mein Freund; vergessen Sie nicht das Ungarland!* "

CHAPTER XIII.

INCIDENTS ON THE ROAD ALONG THE DANUBE BELOW BUDA-PEST.

A BEAUTIFUL but dusty road runs from Buda along the Danube for nearly two hundred miles, through rose-bedecked villages and great plains covered with flocks of sheep and herds of oxen and swine in hundreds and hundreds. Herdboys on horses gallop hither and thither on the moors, perfectly at home on their mounts. Occasionally we would come up with a herd on the move to other pastures—an amusing scene. For a mile or more nothing of the mass could be seen but a thick column of white dust moving along the road; then, as we came nearer, a herdsboy or two with their long whips could be indistinctly made out on the skirts of the dust column as they strove to keep the wilful grunters to the straight road, and finally the noisy chorus of grunts and the powerful swinish perfume dispelled all doubt as to the nature of the moving mass.

This is truly a pastoral region, an Arcadia, rich in the finest corn and wine. Sometimes at a bend of the road or river we came within the rushing sound of the mill-wheels in little colonies of mills moored in the Danube; sometimes a ridge of hill, green with vines, and dotted with white cottages, rises athwart the plain; and the lordly Danube is ever there bounding on in its majestic course through empires—a river to rave about by day and night,—

> "The wandering stream,
> Who loves the Cross, yet to the Crescent's gleam
> Unfolds a willing breast."

The peasants are well-to-do, as their good dresses and contented air bespeak them to be. Some millers on the Danube make snug little fortunes, and can afford to keep an inn at the same time—their mill on the river, their inn on the shore. People and houses are all extremely neat and clean, and the more so when I passed as they were then dreading the cholera, which latterly did come their way. Yet it was here that the ferocious Danube-valley mosquitoes took their biggest meal out of me, much to the hilarity of my gentle hostess when she roused me in the morning and saw "the spotted leopard" they had made of me. I had persisted in choosing my bed for coolness' sake on a rude couch beside an open window; and so they had swarmed in and buzzed and busied about my body all night. One man who had insisted the night before on being told my profession, and who had got for answer that it was none of his business, jocularly remarked that, though "it was none of his business," the only remedy was to rub me up in a butt of brandy.

Though I found occasionally some very rough and rude customers in Hungary, yet, I must say, fine faces, fine eyes sparkling with vivacity, fine manners, free and natural, kindness and politeness are the rule.

Below Duna Foldvar the road got bad again and the wind blew dead in my face. What can be more absolutely perplexing to a bicyclist than a strong wind on a bad road? A glorious instrument is the bicycle, when the road is good or the wind still; but, given a bad road and a strong wind, it is a miserable failure!

> "Then the tired jade the wheel forgets to hurl,
> Provoking envious gibes from each pedestrian churl."

Nothing could be more irregular than the style of driving here. Drivers lie down to sleep in their vehicles and let the beasts wander at will. Since 1876 the rule of the road in Austria-Hungary is "keep to the left." But the road-keepers, who only macadamize one side at a time, do their best to render this rule futile. A peasant on the top of a laden waggon of wheat drawn by two horses was coming along, as usual on the wrong side. As he paid no heed to my shouts, I went to my right. So did the horses in a fright. Too late he bawled out piteously to the horses as he pulled in the reins, "*Né, Né!*" The rickety concern toppled over and he descended double quick from his fifteen feet elevation, and all the sheaves upon him. When I got them cleared away, he rose up groaning and moaning; he had fallen on his arm. The cart was twisted out of shape, the ropes and reins all broken. After spending an hour, mending and loading the cart again, what was my disgust to hear the wretch demand pay for the *Frucht* spilled. Some bitter altercation followed, in which I threatened him with prosecution, till he whined out in broken German, *in Gottes Namen* to give him a *Gulden* for he was an *armer Mann* (a poor man). After that who could resist?

In the pleasant village of Bar, I was told that Igali Svetozár —the Hungarian that accompanied Stevens from Pesth to Belgrade—lived there. He was not at home. Not far on two bicyclists met me. They thought I was Igali; and I had made up my mind that one of them was he. We were both wrong. They were the captain and another member of the Belgrade Club, riding on to Pesth.

Early in the forenoon we reached the battle-field of Mohacs, twice fought, first in 1526 when the Turks disastrously crushed the Hungarian power, then a century and a half later when the victory was reversed. As the ground for a decisive battle, enclosed as it is towards the east by the Danube and towards the west by a semicircle of hills, it appears equal to Marathon and in some respects even to Waterloo, which Byron thought the best field in Europe and "wanting little but a better cause." In the inn at the barracks square, Captain Armin Mariantsik of the Hussar regiment stationed at Mohacs, brought Igali who chanced to be in town. When Igali came I addressed him first in English, but he looked at me in dumb surprise, no doubt thinking me another Stevens of one language. He was bound on farming business to Fünfkirchen (the town of the five Turkish mosques), but he postponed it on my account till next day. A bold, strapping fellow is Igali, and as kind as he is bold. In the Casino he introduced me to the officers at mess, then left me in their keeping for a time. The first lieutenant took me to his quarters; showed me his war-horse which neighed at the sound of his step and laid its head at his feet in token of welcome; then in subdued tones he mourned over the photograph of his lost English sweetheart and told me how she had been won and how she had died. We all went together down to the quay, and saw there waggons of the famous brown coal of the district, which according to the captain is the best coal known—a verdict which I suppose the Welsh, Scotch and Belgians will hardly accept. Then we rowed gaily across the Danube, and bathed in its rushing stream.

In the evening we dined in the vine-covered court of the hotel that Igali styled the "Cyclists' Touring Club" headquarters, though evidently used as such only by himself and a neighbouring count who has a craze for the sport. While we enjoyed our dish of sturgeon, caught in the Danube,—an article considered a rarity and delicacy elsewhere, but here cheap and common enough—Igali told me stories of Stevens: how he insisted always on going first in riding, how he seemed like me insensible to the great heat and to fatigue—"but you are Englishmen," said Igali, "you stick at nothing in the way of travelling"—how he often mistook characters, as when he indulged in a remonstrance against the class distinctions of aristocratic countries, because Igali had chastised an impudent vagabond whom Stevens took for a shepherd, how finally the only sound he uttered of his own accord all day was whistling to the tune of "Yankee Doodle."

All the time we were dining and discoursing, a band was delighting our ears with typical selections of Hungarian airs. The Magyar music is wild and sometimes weird and unearthly, but it is sweet, pathetic and mournful. Its prevailing tone seems to me to be a mingling of sorrow for the unfortunate past and of rapturous aspiration for the hopeful future. If the couplet—

> " Chords which vibrate sweetest pleasure
> Thrill the deepest note of woe "

can be taken as a standard of true music, then the Hungarian music is of a high order.

CHAPTER XIV.

THROUGH SCLAVONIA AND "THE MILITARY-FRONTIER."

A ROVING life, a rolling life, that is the life for the young and free ! What pleasure could be purer, healthier and keener than to be up fresh in the early morning when the rising sun is casting westward long shadows of hills and houses and trees, and all nature is sparkling with new-born joy ? And if at the same time the rover is speeding along on his wheel with a strong "wind that follows fast" on his back, on with little effort over sand and ruts and stones, on through new and glorious scenery, the pleasure becomes overwhelming in its intensity.

Such was my happy lot that day I entered Sclavonia. Here my meagre vocabulary of Magyar proved of small avail ; for the people speak Sclavonian or Servian, and less German even than in Hungary proper. The people look decidedly more Oriental as we approach the gates of the East ; they are smaller in features and crueller-looking. All this southern district of Austria is under martial law, as can be guessed from the greater number of soldiers and fortresses.

Essegg, the capital of Sclavonia, is about the worst of all the difficult places we had to enter and get out of. It is a wonder to me how the Turks ever got in to destroy it so often as they did. Marshes, sand plains, thickets and forests, streams and river combine to fortify it by nature, and with its fortress make it one of the strongest strategic places in Europe. Making for its towers, I found myself on the banks of the Drav, two miles from any bridge ; yet the towers of the town were just across the water. Instead of retracing the forest path I had come by, I foolishly forced my way along by the banks, and after an hour of pushing, lifting, dragging my wheel through dense pathless thickets, succeeded in regaining the high road. But much the same experience awaited me on the other side, this time through vast moors where the sandy rutty paths crossed each other and branched off most bewilderingly.

Here more than in other parts of Austria it is a puzzling matter to get an accurate idea of distances. It is most annoying, as well as stupid, when you ask a distance, to be told not how far it is, but that it will be so many *Stunden* (hours) for *you*. The simple folks have the presumption to calculate your speed for you, though all the time they have no idea of a bicycle. The Austrians generally forget that the *Stunde* is a measure of distance ($2\frac{2}{5}$ miles) as well as of time (one hour).

It was evident that a cycle had never before gone this route round by the south of the Fruska-Gora mountains. Crowds of people thronged round us at every stopping-place. All the children ran away in fear when they saw us. In one village a number of children who had been playing on the road ran within a crucifix inclosure, no doubt remembering what they had been taught, that the cross gives protection from all dangers; and there they cowered till we were out of sight. We were tearing along a grand bit of road near Mitrowitz, the sun glittering on the bright steel parts of the machine, when we came up behind a big girl. She fled, shrieking, at the first view of us, and, as we gained on her, her shrieks and her pace increased, till she fell down in a faint. On her recovery, I could make out from her that she had thought it was an evil spirit of fire pursuing her. Poor thing! she must have had a bad conscience, indeed.

People at home have no conception of how exquisitely rich and beautiful the land is in those regions. One could linger by the Save, and gaze for days untiringly on its deep blue waters, as blue as the Rhone or the Archipelago. The endless tiers of moor and hill and forest are seen at times from a high point on the road, as they stretch away on the north to the fortress-crowned rock of Peterwardein, the Gibraltar or Ehrenbreitstein of the Danube, and to the south till lost in the far distance where the true East begins at Belgrade.

Owing to my being misdirected by two officers at Ruma, it was my lot to traverse the heart of this wild country. For twenty odd miles the only road we had was a forest track only about two yards wide. On this road we overtook many long trains of gipsy caravans on the move or encamped in some green hollow beside a rivulet. Towards evening, on entering Golubrinä—a township embedded in the heart of those forests —my journey and my life were well-nigh ended together. A stampede of fifty horses which had been feeding on the common followed me up the long street; horses to right of me, left of me, behind me, before me, close on every side, all snorting and neighing, plunging and tearing along—men and women with whips and poles trying to stem the living torrent, and we in the thick of the throng.

Indeed I fared badly altogether in that place. The only decent food the man at the dram-shop could give me was some wretchedly prepared omelette; and all the while I was eating it, dirty mangy-looking vagabonds came about me plying me with questions which I could not understand about myself and my vehicle, and getting enraged because I would not or rather could not answer them. My only pleasant remembrance of the place is of drawing water from the deep well among the rank luxuriance of the garden, and having a proper wash there, as the deep stillness of the darkening twilight settled over the earth. But the religious calm and sense of purity the outside scene had instilled into me was rudely perturbed by the scene of loathsome manners inside the house. There a number of half-tipsy boors were gobbling up some ill-smelling stuff, smoking foul tobacco, and ejecting their expectorations all about the floor. There were two beds in the room; one I occupied, the other was for the innkeeper and his boy-servant, while a tramp rolled himself up on the floor in a mat. When they went to bed they first closed door and windows and shutters; so that not a breath of pure air could enter to clear out that abominable atmosphere charged with the nausea of bad cooking and the stench of foul breaths. No sooner was all quiet and I had sought to smother the outward discomfort beneath the bed-clothes than straightway began a quick cavalry charge across my body on the part of those brown-coated soldiers that delight to carry their war and pillage into the very haunts of peace. There was no mistake this time; it was war, war to the blood. So jumping out of the bed, at the risk of being brained by the landlord for housebreaking, I banged open the shutters, drew on some clothes, and lay down on a chair with my head on the window-sill. O the misery of that half-waking, half-sleeping waiting for the morn! Sometimes (in my dreaming) I was lying on the bleak moors with the cold wind chilling my blood, sometimes I was hanging by the arm over a swift rushing river, while the cold stars mocked my agony by their seeming tranquillity, sometimes I was falling with my wheel, falling, but never reaching ground. When the early cock crew, and the first shouts of the oxen-drivers were heard in the street, these sounds seemed to me to come from a far-off world that I had left long ago.

CHAPTER XV.

SEMLIN AND BELGRADE—SERVIAN PEOPLE AND POLITICS.

At last when clear light came back about half-past three, we were on the last stage of the road to the beginning of the real East ; and in a few hours were in sight of Semlin's walls and Belgrade's high-built minarets. Eight hundred years ago Semlin was the scene of the first victory in the disastrous First Crusade. Peter the Hermit with forty thousand followers, had passed safely from Peterwardein (hence the name), but, to avenge some crusaders of a former band who were impaled on the walls, he stormed and took the town. On the Zigeunerberg in the river is still seen the ruined castle of John Hunyadi, the Hungarian champion of Europe against Asia, "the White Knight," whose name the Turks corrupted into *Jancus Lain* (John the Wicked) as a bugbear with which to frighten their naughty children. When he had completed his glorious defence of Belgrade against the Turks under Mahomet II., he died on this spot ; and the sigh of the Ottoman Prince, in that he could no longer hope for revenge against his only triumphant antagonist, is the fittest epitaph a warrior could obtain.

While from the ferry steamer that crosses to Belgrade I was watching the noisy broods of water-fowl on the mud island at the junction of the Save and the Danube, a hand was put on my shoulder and a French voice said to me, " I sink you Ingleesh." To try and "put him out," I answered equivocally in German, " No, but I am Scotch." At which, however, he laughed and said in French, that it was all one, but that if I hated the English so much we would speak in French. He was a young French-Swiss, rejoicing in the name of Charles the Drover (Charles Bouvier). True to his name and its roving propensities, he drove, not oxen, but, what is more congenial to the degenerate Switzers of nowadays, his trade as waiter through the countries of Europe. Asking me if I had not been bewitched by the charming freshness and beauty of the Hungarian women, I answered, "Yes, they are almost as beautiful as English women." "Oh!" said he, "far more so; the women I saw in England are too fine, too delicate and too haughty: *c'est vrai, la jeunesse anglaise est belle, la plus belle du monde, mais après, après—non!*"

It was the 30th July when we were at Belgrade. From Hamburg to here, including stoppages and three days' illness, we had taken twenty-four days, and by putting up usually at country places, and living on common wholesome fare, such as bread, soup, eggs, fish, veal, beer or wine, I had spent only 5*l*. What use is there to fare higher? It would not improve one's powers of endurance.

Belgrade lies picturesquely on a high promontory formed by the Save and the Danube, which together separate Austria-Hungary from the eastern land of Servia. This is something like a boundary—"a natural frontier"—not your wretched ten-feet wire fences, nor your shallow puddles that a child could cross. A magnificent situation has Belgrade, "the White City," high up, covering all sides of the promontory with its crumbling Turkish mosques and minarets and ancient fortress, its new modern buildings looking grotesquely out of place, and its many steep narrow stair-like streets; while undulating hills, gay with varied scenery, run far up behind .t. Below wind the blue Save to west, and the dirty-green Danube to the north and east, and across them stretch away into dimness the fertile plains of Hungary.

The traveller who has never before been in the East does well to stay a time in Belgrade; for in more than its geographical position is it the key to the East. Its houses, its race of people, their costumes and manners, are all strange to him, and of a character that he will see more of in more decided forms as he advances into the lands of the morning sun.

The people are very dark in complexion—almost black. They are on the whole a thriving community, but in several parts of the town, particularly about the *Dortschula* (Turkish quarter), look very poor. As Christians the peoples in proximity

to the Turks have carried their revolt against Moslem customs
o the perilous extreme. In contrast to the enforced abstention
of women from public life and work under the Moslem system,
the Christians hereabouts make woman their slave, their maid-
of-all-work, in the dirtiest and heaviest labour. Nowhere have
I seen a greater degradation of woman than here in the principal street, the *Teracia*, where a woman was engaged in carrying
a hod of mortar up high scaffoldings at a new building. It seems
to me that even the confinement of the harem is more humane
and more desirable than such barbarity.

"It's O! to be a slave along with the barbarous Turk,
Where woman has never a soul to save, if *this* is Christian work!"

Servia is in a critical and anomalous condition as regards
politics. It has three parties in the government, one anti-
Turkish and favourable to Russia, another with inclinations
towards Austria and the West, while the dominant one—a
mixture, I suppose, of these two—is for war and aggrandizement.
From citizens and peasants, as well as from a journalist—into
whose favour I slid by pronouncing the English names in a
German copy of "Oliver Twist"—I gathered that Servia was
then preparing for another war on Bulgaria. But the forcible de-
thronement of Prince Alexander—with which Servia may have
had more to do than outwardly appeared—has altered the face
of affairs for the present at least. What I could not comprehend was the peculiar hesitancy in their policy. Though every
one laments that trade was ruined and occupations lost by the
last war, though they feel, in common with all the small nationalities in Eastern Europe, that antipathy to Russia that the fox,
in Horace, feels against the lion,—

"Quia me vestigia terrent,
Omnia te adversum spectantia, nulla retrorsum," [1]

yet they sadly shake their heads and say that war must come.
Russian gold and promised aid must have something to do with
this anomaly.

In connection with this it seemed significant that the Czar's
portrait should be hung up in houses along with that of King

---

[1] "Because the footprints terrify me, all making towards you, none
back from you."

Milan. The relationship of the two by marriage does not appear sufficient to account for the fact. For on the part of all the various peoples on the Continent it is odd to observe the attempts to make and think themselves a nation distinct from every other. So they hang up in public and private everywhere, as a sort of visible embodiment of their patriotism, the portraits of their particular rulers—Kaiser Wilhelm in Prussia, King Albert in Saxony, Franz Josef as Kaiser in Austria and König in Hungary, King Milan in Servia, King George in Greece; but, strange to say, I only once in Turkey saw a portrait of the Sultan.

The opinion which I at first formed that in time of peace at least the Servians are not the cruel, bloodthirsty brutes we in the West think them to be, but on the whole decent quiet folks, I had afterwards no great reason to alter. Their taste for war is natural in a young state; and if it be true that they can bring 200,000 men into the field, they are in a fair way to succeed. But the physique of the soldiers must first be improved, for they are as small as Belgian soldiers, have worse legs, only step better. As I was scrutinizing a regiment on the march, a Servian gentleman, who turned out to be Terzibaschits to whom I had a card of introduction from Vienna, depreciatively remarked that it was "*pas grande chose.*"

If the nation would only work hand in hand with the kindred state, Bulgaria, to form a powerful Balkan confederacy, I could heartily wish the Servians all the success and prosperity possible. But I fail to appreciate a people, who know they are doing wrong, who know they are shedding almost their own blood, in killing Bulgarians, and yet insist on war. Their land is fertile, but they say that they are too poor to buy plant to work it, and war may bring money—a rather risky policy. In Semendria there was, besides the omnipresent shows of the defeat of the Turks in the long past centuries at Vienna and Buda-Pest, a panorama of the late war with the victories of the Servian arms loudly displayed throughout it. So too, on articles of sale, such as match-boxes, the Servian flag is seen triumphant, while the poor Bulgarians are lying beneath, dead or dying. Ah! the young cub has once tasted blood, and he wants more.

The simple hotel at which we put up in Belgrade was such a

charming retreat with its tree-flowers and vine-embroidered terrace of bedrooms that I did not divulge its name to the cyclists I met at the club. They would doubtless have been shocked at my selecting such a low place, and been for transferring me to the more stylish Hotel National. This is always the way with cyclists, especially continental cyclists; they must have all their comforts with them: they cannot "rough it" or leave their set style of living.

At the premises of the two-year-old Belgrade Cycling Club, which counts among its members some fine energetic fellows, I "made a declaration" in their visitors' book. Of three strangers who have recorded their tours in it, one is a Buda-Pester, the others are Stevens and myself. Next afternoon, after superintending the making of some spokes in a gunsmith's shop where were all manner of ancient weapons, swords and pistols, blunderbusses, carbines, and rifles, we were escorted out of the city some kilometres on our way by half a dozen of the club members.

CHAPTER XVI.

SCENES IN SERVIA.

THROUGH half the length of Servia runs Trajan's Roman road, along which are still left many Roman architectural remains of interest to the student-traveller. At first it runs through wild and beautiful hill country, up and down near the Danube, affording some superb views of river and long islands wooded to the water's edge. Certainly all in all it is a good road, but does not deserve the inordinate praise bestowed on it by Stevens when he said in Belgrade that it was better than British roads. This is the road along which passed "those promiscuous multitudes of savage beasts, without humanity or reason," incited by the vehement persuasions of Peter, the little hermit, to burn and plunder and fight their way to rescue the Holy Temple, and kept together only by the fear of his keen and lively eye.

When darkness fell that evening, I was doing my utmost to reach the distant lofty towers of Semendria. But terrified at the awful hills we had to climb and descend at every turn of the river, I was glad at last to stop at a low-roofed porched house among fields of tall maize. Here by signs I got something to eat, and had coffee first made for me *à la turque*. The fireplace usually faces the front door in Eastern houses; in the solid stonework or brickwork there is a small aperture, in which charcoal logs are smouldering all day and night; there appears neither smoke nor light, but on the white ashes being stirred some red is disclosed, which does the cooking. A tiny pan, about the size of a brandy-glass, is half filled with coffee and sugar, then filled up with warm water and put among the charcoal ashes till the liquid boils. When served, no one can complain of its weakness; but its intense heat and jet blackness rather startle the novice.

It is curious to note how the glasses and jugs for beer and

wine differ in the various countries and districts. In Germany generally, beer is served in big pint glasses; then as one goes into a wine district, the beer glasses get smaller while the wine glasses get larger: in Servia both kinds have dwindled down to tiny three or four inch tumblers, indicating that both beer and wine are scarce. Indeed a good traveller could tell, even though he were blind and deaf, the country he was in by feeling the size and shape of the liquor glasses.

A very old place is the town of Semendria, with its caves and Roman remains, its ancient houses and its richly-endowed church; and a most remarkable spot is its fortress. It stands on a bend of the Danube where the Jessava falls in. Built by the first Servian prince, in size and strength it still is appalling. It is a triangle, and has an outer wall of circumvallation. The walls are 100—150 ft. high, and castellated, with massive square towers rising on them every fifty yards. Figures of deities, arched windows, staircases, and shabby modern erections are all most oddly jumbled together. Inside are bands of soldiers at work or play, amid groves of the most luxurious vegetation; fruit trees of all sorts, plums, apricots, pears, apples, and berries, let fall their produce almost unheeded. And the fauna is as prolific as the flora. At every step some rabbit or hare or wild bird is disturbed, while snakes and salamanders and weasels dart in and out among the grass and the broken walls.

The Græco-Servian church here is an exquisite building out and in. After ten minutes' ringing of the great bells, I expected a crowd at the service on Sunday; but only the priest, the sacristan and myself were present. It was gone through rapidly, of course. All was cold and lifeless. Surely one man, even though he be a *caloyer* (priest), is not enough to represent the spiritual life of a whole town! What a killing effect on the life and tone of character among a people must such lifelessness in religion bring about! Give me, after all, not this gorgeous gilt grandeur with its coldness and its lifeless forms, but even a poor barn in Prussia with a crowd in it singing heartily together some Luther's hymn or Psalm of David. Yes; *Ichabod* can be written over the portals of the Greek Church. Religion has gone from that church and entered the common life. I see it in the awe-struck looks when a funeral passes by; I hear it in the mournful lullaby the mother sings to her babe; I hear it in the melancholy drone, grating yet pleasing, that rises from the harvesters in the valley, and sounds as if imprisoned souls were moaning their captivity.

If, as people say, we are to judge the barbarity of a people by their risibility, the Servians must be very barbarous. All along the route the peasants come running out of house and field to see me, to stand and "stare with wonder's lingering dread," till we have passed, when out comes the loud "Ha! ha! ha-a-a!" in all sorts of keys and voices (but chiefly soprano). Three or four hundred yards away, still follow the cachinnations of that half-wondering, half-idiotic laughter. One cannot help imagining that something extremely amusing is the matter with one's self.

One day a man was driving a cart half-laden with cut grain loosely placed, on which he sat. While he gazed stupidly at me and laughed, his horses shied, and made off over the ditch, through the field and back to the road again. The telegraph wires, which are very loose and low in Servia, caught him and the grain and tossed both over together, while the horses stopped short with the shock. It was now my turn to laugh This time I left him to himself—as I did not wish to pay another *Gulden* for other folks' stupidity.

A comical case was this other one too. Two great bullocks tied together by the head and led by a man holding the rope between them bolted on seeing me. The rope caught him low down; he was carried a yard or two, and performed a somersault, still holding on by the rope.

About six one morning I was swinging meditatively along, when I heard heavy steps running behind me. With a start I saw a skull-capped, fierce-moustached, Oriental-dressed man making the wildest grimaces. Instinctively my hand went to my revolver pocket and my feet plied the pedals faster. The latter act soon placed distance between us; and then I knew from the shouts of laughter and disappointment of the onlookers that it had been meant for a race.

The dogs are still most persistently annoying. One big brute got into a perfect paroxysm of rage at the sight of me, burst his chain and would have sprung at the saddle, had he better known the machine. Three dogs, say, come from one house and another. At first they only stare; then comes a growl. Another makes a dart out from his kennel, and is slowly followed by others. At last some braver spirit bounds straight for the wheel. Instantly the street is alive with canine life in all shapes and sizes, and the air is made hideous with a perfect pandemonium of sounds from the thin transparent squeak to the big deep bay. On I speed through (or over) it all, and a muffled noise from a field or behind me tells how some champion has come up too late for the fray, and discovers he has not courage enough to carry it on single-handed.

The curiosity of the people is sometimes intolerable. They crowd round whenever I halt (so much so that I even dreaded to stop and get a drink at a well), they touch and push the bicycle about, trying to comprehend it, chattering like magpies all the time. When I enter a place, at first only a few boys and girls begin to follow, then others, and men and women swell the crowd, till, before I get through the mile of street, it surges from side to side, stopping all other traffic, while the hubbub is infernal. When at last clear of the cobbles, I vault into the saddle, deafening shouts and laughter arise that sound most like derision.

The queerest speculations as to the bicycle are elicited. One man explaining it to his fellow-citizens touched the bell and gravely stated that the *electricity* was kept there! Another wisely informed me by signs that the pedals were for the knee-bends, and the handle-bar for the arm-pits!

That the people here speak only Servian was to me a great comfort. No more would I have to answer, "Where from?" "Where to?" "What is your object?" "What your profession?" "What countryman?" "Are you paid by your Government?" and a score other more or less impertinent questions. Yet it was a discomfort too. For whenever I wanted to ask the road or distance, or such like, I had to begin: " *Spricht Jemand Deutsch hier?*" " *Est-ce qu' on parle français ici?*" " *Homileite ta Hellenica?*" " *Parlate italiano?*" Judge of my disgust when I usually found no one to speak any of the languages—but only Servian, and they pride themselves thereon. Often, however, Greek or Italian was spoken, where French and German were unknown.

Late one evening I found myself on a high ridge of wild

forest country above the valley of the Morava. Rain came on, and reluctantly I put up at the first house I found. Such squalor, such a lack of the comforts of life, such brutishness, ignorance, and inconsiderateness on the part of the men and women in it I had not expected to see even in Servia. I reconciled myself when I recollected I was up among the mountains. Nearly every one was drunk, and kept up singing and roaring till near dawn of day. I pushed the bed against the door in the room they gave me; but the men broke open the window and shone in lanterns upon me in bed. They wanted me out to perform on my machine for their amusement. Surely this was the stuff, at last, out of which sprang "the Bulgarian atrocities." With the promise from me that they would see me start at half-past four in the morning, they left me in peace and returned to their rioting. I had scarcely got three hours of sleep when thundering knocks at door and window awakened me. There were the evil-looking faces at the casements grinning under their fantastic caps of the Glengarry fashion and calling out with renewed thumpings, "Get up, get up; half-past four, half-past four!" There was no alternative, I must get up. To my request for a basin and water, the grim slut of a hostess answered that they kept no such things there. On getting outside, ready to start, I was nearly massacred by the expectant ruffians, because the road, rising far up from the inn at a gradient of nearly 50° made mounting impossible. This fact they could not understand; but nevertheless the expected exhibition for which they had either kept a late vigil or made an early rise did not come off. So, after all, I had my revenge, though unexpected.

Near Alexinatz the people saw me from afar, and met me in crowds of hundreds. So completely did they block me that only on showing my revolver could I get into a restaurant for some food. There the hostess and her sister, big strong young women, wearing the national dress—a red vest and chemisette, and a little fez on the head—as we sat on a long sun-shaded balcony among roses and vines, insisted that I should have every second pull at their cigarettes—an odd custom, I thought; but they tell me it was to show they were in love with me. In getting out of Deligrad, farther on, 200 or 300 men ran before me half a mile to the top of the steep hill outside in order to have a sight of me mounting.

CHAPTER XVII.

SERVIAN SCENERY—"NEW SERVIA."

FEW countries can vie with Servia in beauty of scenery. Beautiful verdant valleys, well-watered by many rivers, long lofty mountains rising above one another till the eye cannot follow the view, great deep wild ravines cleaving their sides in all directions clothed from top to bottom with forests, all make a landscape that Switzerland can scarcely match. Especially is it so from Nissa, the former frontier town of Turkey, southward through the fertile valleys and the wild but magnificent mountains, including the Miowatski, in "New Servia." This is the name given to the slice of Turkey carved out to Servia in the famous banquet of the nations consummated at Berlin on the 13th July, 1878.

A famous place is Nissa. Peter the Hermit's hordes sustained their first great defeat here when their cruelty and lawless rapacity roused its inhabitants against them. In its *palanka* (suburbs) is said to stand a tower made of the skulls of Servian rebels, telling of later deadly struggles in this vicinity between the Crescent and the Cross. But Nissa is best known as the birthplace of Constantine the Great; and a meet nurse it is for a man of imperial ambition. Away eastward up the Nissava river tower huge dark masses of mountain; northward and southward the plain and river of Morava stretch and wind among the glowing yellow hills.

No lovelier country have I gone through than that from Nissa to Leskovatz and on to Vranja. After crossing at Tschetschina a ruinous bridge of wooden piles over the Morava which runs as clear and fresh over its rocky bed as any Highland stream, -we followed an almost straight road for thirty miles with rich fields of maize and corn and melons, and groves of beech and oak and poplars and fruit-trees on each side. Avenues of acacias and beeches sometimes extended as much as six miles in an unbroken bee-line. Nothing could be more romantic than the occasional glimpse of a secluded village with its mosque and minaret rising through such a fairy scene.

The military were in strong force at Lescovatz; hundreds of huts made of poles and turf or branches were standing outside the town; and the roads were gay with uniforms. The stirring martial music heard as we approached in the gloaming heightened the ineffable charm the fairy-like spot had cast over my senses, and deepened the contrast of the outside appearance to the dirty, prosaic, old and yellow look that things wore inside. I rushed despairingly about the crooked narrow streets over cobbles that for age and size might have been laid by the Goths, seeking for lodgings and finding none, and followed by crowds of yelling bloused and crimson-capped rascals at my heels. At last I unearthed the young mill-owner whose name they had given me at Belgrade, but only to find an inseparable barrier between him and me, for he spoke "only Servian." Luckily an Italian workman from Florence saw me and took me to an inn such as it was.

On leaving next morning, having been thoroughly exasperated at the jostling given me in the streets the previous night, I adopted the dangerous plan of showing to the troublesome crowds my revolver cocked—but safely locked. This kept them at a comfortable distance, but so persistently did they follow me that out of spite I did not afford them the desired spectacle of seeing me mount till three or four miles out of the town, by which time they had decreased to only two or three. But not before they had perceived my malignant purpose, for they ran along the fields and from the cover of the trees threw stones at me, luckily with small effect.

From Nissa, where Stevens and his Belgradian escort turned eastward to Pirot, as had done the Hermit and his hordes centuries before, I am the first cyclist on as far as Salonica. May there never be a second, is my prayer—for the second's sake. No traveller seems ever to have gone this route. Still let lovers of the terrible and grand come here, and go no more to Switzerland. All around are mountains, torrents,

F

and ravines, rocky and sandy steeps with stumpy bushes of hawthorn, oak, and beech clinging to their sides. Halfway up are cottages with fields of corn encircling them, up again are rocks and trees, and higher still bare summits. Herd-boys are piping to one another from rock to rock, tending their sheep and goats and black thick-horned cattle.

The peasant women are quite Oriental, with their chequered scarf and hood and striped petticoats, their rings and crosses, and other tawdry ornaments. The boys are also Oriental, for they run about with only a coarse linen shirt open down the front and reaching only to above the knees.

At one small mountain inn of one room and windows innocent of glass, while I slept during the heat of the sun, a girl came in. It seemed in my dream as if I were lying on a mountain top, and the mist was whirling around me to cool me from the terrible heat; I heard the trees waving in the wind and the cataracts begin to roar: then a wailing from the valley smote my heart as though for the funeral of some loved one. The girl was singing to me, as she plied her distaff and wool, singing in weird mournful tones, that rose high then died away like the wind among the trees on the mountains.

The shepherd-boys have all pipes or whistles, and play a monotonous air, like the double motion of a saw. Wandering bands go about with banjo and fiddles, and play so weirdly yet so sweetly that it is hard to imagine such strains possible from such tawny, ragged, ill-favoured creatures.

Say what they will, England is still high in favour with these Eastern people. Several times I was taken for a German and coldly received, but as soon as they learned I was English, they could not make enough of me. One man in Semendria, gazing with admiration on me, declared an Englishman to them was *wie Gott* (a very god.) At a station, on the new line which a Belgian firm is constructing, the host, a tall, handsome, strong, frank-faced man, clapped me on the back when I told I was "*Ingleese*," and, with a "*Bravo! bravo!*" squeezed my hand affectionately. On the other hand, though they are dead against Russia, in a discussion some Servian gentlemen and I had at Vranja, the general opinion came out that the Russians make the best soldiers. Why? "Because, while the Englishman is too well-off to fight, and the Frenchman cares for his *toilette* as much as for glory, and the German loves his beer as much as his Fatherland, the Russian has only two thoughts and for these he fights till death—first, *Kaiser*, second, *Gott*." It was no use my suggesting that the Turk would by that reckoning be better still, for his chief thought was *Allah* (God) and his next, a perpetual Paradise to be gained by a brave death. Such words were treason there.

CHAPTER XVIII.

SORE TREATMENT AT THE TURCO-SERVIAN FRONTIER.

TRULY the Berlin Treaty was very impartial to Turkey! Had the deputies of the great powers present at it seen the fair fertile land they sliced off for Servia and compared it with the land south of Vranja, the present frontier-town, I think even they would have questioned the fairness of the award. There is nothing now to be seen but long barren plains, almost treeless, and interminable ranges of brown bare mountains, south, east, and west.

Vranja itself is still very Turkish, very Oriental—fair without and foul within. Without, as it lies clustered together at the head of a long valley on the shoulder of a hill, with its whitewashed mosques and numerous heaven-pointing minarets encircled with poplars and gleaming against the dark background of precipitous hills, it is a sense-captivating sight. Within, its mud walls, its close alleys, its mud or sun-dried brick hovels, its gutters and smells, its only drain flowing open down the main street, dispel all fair illusions. Yet to the student it is interesting by the very novelty of the life it displays—the long rows of open shops with the owners and friends lounging at the entrances, the curious commodities such as sandals and caps, and ornamented weapons for sale or on manufacture in the numerous shops, the pack-mules and donkeys laden with fruits and vegetables being goaded along, and above all the conspicuous dearth of women in the streets.

Three or four hundred persons of all ages followed me through the town, and amid cries of "Bravo! Ingleese," I raised my cap, and started away to brave the Turks. Eight miles south is the frontier line between Servia and Turkey. The fellow at the station there could not read my passport, and knew neither French, German, nor Greek. But he sent me back on foot to Vranja for a police *visa*. This I got from a fellow who evidently did not know what my passport was. At the exit of the town it was again *visaed*. At the frontier again about 8 p.m. the man would not look at my papers till he finished eating, which was in three-quarters of an hour. And then he pronounced my passport still not good; why, I could not make out. So off I bounced towards Turkey; but at the half-way hut, a guard of soldiers with fixed bayonets blocked the way. Every motion of mine they followed and twice had their bayonets an inch from my breast. Oh, it was galling to a free-born Briton thus to be thwarted and confined by those swarthy skunks on the very land that his country had helped to give them! I raged and ramped about, and roared out towards the Turkish lines the name of Abasy Effendi, a worthy officer stationed there. But all in vain. The whole Servian guard turned out and hemmed me in as if I were a wild beast. Trying to get back my machine, all I got from them was, as they pointed back, a thundering "*Marsch!*"

There I stood in the cold dark night, without a person at hand from whom to ask an intelligible explanation or advice, eight miles from any known lodgings, footsore and tired out with the day's excitement and exertions, my wheel and viaticum locked up in the guard-house—it was a desperate case. Still indignation buoyed me up, for I saw well enough that the man at the custom-office had taken a spite against me. Flinging myself into the room where he sat drinking and smoking with a malicious smile of triumph on his face, I shook my fist at him, threatening him with the consuls and emphatically repeating that I was *Inglese*. Whereupon up rose the blackguard, shook his fist at me, ejaculating, "*Serbisch, Serbisch!*"—meaning tha Servian was as good as English any day.

The goodfolks of the house, secretly sympathizing with me, gave me a small bedroom. Early in the morning the innkeeper made me to know that the French railway station-master was coming by. When he did, I told him my case. It turned out that a mention of my machine was wanted before I could pass, and that I should have once more to trudge back to Vranja for it. "But," said the Frenchman, "why didn't you give him some francs at first?" Well, this is how trade flourishes in the East! *Virtus post nummos*, is the rule of life there. If you want to keep the law, the only way is *money;* if you want to break the law, or get it broken for you, then—*money*. The prime, sole object of the law is *money*.

The magistrate in Vranja, when I appeared for the second time before him, was furious, and immediately armed me with a private official order to let me pass. My case by this, the third time I was in Vranja, was well known; and, when I finally left on my wheel—which the Frenchman had rescued from sequestration—the town was waiting in its thousands and cheered me off with a regular ovation.

With the desire to get the punctilious fellow made an example of, I set the British Embassy at Belgrade to investigate the case; but after some correspondence in which it transpired that the fellow denied the most serious charges, it was decided best to let the matter pass, in consequence of the strained condition of affairs in the East.

CHAPTER XIX.

RECEPTIONS IN TURKEY.

AFTER my escape from Servia, to reach Turkey, where I already knew of a friend in the person of young Abasy Effendi, who speaks fluent French, was like getting home. So this was Turkey, the place I had been warned of all through Europe, had dreamed of and dreaded as a lair of cutthroats and bloodthirsty barbarians! Disillusions, as well as disenchantments, are scattered plentifully about the traveller's path.

The Turks were in great force about the frontier station, and received me without any fuss. Abasy brought out the Chief of the Customs to see me. But there could be no thought of business till I had first performed on my wheel before them all in the courtyard. As the thing circled and curvetted beneath me, the intense amusement and wonder depicted on their faces was a treat well worth the trouble. The Turk, reversing in this and other cases all our practical Western maxims, puts pleasure before business; but the fact that he still keeps a keen eye for the latter was shown by his exacting, as the best reward for the pleasure it had afforded him, a duty of twenty francs on my machine. Thanks to Mr. Blunt, our influential Consul-General at Salonica, this sum has since been refunded.

There is little traffic on those Turkish roads. Once in ten miles you may meet a train of waggons drawn by oxen, and usually laden with grain, or a band of men on horses with baggage strapped all round them, but, for security, travelling is all done in company. Only once did we meet a solitary traveller, and he was a Servian, well-mounted and well-armed. Everybody travels armed, at least with pistols, and usually also with sword and gun, and cartridges strung ornamentally round the body. What was my poor little revolver against all that! I hid it away in very shame. Sometimes the aspect of the wandering bands was most ferocious. Once or twice in lonely parts I was stopped and examined, but always, either through coolness or a show of assurance managed to get clear away.

My first day's experience of Turkish weather was not promising. On the highlands a tropical rain had drenched me and in the plains the sun made my wet clothes feel as if they were boiling on me. But on subsequent days I had good reason to long for the rain that never came. Yet no one need complain of the scarcity of drinking-water on the Turkish roads; for, thanks to the religious imposition of washing the hands before prayer, fountains are found at convenient distances, and some of them in most romantic spots. Indeed, many of my pleasantest reminiscences are centred round those fountains. On the brow of a hill, or nestling in a glen, almost hidden by flowering heath and tangled brambles, bushes black with big berries, the fountain spouts out its clear, copious stream through an oblong slab of handsome stone or marble into the bowl and then into the lower trough. Sitting quietly there enjoying a morning midday pipe, I have watched many a picturesque scene—big, brawny-armed Bulgarian women (Bulgarians chiefly cultivate the *tchifliks* or farms of the Turkish proprietors) filling barrels with water; itinerant families cooking and eating their scanty meals around the spring.

Near Kumanovo, after having traversed hills all day, I came upon a strong body of troops, some thousands strong. Such a medley I never saw. There was no order in their march. Baggage-mules, infantry, cavalry—some in line, most out of line—crawled along higgledy-piggledy-wise. The horses were poor in the extreme. The men were sturdy, brave-looking fellows, but most shamefully accoutred—rags on their backs and ropes on their feet. As I passed the main body, I shouted, pointing to myself, "*Ingleese*," and "*Viva la Turca!*" Whereupon officers and all waved their hats and shouted, "*Bravo!*" It was an inspiring moment. When we were well past the main body, at a place where the path ran along a slope above a river, when my breast was swelling high with the tide of emotion, a straggler, as much from ignorance as from wantonness, thrust his sword amongst the spokes behind the forks. To his speech less dismay he beheld us rolling and sprawling down the bank. Luckily I only got my wrist slightly twisted.

After crossing a river by difficult stepping-stones, we came to the Douane at Kumanovo, a strong garrison town. Nobody spoke anything I understood; so my score of Turkish words had to be aired, till eventually a Greek innkeeper came to my aid. We went down a street through which ran a broad clear stream swiftly. His inn was a long, rambling, lumbering den, with endless turnings, outs and ins; stalls, wine-butts of giant dimensions, ladders, garrets, and bare rafters made up this old-world abode. Many of the soldiers whom we had passed came flocking in, stabled their beasts, and lay down in rows on the raised boardings.

In the evening I went down to see, but especially to be seen, for I was the great centre of attraction and received with marked civility everywhere in the town. Seeking for something sweet to eat, all I could find, besides the never-absent pears and melons, was a kind of insipid floury confection in stalks, and also Peak, Frean and Co.'s biscuits. After being freely offered to taste all sorts of abominations, I hit upon loaf sugar as the purest and best sweetmeat available there. On my return to the inn, the soldiers had lain down for the night. Some were thumbing and mumbling over yellow pages by the light of rude, open lamps; others were crooning melancholy airs in that peculiar strain that only Easterns can produce, while only a few were hilarious. In the daytime it would have been with dread and misgiving I should have trusted myself to lie down among such a wild, promiscuous herd; but sleep is an irresistible dispeller of prejudice and distrust, and by-and-by the landlord and I betook ourselves to a garret and slept on mats *à la turque* as soundly as if in a feather-bed in a locked bedroom.

In the morning gendarmes conducted me to the governor, who received me well. He and all his officers were seated, Turkish fashion, on divans. After my passport was examined by all, it was sent off to be officially prepared! A young Turk was brought who spoke French. Then followed an hour's close questioning, and an order to ride my machine through the town to demonstrate to the people. Every man and boy turned out —the women peered out of windows, and over walls—to see me perform, and the soldiers had hard work to keep room for me to move. Then a private performance took place in the governor's courtyard, "attended by the nobility and gentry."

Those Turks are strong-built fellows, handsome of face and figure. As for the women, what I saw of them behind the ugly white bandages on their faces did not make me long to see more.

At the Douane all sorts and conditions of privileged men came to call on me, among whom was a Sheik (priest), a tall, grave-looking, white-apparelled, turbaned personage, also a merry-faced Bey from Constantinople, with a soft mellow voice. Then came a French-speaking captain to bid me wait for the chief military man of the district, Sabit Pasha, who had heard of me. At last the great man arrived. After salaams were over, and boots off, we all sat round a beautifully-draped inner room. Coffee was served by a tall servitor who bowed himself nearly to my knees each time he gave or took away the tiny cups. Then cigarettes were lit. And now for the conference. It touched on all subjects of European politics, especially on my views of Austria and Servia as gained by my travels.

Thanks and congratulations were then interpreted to me, also an offer of a mounted escort, which I declined, and also a request that I should ride through the town in order that the Pasha might behold the working of the wonderful "flying horse of iron."

Over a wild bare mountainous country, where the road often ended in a ravine with no bridge to cross it, but I had to lower myself and wheel down a steep tortuous path, cross the torrent, and crawl up the other side, there was not a house except some few empty khans all the way to Uskub. When nearly famishing I crossed a field to where some harvesters were at work beside a hut, and asked for *yekmek* (bread), but only got a *yok, yok!* (no, no), and the same when I asked for *soot* (milk)—they could not spare any of either. Farther on in a tent-shaped hut of mud and straw I ate some boiled eggs and bread, worth a few pence there. Too late I discovered to my dismay that the only change I had was a few Servian *paras*, not enough to pay. Before trying them, I looked outside to see if the way was clear for an escape if necessary; but the road was one long rapid descent and full of ruts and stones, which would make mounting out of the question. The men seated there with guns and pistols all around them, refused to take the money as being neither current nor enough. On my showing them a twenty-franc piece, they wanted to keep it, declaring they had no change. But that bargain would not do. Then they drew their long knives, angry that I could not pay for what I had eaten. This reminded me how much they prized English pocket-knives here. So mine was bartered for my meagre mess.

CHAPTER XX.

DIFFICULTIES OF TRAVELLING IN LOWER TURKEY—IN CUSTODY.

At Uskub, on the Vardar, was a nice little hotel, where the presence of Greeks and Frenchmen engaged at a new railway made me feel at home. There was no small difficulty in finding it out; but a revenue officer, who came running breathlessly after me in the belief that I was trying to evade the search that is made at every Turkish town, when he heard I was English, only made a show of searching, and directed me to the Greek inn. There an English lad and his mother found me out, and took me to their house. On crossing the bridge they had to bargain with the sentinel at the guard-house there to let me pass when I returned—for the law permits no passage from one side to the other after dark.

The town has an exquisite situation in the valley and on the river, and besides the imposing citadel and one or two old towers—of Venetian origin—has dozens of airy-like minarets and an old crowded cemetery on an eminence above the town. Here I saw the first beggar on my route since leaving Austria; it was an old filthy hag muffled up and croaking out impending blessings on the Effendis that would give her a few *paras*. They tell me that begging was unknown till the Franks came —that is the name in the East for all Westerns.

The country around is most desolate and barren of people. All the way to Keuprülü, thirty miles, there were not more than half a dozen habitations visible. At the beginning of an hour's most arduous climbing some thousand feet on to a ridge of mountains, being parched with thirst from the scorching heat, I went up into a high cottage where in an open verandah sat two Turks wearing the *fezi* and baggy trousers. They gave me bread, butter-milk, and some juicy scraps; for which I gave them a five-piastre piece (1s.) They said they had no change. As usual, of course, they must see my passport and papers—every Turk constitutes himself a custom-house officer over you—then they rifled my pockets and felt me all over, then turned everything out of my knapsack. But they did not find what they sought, for my *gold* was hidden in a secret pocket in the lining of my breeches. Dissatisfied, they found a fault in my passport (save the phrase! they could not read a word of it), and ordered me back to Uskub to put it right. Saying I would, I got on to my machine with the head facing the way I had come, when to their surprise and rage, I suddenly wheeled round and sped with fear's fleetness up the road. Every second I expected a bullet to come whizzing up; for they had both pistols and guns. Not till I had scaled the heights and once more was on my willing steed did I breathe freely.

A more terribly hilly, aggravatingly up and down road, there could not well be than over that ten miles of ridges to Keuprülü. As far as could be seen on every side rise peaks after peaks of great height. The town lies in the hollow of the mountains; through it passes the Vardar (Homer's Axios). When the lamps in its 5000 houses, built from the river high up the sides on both banks, are lit by night, the scene is enchanting.

At the bridge, when I was being followed by nearly a thousand people, the gendarme pounced on me, dragged my machine and me into the guard-house, fixed his bayonet, and made me produce every article I possessed. Maps, cards, books, pins, revolver, and various little trophies I had collected, all fell under dire suspicion. As for my wheel the poor thing was thought to be an instrument by which I, a brigand or auxiliary of brigands, might the more swiftly carry off booty to mountain fastnesses. So, at least, I made out from the babel of tongues that clamoured about me. At my oft-repeated call for the pasha, they conducted me to the police quarters above the river dam. But the pasha could speak only Turkish. An Italian pushed forward out of the crowd that now swarmed in many hundreds around us. Between Italian and French, the pasha at last was aware of what my character really was; and he telegraphed to Constantinople for instructions. I was told that on no account must I cross the mountains, as they were officially known to be full of brigands, that "affairs of brigandage" occurred weekly; people disappeared, nothing more being heard of them, since they were probably thrown over the terrible ravines that cluster thick around the awful *Demir-Kapou* (Iron Gates) quite near here. Indeed in this same province of Monastir not far from here, a formidable band of brigands, about two months after I left the district, robbed a merchant's caravan, set fire to a village, and massacred seven persons. Moreover, the Turkish authorities are very chary of travellers in Macedonia, since they were forced by Britain to pay up the ransom of one or two who had been carried off by the brigands. One gentleman, after attending a performance in Salonica, entered a cab in order to proceed to his country residence, but found he had been entrapped: and 10,000*l*. of a ransom was the penalty for his mistake.

The answer to the telegram came in an hour or two, to the effect that the magistrates were to send me on by rail, as the Government could not undertake the risk of letting so conspicuous a traveller as I was with my wheel pass the mountains. Meantime a clerk had taken a minute inventory of all my belongings, and also recorded my verbal deposition. My effects were to be returned to me in the morning, only if I went quietly off by train the few miles down to Salonica. The whole town was gathered round me in the street, on the river-banks, on the bridge and on the railroad, and to such a concourse of spectators I was made perform along the railway. But, no doubt from an exaggerated notion of the machine's power and speed, a gendarme was sent on in front to see that I did not escape!

Afterwards they put me in the best room of the police-station, fed me with cheese, bread, wine, melon, and coffee, and left me to sleep on the divan. The turbaned Turkish servitors served me so urbanely and solemnly that for some time I could not think of partaking in the presence of such august individuals.

Without a doubt there are fine men in Turkey; and it is a pity their manners and life are not freer. For then those strong, healthy, bold-looking youths would not, when they come into prime, become so strongly marked with the look of cruelty and ferocity that most of the grown-up wear. I had a rare opportunity of narrowly examining their physique and appearance, as I reclined at the open exposed window of the guard-house. They flocked up all evening and sat down on the wall overlooking the railway bank opposite me, and there while they satisfied their curiosity on me, I took good and leisurely stock of them.

CHAPTER XXI.

"SPEED THE PARTING GUEST"—FIRST SIGHT OF THE ÆGEAN.

IN the morning it was announced to me that I might go and see the town. At the bridge the gendarme who had given me such unceremonious treatment the evening before, now gravely and humbly saluted me as I passed. The market-place where at least three gutter-streams cross and recross each other was already thronged with sellers of provisions and fruits who had come with their strings of donkeys from the surrounding country. Fresh grapes and figs, selling at about a penny an *oke* (2 lb.), nuts, melons, pears, apples, plums, apricots, peaches, besides heavier and wholesomer fruits of the earth, were all being bought and sold as soberly and eagerly as if the transactions involved sums important to the stability of the Bourses of Europe. On my expressing surprise that such a large town had no more serious trade, a labourer, who had been in Austria, replied to me in one of those humorous reversions of Western sayings, "It is a good wind that blows nobody ill." By this he meant that the railway had destroyed all the trade of Keuprülü, which formerly consisted in carrying the grain of the inlands down the Vardar to the sea. Indeed there is still so much hostility of various kinds that the line has to be guarded at frequent points along its course.

In the custody of a soldier, who carried the bread, black wine, and [1] *kanati* for water—the usual provision for a journey—I proceeded to the governor's house to recover my passport. There, in a grand, wide, lofty room commanding a view of the town and slopes, the *Kamakan* introduced me to his chief officers, and evidently, from the merriment among them, told my story and captivity. Several times he clapped his hands—for the Turks have no bells and are too sedate to encourage a useless

---

[1] An earthen jar with a long narrow neck and wide body.

expenditure of voice—and a servitor appeared, taking off his sandals before he entered, and delivered various papers which were discussed and signed. Coffee also, which is the necessary prelude or accompaniment of all serious business, was passed round to all of us. No wonder the Turks become so yellow and smoked when one considers the excessive amount of coal-black coffee they daily consume.

By-and-by, as train-time drew near, the kind old kamakan, who had wished me a cheery *Saban hiresem* (good morning), when I came in, now rose and shook my hand—contrary to Ottoman fashion—then patted me admiringly on the back and wished me *Urlarula* (a good journey). But the soldier did not quit me till the train was on the move.

It was indeed a terrifying country we passed through— mountains, mountains everywhere, closing in till only their perpendicular sides, the Vardar, and a patch of blue sky are seen. Then come bare, bare hills, and sandy plains, above which in the distance rise Mount Bermius and Mount Olympus in conspicuous majesty. At last the sea—$\theta\alpha\lambda\acute{a}\sigma\sigma\eta$! $\theta\alpha\lambda\acute{a}\sigma\sigma\eta$! No matter what sea : any sea is good enough after so much land! $\Theta\alpha\lambda\acute{a}\sigma\sigma\eta$! was the joyful shout of Xenophon and his Ten Thousand when they first saw the sea after escaping from the heart of Asia ; and now, after long centuries of blood and fire and terror have passed over these lands that enclose it, $\theta\alpha\lambda\acute{a}\sigma\sigma\eta$ is the sound I greet it with. Children of the wave, born on ocean's lip, they could not live happily away from it long! freedom is the word by its murmur and its roar it has sounded to them, to Britons and to me. And round about these shores, as far even as the Black Sea, which probably the Ten Thousand at first mistook for their own Ægean, their true modern countrymen are swarming and flourishing still with renewed vitality, promising to outstrip all their neighbours and former oppressors, not only in what pertains to the sea, but in all the arts of peace. War and oppression and ruin have done their utmost to uproot the Greek race and language; but here still unchanged remain the "old poetic mountains," the same calm sea, the same Hellenic speech, and a relic, slumbering indeed yet living still, of the ancient Hellenic spirit.

Though there is room for grave doubt whether the Greek, especially the Greek peasant, is morally the superior of the

Turk, since he has neither the fine physique nor the soberness and solidity of the Turkish character, there is no doubt whatever that he is not the Turk's inferior in all that pertains to administration and commercial enterprise. This was at once manifest in Salonica. In striking contrast to the stagnation and backwardness of places completely under Turkish guidance, here was a town full of bustling activity, where Greek shopkeepers, Greek merchants, Greek works and Greek ships have dispelled the lethargic sleep of Turkish fatalism.

But the peculiar position of the Turks in their Eastern home in Europe, environed with hostile races and hostile religions, yet retaining their distinctive habits and tastes, deserves fuller consideration.

CHAPTER XXII.

AN ESTIMATE OF EASTERN LIFE.

To one brought up in Western Europe how strange all things appear in the light of an Eastern sun! Buildings, costumes, manners, speech, all are strange. The sky does not look the same, but one nearer Paradise, not the dull grey that makes men burrow themselves in the busy practical affairs of their little life, but the deep mystic blue that steals the soul away from self to dream of the great eternities. Even the earth is not the same, it is wilder, ruggeder, browner, richer ye barer: for the sun and the sky, while they reflect their own richness on the earth, seem jealous that man's abode should engross his thoughts that are due chiefly heavenward. Mould, the deep mould of ages, is thick over town and vale and hill. There seems little juice and sap left in land and people. Only let me lie where I am, they seem to say, let me enjoy what I have and be content, or if I am not content, let me dream I possess what would make me content. This spirit of dreaming rather than of doing is both the charm and the curse of the East. It gives its tone to all work and life, social, religious, and political, with the result that there is very little accomplished of either. The Turk reverses the common maxim, and luxuriously declares, "What can be done to-day were far better done to-morrow."

The constant dread that haunts the stranger in the East is lest he too come to look at life as the Easterns do. For to every sensitive mind there is a subtle charm in their life, a sensuous glow of warmth that makes one insensible to the cold thoughts he has brought with him from the West. All the Franks I met have succumbed more or less to this influence;

but none more entirely than one who found me on the banks of the Vardar. Here amid the ruined remnants of Roman and Venetian sway, beside Homer's Axios as it sweeps on to the blue Ægean, through the yellow plains and bare brown hills of a Macedonian upland, my last thought would have been to meet an Englishwoman. But, before my iron steed and I had been an hour in the town, the news had spread like wildfire and reached her ears that an " Ingleese " had come from the mountains on "a flying wheel."

So her son and she came along to the Greek inn where I was busy at the open window furbishing my Hellenic lingual stores ; and at the single sentence pronounced in musical English tones, " Is it true you are English ? " my heart was back again across the long continent to the brave land that is girt by the sea. She is a daughter of a noble family, and withal a gifted authoress, but her French husband's faithlessness has made her choose her home where she can best forget her sorrow, in a land where all the glory is either past or hoped for in the future, in the dreamland of the glowing East. Sitting that night on the balcony as the clear crescent moon rose over the mountain peaks and shone on us through the trellis of vines, listening to the solemn tones of the Mussulman family at prayer across the courtyard, it was natural we should speak of religion. With the last "*Allah Hu!*" of the Muezzin floating on the night-breeze to us from the minarets—a sound weirder and sweeter far than of any bell in Christendom—the religion we spoke of could not be a narrow thing that shuts out any human soul, but the truer and nobler that holds all men brethren in the kingdom of God.

She wondered that a rover like myself should care for such serious things, and on being informed that, before many months were past, my vocation would be in the Protestant ministry, she sadly said it was a mistake. " Can you believe all you were taught when a child ? " To this I replied, " Yes ; but with the added light that reason and experience have given : for nothing is truer than the universality of religion in men's hearts, and the superiority of the Christian spirit in peace, humanity and charity." For her part, she said, life in the East had set her at war with creeds and doctrines, and she could not again live with peace of mind in England ;

all that was best in the Cross was like the best in the Crescent, and she preferred to live where she might blend most easily the beautiful and the good in an unfettered religion of the heart: but yet she could not be a Moslem, for in that system,

> "Where woman's parted soul shall go,
> Her Prophet had disdained to show."

Perhaps, after all, she was not far wrong; for to the observant mind there is much in the Crescent akin to the Cross. Some of the noblest Christians have owned this truth and acted accordingly in their dealings with Islamism; and none more markedly than Gordon the warrior saint, who, though a fervent Christian, yet won the esteem and affection of the Moslem world. Of a truth there is a fascination in Turkish life that only those who *will* not can fail to feel. Their firm belief in God's guidance, their calm enjoyment of peace, their stoic fortitude in adversity, their undaunted daring in the battle, their heroic contempt of death, all command respect and even envy.

The same men, who in the chamber, with their [1] *chibouque* and [2] *comboloio*, are the gravest and most silent people on earth, when in the battle-field before the foe are the most animated with resistless fury and dauntless courage. What though in the ages past this fury, this courage arose from their conception of *Jannat al Aden* (the perpetual Eden), from a desire

> "To plant the Crescent o'er the Cross,
> Or risk a life with little loss,
> Secure in Paradise to be
> By Houris loved immortally,"

there is no absolute necessity it should always so arise. Often already they have allied and fought bravely side by side with Christians, and may yet fight as bravely again. Never shall I forget the welcome the Turkish regiment gave me on the mountains, when a thousand caps were waved and enthusiastic cheers echoed among the rugged hills. O for a sound of those voices and a sight of those faces as they rush against invading tyrants with the loud repeated cries of "*Alla, il Allah! Allah Hu!*"

Who will say there is no greatness in Turkey? Look at

---

[1] Pipe. [2] Rosary, or bead-string.

Osman Pasha. A nation that could produce such a man must have within it the makings of others like to him. Had there been another Osman Pasha ready on the spot to take his place when he was taken from it, Plevna, says Archibald Forbes, had been won by the Crescent. There are fine manly people still in Turkey, who if properly governed would yet rise to something like their lost glory. All the better classes whom I met, beys and sheiks and kamakans and pashas and upper officials, appeared to me wise and able, good all-round specimens of men; and they certainly showed themselves towards me kind-hearted and charitable and hospitable—thus carrying out in practice the two great virtues of Charity and Hospitality, which the Prophet enjoined as the first of duties.

It is a pity that they are so badly governed, that their supreme administration is so conservative, so lax and so corrupt. The people have not a chance. All is in the hands of the sublime Porte. What avails it that they are brave, enduring, and fiery soldiers, if all their temporal reward is black bread and sour wine, ragged sacks for coats, and coarse ropes for shoes? They are fleeced, literally fleeced by the government, which hands over to pashas and commandants and priests the entire revenue of the land, and while these live in luxurious ease and plenty, the people are left to pick a starvation meal from uncultivated fields or barren moors.

But let it not be thought that all the better classes are willing abettors to this suicidal *régime*. For some of them have told me that they know with sorrow these existing evils, but dare not move a finger or utter a word against them. To do so is certain death. Reformers or innovators have no place in that land. Not long ago a certain young man of high birth and office betrayed by word and action his Western views and desires for reform in assimilating Western ideas. He was a polished courtier, an accomplished scholar, and popular withal. But one morning the man, who had been the evening before in perfect health, was announced as dead of apoplexy. A little drop of poison had settled for that time the rising movement for reform. The best men amongst them are well aware that as sure as their government goes on resisting and not assimilating Western civilization, so sure must they be driven inch by inch out of Europe. On every side this expulsion can be traced not line by line, but mile by mile. The "trail of the Turk," but not the Turk in person, is seen from the Danube through some of the finest country in Europe, through the Morava valley to far south of Nisch. Whole provinces have been cut off both north and south; and Russia is ever watching her time to pour her ruffian hordes over the devoted land.

If only the Turk would head the torrent of new life that is pouring in on him, he might still be safe and conquering, if only he would consent to progress—and why should not Islamism progress in newness of life and thought as well as any other system?—but no; the torrent is bearing full against him and he will be carried remorselessly away. *Kismet, Kismet!* it is fate, it is fate! I am far from being an out-and-out "Turkophil." But in these days when the weak is being so much protected by the strong, when small nations are being so much bolstered up by the great, it is with regret that I view the desertion, the inexorable sweeping into the sea of that brave race that once was the strongest and proudest, and the desolation and lawlessness of their country that once under Solyman the Great was the best governed in Europe. My sentiment at this sight is akin to that of Poe in describing the ruin of a noble mind,—

> " Ah, let us mourn, for never morrow,
> Shall dawn upon it desolate."

Their very faces plainly tell that the Turks are out of place in Europe. The melancholy of the East, soothing though it is, is graven deep upon them; and the very elevation of their joy that breaks out at times, by its contrast with their melancholy, points to their earlier home amid the greater contrasts of the fiery East. Their life is meant to be spent, not where it is a toil and a misery to live, but where it is a warm sun and a garden of roses. But those sons of the East, transplanted on a barrener soil, are out of their element, and all has gone wrong, and will go wrong: barrenness, bareness, rottenness point to the coming dissolution. They are as much out of place as a Spaniard in Britain, or as a deeply-regretted Mohammedan friend of mine, Aurung Shah, from India, was out of place in Scotland. For three years, while at the University, he never ceased to pine for his warm sun and garden of roses, till consumption made him its prey. Lying in the Glasgow Western Infirmary, conscious that he was wasting away, he gave me a message to write to him from Turkish land and tell him of the race he had longed through life to see. But ere my letter reached him, he was where there is neither Cross nor Crescent, nor East nor West, but only the faithful, the pure in heart.

CHAPTER XXIII.

IN SALONICA.

FEW towns of the ancient Greek world have greater interest past and present than Salonica on the Ægean. Every epoch of history has eft its vestiges here. The seven-towered citadel, once the acropolis, "thrice destroyed and thrice rebuilded, still it watches o'er the town." Like a phœnix the town has risen from its ashes after each successive destruction; and its white walls encircling it five miles round show the handiwork of all the ages, Hellenic upon Cyclopean, Saracenic upon Hellenic, Norman upon Saracenic, Turkish upon Norman. Climbing up the side of its rugged cliff that faces the glorious Mount Olympus across the gulf, surrounded by plantations of cypresses and plane-trees that the luxurious Turk loves to rear, and by orchards of figs and olives and melons that the practical Greek prefers, as it is seen from the long bare Vardar valley it looks a soft daughter of the East waiting to be wedded to the manly West. Before a year is over this wedding should take place, for then the new railway from Salonica to Belgrade will have been opened and direct land communication be established from London to Salonica in four days. The town will then be a station on the shortest highway to India. For that its excellent quays, harbour, and roadstead make it admirably suited.

But even apart from its geographical situation and commercial prospects, this place is full of interest. Here are Roman triumphal arches built by Aurelius and Constantine, Greek and Roman temples converted into Turkish mosques and Christian churches, Byzantine structures and Venetian castles. One of the latter, a huge round tower, stands by the shore, and is used for a prison. Its lower stories are reserved for venial defaulters and, according to the gravity of the crimes they have committed, the prisoners are raised a story higher till only brigands and murderers occupy the highest, round which sentries pace day and night : this gradation is made not only to prevent escape but to make the worst criminals suffer most from the stifling heat. The triple arch of Constantine at the west end of the chief street—part of the great Via Ignatia—is now dilapidated ; the bricks are falling fast from the upper parts; but underneath on the solid walls are still seen Roman carvings and letters, side by side with stalls of vegetables and fish. The marble arch of Augustus at the eastern entrance has been used as a quarry for the walls and the quay, and the sole relic of it is now, owing to the intervention of Rev. the Mr. Crosbie, Scotch Missionary to the Jews here, deposited in the British Museum.

It was in this vicinity that Cicero lived in exile for sixteen months, till at the end "all Italy brought him back on its shoulders." In the mosque of St. Sophia is shown the βῆμα or pulpit from which St. Paul is said to have preached to the Thessalonians,—Thessalonica being the former name of which Salonica is an abbreviation. There once stood, between this church and the sea, a vast area of a Hippodrome, in which the Roman emperor Theodosius saw fit to massacre 7000 of the citizens.

For the classical scholar, the Christian student, and the antiquarian this town is a feast of deeply interesting memories. The ethnologist, too, has ample scope for curious observation. For here are 40,000 or 50,000 Jews speaking a medley of Hebrew and Spanish, descendants of Spanish Jews expelled from Spain in the seventeenth century. Wherever one goes among the long narrow alleys and under the rickety wooden arcades, Jewish costumes and Hebrew shop-signs are found predominant. The richest citizens are Jews. More than thirty years ago the Church of Scotland established here a Mission for the conversion of the Jews.

The Missionary naturally takes to the Jews, but possibly if he had closer pecuniary dealings with them, such as a young French valet had whom I met on board the steamer to Athens, he would see them in a truer and darker light. This young man, quiet and intelligent, had engaged to serve for three years with a Jew, the richest man in Salonica ; but falling ill of the *maladie du pays* (malarious fever) he was brutally compelled to hang on at work till the doctor ordered him to leave the country for his life. The Jew thereupon withheld his wages on the plea that his term had not expired, made him pay the doctor's bill, which however the doctor would not accept, and sent him home as a deck-passenger! Had it not been for two of us, his fellow-passengers, begging a berth for him to Marseilles, the Jew would have had to answer for a case of neglect involving manslaughter. Let the Jews mind their own: we need our money and energy for our own poor and ignorant at home.

Besides the Jews, Salonica affords another ethnological study, in the Greeks. These carry on most of the export and import trade of the port. Indeed the quarters about the harbour are more Greek than Turkish. The fame of my journey had reached Salonica, and as soon as I took my first stroll through the town, Greek gentlemen came up and addressed me as ὁ κύριος Ἀγγλικὸς (the English gentleman). Before long they had introduced me to various coffee-house circles; and discussions about Greece and its future went briskly on. It was an unspeakable delight thus to sit or saunter on the long quay in the moonlit nights in the company of true patriotic Greeks, speaking the language that St. Paul and Cicero spoke when here long ago in the twilight of the ages, and gazing along the sparkling gulf as hill rose after hill, and mountain after hill, and summit after summit up to the triple peak of Mount Olympus, the cradle of Hellenic life.

We hear much of the dispersion of the Jews, but seldom think of that of the Greeks. Yet it is a strange fact that out of Greece and scattered over many lands there exists a greater Greece; in Turkey alone the Greeks are double those in Greece. Wanderers like the Jews, originally only a small nation like the Jews, and like them too in having nurtured greatest and best of what is spiritual and intellectual in humanity, they have been like the Jews accused of a lack of patriotism. For, although in every city in Europe are located wealthy Greeks whose money and influence might speedily reform and establish their native land, yet they live and die away from it. But it should not be forgotten that those sojourners can best serve their country out of it. In Turkey they must effectually paralyze all efforts made to enslave or injure Greece again. Probably long before the expected return of the Jews to the birthland of their race and its glory, those outside Greeks will have gathered to their mountains and valleys again, and made ancient Hellas once more a green and fertile country, not the mere corner that it is at present, nor the heterogeneous groups of hostile townships that proved its ruin at the time of greatest glory, but one united nation, a nation of mountaineers and mariners, from Macedonia to Cape Matapan. But the times are not yet ripe. Therefore, ye Greeks, work on, as ye have begun, but have patience!

Having three days to stay in Salonica, I had plenty of time to roam about, to think over the past, observe the present, and dream of the future. I went out in a *caique* shaded by an awning, and had a swim in the gulf. At the instance of the Chief of Customs, I showed what a perfect instrument a bicycle is by riding on the quay among bales, and barrels, and ropes, and chains, and on the edge of the quay wall. Tired of the town, I went out into the country; but soon returned when the unhealthy air of the miasmatic swamps began to influence me. These swamps used to extend along the very shores under the town, and must have made it a hotbed of fever. Outside, the black, big-horned cattle are still seen weltering in the mud, while the sun bakes or steams their backs till they look more like crocodiles than oxen. Happily when I was there the town was rejoicing in a wind from the south-east; they tell me that when it comes from the west or north, life is almost insupportable. So in this instance too the Easterns reverse the Western saying, "The wind in the east is good for neither man nor beast," for they say "The wind from the east comes from Paradise, bringing health and life and wafting blessings from Mecca."

CHAPTER XXIV.

ON THE ISLE-SPANGLED ÆGEAN.

UNDER the auspices of a *cawass* from the Consulate, that is, a servant dressed in the ancient Slavonic costume still worn by the mountaineers and farmers of Greece—a long white kilt and ornamented braided jacket, and belt containing silver-mounted pistols and dagger—under his auspices my wheel and I were taken in a small boat to the custom-house. There I landed to procure some provisions for the passage on the French steamer to Piræus. My remnant of cash did not warrant me going higher than third class. Then began my experience of Greek duplicity. In one street I bought some bread, and laid down a two-drachma piece, and received one back, as I believe. On the quay at a stall I chose two large melons; and while I was getting change for a large piece of silver, the baker came up breathless declaring that I had lifted both drachmas of the change and had forgotten to give him one. Being in a great hurry, for the steamer was blowing its whistle for departure, I remonstrated, but paid up. When once more on the *caique* rowing towards the steamer, I discovered from the change left that the fruit-sellers had taken advantage of my confusion, given me back my change minus the price of the melons, then, on my asking how much it was altogether, coolly permitted me to pay them over again. The boatman hearing me inveigh in English against the cheating rascals, uttered a few isolated English words of disapproval at their roguery; but as soon as we reached the gangway, he showed himself as great a rogue as they: for not content with the *Medjidieh* (3s. 6d.) I gave him, he claimed more for having spoken English!

From all these exactions I stepped on board, a poorer but a

wiser man. There is a saying in the Levant, that "a Turk cannot touch money without dirtying his hands." The Greek seems to have closely imitated in this respect his old oppressor; it is still true of him—

> "Still to the neighbouring ports they waft
> Proverbial wiles, and ancient craft;
> In this the subtle Greek is found,
> For this, and this alone, renowned."

Surely Greece is a land of melancholy contradictions. The Past, wondrously fair and inspiring, and the Present, wondrously poor and disappointing, face each other well-nigh irreconcilably. Still smarting under the sense of having been duped, I leant over the side of the ship and watched the receding hills of Macedonia, till, as the bold precipices under St. Elias mount came in sight and the sun in unclouded grandeur seemed to rest for a while on Mount Olympus, all the wretchedness and meagreness, and prosaicness of the present were drowned as in a Lethe rolling rapturously with golden memories. There, among those lofty peaks, 10,000 feet above me, where now Helios, Apollo the Sun-god, is still reigning supreme in a blaze of ineffable splendour, once in the spring-tide of Hellenic history rose the high court of the gods, and of Zeus the Lightning-darter. There, under its shadow, amid the wooded valleys and plains of that beautiful Thessalian country, grew up those cherished traditions that were the comfort and delight of a departed race of heroes, and have been ever since the joy of cultured minds; there, among those woods, where now stands a fortress-monastery, and where matin and vesper bells call to prayer and hymns in praise of the lowly Galilean, once rang the wild revels of Bacchus and his tameless Bacchantes. And here under Zeus' throne, we, a motley crew of petty moderns, are bounding ruthlessly over Poseidon his brother's dominions, unconcerned though Æolus send us a breeze to follow or to face us, and with no more remonstrance from Poseidon than an encircling line of flashing phosphorus as we drive on into the night.

Away before us rose first the conical peak of Ossa, and past it the long ridge of Pelion, forming outposts to Olympus, "to sentinel enchanted land." They look like stepping-stones up from the south to Olympus; and it was natural for Homer to seize this idea and make the Titans pile Pelion on Ossa in order to reach the gods and pull them down from Olympus. Virgil reverses the order and puts Ossa upon Pelion, while modern critics gladly snatch at the seeming incongruity of placing the broad Pelion on the peaked Ossa as an instance where old "Homer nods." But if the giants came from the south they would not be so unmethodically mad as to pass by Pelion, go on to Ossa, carry that back and plant it on Pelion, then try to step across the some sixty miles to Olympus: they would rather, like the practical sons of Earth that they were, take the lower mass, Pelion, that first came in their way, throw it up on Ossa till its back of some twenty miles would help to fill up a somewhat similar distance between Ossa and Olympus. Oh no, Sir Virgil and ye wise modern critics! old Homer knew his country better than you do, and, blind though he were, is more than your match!

Turning from such thoughts as these, I sat down on a barrel amid the filthy disorder of the French deck, where Jews and Turks and Greeks and Asiatics of all ages and of both sexes had already secured their sleeping-ground, and there I ate my supper of bread and cheese and melon. The *maître d'équipage* (boatswain) was the only officer on board who showed me the slightest regard either as an Englishman or a gentleman. The others all despised me for going as a deck-passenger; when I first came on board I asked the mate where my bicycle might safely go, but he shrugged his shoulders, and contemptuously remarked, "*O ma foi, non;* deck-passengers must look after themselves."

The boatswain, however, gave me a piece of rope to lash it to a rail, and let me put my knapsack in his own berth. "Don't leave even that belt outside," he said, "or you will never see it again." He was right. When I rose during the night from the hard corner where I had coiled myself, there was nothing left of my melons but the seeds. Next day my store of bread and cheese also disappeared from their place of hiding; and so my stomach and its needs were left to the tender mercies of the place-proud cook. With the view of buying something from him, I ventured into the galley; but had scarcely put my nose inside, when round turned Monseigneur the cook, and with that cool, stinging tone common to French officialism, ordered me outside: his imperious "*Mettez-vous dehors !*" still jars, repellent and irritating, on my ear.

Nothing can be more offensive to one accustomed to deference than to be compelled to submit to the petty tyrannical humours of inferiors, when chance places him in an apparently ignominious position. However, I had full revenge; for from that time till we entered Piræus, I hardly ceased to revile and laugh at the disorderly French arrangements of the ship and compare them with English. In the hearing of the officers, whenever any French speaker was with me, I loudly declared that in all the British companies' ships in every part of British waters, I had sailed with some of the wildest characters, and no one had ever dared to steal a pin from me, because British discipline would at once have found out the culprit. Moreover, I maintained it was the crew not the passengers who were the thieves. Of this indeed I was pretty sure, for one little foul-mouthed Marseillais knew where my eatables were. I knew at first sight that he was a practised hypocrite. With that peculiar ludicrous gravity of voice and manner that a Frenchman puts on when he wishes to make you think him your friend, that will look after your affairs as faithfully as he would his own, he professed that my wheel and eatables would be perfectly secure. There is small doubt it was he that looked after them rather closely. No doubt by way of compensation for the loss of my food, his gang generously passed the salt-water hose over my wheel, and left me a large legacy of rust ! Whenever a Frenchman looks grave of his own accord, be sure there is something false, ridiculous or mischievous, "lurking beneath his owl-like solemnity."

Among the cabin-passengers were some rich Jews and Greeks, two Italians, a Frenchman, and an Armenian. The latter, hailing from Marsonan, Asia Minor, and called Garabed Azhderian, when I first saw him was telling the Italians and Frenchmen how he was bound for England and America to prepare to become a professor in his native land, and was pouring out his national and spiritual aspirations. The Frenchman threw cold water on all his enthusiasm: "Your country will always be backward till you fling out religion and all its votaries, and then become prosperous, as France has done." Garabed could not agree with him, but pointed to Britain and America as contrary cases, and said he would have nothing altered in his country's life except ignorance and vice. Hereupon burst forth the usual French denunciation of Britain as crammed full of very poor and very rich, always at each other's throats, as hypocritical and utterly selfish, caring only for money. The Armenian opined that it was right to be selfish when one could at the same time best serve humanity.

I thanked him for his defence of my country and of religion; and asked the Frenchman if he had the heart to revile religion amid such a scene, within sight of Olympus, on "the harbourless coast of Pelion," where the elements fought against the tyrant of Asia, and on the side of the brave men who away over at Thermopylæ were dying for their liberty, their country, and their gods.

CHAPTER XXV.

AT VOLO.

AFTER passing through the waters of Artemisium, where the Greeks first withstood the Persian fleet, and where also Frank Hastings on the side of the Greeks wrought havoc among the Turkish fleet with his "Karteria" (the "Endurance"), the first steam man-of-war, we doubled the promontory of Tricheri, the ancient Aphetæ, whence Jason set out in his Pelion-pine-built Argo to fetch the Golden Fleece.

As we passed by the rock-built town of Demetrias, one of the three "Fetters of Greece" under the Macedonian sway, a significant glimpse of Greek family life presented itself. A young manly fellow stood on the ship's prow and waved a handkerchief as he looked expectant up to the houses high up on the cliff. A pure and guileless affection was shining from his face as he watched; a happy smile suffused it when he fancied he saw an answer; disappointment and sorrow gradually settled on it, and the handkerchief fell by his side as no answer came: till, at the flutter of something white from a house in the wall, up went the handkerchief again, and a radiance of blissful happiness seemed to fill all his being. There is high hope for Greece when she is thus fostering the purity of family ties.

The ship anchored at Volo for half a day. The town lies at the head of the Gulf of Volo, part of it on the shore and part of it some thousand feet or so up the steep sides of Pelion. The higher position with its walls looks inaccessible and very insecure owing to the many ravines that lure a way for torrents through it. But the Greeks chose sites for towns at a time when pirates and enemies from the sea were more to be dreaded than the devastation of torrents.

The superiority of Greek over Turkish rule was at once apparent in broader streets, better sanitation, and finer buildings. The Greek soldiers are incomparably better clad and cared for than the Turkish, but they are much slighter and smaller. But the Acarnanians, the mountaineers dressed in petticoats or *fustinellos*, are certainly a match for any Turks. It was they who did the recent fighting on the frontier not far from here. They are named οἱ εὔζωνοι, the well-girt; and they are well girt indeed. Their kilt is made of a thin white linen stuff arranged in layers of folds that stick out bushier than the dress of a ballet-girl, and contains as much as forty yards sometimes, I was told. When once I was indiscreetly making light of that style of dress, a Greek gentleman rebuked me with the remark that it was not only the most ornamental, but also the most useful possible: for, when proper materials were not at hand, it could be used as a sail at sea, as a sheet to sleep in, as a sack to carry things, and in battle as a flag of truce or as lint to bind up wounds. Surely such a commodious uniform should be adopted without delay by all the armies and navies of the world! There is another cumbrous dress whose utility I also found out. It seems that the great baggy trousers, sometimes all of one piece but tagged at the foot, act as a fan or a pair of bellows when the wearer walks about, and so keep him cool in the heat of summer.

Sitting in the acacia-shaded court of a coffee-shop in a quiet spot at the back of the town, I did my best to follow and join in the discussion about the frontier troubles. When the men discovered me to be English, they treated me all round to coffee and *loukoumi* (penny stalks of 'Turkish delight'), and received in return my views of the question, to the effect that Greece was not yet ready to fight, and that Turkey would have once more enslaved her. These views would have provoked a show of hostility against me, had their delivery not been jocularly interspersed with ejaculations in my broken Greek against the big bold ants that kept swarming over my neck and face and hands, greatly to the merriment of my comrades. The Greeks would not believe that the Turks could have been able to reach Athens and overrun Greece; they already think their little army and navy a match for any first-rate power, and easily for "the sick man, the Turk:" moreover, have they not at the head of each armament their French commandant-general and French high-admiral! The Greeks are slow to believe that France is not now, if indeed it ever was, the best place to go for either an admiral or a general.

Indeed there is nothing more galling to a lover of Greek life than to witness the absurd attempts that have been made in Greece, especially about Athens, to acclimatize French manners and costumes and modes of working. Government, administration, and education have been modelled on French plans. It is absurd to see Greeks dressed out in the spruce but artificial fashions of Paris; it is wrong and ruinous for them to rear their children in the effeminate, coddling, and cramping style in vogue among the French, preventing them from that free and manly life in the open air engaged in hardy sports that is more after the true Greek spirit and tradition. Although in lively temperament the Greek is akin to the French, yet his element of religious seriousness severs him hopelessly from any real assimilation with them. There are not wanting signs that the Greeks see in Britons a more congenial and elevating example to follow in literature, education, and administration. Nevertheless, let them hold by their own great models in life and character is the sincerest advice a friend can give them :—

> " Trust not for freedom to the Franks—
> They have a king who buys and sells :
> In native swords, and native ranks,
> The only hope of courage dwells."

The Greeks hold firmly by their Church and its rites, although they do not put much life into their ecclesiastical service. A Greek funeral is a grotesque affair. The first one I saw was at Volo. As it passed, the men with me stood bare-headed in silent reverence. First there came an old man bearing a black board with two white lines transverse and a white cross drawn between them on it; then came a group of bare-headed boys, and a young man before them, chanting dolefully; next passed six old *kaloyeri* (priests, or good old men), all robed in white; then the coffin borne by men in red caps, then relatives wearing a white band loosely tied on their right arm; these were followed by a motley crowd clad in various costumes: and to end all, two big dogs marched staidly in the rear.

An amusing story was told me about the American Mission at Volo. As may well be understood, the Greek priests have no sympathy with evangelization; indeed they seem not to comprehend what is meant by it. When the Mission was started the people showed great aversion to it, especially when the school began to attract numbers by its cheapness and superiority. One day a quarrel arose between boys of the rival schools, the Greek Orthodox and the Protestant. The lady missionary rushed out to defend her pupils, when unluckily a ripe fig, aimed at one of the scholars, caught her on the back of the head. Ah! then there was raging and waging. Alas! for the poor Greek offenders, ye shall all be exterminated. What a volley of threats rained on the devoted people of Volo! They had dared to raise the hand of violence against the Lord's anointed, and they shall all be cut off, yea, they shall be swept away as surely as were Pharaoh and his host. The majesty of the Stars and Stripes has been assaulted. See how the Stars dart forth portentous gleams of angry brightness as the banner waves in the breeze! see how the Stripes are lashing the air as a figure of the coming wrath! Forthwith a message flies on electric wings to Athens: "Our flag is insulted; the station is attacked; we are stoned in the public streets. Send round our gunboat, or we shall all be killed." Next day the American gunboat arrives, and a boatful of marines armed to the teeth invades the town. "What is this all about?" demands the captain. "Oh! is that all? Hang all you darned Mission coves. I guess you think we have nothing else to do but trot about after you, and give you a good dinner for nothing when you come on board." Then out speaks the Greek *kaloyer:* "Lady, what do you come here to do? To preach the gospel and life of Christ? Well, what does He say? 'Bear persecution for My sake. If any man smite thee on the one cheek, offer unto him the other also.' But what do you do? As soon as a child hits you by accident with a harmless fig, you send immediately for guns and soldiers to come and bombard us! Ah, my dear lady, you had better go home straight to America, if you have nothing nobler to show us than that." The old priest scored that time.

CHAPTER XXVI.

FROM VOLO TO THE PIRÆUS.

AMONG our deck passengers were two brothers, Belgians. They were of that remarkable species of modern adventurers who are content to rove about Europe or the world, settling somewhere till they have made some money, then travelling about till it is spent, or till they find a more congenial sojourn. Of such also was the Swiss I met at Semlin.

One of the brothers was a well-educated, sensible fellow, by trade an overseer of labourers on railroads or in mines. He had been out on the Canadian and Pacific Railway, but lately had been in Greece, and was now bound for America again. He had no love for the Americans, except in so far as they had never pressed him to pay his bills when he was hard up, so that he had come away with the firm but questionable conviction that people out there would never let any one starve, though they had no money; he hated the English, for he said nobody in England would give you a bite if you could not pay for it; he hated the French as weak and frivolous; he hated the Greeks as foolish, stupidly proud, and ignorant: in fact he was a cosmopolitan hater, such as Johnson would have gloried in meeting.

The other brother was indeed a character. He went about with a perpetual smile on his visage, accosted everybody, hob-nobbed with everybody; his eyes were always filled with a half-drunken, wholly comical expression that betokened the utmost good humour and good fellowship. He was an immense favourite with the Greek families, and in his way carried on elaborate dialogues among them. But all I could discover of his knowledge of Greek was " begun, continued, and ended " in ὄχι (No) and μάλιστα (Yes). This rich vocabulary of his he profusely supplemented by an infinite variety of the drollest gestures and grimaces, the success of which was ever being announced by bursts of hearty laughter. His more sedate and cynical brother, who fondly addressed him as *mon pays*, declared of him that he was a great man among the Greeks, indeed a greater Philhellene than Byron, for he had actually fought on the frontier in the Greek ranks and in the Greek uniform against the Turks! It was peculiarly amusing to watch him as he lay on the deck or on his mat and listened to some Greek playing on the guitar, and crooning some sad weird "lilt o' dule and sorrow." The Greek, fancying his listener understood and appreciated all, would pour out his soul in impassioned music and song, till some wilder strain or weirder wail would excite in the prosaic Belgian nature the sense of the ludicrous, and the droll fellow would be over beside us telling what barbarous sounds he had been hearing, and how he had cheated the wily Greek by his make-believe of attention.

Nothing breaks the monotony of the long sail down the rugged east coast of Eubœa, except some distant views of islands, and on the land occasional glimpses of ruins on cliffs or villages embedded among orchards and forests of oak and pine and elm and plane trees.

There seems little or no trace left of the Turks, who formerly swarmed on this island. Indeed, they say that all that is left of them to remind of their former predominance is the fez, the narghile, and slippers, worn by the Greeks generally. The old saying that the Turks of Egripo (Eubœa), the Greeks of Athens, and the Jews of Salonica are the worst of their respective races can apply no longer unless in the latter case; for there are no Turks now in Eubœa, people say, and progress and education in keeping with the ancient Greek spirit have relieved the Athenians of the unenviable distinction.

At early dawn we neared the renowned land of Attica, and numbers of the French-speaking passengers gathered round me as I pointed out and told the stories of the many isles we were passing or sighting. All were eager to know what were those noble columns gleaming white across the blue waters and against the yellow hills behind. There they stand in the vestibule of Attica, in number twelve—like Apostles, sent into modern days, of that fair religion which made men enshrine the noblest thoughts of the soul in enduring sculpture. Towering above the rocks of Cape Colonna, 300 feet below, they have weathered the gales and salt sprays of twenty centuries, and still they stand in airy loveliness. Poseidon (Neptune), to whom along with Pallas Athene the temple was dedicated, has watched over them, and through all the storms he has raised and quelled through all those ages has spared them, while many a fair fabric he has wrecked on the breakers beneath. This is the actual scene of Falconer the sailor-poet's "Shipwreck:"—

"Here in the dead of night by Lonna's steep,
The seaman's cry was heard along the deep."

Burns says of Falconer, "He was one of those daring and adventurous spirits which Scotland, beyond any other country, is remarkable for producing:—

'Little did my mother think
That day she cradled me
What land I should travel in
Or what death I should dee.'"

After rounding this famous promontory of Sunium, we came into view of Ægina, Salamis, Hymettus' purple steeps, the factories of Piræus, and the graceful queen of ancient cities, Athens herself, as her still noble remains rise through the pellucid air of Attica amid a scene whose every spot is classic ground, where every name sounds like the rustle of bygone ages.

CHAPTER XXVII.

THE PIRÆUS.

No adequate notion of the wonderful prosperity of Piræus can be obtained from the sea till the ship comes into the narrow entrance to the largest of the three fine natural harbours. Inside this are moored large English, French, Austrian, and Greek steamers, coal steamers, cattle steamers, mail steamers, passenger steamers, and sometimes gunboats and ironclads, besides a forest of sailing-craft and gaily-painted pleasure-boats. Broad streets traversed by a tramway, and well-built houses lining the long quays, factory chimneys throwing out their smoke overhead, the whirr of mills and machinery, and the whistle of locomotives—all proclaim the marvellous stride of progress the ancient historic port has made since 1834, when there were only a few *caiques* in the harbour, and no trade, few houses, few inhabitants, but only decayed hovels and crumbling walls and pestilential marshes.

This port once fortified on an immense scale by the old Athenians with circumscribing walls and the famous Long Walls of four to five miles in length—all of which have left remains that prove their great strength—may still be made as stout of defence as ever it was, and may yet be the scene of decisive struggle when new Greece comes to fight again for progress and independence. When once the Greeks have begun to develop systematically the internal resources of the country, have opened up traversable highways and planted trees to attract moisture to the at present parched soil, then Piræus must be a place of first importance.

In spite of centuries of slavery and oppression, the Greeks have remained essentially lovers of the sea. Their merchant marine finds its way into every country in the Mediterranean and Levant, outnumbers that of Russia, is a rival to that of Austria. If only they would change their sailing-vessels into steamships, their natural maritime genius would easily give them the lead on the seas in the East. Thanks to Frankish engineers,—especially to my uncle, a Scotchman, who has been decorated by the Greek Government with the highest honours for his services in training Greeks for marine engineering,—they are already in a fair way to reach this desirable position.

It was an easy matter finding out my uncle's abode when I landed. Everybody knew Κύριος Ζδῶν (Mr. John), as they call him. His engineering and shipbuilding yards, called Μηχανουργεῖον ὁ Ἥφαιστος (Vulcan Foundry), employ the largest number of hands of any public work in Greece, and his establishment is the second largest of any kind there. When he started business some twenty-five years ago there was only a flour-mill or two about the place; now there are dozens of factories of various kinds, especially in opposition to his.

The first Greek who spoke to me after landing was an Athenian editor; another called on me shortly after: and, as in other important places on my route, before long the newspapers had made me a noted character. Wherever thereafter I went, people had read or heard of me; and many a time my musings over some ruined relic of the past Greece were disturbed or diverted to the meagre present by whispered remarks about such prosaic things as myself, my wheel, and my exploits.

It is curious that, while Athens and the Piræus have some score of newspapers, read by almost everybody, there should be such a scarcity of books that hardly one is seen in house or street. It looks as if their ancient character still predominates in the people as narrated in the Acts when Paul visited Athens: "they spend their time in nothing else than either to tell or to hear some new thing." Hence they take to newspapers rather than books, as giving them the newest possible matter to tell or hear.

My life at the Piræus was very quiet and pleasant. Up in the morning at the blowing of the steam whistle, in time to see the sun rise over the shoulder of Hymettus empurpling the heights that still are famed for flowers and bees, we would go to bathe in the limpid waters of Phalerum Bay, or stroll along the shaded streets and quays. Sometimes we would take a drive to the olive groves and vineyards and orchards that cover the plains between the Cephissus and Ilissus of classic fame. These are possessed by men of property—and my friends to be in the fashion have theirs—and by gardeners who rear and sell the produce in the Athenian markets. They are irrigated by deep-sunk wells worked by an endless chain of buckets which pour the water into a trough, whence it is led by channels all through the grounds. A horse or bullock turns the chain, after the manner of a threshing-mill.

We went once to visit some old dependants of the family. They lived in a walled enclosure on the top of one of Piræus' rocky heights. Inside this parcel of ground—enclosed by my uncle, because property, though easily acquired, can be confiscated by the state if not precisely marked out—are some ancient deep and solid-built wells and passages cut out of the rock. The Greek women there received us with characteristic cordiality, brought us each the usual glass of water and spoonful of jam—which constitute the conventional token of hospitality—and at last, after a volume of naïve insinuations and questions, sent us off, each provided with a bunch of strong-smelling mint to protect us from malarious vapours on our way home.

But it was no pleasure walking about Piræus in the excessive heat of the day in August. No rain had fallen for the past three or four months, and not a blade of green herb, unless where artificially watered, was present to relieve the senses from the arid yellow bareness. Wherever a breeze sprang up, it only added to the discomfort, for it caught up the dust and sand, and whirled it along the streets in tall thick columns high up from the ground into the air some hundreds of feet at times.

Still the coolness of the evenings and the serene beauty of the nights were ample compensation. Sometimes we sat on the terrace at the top of the house, but oftener we rambled about the various pleasure squares. Every night these are filled with people sitting before the *cafés chantants*, where bands of Italians, Germans, Bohemians, and Armenians—chiefly girls—sing and play and dance. I never saw anything so wild and grotesque, so lascivious and meretricious as the dance of an Armenian woman performed here every night, to the accompaniment of music, a dance that had in it every possible grimace and contortion that could have graced or disgraced the most furious Bacchante. And all the while that these revels are going on, waiters are bawling out their orders over the heads of the seated multitudes. Perhaps at the most interesting point of the dance, or the finest passage in the song or music, a yell at your very ears will announce to all the assemblage that you have ordered, say, τρία γλυκοῦμι, δύο καφέ, ἕνα λεμονάδαν, ἕνα μαστίχαν! The first word is for 'Turkish delight,' the last for 'mastique,' a kind of peppermint drink that turns into a milky whiteness when mixed with water. These, with lemonade, resinous wine, coffee, and cakes of pastry (3*d*. each), form the gastric dissipations of Greek life. Add to this the smoking of cigarettes and *chibouques*—not confined to the male sex—to light which the waiters always bring you out a bit of red-hot charcoal on a platter.

CHAPTER XXVIII.

A TRIP TO ÆGINA.

NEARLY all my friends were in a dead-and-alive state of health, suffering from the fever. To get free from this, some of them went down with me to their summer-house in Ægina. This ancient island Queen of Hellenic seas, styled by Pericles "the eye-sore of Piræus" on account of its position facing that town and rivalling Athenian maritime power, is now better described as the eye-salve and convalescent home of Attica. For the absence of marsh-land keeps the air pure and the climate salubrious; and long sweeping views can be enjoyed from it of the magnificent amphitheatre of hills—now only bare declivities—of Argolis and Attica, and of many hallowed spots whose names shine conspicuous in the heirloom of history.

But Ægina is but a sorry shadow now of its past greatness. Where in the palmy days its citizens numbered 200,000, only 6000 can be supported now. Only one solitary Doric column is left in the town, to sadly tell of its departed kindred of beauty wrought in stone—a beauty pre-eminent in a land where beauty was the rule.

We took our morning baths off the moles and lighthouse of the old oval harbours, which once sheltered goodly fleets and daring mariners. The tideless sea has not covered them, but time and weather have eaten and honeycombed their tops till they are the very embodiment of hardy old age, wrinkled of skin, yet hale at heart. Nothing can infuse a deeper sense of immutability or deathless old age than this spectacle of masonry built in centuries past beside this sea without a tide :—

> " There shrinks no ebb in that tideless sea,
> Which changeless rolls eternally ;
> The rock unworn its base doth bare,
> And looks o'er the surf, but it comes not there ;
> And the fringe of the foam may be seen below,
> On the line that it left long ages ago."

Right across the island over the mountain from the town stands one of the most ancient temples in Greece, said to be that of Zeus Panhellenius (God Supreme of all the Greeks). We bargained with a muleteer to take us up the six miles to it. My cousin John was mounted on a sturdy mule, and I on a bony white gelding, with neither reins nor stirrup, and only a skin stretched on four pins for a saddle. In spite of the guide's repeated assertion that his horse knew the way, I made reins out of a rope. It was well I did so, for the horse was so badly shod on one foot that he was constantly stumbling over the stones and rocky ledges that composed the execrable mountain path. After we had passed the ruins of the mediæval Venetian town on a pointed hill about three miles inland, it seemed to me that we should have gone north. But the fellow maintained he had been to the temple hundreds of times, and therefore knew the road to be south. However, after an hour's scrambling through brushwood and groves of fir-trees—bled at that season for resin with which to preserve the wine—we came in sight of the sea, but there was no temple in view. We brought our so-called guide to task, and made him confess he had never been so high up the island before. The beasts' heads were now turned north in pursuance of my idea of the temple's position, and when the ground became too broken and full of gaps, I started off on foot, in disgust at the guide's incompetency. My cousin soon followed, and we soon came upon the fair ruins.

> "There a temple in ruin stands,
> Fashioned by long-forgotten hands;
> Two or three columns and many a stone,
> Marble and granite, with grass o'ergrown."

By this time it was high noon, and we were hungry. From a high rock we 'cooied' and signalled to the fellow to bring up the animals. We looked for water all about, but could discover no spring, only a dry cave leading beneath the temple into the rock on which it is built. We had therefore to content ourselves with the melons we had brought, and some locusts we had gathered on the way. The animals got their share of these, and then set off on a foraging expedition of their own among the rocks and crevices in search of the sweet-smelling thistle which grows profusely on Greek soil.

On all sides except one the temple, standing on the shoulder of a hill and topped by a higher hill, is shut in from the sea. Below, on that one side, lie wooded slopes clothed luxuriantly with vineyards and gently bending towards the lovely bosom of the Saronic Gulf. With no village near—nothing but nature and this fair but melancholy monument of forgotten art,—the place is a soul-entrancing solitude. Here at least no jarring sounds of empty modern life, no jarring sights of un-Hellenic garbs and manners can clash with thoughts of the brave classic Past. The sound that fills the air from yonder chestnut-tree is in keeping with my thoughts; for it is the chirping whir of the classic τέττιξ or cicada. To the mind there is neither space nor time; and as I listen I see the Homeric heroes starting up in the midst of the *agora*,

Goodly orators, like the cicadæ which sit on a tree by a wood and send forth their lily voice.[1]

When we got back to the town, the 'guide' invented some pretext, as is the fashion, for claiming more than his bargain. "The bargain or nothing," we said; and the fellow chose the latter. All evening he tormented the servants by demanding in to see us, till at last the sharper feminine wit of one of my cousins put the crucial question to him, "Who guided to the temple, you or the stranger?" That settled him. We had many occasions for testing the native wiliness and propensity to cheat. Sometimes we catered for fruit, bread, and fish. At first I in my broken Greek would make the selections; then when the sellers and I were haggling over the exorbitant charges, my cousin would interfere. The sellers would begin, "Oh, I beg your pardon, effendi—." "Don't 'effendi' me, if you please," my cousin would say, "I'm not a Turk, but a Greek." "Oh! then, if you are his dragoman (interpreter), we'll go shares." And so on, till they were made aware that we were up to their dodges and knew the market prices.

[1] ἀγορηταὶ
ἐσθλοί, τεττίγεσσιν ἐοικότες, οἵτε καθ' ὕλην
δενδρέῳ ἐφεζόμενοι ὄπα λειριόεσσαν ἱεῖσιν.
Hom. Il. iii. 151.

CHAPTER XXIX.

MODERN GREEK SPIRIT—A CONTRAST WITH THE PAST.

IN an ancient land like Greece, the thoughtful stranger is never at peace. He wishes to get away back to the Past and live in it; but the Present kills all his fine feelings—defiles, demeans the Past.

> " Out upon Time! who for ever will leave
> But enough of the Past for the Future to grieve!"

Yet, through the weakness and degeneracy of modern Greek life, can be traced the characteristics of the ancient and classical. The Greek women have still a deep sense of pride, traceable even among the lowest classes, which no doubt is a sentiment left from the times when the freeborn did no menial or even manual work, except by way of education or for the good of the state. A Greek woman will not appear in public unless arrayed in her best. In Ægina I often wondered why our water in the *kanati* was not replenished during the daytime, seeing that there was a well just in front of the house in the square. Said our Greek maid with a tone of offended honour, "Do you want me to go down for water before all the folk in broad daylight?"

The cunning and subtle power of overreaching displayed in the modern are the lineal descendants of intellectuality in the ancient. But "what a falling off is there!" The following story, told of a now wealthy miller in Piræus, has a ring about it of a practical joke from Aristophanes or Lucian:—When very poor he sat on the quay and sold roasted heads of maize. Then he kept a wine-shop in company with another man, till they had realized some money and wanted to split partnership. They made a literal division into two halves of the stock in trade, but could not agree about a solitary barrel of vinegar

"Thou hast no need of vinegar," said our hero—the Greeks all 'thou' and 'thee' one another as of old—" and I will give thee 100 drachmæ for it." "Oh!" said the other, "I'll give thee 200 for it." And so on went the bidding up to four figures, when they grudgingly agreed to open it. Both of them had, unknown to each other, been for years in the habit of dropping odd drachmæ through a slit into this barrel, which was labelled 'Vinegar,' but was in reality now crammed with silver coins. Imagine the sensations of the two rascals as they eyed one another across their secret bank, and realized that their sharpness had cut themselves!

It is a hard struggle to get back to the Past, when all around is so changed! This surely is not the Greece of history. Thy hills that once were green with woods and vines are now bare and treeless! Thy towns are in ruins or have disappeared! Thy sons are mixed with foreign blood; they like to follow now, nor yet have learned again to lead, as in the brave days against the Persian hordes!

At first I thought to visit all the sacred spots round Athens on my bicycle; but soon gave up that mode of locomotion when I found its presence made the process of getting back to the Past harder still. To hurry indecently over ground where trod Solon and Pericles, Plato and Demosthenes, and many more of the Past's great ones, through the groves of Academus or by "the whispering stream of Ilissus," was pure desecration! What has a bicycle to do with Greece, with the Past? It is there in discord with the simplicity of past Greek life and thought. Well might the δαιμόνιον, ' the little spirit' that Socrates carried in his breast, and that would not permit him even the simple luxury of a good pair of sandals, well might it raise him to repel such an artificial intruder from his favourite haunts. Put it away and walk, as he did, on foot! Ponder, with him, and laugh over the vanity and would-be wisdom of the crowd!

I made a pilgrimage to the tomb of Themistocles, on the promontory of Piræus. It is embedded in the rock on the shore of the blue Ægean over against Salamis. Broken columns, drums, and slabs lie scattered around it, all encrusted with salt as if ocean were drying its tears of mourning. And the tide that never changes washes over the hero's grave, as if the waves of the gulf where he did so much for his country would wash away the guilt of treason. Truly,

> "Greece is no lightsome land of social mirth,
> But he whom Sadness sootheth may abide,
> And scarce regret the region of his birth."

This is the shore whence Nicias with his triremes and heavy-armed sailed to conquer Sicily. Here was heard the trumpet for silence, then the voice of the herald and the crowds in prayer for success that did not come. Now all is dry and bare and leprous-like with ruin. Yonder is "Xerxes' Seat," "the rocky brow that looks o'er sea-born Salamis!" This is the tomb of him who destroyed the fleets of Tyre and Sidon! But where now is the living patriotic spirit that made of Salamis and Marathon watchwords for freedom? Instead of a great Greek admiral, see yonder, in the place of honour, stands the house of a mercenary, a Frank, the Lord High Admiral of modern Greece! When I see this excessive adulation of the French in Greece, my feelings are ruffled with anger like, in the song, "the wee bird" that "cam tae oor ha' door," when it saw the foreign redcoats :—

> "O this is no a land for me!
> I'll tarry here nae langer."

Let me get away from *this* Greece, back to the Greece of my Thucydides, Sophocles, Demosthenes, back to the Greece of my thoughts and dreams, the Greece of history and the past!

> "A man's best things are nearest him,
> Lie closest at his feet;
> It is the distant and the dim
> We go so far to meet."

But, patience! this still is Attica; there still is Salamis, there Athena's citadel, there the Parthenon, there Hymettus, Pentelicus, Cithæron. Eternal hills, ye never change! eternal Art, thou speakest still! And you, Greeks that are left of the ancient stock, hope on, but work! Roll back the clouds of ages of gloom! Wipe out from your land and from your spirit the traces of oppression, fouler and more life-sapping than would have been the Persian, an oppression that has converted a nation once proud and self-reliant into wily sneaks and cringing cowards and servile imitators!

Nevertheless, with new-gained freedom has come back some of the old courage. Already it is burning to recover land that once was Greece. It is there, and will speak again. But what if it be too hot and premature? Ah! then, again it will be hopeless. Greece must grow again, or she will be like the son of a great man with all his father's ambition but none of his ability, or like an old man recovered from a disease who thinks he is as strong as in his manhood, tries his strength, but finds only regret for its loss. Greece, if she be not careful and cease aping the ways of foreign powers, may win the fate of the foolish frog that envied the bull, and burst in trying to make itself as big.

CHAPTER XXX.

A PILGRIMAGE UNDER DIFFICULTIES TO MARATHON.

BESIDES a trip to the prodigious ruins on the Sacred Way at Eleusis. I had one on wheel to Marathon.

My cousins were at Cephissia, and I was to bring them home by rail on my way back. From Piræus a grand road runs, through Athens, on to Cephissia. There I was misdirected, and found myself at midday at Tatoe (Decelia), the king's palace. Thence the soldiers sent me across country. That was a false step. Before the end of·five miles the path lost itself in fields. Some miles I pushed my wheel over fields, brooks, through thickets and pathless wastes strewn with marble chips. In the northern valley of Mount Pentelicus, the guards at the station, placed there against the brigands, treated me to bread, eggs, wine, melon, and a smoke, and put me on the path to Stamata. Thence I made for Vranú (the ancient village of Marathon), but the Greek villagers would not direct me properly; everything with them is just κάτω ἐδώ (down here)—everything is quite simple to Greek minds. What appeared the best road—a mere sheep-track—at length disappeared down steep sides over fallen rocks and trees and briars into a deep wooded glen. At the bottom ran a deep clear stream brawling over immense rocks, and over it perforce we picked our way. Once a slip launched us knee-deep into a boiling lynn. No path was traceable on the other side. Up, up again over prickly bushes and mud and shingle, through pine forests whose soil was slippery with the growth and decay of centuries. Down again to the river's side, but still no path. Gorgeous plants and flowers exhaling rich odours, and gay-plumed birds interested my attention for a time, but when three hours had been spent wandering up and down the banks, but always down the stream, and the sun had reached the top of the thousand-feet cliffs that towered around, despair laid hold of me. Leaving the wheel, I climbed the cliffs, and saw the windings of the stream, three or four miles more, and then the village of Marathona (not Vraná) among its cypresses down far in the valley. After twenty minutes' search I recovered the wheel, and giving up the attempt to trace the river to the plain, for the banks were so steep and shingly, and the vegetation so dense that further movement was impossible, I tried to make a way up the cliff. But the stones and the sand slid under my feet, and the machine fell back on me. One foot up, then a slip, a fall, and a nasty bruise, until utterly exhausted, my machine entangled in thorns, and a big rock above us, I despaired of extricating it out of such a frightful place. The thought, however, of what the world would say, and the crash of a huge tortoise through the brush-wood, suggesting the presence of other uncanny creatures, combined to nerve me, and shouldering the wheel, I climbed inch by inch slowly and fearfully up that in many places seventy-degrees gradient of rock and sand and thicket. When we reached the top it was already dark, but the light of the brilliant stars showed me a field of grain down in a valley. There was a path which led three or four miles down to a river. I was making a soft place to lie down for the night, when the bray of a donkey led me on. It came from a field beside a mill, and there they spread straw on the ground beneath some trees and gave me a coverlet. A young Greek shared this primitive couch, and talked incessantly. The sense of rest and peace, as I lay and smoked my pipe, and chatted with the Grecian, and watched the rising moon, was most sweet and deep. Up at four, and over five miles of mountain road to Marathona, then ten miles of sandy road out of "the pleasant mead of Marathon," and my troubles were over.

The want of water is the greatest obstacle to travelling in Greece. At one spot on the shoulder of Mount Pentelicus, when gasping for water and broiling in the sun, I followed a track that seemed to lead to a well. A well there was indeed, but it was deep. At hand was a cell with a dish like a bucket. Joyfully I rushed to bring it, when to my infinite disgust and pain, it was seen to be a religious lantern! Such a sell is surely enough to knock all religion out of one's head.

CHAPTER XXXI.

CORINTH—THE EARTHQUAKE.

AFTER a fortnight's stay at Piræus, the wheel and I departed for Corinth by rail—a narrow, jolting, French-constructed, rickety affair. The train crawled along the coast past the lovely bays of Eleusis and Megara, and along the terrible Skironian rocks. On the narrow road—the Κακισκάλα, or Evil Way—that still winds round these, the famous robber Skiron had his lair. Here he stripped his victims, made them kiss his feet, and while so occupied kicked them off the ledge, so that they fell sheer down some 700 feet on to the rocks that shine white through the shallow blue waters, where a great tortoise robbed them further of whatever life was left in them.

Gangs of labourers, chiefly Italians, were busy at the projected canal across the Corinthian Isthmus as we passed. The natives, who maintain that the one gulf is lower than the other, will never believe in the feasibility of the project till all doubt is solved in the fact accomplished.

I put up at the Hôtel de l'Isthme in New Corinth, and there met a young Athenian, who also was bound next day for Patras. After dinner I proposed to walk to Acro-Corinth, which here dominates everything, although it is five miles away. He, fired somewhat by contact with British enthusiasm, declared he would accompany me. Off then we started in good style—he proudly making known to every person we met the, to him, wonderful enterprise we were bent on ! But, alas ! for fickle Greece, we had gone only about two miles in the hot sun on the unsheltered road, when the would-be champion, seeing before him more miles of white dusty road and the giant rock, towering its head higher as we drew nearer, to be climbed at the end, thought better of his unwonted enthusiasm, and with many a transparent excuse left me. A gentle riddance! Greece is not Greece to me in the company of a Frenchified Athenian.

Forward! or, as the Greeks say to their donkeys, Ἐμπρός! There against the golden sky frowns in its vastness and blackness that gigantic citadel. Talk of the Athenian Acropolis, or of Ehrenbreitstein, or even of Gibraltar! They are dwarfs beside this giant of nature crowned with the strength of Greek and Turk and Venetian embodied in massive battlements.

For miles now on either side of the road are far-stretching vineyards, where thousands of clustering grape-bunches, green, blue, and black, tempt the wayfarer. But yonder hut of branches raised on poles, and the ominous protrusion of a gun-muzzle may well make him prefer his thirst to a heavier repast of lead. For the vineyard-watchers think little of shooting any meddler of their vines. In one of the Athenian journals I read an article, occasioned by the death of a man who had been so shot, and entitled, "Is a man's life not of more value than many grapes?" Until the law forbids the present free use of fire-arms in Greece and Turkey, civilization must advance slowly in those countries. In Turkey I was repeatedly warned never to show my revolver, for any one might then shoot me with impunity, on the ground that he did so in self-defence before I could shoot him.

As at Marathon, so here, it was my lot to take an extraordinary route. Before I found that I was on the wrong road to make the ascent of the rock, I was half round its base on the east side. Looking up at the beetling crags, I saw a possible track, and asked a white-kilted, gaily-attired Peloponnesian, who was passing mounted on a mule, if I could get up that way. He laughed and said, "Yes, if you are a monkey." However, with the help of a stout stick I cut, up I got till near the crenellated walls, when I saw that even a monkey could not go farther up unless he could stick like a fly to the overhanging bluffs. But I crept round till above Old Corinth, and reached the orthodox entrance.

On the summit is obtained one among the very grandest and most varied panoramic views in Europe—southwards the massive ramparts of the Morea; westwards, Mount Cyllene, clothed with dark pines, and Erymanthus; below these the long winding Gulf of Corinth with its beautiful shores; northwards, in succession, Parnassus, Helicon, Cithæron, and Hymettus, with Athens, Ægina, and Salamis; then the Ægean with its countless isles. These isles, "mountains of Greece scattered over the sea," arid and barren of foliage as they are, present a most peculiar, almost comical, appearance when, seen from this height. It is said they gave the name Ægean to their sea—the word " Ægean" being derived from αἴξ, a goat, and hence means " the sea of goats." To my fancy this sea looked like a great washing-tub filled with water deeply tinged with "washing blue," and the isles not so much like goats as parts of clothes left in the tub to bleach, and puffed up above the surface by the imprisoned air.

While I was picking my way among some mediæval remains, I felt a sudden change in the atmosphere. Hitherto the ground and air had been as hot as an oven. No rain had fallen for months, and the weather had been hotter than experienced for twenty years. But now, about five o'clock in the afternoon of the 27th of August, a gale of wind came from the south-west, bringing with it great black clouds, and thunder and lightning, and a deluge of tropical rain. The scene then, as I "stood on Acro-Corinth's brow," and watched the storm sweeping up the gulf and buffeting those grand old poetic mountains, was one I can neither forget nor justly portray. There was just time for me to escape round to the north side, where I crouched under a gateway at the head of a gully filled with a wilderness of fallen stones and rocks, when the full fury burst upon the mountain. By-and-by the water began to pour down from the higher ground, and forced me to make all speed I could down to the plain.

When I reached Old Corinth, and was standing for shelter under covert of an old wall, a little boy and girl appeared on the top of it, offering me old coins and other excavated relics for sale. They went away, but soon were back again, saying their father wanted me to come inside the house. It was merely a mud and stone hovel, but was very roomy. On the floor squatted the father with a bandage round his head. His handsome spouse set bread and cheese beside me on the floor, and he called over a goat and milked as much as I required. But the boy was not contented until I bought my choice from his store of antiquities, which he kept in a sort of garret up a ladder. Then, as he took me through the miserable streets, he enumerated the wonderful things he could do for me and show me if only I would give him a drachma too.

The storm, which was the precursor of the great earthquake that passed over Greece that evening, was now nearly spent, but the evaporation from the parched land was great and rapid, leaving the ground and air perfectly cold. It was noticeable that the storm and the earthquake followed the same course, from S.W. to N.E.; so that the one may have more to do with the other by way of cause and effect than is generally supposed.

Thus another storm had passed over Corinth's Seven Doric Columns, that have stood for six-and-twenty centuries—all that is left erect of a city renowned for splendour and luxury. To think that round this desolate, forlorn spot—where now, since the earthquake in 1858, are only a few wretched hovels and sheds, and a few rude, ignorant peasants—once gathered the flower and wealth of Greece for the Isthmian Games, once lived and taught St. Paul during eighteen months, once thronged, in the height of its power, a population of 300,000, record says, engaged in prosperous commerce ! All that glory is buried now, and the Seven Columns alone are left to tell *hic jacet*.

About eleven o'clock I retired to bed at New Corinth. My room was in an outhouse in the courtyard, with vines trailing about the frameless windows. For a time I lay reading by the light of a wick stuck in a cork swimming in a tumbler of oil which stood on the sill, but I dropped off asleep. I was awakened by a feeling as if I were in a small boat on a choppy sea,—head down and feet up, then a sidelong shake, then feet up and head down. Fancying I had at last caught the fever, I sat up, but was instantly thrown half over the bedside, and the lamp was upset with its oily contents on to the bedclothes. Then cries and shrieks were heard, and a sound as of people rushing downstairs within the main building. Then after a sharper shake and a long rumbling gradually dying away, the queer feeling was gone. All this took only some twenty or thirty seconds. Had the shock lasted only a few seconds more, all Corinth would have been, they said, in ruins.

The landlord, a young Greek, came in to me as I lay trying to sleep, and asked me if I was not afraid, and why I had not run out. "Oh!" I said, "I don't know, unless it be that an Englishman is not easily frightened." He told me that all the people were in the streets, and many of them undressed, for they were afraid to stay indoors, as long as another shock was expected. The poor fellow was trembling all over, and his hand was clammy with a cold sweat, as he talked, in a way that was more a prayer to God than an address to me, about the helplessness of man on an earthquake. "He cannot fly, he cannot climb a tree, he cannot hide in a house or a cave, he cannot even on the sea, anywhere escape: he can only go to God."

CHAPTER XXXII.

SCENES ABOUT PATRAS.

As the steamer—which I easily recognized as the "Raven," an old Glasgow boat, though now bearing the Greek equivalent Κολοιὸς—sailed farther westward, the vegetation became richer, and the scenery wilder and more beautiful. Greece is marvellously fair as seen in the Gulf of Corinth. We anchored for a while in the harbour of Ægeum or Vostitza, whence come the finest currants, and had a good view of its cliff-built town, and the huge plane-tree fifty feet in girth in which St. Luke is said to have lived, and which is hollow and has been used as a prison. Many English steamers lay here, and more at Patras, which we reached in the evening.

Patras is the most important emporium in Greece. Its quay is crowded with seafaring men of many nations. Its streets, broad and straight, are thronged with well-dressed, contented-looking people, strong, proud, and fine-looking. One can walk all round the town under the pillared verandahs, where are good shops of every description, without being exposed to the sun. It has gas, gravitation water, watering-carts, auctions, theatres, and suchlike modern amenities. Its situation is perfectly beautiful. From its mediæval castle, 400 feet above the town, the prospect is ethereal in its loveliness, embracing Zante, "the flower of the Levant," Cephalonia, Mesolongi, where Byron died the snowy heights of Guiona and St. Elias, and many another lovely mountain rising high over the calm blue waters, while close below is the green smiling plain of currant-vines and olives.

My uncle's agent here put me up at the best hotel, where I had many a discussion on the balcony with young German and Greek merchants. The agent had secured a passage for me to

London, by a "currant-boat," which was not ready to start till three days after. Hence there was plenty of time for me to saunter about.

On Sunday, while I was loitering about the shore near St. Andrew's Church, two negroes passed me talking English. They informed me that they had come over from America to Italy, and had been working at odd jobs since then, such as on the Isthmian canal, and were now on a Greek ship. As I showed them the spring with an ancient Greek inscription above it, beside which in a cave St. Andrew, the Apostle, lived, and the spot beneath an olive-tree where the Romans crucified him, the reverent look on their dark faces was as good to me as any elaborate service in a church. "Ah!" said they, "dem ole good men were not afraid to die. We be glad they die, for now de black men hab better life, and nobody stop dem now no more to go where dey like."

The Greeks say that the Apostle's bones lie below the church here; but a Scotch tradition has it that Regulus, a disciple of his, carried them with him to St. Andrew's in Fife, where a square tower still remains of the church he founded, and hence, too, St· Andrew became the patron saint of Scotland.

That day little else was talked of in the street groups and the shops but the earthquake. Besides the usual cries of ὡραία σῦκα! ὡραία σταφύλια! (fresh figs, fresh grapes), there were mingled also those of newsvendors selling the latest telegraph messages περὶ τῶν μεγάλων καταστροφῶν! (about the great catastrophes)— dwelling on the last syllable 'ōn,' and producing a most musical and melancholy effect. Whole villages had been wrecked round the coast, and some hundred people killed. One or two slight shocks occurred while I was in Patras, amusing myself but especially the natives by wheeling along the streets, so that I have the peculiar distinction of having ridden a bicycle on an earthquake!

Everywhere I went, I was greeted with shouts of "You speak English?" which constituted the English vocabulary of the Greek populace. But the brokers and one old fellow, a wholesale wine merchant, speak admirable English. The latter, named Valerios Kaligeros, was about the coolest foreigner I ever met. He had evidently derived his *sang-froid* from the company of English aristocrats, for he had been a courier throughout the

Levant. He sat at a table beside his door, clad in a stylish white dress, and seldom spoke more than a sentence of a very few words at a time. The trenchant way in which he polished off the character of certain persons he knew, and the various nationalities, either by a sneer or a shrug, or a supercilious turn of the head, was most entertaining : " What do I think of the French ?—squeaking dolls ! The Germans ?—humph ! The Greeks ?—poor things ! I tell you there is only one race that deserves to live, with any enterprise in it, and that is the English. I know it."

CHAPTER XXXIII.

HOME AGAIN.

ON the last day of August, the "Sinloo" steamed out of Patras Gulf with my wheel and me on board. All that the wheel had lost since its disembarkation at Hamburg was the Underwood odometer, which, loosened by inquisitive hands, had dropped off among the mountains of Servia, and the bell, which, caught hold of by a stupid Greek boatman as we were lowering the wheel down the ship's side, had sunk "with a gurgling sound" to its rest at the bottom of Patras Bay. The machine, a "British Challenge," also took me over the journey which is the subject of the following "Group of Wanderings," and after having been ridden by me about 6000 miles, is still perfect and strong in all its parts.

There were also two young Greeks on board, with whom I kept up my Greek all the way to London, in describing to their wondering senses the power of Britain on the seas.

We passed through the straits of Messina, between Scylla and Charybdis, past the Lipari Islands and Stromboli, "the lighthouses of the Mediterranean," and anchored for a day in Gibraltar Bay. On the rock I had a ramble with some of the "rock scorpions," as sailors facetiously term Gibraltar's natives. Very proud these are of their British rights, "We are British, every bit," they say, "and speak English as well as any in the empire; we have nothing to do with those skunks, the Spaniards."

It was the 8th of August when I finished near Salonica the bicycle part of this journey, which part therefore occupied, including stoppages, thirty-three days, and was a distance of about 1500 miles over some of the worst, most mountainous ground in

Europe. On the 12th of September I was in London, and next day in Glasgow. I visited the Indian and Colonial Exhibition, which I found superior to the Antwerp and Edinburgh ones in all respects save the building, which is a mixty-maxty jumble.

ITEMS OF COST.

	£	s.
Leith to Hamburg	2	10
Bicycle ride	8	0
In Salonica and boat to Piræus	1	10
In Greece (where, of course, I was my uncle's guest)	0	10
To London	8	10
To Glasgow	2	0
In all	£23	0

For some time after my return, my friends chid me on my changed and fierce appearance; but I reminded them of what Wordsworth says of Peter Bell :—

> " There was a hardness in his cheek,
> There was a hardness in his eye,
> As if the man had fixed his face
> In many a solitary place
> Against the wind and open sky."

Part II.

ON WHEEL UP THE RHINE VALLEY, FROM AMSTERDAM TO GENEVA, AND BACK BY ANTWERP.

CHAPTER I.

FROM CARLISLE TO HULL.

On the 9th of July, 1885, when going out of Glasgow at dawn, the loss of a valuable assortment of screws and nuts so disconcerted me that after a vain search I could not but take the occurrence as an ill omen, and thought of going by rail to Hull. But when a friend, who had seen me start, came to the house with the lost parcel, which he had found in the street, I hailed the omen as good. To save riding over known country, however, I went by rail as far as Carlisle, then started for Hull on wheel.

Through Penrith and Appleby we made east over the Westmoreland moors into Yorkshire. It was somewhat tough climbing over the stony hill road between Brough and Bowes, passable enough in daylight, but, when darkness fell, too dangerous for me to have risked the descent into the Yorkshire vales. My first adventure befell me not far from the sheep-farmer's house where refuge was graciously given me for the night. At a rise and turn in the road where the dry-stone dyke was low and broken, a bull stood pawing and bellowing. He had evidently made up his mind that we had no right to pass by his territories, for the nearer we came the wilder he became, until he was like to tear down what of the wall was left. The shepherd who, after some minutes of anxious dilemma on my part, came up and took us past the brute, said he would have made short work either of the wheel or me if I had attempted to pass alone.

It is a lovely but difficult country to ride through between Bowes, by Barnard Castle and Richmond. Long hills and many streams have to be crossed and some of the hills are dangerous. The long, steep and winding one above Richmond that passes the barracks, I went down mounted till the traffic in the street above the terrace stopped me. The scenery is among the fairest in England. The old priory and the great Castle of the once royal House of Richmond, the river and bridge and quaint town in the midst of woods, form an interesting study. The thick walls of a Maison Dieu, dating back to the Normans, attracted my attention; the small rooms still are intact where many a knight no doubt has been nursed, and its gardens, that must have been the scene of many a happy convalescence, still slope down to the river. The whole has been acquired and saved from demolition by a monumental sculptor with antiquarian tastes.

After joining the highroad between Edinburgh and York, my way lay through typical Yorkshire country, past one source of the Ouse, near which I saw through an industrial establishment for vagrants, and on through Boroughbridge to York. At a farmhouse on a long moor when I asked for milk, the maid, to my wonderment, smilingly ushered me into the drawing-room, and told me her mistress would be down directly. Meantime a cloth was laid and preparations went on for a regular tea. At last, afraid that some misconception had arisen, I declared I could wait no longer; and was just going out when the young fair mistress, brought down by the maid to prevent my departure, and with some parts of her toilet not completed, stood before me in a radiance of smiles and blushes. On no account would she hear of my leaving, until I explained that I was a mere passing stranger and did not even know her name. It seems she was expecting a cousin of hers whom she had not seen since childhood. He had promised to surprise her some day by coming on his bicycle ; and when she saw me enter the yard, thinking it was he, she ran upstairs to adorn herself for the dear occasion. I wish I had been that happy cousin, for " her bright smile haunts me still."

There were three great Minsters visited by me on this journey, York, Cologne, and Strasburg ; and in spite of preconceived notions I love most that of York. It possesses an air of calm repose and graceful yet solid beauty, the like of which did not impress me when gazing at the wilder and more imposing structures of the other two. The situation and surroundings of these latter lack the freshness and cleanliness that York Cathedral has, and somehow made me think of misery and superstition, of war and cannons, while at York the whole place breathes peace, poetry, and romance. To live under the shadow of its grey pile, within sound of its chimes, must be in itself a culture of no mean order, a constant weaning of the soul from the grosser things of the world.

In the remarkable, clean and pretty town of Beverley I saw the curious wood-carvings in the Minster and also the carved house-front of the carver opposite. The militia encamped on the moor reminded me of the royal army that lay there in 1642, when the signal for the Civil War had been given by the citizens of Hull shutting their gates against their ill-fated king.

CHAPTER II.

ARRIVAL IN HOLLAND.

AT Hull we embarked for Amsterdam by the steamer *European*. On Sunday morning we came up to the lofty sea dykes of Holland, and waited our turn to enter the Amsterdam canal at Ymuiden, fourteen miles from the capital. Here a large Glasgow sailing-ship from the East Indies was being worked through by the capstan. The sailors were merrily singing their "homeward bound," as they chased one another round on the spokes, and the capstan clinked with its metallic sound like a joyous accompaniment to their song. All seemed beside themselves with joy that the long six or eight months voyage was over and they were near home again, all except one Hindoo, tall and solemn, who opened not his mouth nor let even a smile of approval light up the gloom of his face—no doubt he was thinking of sunnier skies and darker skins that were dearer to him than aught his mates could show him in their climes, far from his home in the glorious East.

Round about us on the piers and banks were crowds of Sunday-dressed Hollanders, all the men smoking, the women chatting about us strangers, the children more unconcerned running about the steps in their spotless white dresses and stockings, which are in keeping, but do not set off, their pale complexion. While we lay there, a dispute arose between two Dutchmen, which set the whole place in confusion and uproar. Judging from the terrific noise, I ran up expecting at least to see a little sparring, but found the two only yelling defiance into one another's faces. Our captain dryly remarked that I might have known foreigners better than to look for a fight from them: "They fight like women, with their tongues, not fists." One should expect to see more firmness depicted in the physiognomy of such an energetic, practical people as history shows the Dutch to have been; but no—there is an evident lack of stamina, and a sort of deeply-marked eccentricity plainly written on their faces: there is a something in them that detracts from one's ideal of what " proper men " should be.

The canal rises above the country in many parts, and branch ones join it frequently on both sides. From it you have an endless view of waterways and meadow-lands and villages with spires, whose tops seem almost on a level with the ship's deck. Wildfowl abound among the tall reeds that line the banks, and now and then a pop of a gun and a curl of smoke tell of the presence of boats and sportsmen, though they are lost from view among the reeds that grow far into the water. Great farmhouses stud the country, with only some ten feet of a ground wall, but with sloping pyramidal roofs that rise some scores of feet, round which at intervals run galleries that indicate the various storeys.

The sight when the canal widens into the Ij (ee) is unrivalled. The broad sea inlet covered with skiffs and trim sailing-craft with weather-boards, the immense timber enclosures, the long quays and docks crowded with vessels, the houses and spires of the pile-built city surrounded by water and traversed in all its parts by water, the huge blocks of stores, the high, narrow warehouses ranging along the lines of traffic, all bespeak the still vital prosperity of what was once the wealthiest, busiest centre of the world's commerce.

Taking a stroll through the city, I found the people as much given to pleasure-seeking on Sunday as the French, only in a heavier and clumsier style. The churches, however, such as the Oude Kerk and the Nieuwe Kerk, were fairly well attended, and they are places worthy of worshipping in. The worshippers were all well-dressed, as in Britain, not with a considerable admixture of working-day clothes, as in France. Indeed the whole town seemed entirely given over to the respectable classes, for nowhere could I see anything but gay scarfs and shawls, white linen and smart suits. In this respect Amsterdam is like our towns, where on Sundays the poor and the shabby and the roughs retire from public view like wild beasts to their dens for the day.

Nowhere do such clouds of smoke ascend as incense to the

great Unnamed but constantly worshipped modern god of Tobacco as in this city on the waters. No doubt the moist atmosphere tends to preserve for the Dutch their proverbial pre-eminence in this worship. The "weed" is grown in the country, and cigars sell at a trifle. Nowhere is the practice regarded as so venial a fault on the part of the young. Near the Palace in the Dam square, when passing through an alley, I remarked a family seated on the raised stone pavement; all except the females were puffing vigorously at their pipes or cigars; but my staring surprise at beholding two youngsters of very tender years gravely and serenely doing their duty towards big fat cigars as long as their face, right under the nose of papa and mamma, was too much for the gravity even of Dutchmen.

Like Salonica, another sea-port in a similar position at the opposite corner of Europe, Amsterdam has been a city of refuge for persecuted Israelites. Hebrew signs are not uncommon in many narrow streets and on the canal banks. One's thoughts naturally turn to the greatest of Israel's children born since the final dispersion, to Spinoza, persecuted here by the persecuted, an exile from the exiled, for little else than that he had a wider conception of God than they had.

Many monuments still remain to suggest the brave old days of Holland when her flag was supreme on the seas; but none is so memory-stirring and fancy-begetting as the Weeping Tower. Here the hardy world wanderers parted from their friends: many a solid trader has here bestowed his last blessing on his boy and his "venture;" many a snug ruddy Dutch maiden has here watched the fading sail that wafted into the Zuyder Zee, onward to distant unknown lands to find his fortune or his grave, the lad whose heart was hers, and hers was his, for whom now she wept, shedding her warm tears beside the cold walls into the cold water, like Jacques' deer "adding her sum of more to that which hath too much."

It was closing time when I reached the Park and Zoological Gardens, but the soldier at the gate seeing my C.T.C. badge, saluted and let me pass, though he locked the gate behind me. This was the only time I ever wore that badge when abroad; it gives foreigners, who set more store by decorations than we do, an exaggerated notion of one's importance that rather interferes with my style of travelling.

Early on the 13th, a great crowd of clerks, piermasters, labourers and sailors, who had learned that I was bound on the wheel for Geneva—an enormous distance in the eyes of Dutchmen, whose whole country is only about one hundred miles by one hundred, and who never stir from home unless they can get a ship or a train or a carriage to convey them—saw me start from the ship's side, but their sluggish Dutch temper could not fire enough to give me a parting cheer.

CHAPTER III.

ALONG THE PAVED DUTCH ROADS.

FOR many miles the road ran along the canals, thus giving at once a view of the varied traffic on these, and a panorama of the wonderfully fertile lands. The cottages and farms are more numerous than on any other route I have ever been over. The country is one huge kitchen-garden; everywhere are fields of turnips, mangold-wurzels, cabbages, maize and oats, and wheat. Trees line the fields and canals that cross and recross in bewildering mazes; gay barges show brightly through the foliage, beside quaint high-roofed steadings surrounded by shaded meadows where the deep-hued cattle browse and low all the summer day; every cottage has its garden, every garden has its beds of tulips and marigolds and asters and roses; even the waters share in the general fertility and fringe their sides with lovely floating wildernesses of lilies in every tint of white and red and blue and yellow. Now and then we pass clusters of villas almost buried in a wealth of flowers and verdure; their names tell the stranger that they are retreats from a life in the great marts of the land and its colonies, to enjoy into green old age a well-won ease amid scenes whose charm a Dutchman alone can fully revel in.

Owing to the soft nature of the soil, the roads have throughout been paved with small tiles or bricks, about 6 in. by 3 in., which make on the whole a good level surface. In some places, however, where they have not been lately replaced, it is very sore riding over them. Whenever there is anything like a hill, they are sure to be in a ruinous state, but that is very seldom; hills cannot be spared in Holland, the highest in all the land is only 330 ft. ! The bicycle does not seem to be a familiar sight on these roads, to judge, at least, from the startled looks of pedestrians, who may chance to be surprised at meals or at rest by the wayside. I can readily credit the story of the Dutchman whom a bicyclist passed at a good speed with his lamp lit, and who fled back into the town and told all he met that "the devil had blown past him on a windmill." His was no improper analogy in a land where hundreds of vulture-like windmills blacken every horizon.

A tremendous thunderstorm broke while we were in a wood, and drenched me through. A woodman led me to a cottage at the outskirt, and there we waited till the sun conquered once more. The whole land was soon reeking with evaporation as the sun put forth its midsummer strength. In such a climate there is no wonder that generation is rapid, both among plants and animals : the only apparent wonder is that the people are not giants instead of comparatively pigmies.

In Utrecht, where canals and highroads, and the Vecht and the Old Rhine are perplexingly intertwined, I had the utmost difficulty in finding the road to the frontier. In shop after shop the same answer was given, "they did not know," or "did not understand ;" several times we had started out of the town and were enjoying the sight of the grand avenues of old trees and the ponds and fountains and parks, when it became evident we were on the wrong track ; the last time we returned, I sat down on a stone bridge, almost ready to cry with vexation that I could not pilot myself better, when luckily two students spoke in French to me and asked me why I looked so forlorn. With gladness I told my wants, which soon were satisfied. Now all my trouble here arose because I could not speak Dutch, and could get none to understand French or German. It is true the students can speak these languages, but that is part of their business; it is not true, as is usually supposed, that almost everybody speaks them.

Dogs are very numerous in the country, and were a source of great hindrance to me. One splendid specimen of a retriever rushed out of a garden near a villa in the so-called hilly country above the junction of the Rhine streams, and after he had got over his first surprise, began making a show of racing. To humour him I put on more speed, which brought out his hunting propensities and made him career around the wheel in wanton gambols. When he had come about a mile, I thought the game had lasted far enough, but not so he; there was no thought in his head about returning. Another mile went by, and still he kept on. With all the pace I could acquire, we flew along the winding road, but it was plain he meant to follow to the end. Afraid lest I should be arrested farther on, on the charge of stealing the valuable animal, I dismounted and made 'inquiries, only to' find that he was already too far from home to be recognized. Discourage and threaten him as I might he would not turn tail. There was therefore nothing for it but to tire him out; and when five miles from where he joined us had been covered, the last I saw of him, as we whirled round a bend, was a black spot like a ball steadily advancing away at the end of a long stretch of avenue. Possibly he had come from England, and had known the pleasures of running out with his old master, but, grown sick of the slow, stay-at-home ways of his new Dutch master, now wished to be back to the old life.

Towards evening, tired and hungry after sixty miles of causeway, I was slowly moving up into the picturesque town of Arnheim, paying no heed to the rabble of children increasing about us. Shopkeepers and householders were at their doors enjoying the cool of the evening and watching the arrival of the dust-covered stranger on the wheel. All at once the hind wheel seemed to rise, and I was thrown heavily on my shoulder. Leaving the machine as it lay, with the speed of rage I darted after the big boy who had done the trick. Up close and down close, through barns and sheds and yards I chased him—all sense of fatigue or hunger gone—till a locked door at the head of a lane brought him to bay. He lay down in the corner, bawling and kicking with all his might, screaming out, as I understood, what would be done to me if I touched him. Meantime a fearful hubbub arose behind, and, before I had taken my fill of pommelling the culprit, a motley crowd of jabbering, vociferating Dutchmen was upon me. Bakers with baskets, cobblers with hammers, grocers tying up their aprons, butchers brandishing their knives, women flourishing brooms and pokers, all had rushed to the rescue of the boy from "the mad foreigner." This great show of force saved the young rascal from a probable ducking beneath the pump. A clamour was raised for the police, as the crowd clattered after me with hissing and hooting. At the mouth of the close, a policeman was found preparing to come up and arrest somebody. Happily he knew some German, and took my side when he heard the tale. But the crowd now vented their wrath on him for defending me and letting me go; and the wrangling was still loud and bitter when my wheel rolled me rapidly from the place. I have never seen a set of people so little alive to the value of corrective justice; and as they growled around me that day, I could not but vividly picture up another summer day, two centuries gone by, when Jan de Witt, the Grand Pensionary, was as foully murdered in the face of crowds of his fellow-countrymen as ever brave man was; and from the howling mob of their descendants, foolishly screening a boy that had done a dangerous trick, I could gather some notion of the blind unreasoning fury that caused or permitted that brutal deed of blood.

Arnheim is the capital of Guelderland; its inhabitants according to an ancient rhyme are: "*Hoog van moed, klein van goed, een zwaard in de hand, is 't wapen van Gelderland*" (High of mood, little of good, sword in hand, is the coat of arms of Guelderland). This ancient character of theirs tallies nicely with my above encounter with some of the present ones. Yet when once we were settled comfortably in a clean little hotel on the Roermondsplein, my feelings towards them were changed on discovering that the brave and chivalrous Sir Philip Sidney, the last of England's knights-errant, had here breathed his last breath, after affording on the field of Zutphen that undying example of humility and self-denial : "Take this cup of water," he said to the wounded soldier when himself nigh unto death; "thy necessity is greater than mine."

CHAPTER IV.

OVER THE DUTCH BORDER INTO RHENISH PRUSSIA.

IT was great fun that night to sit with my feet on a chair in the billiard-room and receive the various visitors who came to see the Englishman who was going on a velocipede to the source of the great Rhine river they worshipped as flowing in its strength from regions whose distance wrapt them in mystery and romance. While they plied me with beer and schnapps, the only answers I could give to all their elaborately set forth questions consisted of "Yes" or "No." Presently an unmistakable French voice was heard above the din of the circus outside : " *Nom de Dieu!* is there not a morsel of *saindoux* (lard) in all this *sacré* Dutch town? *Saindoux*, I tell you, not tallow candles ; I want *saindoux!*" The indignant demander was a French performer in the circus, and he wanted lard to rub his face with, but nobody could understand him. "You're the only civilized person in the whole town !" said he to me, when by my help he had obtained the lard. The use of the word "civilization" and its kindred is the surest test of a genuine Frenchman ; exalted to the uppermost place in the modern French mind, it comprehends all possible virtues and good in life.

As we approach Germany there appear no indications that nature has intended a frontier. There is neither mountain nor river nor wall to show a division of races; but near Millingen a small gunboat moored in the Rhine shows that man has made some boundary such as it is. Indeed I became aware that we had passed into Germany, only when a little boy whom I asked in Dutch words how far it was to Germany, shook his head and said in German, " I don't understand."

Although the people of Holland by no means would be a

party to the Germanizing of their country, I much fear that both nature and the outlook of European politics point distinctly to a date that cannot be far distant when Holland must be Germany.

The first real assurance that we had quitted Holland was the measured time of an instrumental band playing in a school beside the ancient Münster church of Emmerich. Nowhere but in Germany would such music be taught in a school, especially in the early part of the day as it then was. In this matter the nations have everything to learn from Germany, and in this alone is the German education really superior to, say, the Scotch system. Music is perhaps the best preservative of order among the people; it exalts and ennobles life, and renders a humble sphere more endurable to those who have the will but not the means to rise.

Gradually the landscape becomes more chequered, and the indefinable glamour that hovers over historic ground where men have wrought or thought deepens as we move. Across the Rhine is seen near Xanten the remnant of the Teutoburgian Wood, amid whose dreadful gloom the Roman Varus with his three legions met annihilation from the hands of Arminius, the German champion, and his German hordes. The terrible tale is told with graphic pen by Tacitus when Germanicus visits the fatal spot of sorrow (*mæstos locos*): "A half-broken wall, a low ditch—whitening bones in the middle of the camp—as they had fled, as they had fought—scattered or heaped—fragments of weapons and limbs of horses—faces nailed to trunks of trees." Here, where German prowess and independence first stemmed the all-absorbing wave of Romanism, there burst forth the high-toned cradle-song of the great Teutonic race—the Nibelungen Lied; and here its hero, Siegfried the dragon-killer, was born.

At Wesel I got some money changed, and prepared my mind for a long free revelling in the bewitching memories of Rhenish land. The richer public buildings and churches as compared with those in Holland or Prussia proper, told without the aid of statistics that Rome is conquering still by her church where once her sword had been broken.

CHAPTER V.

THROUGH THE "BLACK COUNTRY" OF GERMANY.

My astonishment was great when at Ruhrort we came into a vast district as black and coal-begrimed as any about Birmingham or Glasgow. It is hard to believe that one is by the chivalric Rhine, while far and near furnaces and factories belch forth their sooty volumes ; while coal and iron mines rear their ugly scaffoldings like gallows where freshness and cleanliness are immolated to the god Progress ; while everywhere walk about crowds of hard-worked men and boys whose pale gaunt faces gleam spectrally through the soot and slime that befoul them and their tattered garments ; while in place of quiet rural lanes, rails and cuttings for rails dissect and debase the once fair face of nature. Man too seemed degenerated, for there is as much apparent wretchedness about here as in the coal districts of Britain. As is usual in manufacturing districts, the people are less civil and obliging, more forward and impertinent—children and adults alike. This is one of the reasons why attempts to compare English life and society, which are essentially manufacturing, with their Continental equivalents, which are mainly rural, such attempts as made by Taine and Max O'Rell, end uniformly unfavourable to England, because they leave out of sight the differing conditions. But let them take such a district as this and compare it with one in England, and I feel sure the result will be reversed.

Nowhere else have I had to dismount so frequently because of persistent annoyance on the part of passers-by, or found it so hard to get a clear civil direction as to the route I should take. After crossing the long bridge over the Ruhr, above the spacious harbour where lay hundreds of vessels, we reached Duisburg, whose church-tower had long been the one beauty-spot in the black horizon. But such numbers of prying eyes and meddling hands came about whenever I alighted to ask the way, and clattering tongues demanding what I was doing and generally making light of me, that at last without obtaining any definite direction I went the way that pleased myself, and was in sight of the wilderness of stalks that surround the vast establishment of Krupp's steel-works at Essen, before I knew that we were off the road for Düsseldorf.

Still on all sides are seen factories, furnaces, foundries, and are heard the whirr of machinery and the clang of iron-hammers, and within the short distance down to Elberfeld are crowded more densely-populated bustling towns than can be found out of Britain.

CHAPTER VI.

BEYOND THE SMOKE INTO THE REGIONS OF ART AND ROMANCE.

It was night as we entered Düsseldorf, the city of artists and of Heine and Jacobi; and the lights were shining in Jacobi's garden, that has met with a fate uncommon to places hallowed by the memories of the great and good. It is fit that where Goethe and Herder and Jacobi have lived and communed on the deep mysteries of life, no desecrating brick and mortar should have a chance to lessen the mellowing influence of the actual haunts of past great spirits; but that a society of artists should now hold and hand them down to posterity intact and unsullied is surely fit.

Hitherto the landscape has been flat and of little interest; but from Düsseldorf southward a change towards variety is discernible, until, beyond the towers of Cologne with its majestic colossus of stone-embodied piety, hill and rock and castle mingle more and more diversely with plain and wood and river and town, and the eye of the wanderer is lost in the beauty and ecstatic wildness of new scene succeeding new scene. New and lovely pictures of towns and villages with ancient towers and chapels and minsters, as they stretch along the rough, rocky banks, or lie hidden in ravines, and usually overhung by some grey sombre relic of feudal times still gloomily watching the passes of the river it can no longer guard, spring into view at every turn. As we wheel along the ever-winding road, brooks brawl down the vine-clad steeps, quartz and mica sparkle by the way; great black basaltic rocks, rent and rift tremendously, protrude their fantastic forms with outlines "like the profiles of giants;" and ever and anon through gaps in the clouds that hover over the ravines and the hanging vines, we catch a glimpse of some remnant of Germanic forests as gloomy as the age when in their depths the weird Druid priests searched for the mistletoe, and offered their human victims to Thor and Wodin; and ever by our side is the stream of white-blue waters, bearing with it vessels of strange merchandise and vast-spreading rafts of timber, flowing from its high home among the frozen Alps—a watery way for merchants and travellers now, as in the past days of history it has been such for Roman soldiers and mediæval priests—still rushing on to its grave in the open sea.

To such scenes as these could there be a fitter portal than the unspeakably magnificent 'Domechurch' of Cologne? One often cannot help wondering how under our stinted democratic individualism of modern times such noble monuments can ever again arise. When our age has lived out its course there will be few great enduring structures round which future men's thoughts can gather as to a visible embodiment of its spirit and power. Every man, every community, is too much engrossed in building up each one's own individual material prosperity,— which, however, must cease at the individual's death—to care to unite in some work of artistic beauty and lastingness, some work of love and of the soul.

As we were passing over the cobbles that pave the long Hoch Strasse and Severin Strasse of Cologne, two German bicyclists bugled for me to wait for them. They were having a drink of beer, and looked with that dazed manner, so common in Germany where drinking goes on more or less moderately from morning till night, as if they had already had many more. At the time I was munching, as well as the cobbles would permit me mounted as I was, some rolls and cherries—a favourite repast of mine—and I did not feel inclined to stop for anybody. However, they made up on me at the Severin Gate, where again they must have a drink. As I suspected, it was slow work riding in company with them. They meant show not work and courted attention; vainly decked out, as they were, in ribbons and badges and such unsportsmanlike trifles. Every little inn on the road was the signal for dismounting and taking in some more beer. Indeed it looked very much as if they went by the steam of beer, so often had they to stop and replenish the supply, and so sluggish was their progress. Disgusted with their ways, at length, it was not long till I was far ahead of them, having made up my mind to have nothing more to do with native cyclists.

The roads have at this stage become a pleasure, both from their good hard condition, and from the beautiful prospects they afford. This fact was a great boon to me here, for I could at my ease look around at the rapidly accumulating remarkable features in the landscape. Not a crag or wood or tower or rag of a ruin is there but must be observed as an object of romantic or historic interest; and such is the character of the river's banks, through the gorge all the way from Bonn to Mayence. A sail up the Rhine must be an exquisite æsthetic pleasure, but, for my part, a leisurely ride along the banks, dependent on no advertised hour for arrival, but at liberty to linger lovingly wherever the senses are charmed or the memory quickened, is doubly more enjoyable and inspiring.

First comes the ancient town of Bonn with its walls and terraces and its palace become a university. Above it rises conspicuously the white church on the Kreuzberg, with its Holy Stairs only to be ascended on one's knees, like those at Rome, up which crawled Luther when he heard the momentous words, "the just shall live by faith." In its vault beneath lie a score of dead monks robed still in their cassock and gown, whom corruption has not visited, but Time's pencil has drawn deep withered lines along their ghastly faces. Then across the Rhine appear in lovely shape the Seven Sister mountains of the Nibelungen Lied, clothed green with forests and dotted with ruins, and chief among them the 'Dragon's Rock,'

> "The castled crag of Drachenfels
> Frowns o'er the wide and winding Rhine."

The Dragon's Cave on the hill looms out dark amongst the green vineyards; in it the horny Siegfried, with his doughty sword Balmug killed the beast, set the Frankish princess free, and recovered the hoard of treasure it had gathered: and ever since the simple folks believe its blood has made the vines grow richer, and the wine is called Dragon's Blood. Scarcely have we passed the Drachenfels when above us towers another peak crowned by a solitary crumbling arch, and an island appears in the river with a building on it set among woods. Not quite sure what those objects were, I ventured from my mount to ask a group of neatly-dressed young ladies who were evidently out for a walk. They all blushed and looked away from me, except one whose fair face timidly looking up towards mine did me as much good as her answer, given in sweet German tones, "*Rolandseck und Rolandswerth.*" In the latter name I recognized Nonnenwerth, an ancient nunnery, now a ladies' school kept by Franciscan nuns; and my fair informant probably belonged to it. The crumbling arch is all that remains of Rolandseck, the castle built by Roland after he returned from Palestine, whither he had gone at the call of Charlemagne, and where he was supposed to have fallen. He found his lady-love, Hildegunde, no longer within his reach, but, through despair of him, become a nun. So he built the castle from which he could watch her going to and fro to her devotions in the convent-chapel; and after she died, one morning he was found stiff and stark with his glassy eye turned even in death to where his last earthly hope had flown.

Farther up are the hanging vines of the Erpeler Ley, rooted in baskets fixed in the clefts of the basaltic rocks, great quarries of which break the sides of the hills all the way down to Linz. Picturesque villages crowd along both sides thick and fast. As they are all paved with cobbles, cycling becomes a tedious process, though thereby time is perforce allowed to note the remarkable objects that not one of them lacks. Andernach—an ancient Roman station—is especially remarkable. Its environs are simply enchanting. We entered through the Roman gate and the lofty old walls crowned with verdure. Everywhere are extensive noble ruins, of palace, and castles, towered church of St. Geneviève, watch-tower and gates, all bearing more or less |severe marks of the many captures and recaptures the town has known. On the bend of the Rhine stands the tall watch-tower, beside which now runs a railway, in ludicrous contrast to the tower's venerable appearance. Its beauty as well as its peculiar construction and its antiquity make it a tower notable among the towers of the world. The octagonal tower on the summit of the lower round tower, thus making the whole a tower within a tower, produces a fascinatingly artistic effect.

CHAPTER VII.

WHERE EVERY ROCK HAS ITS *RUIN*, AND EVERY RUIN ITS LEGEND.

COBLENZ, whose very name, corrupted from *Confluentes* and meaning the confluence of the Rhine and Moselle, reaches back to the Romans, is among the most singularly situated cities in Europe. Its beauty and its situation are like Prague's in Bohemia. It has stood as many sieges as Prague has; but now it is, if anything, more important as a strategic position, and whosoever holds it holds the Rhine. The wonderfully lovely blue Moselle bounds it on one side, and the Rhine on another; massive gates and walls and batteries extend all around it in triangular form. On the rocky heights across the Rhine frowns the long fortress of Ehrenbreitstein, "The Broad Stone of Honour," second in impregnability and strength only to Gibraltar and Malta. To the south, high above the town and the Moselle, rise and stretch away in all the impressive loveliness that luxuriance of woods and fantastic shapes can give them, first the Karthause with its double forts where in 1870-71 thousands of French unfortunates spent an unwelcome holiday, and beneath it the Petersberg with its enormous camp fit for 100,000 men, then the Kühkopf (Cow's Head), with its superb view over regions where Cæsar, Goths, Normans, Swedes, Spaniards, and French have fought and plundered all through the centuries. To end this sweep of hills appears sheer up from the Rhine the glorious Stolzenfels, the 'Proud Rock' castle whose pride and fairness the French —the Vandals of fair Rhineland—shrank not from spoiling. Facing it is another beautiful specimen of feudal castle, the Lahneck—at the junction of another lovely river, the Lahn—

which an Irishman, pursuing a better plan than the French, has restored to what it was a thousand years ago.

When we arrived at dark in Coblenz, thoroughly jaded with riding and sight-seeing, it was no pleasure hunting up hotels recommended to me by various people, and finding them all far too pretentious for my pocket or for attaining the object I keep always in view in travelling, namely, to see and know the people. At last, however, a young soldier took me to the Hotel L—, where he was putting up on furlough. There a most enjoyable evening was spent. A *Namenstag* (Christening-day) was being celebrated, and a goodly company of civilians and military, with their fair friends, was present. In truth the Germans know the art of social enjoyment. The wild voluptuousness of the music and songs, accompanied by the most reckless antics in dance and play possible for the brain to conceive or the limbs to execute, was the most sense-intoxicating experience I ever was in. As the hours wore on, beside each man's place at the table were piled up the platters, on which each *Schoppen* (pint) of beer had been served, to show the number of slain each man had made in the battle against thirst. Then came the crowning antic, a screaming farce. The leading spirit began to dance round the room, followed by most of the company, including some of the women. They kept chanting a simple sort of rhyme the body of which contained what they were to do as they followed the leader, and the refrain ended in "*Folgt mir in allen Sachen!*" (Follow me in everything). Sometimes the instructions were to leap over a chair, or kneel before a beauty; sometimes to kiss the hostess or the host, according to sex, as they passed them; and often to perform some feat that was either not graceful or nearly impossible for the women to do, and their attempts gave rise to uproarious merriment. The last series of orders given and sung created a rebellion; when the order went forth from the stentorian lungs of the leader to strip the upper garment, the women seceded in a body. But the young fellows kept on. The fun waxed fast and furious. Off came coat and waistcoat, collar and tie, and the braces were being undone, when—a new game was started.

When the party had retired, a few young clerks and shopkeepers remained with me for a quiet smoke and a chat. Before long, as usual, we were on the vexed question of rival nationalities. They began by decrying the prowess of Britain. I pointed out to them that their union as an empire was but a thing of yesterday, and by no means a firm or universally beloved one among the various States; that Prussia had yet to meet a France soberly governed, sternly disciplined, and ably generalled—not the France she had already met, but one like that of the Revolution when Prussia was crushed—before she could crow as having done the greatest military achievement possible; that Britain was the only European Power whose resources of wealth, soberness, and determination could enable it to hold the foremost place; and that whenever the Emperor William and Bismarck—here they rose to see if the door was shut—had dropped off, then farewell to the military despotism that the people groaned under, and farewell to the temporary elevation of Prussia! Several times during this retaliation of mine they looked at each other suspiciously and whispered to me to speak lower. Knowing very well that I had come round to politics, which is a topic practically denied to German subjects, I taunted them with the fact, declaring that a nation could not be great in any true sense, where liberty of speech was not freely exercised, and where all power and all action hung upon the autocratic will of one man. Finally it was agreed that we drown our differences in another *Schoppen;* and so the discussion ended by drinking '*Prosit!*' to one another all round.

The bewildering frequency with which ruined castles, fair even in their death, appear here along the route is owing doubtless to the narrowness of the defiles and the rapidness of the river, which would induce the barons to build on the inaccessible crags that line their course. Some of the castles are almost within an arrow's cast of each other, and by their very position invited feuds. Such are 'The Mouse' and 'The Cat,' whose ruins still watch each other across the gorge, both falling gradually away, but, if anything, the 'Mouse' falling faster than the 'Cat'—as is but fair in justice to the analogy. Opposite these, on the left bank, are the stupendous remains, the largest on the Rhine, of Rheinfels, a robber-castle, which neither the armies of twenty-six towns in the fourteenth century, nor a French one of 24,000 men in the seventeenth could take.

Higher up is the deepest and narrowest part of the river,

where are whirlpools and the precipitous rocks of the Lurlei jutting out sharply into the water. The echo repeating fifteen times gave rise to the belief that a Siren sat on its top and allured the fishermen as they fished in the prolific rocky basin at the foot.

> "Cool is the air, and darkling,
> Peacefully flows the Rhine,
> The mountain's top is sparkling,
> Where gleams of sunlight shine.
>
> "There she sits in her witchery,
> That maiden wondrous fair;
> Golden-glitters her jewellery,
> She combs her golden hair.
>
> "She combs it with comb of gold,
> Singing a song forbye,
> Whose sweetness can never be told,
> A strange rich melody."[1]

A little higher up, in mid-channel, I saw, as the water was low, the seven rugged masses of rock that go by the name of "The Seven Maidens." The river-god changed the living maidens into rocks, for the sin of Lot's wife, disobedience—so runs the tale.

When passing through Salzig with its vast fields and orchards of cherries, I sought to buy some cherries to eat; but it was a case of "the nearer the kirk, the farther from grace," for already shiploads after shiploads of them had been exported, and none could be had either for love or money.

At St. Goar, beneath the Rheinfels, I had expected, since I came by road and not in the usual manner by steamer, that some public notice might be taken of me. But the ancient custom of initiating visitors when they first came to the town, like all the merry pretty customs of the old free days, has fallen into ill-favour. Nobody therefore tied me to the ring, or made me choose between the water ordeal (which was in reality a good ducking) and the wine ordeal, which was to drink to Charlemagne and other potentates esteemed by the townsfolk. Then after emptying the goblet to have been crowned and made a citizen would have been something worth chronicling, some-

---

[1] Translated (by the author) from the German of Heine.

thing to fit in with the enchantment of the scene. Alas! for the meagreness of this prosaic age; the only living thing that cared to remind me of this toll that once was levied here, was a big burly mastiff, which, enraged that we should pass unchallenged, lifted up his voice and his body against us. But all unavailing; his forelegs were caught as the spokes spun upwards, and he was thrown on his side on the dusty road, while we rolled merrily on.

The number of rocks and ruins in mid-channel is remarkable all about this stage. The stone that is seen at low water off Bacharach is the *Bacchi Ara* (Altar of Bacchus), whence comes the name of this town, famous as a great mart for wines. Its walls and the curious towers upon them remind one that the place has seen much warfare: the French alone took and retook it no less than eight times, and as usual have left their violent marks of desecration in church and castle, tower and town.

The legends that gave the names to these island rocks have all to be dissipated—much to the sadness of the lover of romance—by philological or historical explanations. For instance, there is the Pfalzgrafenstein (Count Palatine Stone), compared to a stone ship for ever at anchor on the Rhine. The legend tells that the Count's daughter got married in the castle here against his will, and here gave birth to her child. Hence the angry Count decreed that every future Countess Palatine should come hither for the term of her 'confinement.' But what saith History?—On such and such a date, such and such an emperor built the castle as a toll-house for tribute.

Then there is the famous Mausethurm (Mouse Tower), near Bingen, in which Archbishop Hatto—who had let the famishing people into his barns and then set them on fire—is said to have been eaten up by mice, sent as messengers of divine Nemesis. They followed him from his palace at Mayence, swam the Rhine, and poured in by thousands,

> "From within and without, from above and below;
> And all at once at the bishop they go."

But what saith Philology?—Mausethurm is merely an itacism for Mauth-thurm (Customs-Tower), so that the island-tower would probably be built by some robber-knight to assist him in his thievish exactions.

My first acquaintance with Rhine wine took place at Bacharach, as was fit in honour of Bacchus. But Bacchus is no fit companion for a bicyclist. The time was midway between breakfast and dinner, so that my stomach was empty and my appetite great. The landord set before me a good-sized bottle which he recommended as wine grown on his grounds. At first it tasted as weak as water, and this fact I remarked after I had finished one half. At my remark the barmaid took to laughing, which the landlord said she did because she knew it would not be weak in my head when once I got outside. However I drank the lot ; and the landlord and barmaid looked on from the terrace while I got on my wheel, no doubt expecting to see a fall. But not so ; I waved them a farewell as soberly and steadily as if no mischief-brewing portion of the god lurked below my vest. It might have been two miles on our way when the windings of the road and the Rhine, numerous enough in all conscience hitherto, seemed to become utterly bewildering. Several times I slackened speed, fancying we were running into a rock or a tree, but, though we kept straight ahead, strange to find, the rock or the tree always got out of our way in good time to prevent collision. And now we had a pretty dance: the Rhine would cross the road, and the road would cross the Rhine, and the marvel to me was ever how we yet managed to keep on the road. Still we kept on for some ten miles, when, in climbing the long steep hill at Bingen where the road turns up the beautiful valley of the rushing Nahe till it crosses the seven-arched bridge from Prussia into Hessen-Darmstadt, determination could effect no more. The deep dust clogged the wheel, which fell sideways; and as I threw over my leg, a buckle on the knapsack tore a gaping hole in my breeches. Deep and fervid was the resolution made on the spot, never again to drink Rhine wine on an empty stomach.

All the way from Bonn, the landscape is shut in near the Rhine ; but now at Bingen it widens out on both sides as we enter the Rheingau, "the garden of the Rhine." Over in the Niederwald, high up on an eminence overlooking this broad tract of lovely land, and, as it were, watching the entrance to the land of romance we have just passed through, towers conspicuously the colossal statue of Germania, 96 feet high and on a pedestal of 80 feet, with 200 figures around it of those who led the late war against France, and all the "Watch upon the Rhine"—a noble monument in a noble spot.

But nature here has little need of art, for few places has she endowed so richly as round Bingen.

> "The river nobly foams and flows,
> The charm of this enchanted ground,
> And all its thousand turns disclose
> Some fresher beauty varying round."

No one can stay at Bingen without rejoicing in its calm romantic beauty, without feeling in his soul the joy and peace that breathe in its air. The spirit of the place is reflected in Mrs. Norton's 'Soldier of the Legion :'—

> "I saw the yellow sunlight shine
> On the vine-clad hills of Bingen—fair Bingen on the Rhine.
> I saw the blue Rhine sweep along: I heard, or seemed to hear,
> The German songs we used to sing in chorus sweet and clear;
> And down the pleasant river, and up the slanting hill,
> The echoing chorus sounded in the evening calm and still."

CHAPTER VIII.

BY THE "LINKS" OF THE RHINE.

BEYOND Bingen the road leaves the Rhine, and does not return to it again to keep close alongside for any length together till near Strassburg, for the windings of the river become now perplexingly capricious. The stretch of country between the great bend at Bingen and Mayence is rather difficult for a cyclist, as extraordinarily long hills rise and fall nearly all the way. In fact I do not remember elsewhere such long pulls varied also by long descents. The views to be had are not only extensive, they are captivating; and gladly would I have lingered long as we gained each top, but that I knew the gates of Mayence closed by ten at night, while I did not know the nature of the country still to be traversed to get there. Great numbers of vehicles, evidently returning from some fair, were speeding home, amid song and laughter from the occupants, male and female, as we neared the many towers and spires and massive fortress of Mayence. There seemed to be a rivalry between them as to the speed of the horses, and when, at a slope, we appeared among them and passed them, loud was the cracking of whips, and long rang the shouts of supposed triumph as one after another passed us up the hill. Judge of the general consternation when, going down the other side, calmly seated with legs over the handle-bar, I rushed past them all and reached the level before they were half-way down. At the next hill two or three of the fastest trotters made up on us, and called out a challenge to a race for the town. We were leading the race along a good stretch of level where, however, the surface, as is common on roads when mud is used as cement and becomes hard as a brick, was peeled off in thick layers by the traffic, thereby rendering riding neither safe nor agreeable. As they gained on us, I turned into the side beneath the trees, where was a softer but an evener track. Finding now that we would soon leave all the competitors far behind, I looked round and shouted an adieu; but just then a branch lower than usual struck me on the head, scratched me smartly, and obligingly relieved me of my bonnet. Thus one of the racers became *hors de combat*, while the rest, with many a merry peal and many a wicked taunt, dashed on without us.

After we had crossed the three powerful ramparts and moats that render Mayence the strongest city of Germany, we got settled in a snug *Gastwirthschafthaus* in a pretty balconied street off the *Grosse Bleiche* (the longest street). There I met some real German characters, with less heaviness about their wits than the Prussians display: a master-cook, whose waggishness would have done honour to a Frenchman; a broken-down, tippling artist, who, if you cared to believe him, had painted all the most meritorious works of art in the galleries of Munich; an officer who was grievously at a loss whether to love me because of my intelligence in military politics, or to hate me because of the attentions bestowed by the sweet daughter of the house on the young English stranger. Indeed, they have sweet, winning, happy faces, those damsels of the Rhine. Perhaps there is no other district in Europe where the people in general are so intelligently happy and contented as along the Rhine; and, of course, this trait shows soonest and best on Nature's second-thought, the lasses.

Judging from conversations held here and elsewhere in Germany, I must insist that elementary education is a rarer thing there than in Scotland, and even in England. One point which there is no gainsaying is that Universal Geography is best known in Britain. The higher classes, indeed, know the geography of Germany and of France well. But the following incident will serve to illustrate the common geographical ignorance: A well-to-do landlady, in a town not far from the Rhine, well-informed and intelligent in what had come under her notice, asked the questions, "How is it Americans speak English and yet are not English? Now tell me, is America in England, or England in America?"

The venerable historic city of Worms on the whole displeased me by its newness—paradoxical though that may sound. For although it is about the oldest site of a city in Germany, famous in history—the Jews claim to have settled there as early as 588 B.C., at the Babylonish captivity—and rich in legendary lore from the Nibelungen downwards, yet only the sacred buildings, such as the double-domed, quadruple-towered, quaintly-figured cathedral, belong to antiquity. The reckless emissaries of the "most Christian" autocrat, Louis XIV. of France, in 1689 wantonly burned down almost all the rest. Therefore I searched in vain for the Diet-House where Luther in 1521 held to his faith, in spite of Pope and Emperor. On the Rosenwald island Siegfried killed another dragon, whence the town arms consist of two rampant dragons or *worms*, which have given the town its odd name.

From Worms the road runs broad and smooth to Mannheim, that very modern town. Mannheim, with its broad square blocks of houses, not called as streets, but numbered like wards in a hospital, is one of the very few mushroom-towns on the Continent, of which America and the British world can produce so many specimens. Business is everything in it; and in this respect forms such an incongruous contrast with its neighbour, the romantic, studious Heidelberg, as, say, in Glasgow the miles of trade-stained quays and streets, warehouses and factories, form with the quiet, old-world Cathedral of St. Mungo which stands in their midst.

As we stood at a music-seller's door in the Planken, the only street that can boast a name, obtaining directions as to the road to Heidelberg, a lady came up and addressed me in English, "Could she be of service to me, for these Germans pretend to know English, while they do not know it?" "Fortunately," I said, "not being a man of one language, I was not at their mercy." She was American; and, from what she said, appeared to be one of those remarkable characters that come across the wanderer's path on the Continent, often in the most out-of-the-way localities, who are self-exiled from all that is English, and who yet in their exile hail with joy the sound of an English voice.

A more delightful spot to live and study in is perhaps not on earth than Heidelberg. The Neckar flows here between rounded hills green to their tops with vineyards or forests. Its vast castle—the largest ruin in Germany, and the noblest even in its ruin—stands nearly 2000 feet above the town and the enchantingly beautiful Neckar gorge; and when the lights are lit in the town and along the banks, and gleam through the trees that grow everywhere here, no fairy could hope for a fairer scene. The beauty of the castle within and without, its wonderful extent, its great variety of tower and court, terrace and balcony, gateways and statues, ivy-clad walls, fountains and gardens, fill the stranger with amazement and rapturous delight. The sun was high above the hills when I entered its grounds; it had long been down before my charmed senses let me leave.

One could easily perceive that the town is accustomed to noisy carousals. Streets, as well as coffee-houses and public-houses, plainly show the student element present among the ordinary inhabitants. A more sprightly air and a greater fastidiousness about the decorations of signs and walls and rooms indicate the presence of young spirits whose student life would be a burden and a danger without those periodical outbursts that tone their otherwise cramped animal energy and bring them more into contact and sympathy with common life. Heidelberg taverns are lively pictures at night. Discussions and speeches, songs and pranks, animate every table, while eating and drinking are going on at every hour. Mottoes and scraps of songs or legends line the walls more here than I have seen elsewhere in Germany. Some of them are exhortations to drink, e.g.:—

> "Trinken lernt der Mensch zuerst,
> Viel später erst das Essen.
> D'rum soll er auch als Gast
> Das Trinken nicht vergessen."

> "Man learns to drink at first,
> Much later he learns to eat.
> So then let him not as guest
> The drinking e'er forget."

Others are much-needed admonitions, e.g.:—

> "Trinkt, aber lauft nicht;
> Diskutirt, aber rauft nicht!"

> "Drink, but do not sprawl;
> Dispute, but do not brawl!"

From my perch at the window of my room in the Haupt Strasse, I watched till a late hour the promenaders and jovial bands of "young bloods" as they came and went, and I overheard many a droll remark, not intended for everybody's ear, resounding in the narrow street between the high houses. For once I had been driven to seek my own company, because in the public room below an old fellow had been pestering me by affecting to speak English. All the time I was at supper and reading a newspaper, he loitered near me, passed and repassed, plainly desirous of speaking, then would go and report to his boon companions, and return to the attempt again. Seeing I took no notice,—for indeed he was not prepossessing with his yellow skinny face and long red nose,—he could stand it no longer, and when I referred to my dictionary for a word, he pounced on me with the momentous statement, "Zat ees Englisch book!" Knowing very well that he wanted to show off his knowledge of English before his friends, I asked him in *German* what he meant. That was an unkind cut to his reputation for English, as was visible both from the smiles of the friends and from his own discomfiture. However, though he kept on plying me with questions and blurting out scraps of his English experiences, all in English, he got not one word of English out of me; and when, evidently resolved not to go back to his friends at the other table until he had redeemed his now shattered reputation, he sat down beside me, I departed upstairs. This is the best method of getting rid of such parasites, whose ignorance generally is equalled only by their "cheek."

CHAPTER IX.

FROM HEIDELBERG TO STRASBURG.

No finer road could a cyclist pray for than the one that runs at this stage along the east side of the Rhine. In constant contrast to the winding "links" of the river, the road is straight for miles almost without a turn. The hills are gentle, but sufficiently elevated to afford an easy extensive view over the low range of hills to the east that form the northern outskirts of the Black Forest, and to the west, north, and south over the wide fertile plain, bounded five miles away by the curvings of the Rhine, and variegated like exquisite tapestry with fields and meadows, and plantings, and villages with their quaint antique clock-towers showing dry and white amid the green paradise of orchards.

It is a very quiet road, with little traffic of any kind except the lumbering hay-carts that carry away the abundant harvests. This fact was evident from the frequency with which we passed yoked horses, left to their own sweet meditations on the road, while their owners or drivers were at work in the fields.

It was owing to this fact, too, that I had my first serious mishap abroad. Between Bruchsal and Carlsruhe, on a long stretch of road where the tall beeches and plane-trees overhanging made a superb avenue, the peasants, whom I could see far down the fields on either side at harvesting, had, following the usual careless custom, left their horses yoked in pairs to the long cumbrous hay-carts wholly unattended and unwatched by the roadside. There were two teams, one on each side, nearly opposite to each other. That on our right faced us; that on the left had their backs towards us. Believing that the animals would show no more spirit than their continental brethren had usually shown to us, I ventured mounted to risk the narrow passage between them. Fool that I was! that passage was like to prove to me the gate of death. For, deeply absorbed in equine ruminations, the first team did not spy me till quite abreast; and so sudden was the start they got that they wheeled quite round in front of me towards the other team; and some part of the cart as it turned knocked me over against the other cart. The other horses now took fright at the commotion and started off side by side. There I clung, with arms entwined among the wooden bars of the cart, and with legs mixed up with the bicycle spokes and forks, hauling it along as the whole cavalcade swept along the road. Not till my voice had reassured them that it was no unearthly visitant that had disturbed their meditations, did they cease their wild career, and allow me time to view the sad havoc made among the spokes and on my clothes. My watch-chain was broken, and some keys and coins attached to it were lost; many of the spokes were bent, but only one required recapping; the knapsack was shifted and twisted so that it was a trouble to me all the rest of the journey.

The first peasant who came running up, followed by a train of women who could hardly run for laughing, I accused of the culpable neglect; but he said they belonged to another man, who was down the opposite field. Some one ran off for him, as I declared I should report to the police at Carlsruhe. When he came up, followed by his train of workers, he was as cool as a cucumber, and laughed me in the face when I said he would have to answer for his carelessness. Placing his hand on my shoulder—which action I resented and angrily forbade him to trifle with me—he said, "My good man, I have left horses by themselves between here and Mannheim in all sorts of positions and never been checked; and don't think you can do it." Enraged at his obstinacy not to admit his wrong, I determined to make a law-case of it, and secured the man that first came up for a witness. Just then an open carriage appeared. I stepped forward and raised my cap to the gentleman and ladies who were in it, explained the matter, and asked their opinion as to the German law of the road. Hereupon up stepped also my proud chieftain, the farmer, doffed his hat and would have spoken, when the older lady silenced him: "The gentleman is talking to us, not you." Their view was that he was wrong and culpable, and they forced him to admit as much. "That is all I want," said I, "the matter may rest there, thanks to you, sir, and to you, ladies. Adieu!"

The views obtainable from the road are still very extensive. Long before we came to them, the green ramparts of Rastadt and the great statue of Jupiter surmounting the Palace-barrack were outstanding objects, and then many miles to the west, wonderfully graceful even from a long distance, the spire and towers of Strassburg Cathedral.

As we approached Kehl—on the Rhine—three miles from Strassburg, an occasional village sign in French, denoted the once proximity of Gallic influence. On the shore at Kehl can still be seen the inmost pier of the bridge, blown up in 1870, which act was the first military event of the war. Now a bridge of boats supplies the place of the stone one. It would scarcely be worth while to build another only to be blown up again at the next outbreak. From Rastadt, which, being a town of the Confederation, is filled with soldiers, Austrian, Baden, and Prussian, and where enormous embankments were being thrown up as we passed—"only for something to do," as a soldier slyly declared to me—till we got into Strassburg, military, and military operations were abundantly visible. Strassburg itself is simply military mad. Ramparts, fosses, embrasures, forts, barracks, infantry, cavalry, artillery, meet the eye with appalling show of strength. One fancies that every second man he meets is a soldier or an official. The bearded, clumsily-built Germans in their ugly, flat-topped, overlapping caps and blue uniforms, go swaggering stiffly about the streets, like veritable masters of creation.

It was galling for me, to say the least, thus to behold what a terribly firm grip the Prussian Emperor has over a city so long French, and owing most of its fairness and its strength to the French, not to speak of its still marked popular sympathy with French life and spirit. Although the people, as a whole, in Alsace have always spoken German, and are of German race, yet before the last siege everybody knew something of French more or less; but now, since Alsace has become Elsass, all is changed. German, and not French, is made compulsory in the schools; all the papers and negotiations of the towns have to be in German. Even the streets have been baptized anew,—reminding one of the ludicrous changes in the Paris street names as the Government changed during Revolution days. Every trace of French occupation is being rapidly effaced; and complaints are bitter and deep, though they be suppressed except in private, that all the old French-engrafted Alsatian stock is being systematically ousted out of the country, and a Prussian one forced in. It is sad as well as comical to find occasionally some deeply graven sign or lettering in French that cannot be removed without destroying the structure, while in glaring fresh new paint, as if to eclipse the old one, its German equivalent is placed by its side. For instance, around Strassburg and along the main roads, Napoleon's milestone-pillars, with the distances cut out on them, are still standing, indicating in capitals, that they are on the "*Route Impériale*," while the German "*Kaiserliche Strasse*" seen on some of them shows the change of ownership.

It was my good fortune to lodge in Strassburg with a French-Alsatian family, and from the various members and from visitors, I first learned what all my subsequent wanderings through Alsace-Lorraine confirmed, namely, that the Germans are still very unpopular, owing to their over-rigorous administration, and their intolerance of French life. In Metzgerstrasse, formerly the Rue des Bouchers, a restaurant-keeper sent me up three storeys to find lodgings. A typical Alsatian girl, strong and fresh, opened the door—she told me afterwards she took me for an officer—and said 'the mother' did not take lodgers except for a lengthened period. However, 'the mother' was pleased to have me for three days, and never was I better entertained. It was not long before they took me into their confidence, and I learned that the father, a Frenchman, had grown tired of his home, and been long unfaithful. He had a prosperous business, yet he gave nothing to the support of his wife and daughter; he came and went, occupying his own room, and that was all they saw of him. The only greeting he had now for his daughter —who made a living by embroidering—was *sale fille*, and for his wife, *vieille bête*. Such a pretty home they had too; I felt inclined to kick the brute downstairs.

Unfortunately for France and her future, this is no uncommon type of a French home. Until some great character arises in

France, possessing a strong personal electrical influence, whether he be a preacher to open French eyes to the sanctity and seriousness of living, or a martinet to enforce morality and discipline, alas! the fondest well-wisher of France must sigh in vain for her salvation.

Yet in spite of the manifest superiority of German character in morality and stability, there is nothing more remarkable in current history, than the fact that the Alsatians, though of German origin, and though made French only in 1681, when Louis XIV., self-styled *Le Grand* and "*Excelsus super omnes gentes Dominus*," by dint of bribery and violation of international faith, took the province under his "most Christian" wing, and though the lower classes have always spoken German and but little French, yet love France more than Prussia. All over Europe I have met Alsatians, self-exiled, because they cannot endure German rule in their country; some of them are selling combs and sponges, some of them are waiters, some of them railway-porters; but all agree in hating Prussia, and in styling themselves Frenchmen yet.

The reason for this preference may be that the French are more amiable, and their life freer and gayer, and that Alsace is really French land with the broad Rhine between it and Germany. To my mind there was much weight in the great cry of the French Revolution days, "a natural frontier!" To any one, who like myself has been on foot at and over so many frontiers, and known their troubles—most of them miserably flimsy, arbitrary affairs—nothing but a natural frontier (a broad, rushing river or a lofty chain of mountains) can commend itself. This should be the rule, until at least we can all as men unite in a common brotherhood, and have a European or a World Congress workably established.

CHAPTER X.

FAREWELL TO THE RHINE.

A CONVENTIONAL tourist, if he knew the pleasures of 'roughing it' and leaving the hackneyed tracks, would envy me often for the pleasant places my lines sometimes fall into on my tramps. Here in Strassburg I enjoyed a Sunday's rest, seated on a balcony high above the street where thronged pleasure-seekers and church-goers. The sun shone through the clematis round our bower just enough to make us feel it was summer. There I sat, read and smoked, or listened to the lively talk of the hostess and her daughter and a girl-friend of hers who had come to see the stranger. They played to me, at first brisk and merry airs; then, when I told them I did not like loud rollicking music on Sunday, soothing strains sweet and low came floating out to me as I sat alone. Now and then deep sounds would reach my ear and deepen my reveries as the bells of the cathedral proclaimed the divisions of the passing day. High over the roofs the spire appeared in all its delicate lace-like tracery, itself 400 feet nearer heaven than we below, and by its giddy loneliness, disturbed only by the doves and storks that sweep and circle about its angles, stealing man's soul away for a season from the sordid things of earth.

About noon I went to the service, and at noon heard the crowing of the cock in the wonderful astronomical clock, and saw the figures of the apostles marching and bowing round the central figure of Jesus. There too I met a cyclist, who told me that the local club had just returned from a run, and were now going to have a dance and a night's enjoyment. Just so, there they were, great heroes in fine new unsoiled suits covered with their fineries. A small run of twenty or thirty miles deserves a round of jollification and self-gratulation for the whole afternoon and evening. Such is the foreign idea of sport—a very little work and a very large amount of fun!

About four in the morning that I left, I was awakened from a sound sleep by an ear-splitting fanfaring and a thunderous roll and clatter of carriages and hoofs on the causewayed street. Looking out of the casement, I saw the whole square and the long street filled with troops of artillery and cavalry to the number of two thousand, detraining through the town on their way to morning manœuvres. It was an imposing spectacle, but indicative of the iron yoke at present round the neck of this people.

When we were leaving the suburbs of Strassburg on our way to Basle, the tire caught in a network of rails and brought us down. A pointsman lent me a strong spanner to adjust the screw of my knapsack which had again shifted. He told me he was a French-Alsatian, and asked if I was not English. "The Russians are carrying their temptation of England too far, and the papers this morning say there is to be war," said he. "The Germans here don't believe Britain has a chance, but I know they are wrong; for Britain is the best governed, most civilized country in the world. Besides, although she has not a large army, yet all her young men are already more than half-soldiers because they go about the world, like yourself just now, undergoing fatigue and hardships for pleasure, fighting with each other at cricket and football and I don't know what more. What must it be when they come to fight for their country? Two to one on Britain!" This speech of his ought to be printed and circulated broadcast over the countries that try to intimidate Britain on the score of her small army.

Now our way ran along the Rhine, through a district seldom visited, containing an endless chain of villages but only one town, the powerful fortress of Neu-Breisach. On the west are the grand highlands of the Vosges, and on the east, the mountains of the Black Forest. The banks are high and picturesque, rich with as wonderful castled ruins as the upper Rhine. The islands in the channel are so numerous that it looks as if you could make a road on the river by stepping from one to another of them. The beauty of this quarter is too little known.

It was high day still when we crossed another frontier, that between Alsace and Switzerland, and arrived in the prosperous city of Basle. In the streets, long winding and narrow, with high houses, could be easily perceived the struggle going on between French and German in language, in customs and in architecture. The German that the people speak has many French traces, e.g. the use of *No* instead of *Nein* for the particle of negation, and in such words as *pikfein*, which is just the French *piquant* moulded into the German *fein*, and the whole meaning 'tip-top.' An enthusiastic admirer of Englishmen found me near the bridge searching for lodgings. He took me through many winding ways and hilly streets to the *Schwarze Ochse* (Black Bull) at the Spalenthor; then he did his best to familiarize me with the Swiss customs and country, and next morning, set me on the road to Berne, to find which without his aid would have been a labour. We passed by the beautiful St. Jakol monument which commemorates the fall of 1300 Swiss fighting against 30,000 French, four and a half centuries ago. It is a touching memorial of patriotism. Helvetia stands wearing a wreath of mourning and looking down on falling soldiers, beneath whom runs the brief inscription : " Our souls to God, our bodies to the enemy ! "

By-and-by we turned into a valley from which there is no issue except over the high hills. Henceforth we must not look for the level roads that we have mostly traversed till now, but for daring paths that wind round precipices, and climb and descend the giddiest heights. While I was alternately gazing at the plains we had left and the heights in front, and wondering if there was no easier entrance into Switzerland than that wild gorge on the hill-top, I found the Rhine, so long my companion, was out of sight.

> " Adieu to thee again ! a vain adieu !
> There can be no farewell to scene like thine ;
> The mind is coloured by thy every hue."

CHAPTER XI.

INTO SIGHT OF THE SNOWY ALPS.

For many a stiff furlong we toiled, mounted up the east side of the valley, passing many villages and chalets set in the rocks, but when a wood-cutter informed me that there were still four or five miles before the top came, it was wiser to dismount. The sun was scorching, and not a breath of air was blowing. Now came long, long steep ascending curves of road, sometimes running far inwards to avoid the beds of torrents, then outwards along the opposite bank, sometimes turning beneath a towering bare cliff, and displaying, far below, the wilderness of firs and pines that have a break only in the centre of the valley, where corn-fields are standing yellow, to begin again and climb the wild steeps on the other side. The far-away tinkling of the bells that hang round the necks of the cows that lead the herd assured me that we were indeed in the land of the Schweitzer.

When at length the highest point of the road was reached, it did not stop for a level rest but began immediately to run down another still wilder, narrower, richer valley. What a sight for a Highlander was there, stirring every emotion of home and country, every brave heroic feeling within his breast! Far over miles of green ridges and deep vales, seeming nearer much than the intermediate land, were the dazzling white peaks of Europe's heart. At such a moment to think of descending on foot would be cowardice. Mount! mount in gallant style; the danger is but spice to the feast of rapturous emotions. For a time the road wound gently sloping past many a peaceful farm, whence children and peasants ran out in wonder at the strange traveller whose like probably never passed that way before. But soon the ravines converged and the cliffs grew more abrupt, and the road steeper and capricious in its swervings and dangerous from the deep sandy ruts caused by the traffic of timber carts. Now we were in at the corner of a bend and beneath us was heard the roar of waterfalls dashing to the valley away beneath, where through the trees the stream was seen in glimpses flowing peacefully past cottages with overlapping roofs amid gardens and fields of grain; now we were in an arcade of mountain-trees growing so dense on either side that it was hopeless to guess whether the next turn would bring us on to a plain or a precipice.

Those cyclists who have ridden over real hill-land will appreciate what I have so often felt in going down a steep road, especially if the scenery be beautiful—I mean a sense of fascination that charms away the fear of danger. Here, for example, although the road was in many places deep with sand, although I knew not what each turn would develop into, and once or twice was fearfully scared because I thought it was not possible to turn in fast or far enough to prevent going over the poorly-protected precipice side, yet my desire to keep on till the bottom was reached grew more and more intense as each danger was safely past.

We were now fairly into the land of *Thals* (vales) and *Bachs* (brooks); these are the terminations to the names of most of the places we now pass. Water in abundance, and milk and cheese found cheap, show the nature of the country. Nothing can be more refreshing than the sight of the village fountains in Switzerland—copious streams perennially flowing out of some animal figured in stone into long troughs round which horses and cattle are being watered or peasant women are busy at their washing. Indeed one could almost tell the country he is in by the nature of the water-supply. In the north it comes forced by gravitation from iron pipes; along the Rhine it comes from oblong-boxed pumps with great iron cow-tail handles; along the Danube the wheel and bucket are used to lift it from deep wells; in the Eastern countries, such as Servia, Turkey, and Greece, a long tree balanced on a tall upright post and with weights at the outside end raises the bucket, attached to a pole, from the well; in hill countries like Switzerland the supply is ever flowing and ever pure. It was at one of those fountains in Langenthal when bathing my face and quenching my thirst that I met a young Swiss cyclist riding an old Howe machine. He took me round to his home in Burgdorf, displaying on the way thither considerable versatility and freshness of character. Patriotic independence breathes from every utterance of your true Swiss gentleman.

It was the time of the great Swiss National Shooting Festival or Wappenschaw held at Berne in the middle of July. As we approached this romantically situated capital of the Swiss Federation, along the banks of the rapid rushing Aare, all sorts of vehicles were speeding homewards into the country. Their occupants were evidently wrought to a high pitch of enthusiasm by the scenes they had been engaged in at their capital, for many a shout of *Vorwärts!* (Forward !) greeted me as they passed. But what is that rolling grovelling thing rattling along towards us beneath the trees? Actually it is an old wooden 'bone-shaker,' ridden by a grisly, greasy individual whose long grey beard and matted locks might warrant his being a grandfather! I was filled with curiosity to speak with such a character; but vain hope! the representative of the early days of cycling "passed by on the other side" without deigning to show the slightest consciousness of the presence of the highly developed modern scion.

The exceptional beauty of Berne cannot fail to excite the admiration even of the most *blasé* traveller. Not to speak of the sublime panorama visible from its streets—more than a dozen Alpine giants of nearly or over 4000 feet, including the Jungfrau and the Wetterhorn, all glowing in the departing sun like white-hot fires—the city itself stands on a rocky platform of the Aare as it rushes past its peopled isles between high banks and verdant terraces, and below its long lofty bridges. Old-fashioned streets with shady arcades along all their course, gateway towers, quaint street fountains, houses with gabled roofs and oriel windows, and many another feature of medieval times, make Berne the most picturesque city of Switzerland, if not even of Europe.

That night it was full to overflowing with strangers from all parts of the country, from France, Austria, Germany, and even Italy. A weary time I had pushing my wheel about from street to street, from hotel to hotel, recommended here and recommended there, but only to find that all rooms and beds were occupied : "You have come too late." In a broad street near the Cathedral I was standing tired and hungry, leaning my head on the saddle and wondering which way to take to reach the fields where at least there would be room for us, when a big hearty voice sounded behind me : "Could your horse carry me, do you think?" Sulkily I replied, "Yes; and your grandmother with you." "What's the matter? Can't you find the way to the *Fest-Platz?*" "Bother the *Fest-Platz!*" I growled, "I want a lodgings-*Platz.*" "Oh ! if that's all, just be easy, you are my guest for the night. Come over here and I'll introduce you to some fine young ladies, and we'll have a glass of wine. Now tell the ladies and me your story, for you English lads have always some fine stories to tell."

As a Scotchman I was doubly welcome everywhere he took me. The Swiss, indeed all Continentalers, have a very warm side for the Scotch. The Swiss and Scots Guards were together the staunchest, bravest supports of the Bourbon Court. Side by side, Scotch and Swiss have stood and fallen on many a red-dyed 'fochten field.'

We drove to the Bears' Den across the Nydeck Bridge, where also was the grand pavilion for the festival. Live bears are kept in the den at the city's expense, in memorial of the founder of the city, who killed a bear on its site, and thence gave it its name Bern (Bären). Into this den, they told me, an English officer fell some twenty years ago and was devoured.

Outside the pavilion a stand, guarded by soldiers, contained the host of prizes to be won at the shooting contests. Inside the pavilion was a unique spectacle : some thousands of holiday-dressed people, sober citizens, and fair citizenesses, mingled with peasants in their peculiar costumes, and shooters in their fresh gay shooting garb—hunter's cap and horn and suit of green—all sitting at benches and tables, and eating, drinking, talking, laughing, while music bands, at each end of the long broad canopied hall, filled the air with melodious discoursings. All sorts of wine and beer and fruits and sweatmeats were being constantly supplied by waiters, both male and female, and the Schützen-Gesellschaft (Shooting Society), of which my friend was a member, had the privilege of partaking thereof along with their friends, *ad libitum.* Among the many introductions I received one is still vivid in my memory, that of a young captain in the Swiss navy—save the term ! it only means the steamers on the lakes. Intensely patriotic, he declared that, although he had served his time on British boats, and risen as high as first mate, he would not be captain on the finest Atlantic linér in exchange for his position among the lakes and mountains of his native land. His only recollection of Glasgow was an amusing one— a fight in Argyle Street between roughs and the Salvation Army.

It was late before we quitted the scene of festivity, and only after my story had been recited a score of times. By the morning trains two or three contingents of shooters arrived, and paraded through the gay old streets, with trumpets and horns sounding, with quivers and bows and arrows slung behind, with rifles and carbines shouldered—a martial array.

CHAPTER XII.

FROM BERNE TO GENEVA IN TWELVE HOURS—A LIVELY RUN.

AT eleven I took a kind farewell of my worthy host, Gottlieb Kneubühler, and started on what in most respects was my finest ride through the finest scenery I have known. At the very outset the road lets one know that it means to dance and leap and caper a bit for many a mile. First it rises on to a long plateau above Berne, giving sense-filling views of long green valleys sweeping upwards till they lose their green in the heights of white snow and ice. Then it takes to dipping deep into ravines, and crawling along up among the woods and rocks on the opposite side. Sometimes it takes five miles of a quiet gradual sloping upwards, unfolding more and more beauties of landscape as it rises, till at the top, the eye is ravished by variety. Then again it dips and swerves and reels, till nothing but a narrow valley is seen, with waving corn and straggling cows and a few ruddy peasants lilting at their work.

Especially is this its nature south of Freiburg, which itself is a fit specimen of ups and downs. Descending a very long and lovely ravine, we come in sight of it as it is built clambering over a rocky peninsula of the Sarine, in its valley and yet over 2000 feet above the sea-level. Before we crossed its magnificent suspension bridge, we rested in a shady park where fountains played. A lady who spoke to me there and also some men, were bilinguists, knowing both French and German. The town is on the border between French-speaking and German-speaking Switzerland ; and a very hard struggle for supremacy is manifestly being fought by the rival tongues. The higher parts of the town are reached from the lower by long flights of steps—reminding one of Edinburgh. The French saying about Morlaix in Brittany, " *De la mansarde au jardin, comme on dit à Morlaix*" (From garret to garden, as people say at Morlaix), might be altered applicably here to "*De la mansarde à la rue*" (From garret to street). For the pavement of the upper street, where the great fountain stands, serves as a roof to houses in the 'Short-cut' to the river below.

Now follow some very long dangerous hills, that think nothing of winding up among woods and mills and hamlets, three or four miles at a time and with as long a descent. The worst begin at the very ancient and very romantic town of Romont. It rises abruptly to 2500 feet, and all around it are old walls and watch-towers, also a massive round tower, and a Burgundian castle, eight hundred years old. Another old castellated place is Rue, just beneath the summit of a hill, as high as Romont, but more precipitous on one side, which is walled in. I had just climbed a steep of four miles, and was glad on the summit aforesaid to mount again. No sooner had I done so than we entered this ancient dilapidated place, which had been hidden from view. The descent was already begun. Loth, however, to dismount so soon, I kept on till the pace became almost ungovernable, and perforce I had to keep the saddle. So into the place we rushed, over the great, partially displaced cobble-stones, over fragments of dishes, old tins, gutters crossing into sideways, and scattered refuse thrown indiscriminately from the neighbouring houses, while dogs and geese and goats and children fled in terror from before us. With brake now full on, still the steep was so frightful that the speed did not decrease, when, oh! horror! the street seemed to terminate in a ditch and a stone wall. When just about to relax my hold, and hazard a stop as less dangerous than the danger ahead, I saw a narrow exit at the end of the houses to the right. Even so, death still stared me in the face, I thought, for there did not appear room enough to turn successfully. Summoning all my courage, I let the machine run first to the left, then obliquely to the right towards the wall; then, on the edge of the ditch, pulled round the machine's head farther to the right in order to clear it, and we shot down the hill—saved. The road at once went more to the left than it had appeared from the end of the street; but, it being still rough with stones and very steep, my tremors did not cease till we reached something like a level. The dust flying off brake and tyre was as thick as flour on a miller over my boots and breeches.

At the last long high hill before Lausanne, I inwardly vowed not to come off going up but perhaps when going down from the top. In one sense it is easier, as it is less annoying, to ride up a hill if it be at all practicable than to walk and push the wheel; it certainly saves time. This I did here up Mount Jorat that rises from the plain for four or five miles to over 2000 feet, past a windmill near the top, or a signal—I forget which—and down some miles to Lausanne on the Lake of Geneva. I count this feat among my best displays of endurance.

For some distance on the top near Les Croissettes the road is level, and gave me opportunity to glory in the marvellous prospect, almost unrivalled in extent and beauty, that lay before me. There at my feet curving its two limbs to right and left away from this central point lies the vast crescent Lake of deep-blue tranquil waters. Here and there graceful lateen-sails, gleaming white in contrast to the blue, are crossing its bosom, or coasting by the rich smiling shores. To the north are sloping hills rich in verdure, and above them the towering forest-ridges of the mighty Jura, as it opposes its dark sides against the Swiss who would leave his mountain home and against the foreigners who would seek to enslave this land of William Tell, the land of the brave and the free. To the east and west at the foot of the green hills along the lake shores is a long line of vineyards, sunny towns, and delightful mansions, nestling amid foliage whose spruce luxuriance reminds one of the well-kept manor-lands of England. Across the lake, the huge mountain masses display their black fantastic forms, run along for a space in solid massiveness; then stop abrupt to show a yawning gulf and beyond it other and higher masses rent and cleft and hurled confusedly; then away above them all, the peaks of cold white snow shining in eternal serenity.

No other region on earth can show such a world of natural beauty combined with such a wealth of deep interest in literature and history. Around these shores have been evolved "thoughts that breathe and words that burn;" many of the greatest "thoughts that strike mankind" have here had their birth. Here wrote the brilliant De Staël; here Byron roved and sang; here Gibbon "sapped a solemn creed with solemn sneer;" here Voltaire and Rousseau kindled the fires that burned the thrones of kings. Yonder gleam the white walls of

Chillon's gloomy dungeons where tyranny trod for ages on aspiring freedom. Far down the lake at its southern extremity appear the quays and climbing streets of Geneva, 'the little republic' whose words and ways showed Europe how to spurn the yoke that Rome and feudal Despotism had in the Dark Ages fastened round her neck.

All the way down the deep woody dell from the Grandes Roches above Lausanne, the road was gay with people—all looking extremely well-to-do—enjoying a walk in the lovely evening light. Several groups we had great difficulty in passing safely; they were so occupied with themselves that they could not hear the sound of my bell behind them. At one of them, where the start caused a lady to run first one way and then another almost bringing on a collision, I could not help exclaiming in English, "I wonder at people walking in the middle of the public highway!" But I was scarcely prepared for the ready answer in silvery English tones, "You would not have run me down, would you?"

From Berne to here for over sixty miles the road has been terribly hilly, but now it runs almost level with the banks of the lake on, thirty-eight miles, to Geneva. When we left Lausanne about seven, the shadows of the Jura range were half way up the Savoy mountains opposite, leaving the lake in shade below. At Morges I had my first conscious view of Mont Blanc, the mightiest giant in this land of mighty giants, so surprising a spectacle that not till I had made inquiry could I believe it was aught else than a dome of clouds.

The air is most invigorating and balmy along this route. Sweet fragrance filled it from gardens and orchards as we rushed along the banks at ten miles an hour, starting the gulls and wild-fowl from the rocks and the beds of streams, past many a goodly cedar, chestnut and walnut and flowering magnolia.

About half-way round, at Rolle, when the darkness was deepest, for the moon was not yet up, I was startled by the sense of some light. It was indeed a majestic sight! From peak to peak the lightnings were flashing and playing, and the whole calm dark lake lit up with the reflections; low muffled sounds of thunder rumbled far away, as if the giant hills were speaking to each other in the night. Then, when some clouds to the south had rolled away, up rose the moon in full fair beauty above the hoary mountains, over the magic scene.

Such a glorious moonlight ride as I now had amid such surroundings was worth a lifetime of slow prosaic ease at home. But by-and-by as we neared the far-glittering lights of Geneva, sleep, which had not got its due the night before, began to make me insensible to all but the necessity of turning the pedals. While in this drowsy dreamy state, I heard some one cry out "*Lumière!*" (light), but paid no more attention thereto, till a man rushed at me furiously out of the shadow of a house, shouting wildly, "*Arrêtez-vous, arrêtez-vous donc!*" (Stop! stop there!") I saw he was a gendarme, and asked him what he wanted. "You haven't got a light!" As I slackened speed preparatory to dismounting he thought I was making off, and caught me roughly by the arm, so that it was impossible to come off without striking him in the face with my leg. In a perfect frenzy of rage at what he believed my obstinacy, he shook the machine so that we fell together on him and nearly brought him to the ground. After all my pleasure of the previous night and the stiff day's work, I had not power left either to resist him or to mount fast enough to elude him. By this time he had drawn his sword, and threatening me in furious language, ordered me to wheel the machine into the guardhouse. There when he had locked the door, he demanded five francs of a fine, which I complained I could not afford, and deprecated his brutal treatment of me for an offence that I could not avoid, seeing that the oil in my lamp would not burn. Moreover, I argued, there was no need for a lamp when the moon shone so clear that one could read by its light. "*Cinq francs, s'il vous plaît, cinq francs!*" was all the consolation he vouchsafed,—"I give you ten minutes to pay up; after that your machine is sequestrated, and the magistrate will decide whether you get it back or no." While he was counting me out the change from a *louis d'or*, I wrote down the name of the place, and was taking a rough sketch of the fellow, when he, suspecting my design, rudely ushered me out of doors. There it was proved that the lamp would not burn. So promising him a summons next day from headquarters, I went my way on foot.

Indeed, fatigue, excitement and hunger had made me so

faint that it would have been foolhardy to attempt a mount. But I dreaded most being pounced upon by some other wakeful guardian of the ways ; and slowly and dreamily I pushed on for the city. It was a quarter to eleven when the arrest took place, about two and a half miles from Geneva ; so that in less than twelve hours, we had done one mile or two less than one hundred miles over Switzerland.

By the time we reached the heart of the city it was midnight, and all but the largest hotels were closed. Therefore I knocked at a little *loge à pied* ('Lodgings for travellers'), which was also a *café restaurant*. It was a partly wooden erection, by the side of a park and beneath the woods round a railway-station. The name was inviting by its classical sound, "*Chalet des Allobroges*," reminding me of Cæsar's definition of Geneva : "*Extremum oppidum Allobrogum est proximumque Helvetiorum finibus Geneva.*" Inside, the place was primitive enough to be tenanted by actual Allobroges, those reluctant recalcitrant allies of ancient Rome. A few rude deal tables and benches, a few bottles and glasses, one or two old pictures on the brown walls, a bare, much-worn floor, three or four rough plates with a clumsy fork and knife laid on each side of them, together with as many rough tanned customers waiting beside these for their late supper, made up the inventory of the room. Willingly I became an additional guest ; and while we were busy at the steaming viands, a knock came to the door. "Who's that?" "The police!" They were not come to make an arrest, but only to slake their thirst on the sly, after an assurance from the landlord that there was no fear of me blabbing.

Then to bed up above a stable, off a loft open at the back, along a ladder to a narrow slit of a room where was a bed with one coverlet, a bottomless chair, and nothing more except ingrained dirt. My first sleep might be over when I awoke and felt that I was not the only living thing in the bed, but that many more were holding their nocturnal gambols. Again I was dozing off, when a distinct feeling of something moving over me roused me, and a quick pattering of small feet across the room convinced me that there were bigger brown things than bugs wanting to keep me company. But what are bugs and even rats, when a fellow is dead tired? Rest and sleep are the only realities to him then.

CHAPTER XIII.

NORTHWARDS—"*spectat ad septentriones.*"

NEXT day I repaired to the *Palais de Justice*, and laid my complaint of ill-usage from the gendarme before the Prefect of Police. I said it was strange that on all the frontiers and countries we had passed, no official had meddled with us till we came to here, the bulwark of the land of supposed freedom. Thoroughly sympathizing with me at the gendarme's abuse of his authority, he forthwith dispatched a messenger to summon him up, and bade me return at four. Accordingly, after a day's pleasure on the quays by 'the arrowy Rhone' and on the lake, I re-appeared at the City Chambers, where the chief magistrate was hearing cases, and ready to attend to mine whenever the fellow arrived. But by the hour when the steamer by which I had arranged to go up the lake was about to depart, he had not made his appearance. Promising that at least he would have the fellow chastised and warned against using violence in future towards strangers, the kind Prefect took farewell of me.

At dawn next morning we left our night's roost at Morges, passed its grey old castle tower and an older one still up its valley, and made for the Juras, to cross into France. Such a feat the people at Geneva and Morges pronounced impossible for a bicycle. But it must be a queer road over which a bicycle cannot go. Even if we had been obliged to walk into France, the glorious panoramas of mountains, the lovely glimpses of Geneva and Neuchatel lakes would have been ample compensation. Yet as I halted on the hill, in sight of the towers of Orbe —after fifteen miles of hard up-riding—I could not help feeling that the beauty and grandeur of these scenes were on too grand a scale to satisfy the eye so much as the narrower yet wilder and fresher scope of Loch Lomond or Loch Katrine.

At this point a waggoner set me on a short cut up to Romainmotier, a distance only of about three miles yet rising in that space 1000 feet. On a sunny brae near here, we passed a young Swiss lady sitting in a shady bower beneath an apple-tree, and reading a French novel. She gave me much pretty instruction in the objects visible on the landscape and about the nature of the passes into France. The latter point was much needed, for the roads are here so tremendously steep and difficult that it would have been no joke to strike on the wrong one and have to retreat.

We skirted the steep sides, loaded with woods, of the deep valley of the Orbe, up past the Dent de Vaulion to near the Lac de Joux, over 3000 feet up, famous for early 'Lake Dwellings' and for its subterranean issues. Then we went round by the lofty Mont d'Or (nearly 5000 feet) through the village of Vallorbe on its side, and up an extremely beautiful rocky and woodland valley, till the kilometric stones on the roadside (there are none in the Swiss part) proclaimed that we had crossed into *la belle France*. France is indeed *belle* among her Juras, such as she is in few other parts.

We were toiling up the hill through Jounge, the French custom-station, when a gendarme challenged, "*Halte!*" and levelled his gun as we kept going on. So again we were led captive. The chief of the customs maintained my machine was new, that it had only been rubbed with mud to make it look old and used, and demanded a duty on its value to the tune of thirty francs. This he said was the recent order of the Government, because it had been discovered that Germans were making cycles in Geneva and importing them into France as old ones and therefore exempt from duty. It was of no avail showing him great cuts in the tires and rust on the wheels. We adjourned to his house to get the receipt; there he suddenly discovered in me a wonderful likeness to his own son then in Paris, and inquired what I, a Frenchman, had been doing in Switzerland. I said I was English, and told him my story, at which he was breathless with wonder. He had been at the Crimea, vividly remembered the Highlanders, showed me his trophies, among which was Queen Victoria's medal, and told me many loving stories of the old English colonel he had served with, and who accidentally had come round that way some years ago and recognized him.

The result of all these revelations was that my wheel was registered as bearing "*traces évidentes de service,*" and I escaped, pocket-whole.

The road still continued climbing higher, but occasionally it would run down long narrow dark gorges where the great arrowy pines seemed almost to meet overhead. After a longer climb than usual, we reached a level, and as usual glad of the rest I at once put my legs over the handle-bar. An abrupt turn— a very common thing on Jura roads—brought us into a magnificent amphitheatre of perpendicular cliffs. So sudden and so grand was the sight that at first I took no notice of how the road ran. It sloped gently along one side to my right beneath some higher slopes; on its left there was no protection from the precipice but two feet of stones and earth. As it went farther in, on the inner or right side rose a wall of rock, and on the outer, the cliffs went sheer down hundreds of feet to where cataracts were pouring and roaring, tumbling and splashing, amid the broken limestone masses. There appeared no outlet to the road ; but, assured that such a good road would not lead the traveller over the cliffs, I ventured slowly down. At length an opening was seen tunnelled out of the rock, forming an archway, but at right angles. This apparition startled me out of my coolness. An inch miscalculated in turning might hurl me down the ravine, down to a fearful death. With an involuntary cry of terror, I ran into a tree projecting from the inner side, and, while the roadside stopped the wheel, held on by the branches for several minutes before my scared senses could be convinced that the danger was past.

Beyond the arch, ran a long deep gorge with the river Doubs (or a branch of it) flowing down through it. We would be some 3500 feet up, and it was a noble prospect that now unfolded itself below and around. As far as eye could reach, rose and fell in ravishing variety wilderness beyond wilderness of red Jura pines crowding the countless hills and dales. Here and there a solitary fir leans over a jutting rock ; down far below, beside the noisy torrent near a village church or green, or round the sloping orchards, flourish the green domes of the bell-shaped beeches, a pleasing yet fantastic change from the tall tapering boles of the pines.

The road now hugged closely and sometimes went under the side of the massive crest of mountain up which I could look five or six hundred feet headlong. As the windings of the road were now visible, clear for some miles, I remounted, and let the machine carry me down at an easy pace. At a bend where the water was oozing in showers through the rock, we met two priests toiling up the hill on foot, and wiping their bald heads as the sweat poured ceaselessly out. They started in a very unpriestly manner as we hove in sight, and as carefully retired to the side as if we were a wild beast on the track. But a respectful "*Messieurs!*" from me brought the smiles to their beaming faces.

At a small village where I stopped to drink at the fountain, a crowd of villagers clustered round my machine that I had left against the wall on the dam. An old man said, that though they had often heard of a velocipede, never had one come that way before, and they had no notion that it was such a fine animal. "How does it go?" "Where's the steam?" "How can it stand itself?" were the questions put to me right and left. So for about ten minutes I stood there in the centre of an admiring throng discoursing in French about the wonders and ways of a bicycle, ending up by mounting and waving back an *au revoir!*

Now we came on to Bourbaki's famous line of retreat from Besançon with his 85,000 men of *l'Armee de l'Est* into Switzerland in February 1871. I pity the poor famished beaten soldiers and their horses that had to toil up through these terrible defiles in the winter over the ice-bound roads. Over the dark defile of La Cluse, frowns the ancient Château de Joux, and its frown is returned by the modern fort opposite— the two forming the massive portals of this great mountain gateway. The gloomy dungeons of the Château—"*ce nid de hibous*"— were once the prison of the versatile Mirabeau, the man of manifold strange wayfarings, "the Pharos and Wondersign, for twenty-three resplendent months, of an amazed Europe—Gabriel Honore Riquetti de Mirabeau, the worldcompeller." Hence he 'stole' away to Holland 'the fair young Sophie, Madame Monnier.' Here, too, the last brave stand was made against the Prussians; and a pyramidal monument looks down on us as we pass and read : "*Aux Derniers Defenseurs de la Patrie.*"

Still 2700 feet up, we passed through Pontarlier, and over another long lofty ridge beyond it, then about ten miles of a constant downhill run, legs over handle.

CHAPTER XIV.

FROM THE JURAS INTO ALSACE-LORRAINE.

THE moon was shining when we passed between the eastmost redoubt of the immense and far-extending fortifications of Besançon. Then came other forts in a valley whence far below could be seen the meandering Doubs glittering in the moonlight. Then the road rushed round below the citadel heights into view of the lamps of the town, and down through an ancient tunnelled gateway to the river's side. Few, if any, other cities can show such inaccessible natural strength as Besançon. With sufficient provisions and ammunition, it might hold out against the whole force of Germany. It is Cæsar's "*Vesontio, maximum oppidum Sequanorum*," and besides the old *Porte Noire* contains quite a marvel of Roman remains.

In the restaurant where I supped there was an old cobbler whose wife had a room to spare. About midnight we repaired to his house up in a narrow alley on the face of the cliff. The houses were very high and old-fashioned, but very picturesque in their grotesqueness. Up we climbed into a court where wooden stairs led up to the various flats, and wooden gangways bridged the space between the houses on the four sides of the court. His abode was in the topmost storey; it was a regular museum of old weapons, guns, saddles, whips and boots hanging or lying about the walls and floors, intermingled with leather parings and the implements of his Crispinian calling. My bedroom opened on to one of the gangways. During the night as I lay on the bed beside the open casement, I heard a rattle and a scraping near my head, and turning saw what looked like a big animal's face. Without another thought I darted my fist at it; then came a yelp like a cat's mewing, and a second later, a dull thud. Conscience-stricken lest in my dreamy fright I had killed some inoffensive creature, I looked out and saw that the gangway did not come quite up to the window, and the glimmering dawnlight let me see the form of 'poor puss' stretched out apparently dead on the stones thirty feet below.

The country north of Besançon, as far as Epinal is still one succession of hills, so that if we had not persevered in riding up the ascents in the road that occur usually every fifty or a hundred yards it would have been a tedious journey for the cyclist on foot. After leaving the vineyards and hills of Vesoul, where a colossal gilt statue of the Virgin dominates the town and the fertile valleys, there are some fine long stretches of an easy descent, with only a turn or two which, however, are very sharp. On one of these descents we had had five miles of ease and leisure to view the glorious unfolding of the woodlands. On the left ran a torrent (the Columbine, I believe); on the right were heights. At one of those exasperating bends we came upon a group of children playing at 'houses' in the middle of the road. To avoid them we had to drive into a crowd of geese in scores, which fled with hideous screams, but not fast enough to disclose in time a big stone lying on the road. We were on it before I knew, and though I jerked aside and flung my weight backwards, we bounded over its side. Upright again on the saddle, I was barely in time to notice with affright that scarcely a foot was between us and the precipitous side of the torrent. With desperate effort I half-wrenched, half-lifted the wheel away from its course, bringing down part of the miserable turf dyke, the only apology there for a fence, —and we sped down the hill as if nothing unusual had occurred.

As we were toiling up another long slope south of the village of Saint Loup, a team of fierce-looking bullocks approached, dragging a lumbering empty waggon, in which the rider was apparently asleep. This is no uncommon thing on the Continent; I have actually seen a policeman stop a horse and car going through a town and rouse up the driver asleep on his dickey. In this present case, as the animals showed symptoms of fear, I hallooed to the fellow to look after them. Too late to be able to control them, he leapt out and ran to their heads, while I saw nothing for it but to dismount—which I had been loth to do owing to the trouble in mounting on the upward slope. They swerved right round, knocking the driver over like a ninepin, and bolted up the hill straight for a ladder jutting out from a tall cherry tree, up which a man hidden in the foliage was gathering cherries. Down rattled the ladder with the man and his load of cherries in a shower, and fell across the oxen's backs. He rolled off and the wheels passed over his legs, while the oxen dashed down over the road embankment, snorting and bellowing, and away up over the fields. While I was bathing and rubbing the poor fellow's legs, a crowd ran up from the village hard by, threatening me with violence for having been the cause of their neighbour's almost losing his life. He and they maintained that I should have come off whenever I saw the bullocks; and not till I had pointed out to them what a tedious process that would be to descend at every such meeting, say, in a day's run of sixty miles, and had in general harangued them for half-an-hour on the rights and rules of the road as pertain to cyclists, did they sanction my departure. Towards evening we fell in with a jolly company of harvesters outside of Saint Loup—the name has a Roman flavour, reminding of Romulus and Remus and their foster-mother, the wolf—returning with laden waggons from the fields. The jolliest of the set and the tallest was the proprietor, who invited me to honour his hotel with my residence for the night. When the grain was stored and the horses, including mine, had got a rub down, we all met *en famille* in the public room of the inn, the host in the centre and we grouped round him. While we were eating, and joking in such way as only a French company can joke, a little man with very greasy hat and blouse came in, and began to cut capers about the room. He called for the landlady and asked her how much dinner she would give him for five *sous*, which would leave him only six for a glass or two of *absinthe*, "and not another *sou* in the world, *pardieu!*" Then he set up the most outrageous drunken caterwaulings intended for songs. "*Pas de chansons!*" shouted the host, as seriously as he could. "I'm not singing," said the droll wit, "you tell me every day that I can't sing, and yet now you have ordered me to stop what you say I can never do! How am I to know when you are in earnest, *Monsieur le patron?*" With such retorts and jokes, he set the table in a roar, and next minute he was busy as ever at his vocal efforts. The landlord was telling me that the fellow had a patrimony which he received in instalments once a month, drank his allowance in a week, and so contrived to beg or borrow for the other three, that he was *ivre fou* (mad drunk) from one year's end to the other. But the man himself, suspecting the subject of our conversation, came over to me and asked what business I had to talk about him as drunk. The landlord said I meant *le petit fils* (the little son). "Well, governor, that's queer; if you let your youngster get drunk before your very nose, I'm off to tell the *curé!*" And out he actually scampered on his message, leaving us all convulsed with laughter at his drollery. Between five and six next morning the first object that met me in the stable yard was the lithe form and red besotted countenance of this irrepressible, already as drunk and as jolly as if he had been at it all the night.

We are now on the western slopes of the Vosges, and a beautiful country it is—majestic mountains and the valleys of the bright glancing Moselle, ancient ruined castles above clean pretty villages, mineral springs and fir-trees diffusing fragrance. At Epinal we join the Moselle at its falls, and we keep mostly by its charming blue waters and green meadowy banks till near the end of our journey.

The noblest road that perhaps I have traversed is that between Epinal and Nancy. Whoever made it—the Dukes of Lorraine or a still greater, road-maker, Napoleon I.—it has been made with a purpose, which most roads seem to have lacked, namely, to keep as straight as possible and to avoid at the same time all avoidable hills. Between its scarcely broken double chain of tall dark poplars, strong and straight, it leads the wayfarer on through pleasant villages and pleasant meadow-lands, where corn and wine "cheer the labouring swain."

But at several points the road does take a dance—just by way of showing that it can do so like its kindred—and for a mile or so looks like giant waves rolling to the shore. On the descent of one of these, a horse was being held beside a wayside inn with his head away from us. But whether he heard the rush of the tire under the brake-spoon or caught a sidelong glimpse of us as we approached, he suddenly backed out towards the centre of the road, just as I was going to let go the brake-handle, and have a run and a rest for the legs down the remainder of the hill. Luckily, the remembrance of a similar equine freak at home—when the rim of a wheel I was riding was driven against the kerbstone and bent inwards one-third of the radius—had made me slow down before attempting to pass. I therefore leapt off and held back the machine from expending its acquired force downwards. Two seconds later, and we should have rushed right against the body of the horse.

Leaving the Moselle, we went up a series of wavy hills through high-built villages on to Nancy, on the banks of another river, the Meurthe. In Nancy we put up at an old soldier's, who kept a restaurant and a number of bedrooms for mechanics working in the great embroidery manufactories. They let me have a corner in one of the big beds, along with a strapping young fellow. In the same room were three other beds, two in each. It was like a barrack next morning when we all got up and busied ourselves about dressing, bandying jokes at one another's expense.

Some five miles north of Nancy we rejoined the Moselle, and followed it to Metz. Near Voisage we met the first German milestone in Lorraine. It is strange to find a frontier here where none exists by nature, and as strange to notice French names still predominant in signs and places, while only the post-office, the barrack, and such official buildings, show the German. Farther into the country, attempts are made to get German names made popular, e.g. Diedenhofen for Thionville, Gross-Oettingen for Hettange Grande. The people seem more French in nature than do the Alsatians. I thought it very singular to be speaking to people on the road in French, and when an officer passed and asked a question, to hear the same people replying readily in German. They seem all to lament the loss of their French connection, and to regard the Germans only as temporary masters. Many a long sad account I got as we went leisurely along this fatal ground, accounts usually showing up the heroic bravery of the French soldiers, and ending in condemning bitterly the terrible mistake of the Metz capitulation. Grave-yards were pointed out to me all along the route, where wildernesses of tombstones dating from 1870 gleam white in the sunshine.

The nature of the roads changes at once when we have passed the frontier, much to the discredit of German administration—unless perhaps they are kept in disrepair, to harass French troops in some future siege of Metz! For twenty or thirty miles they are nothing but deep beds of sand, or rather of fine dust. This fact I found out to my cost when racing a dog-cart into Metz. The driver was much excited because all his attempts to pass us proved futile, and latterly, when nearing the outlying forts in this beautiful valley, he whipped up his horse and urged it on with frantic shouts, so that we became neck and neck. Hollows were now becoming frequent on the road where the traffic was greatest nearer the town, and in one of them we stuck, much to my discomfort and against the appearance of my apparel, besides the loss of the race.

Not one foot is there about Metz but has its sad tragic memories. Yonder is Gravelotte, where 8000 men were killed in ten minutes, and round which a great struggle was fought that cost the victors more blood than it cost the vanquished, fewer though these were. And this is that great stronghold, Metz, which witnessed perhaps the most stupendous surrender in the world's annals. When will France see a general worthy of her past, to save her from such deep shame?

CHAPTER XV.

THE LAST STAGE HOMEWARDS.

In Hettange Grande we put up at a private house to which I had been recommended when in Nancy. The master was full of anecdotes of the war, so exciting that a good book could be written on them and such as are obtainable along this quarter. The room I slept in accommodated twenty-five Prussians when on the march against Metz, and the rest of the house had fifty. The peasants complain of the gross brutality of the Germans when hereabouts, compelling them to do menial debasing work, and making tyrannous exactions. On the other hand, they say that those who spoke or understood German were less outrageously treated.

Next we made for Luxemburg, a state which has been nicely sliced up and promises before long to disappear. One part of it is now in Elsass-Lothringen, the central part is Dutch, though in character no more suggestive of Holland than Gibraltar is of England—another part is Belgian. The people here must always be in doubt about their nationality, and sigh for the Millenium to come and end the internecine quarrels of kings and cabinets. The castled heights of Luxemburg city have held, as their masters, Burgundians, Spaniards, Frenchmen, Austrians, Prussians; and whoever can hold them in future so as to use them—they are by treaty at present abandoned—will hold perhaps the most formidable point in Central Europe. As it is, the solid rock walls, the deep precipitous natural moats, the gardens and terraces, and over all, the frowning forts, without gun or soldier to remind of modern days, form a most striking picture of what a strong city may have been in the days of chivalry.

After crossing to Arlon in Belgium, I discovered we had done 1100 miles of a bicycle journey, and that through the most historic lands in the modern world. Therefore I went straight to the railway station, and there while waiting I addressed a charmed audience of passengers on the subject of my adventures. "*Rien que les Anglais pour cela !* " (None but English for that !) was the repeated cry.

At Antwerp I visited the International Exhibition, then took boat to Hull, and thence train to Glasgow.

The whole journey took twenty-three days. My average daily ride was sixty-five miles, with a baggage of 10 lbs. The cost was 8*l.* 5*s.*, as follows :—

	£	s.	d.
Steamer	2	0	0
Trains (excursion ticket from Hull to Glasgow)	1	12	0
Lodgings	1	2	6
Food and incidental expenses . . .	3	10	6
	£8	5	0

Part III.

"ON THE TRAMP" IN FRANCE AND BELGIUM.

CHAPTER I.

TO NEWHAVEN—MY LIFE IN PARIS.

In the summer of 1881 I left the Broomielaw of Glasgow by a steamer bound for Southampton. We put in for a day at Waterford and for another at Plymouth. From Southampton I walked to Portsmouth, made my way partly on foot along to Newhaven, whence I took the steamboat for Dieppe.

The passengers on board were nearly all French. It is bad enough to bear company with English people when the sea is a bit rough, but with French it is intolerable. One young woman, worse than the rest, kept shrieking shrilly all the night, "*Je vais mourir!*" and gruffer tones were heard occasionally answering her, "*Meurs donc! et laisse-moi tranquille!*"

Having been formerly on a tour through Brittany and Normandy, I did not now linger in the provinces, but went straight to the capital. Eleven o'clock at night saw me emerge from the station into the dazzle and the whirl of Paris streets. I made my way to the Rue des Acacias, near the Arc de Triomphe. A young Frenchman whose friendship I had won on a former visit to France, occupied a room in this street.

The outer grated door—as is the custom in Paris—was shut. After a short wait some one with a key came up with whom I got inside the close. My friend was not in his room; but some time after midnight he stumbled over me in the dark passage fast asleep with my knapsack as a pillow.

This was my mode of life in Paris. The room which he had invited me to share was on the ground flat looking into the landlord's orchard, and not more than ten feet square. He had furnished it with two chairs and a table. For cooking he had a kerosene lamp, a few saucepans, a coffee-pot, and other table utensils. We took two regular meals a day, breakfast at eleven, and dinner at 5.30 when he returned from his office. This arrangement left a long interval for sight-seeing. Our hour for rising was seven, when we had coffee, after which I read till half-past nine, when I made the bed and did up the room, then went out and purchased provisions for breakfast, and on my return set to cook them for the arrival of my friend. Each meal never cost us more than a franc, that is, fivepence to each of us. He did the catering and cooking in the afternoon. Breakfast usually consisted of a cutlet of mutton, bread, butter and cheese, wine, cherries or other fruit, and finally coffee; dinner, of the same, with sometimes a variety in the shape of tomato sauce, soup or fried potatoes. Bread, wine and fruit, of which we consumed most, were the cheapest items, we buying wine at 7d. per quart and diluting it before use. Other items, such as salt, pepper, sugar, butter, cheese, are very dear in Paris the taxes on them being very heavy.

CHAPTER II.

ON THE ROAD TO BRUSSELS.

ONE day at noon I left Paris by the Rue de Flandre, to walk to Brussels. At the Porte de la Villette, a custom-house officer of whom I inquired if I were on the right road, looked at me with such a look of astonishment and semi-incredulity as only a Frenchman could assume, then added, looking first at my equipment, then at a brother *douanier*, "*Amusez-vous bien!*"

At Le Bourget, seven miles from Paris, stands one of those monuments, found all over the north and east of France, which must have an exciting influence on the minds of the young that spring up after those who remember the horrors of the late war have died out. They will have no thought of suffering, but only of wiping out the disgrace their country has sustained. The inscription is significant: "Bourget, 30 Oct., 21 Dec. 1870.—Ils sont morts pour defendre la patrie. L'épée de la France brisée dans leurs vaillantes mains sera forgée de nouveau par leur descendants." (They died in defence of fatherland. The sword of France broken in their valiant hands shall be forged anew by their descendants.)

It is a great mistake to take one's notions of French life and character entirely from Paris. The country people in their simplicity of manners and modest gentleness form a great contrast to the Parisians; indeed they are the salvation of France. Everywhere from them I have met with kindness and interested regard. I can look back to many pleasant times I have spent beneath the roofs of the French peasantry when on my various walks; and many are the families among them whom I place among the number of those I meet for a little, am happy with, and leave with regret. The Parisians are usually n great ill-favour with them, on account of their frivolity and changeableness.

The forests in France are the most trying parts of a pedestrian tour. Sometimes they are as long as four miles without a break. Somehow it often happened to me that I passed through one after dark. The silence is frightsome in those lonely depths, unbroken except by the rustle and cry of some animal startled by the sound of the footsteps; the imagination vividly conjures up all sorts of figures and chances—every tree becomes a robber, every stone or post a phantom; every sense is alert and life is intense. From such a one I emerged the first night, and welcomed the glimmer of the lamps of Senlis.

At "*Les Trois Deserteurs*" I found a happy convivial circle drinking, smoking, and jesting in the flippant way that only Frenchmen can.

The host's daughter conducted me into a tumble-down court and up a flight of steps which evidently must have been in constant use since long before the days of the First Revolution. Within an apartment at the top, everything had the same worn-out, antique look; it was a barn-like place with great black rafters, and long high walls that had once been whitewashed, but had nothing to relieve their painful nakedness and dreariness, except, on one side, a monstrous gaping fireplace, grateless and quite alarming in its openness. The floor was of smooth, hard, red brick and quite bare. The two beds were each capacious enough to accommodate an ordinary family—they must have been made for soldiers; indeed the whole place had that appearance—and withal they were so high that it was quite a gymnastic feat to scramble into them. The morning sun shining through the casement and the silver-tongued bell of a neighbouring steeple awakened me in delightful bewilderment.

The first object which struck my sight on looking out was an old ruined tower on a length of old wall. It was one of the twenty-six towers of ancient Senlis. It was at Senlis that the first indication of cheap living was apparent, it getting cheaper as one advances to the North of France. Here I learned that the road which I was pursuing was Napoleon's great road to Waterloo. The whole length of it is causewayed, and in many parts would seem not to have been repaired since he used it.

Through another long forest, I came to the historic town of Compiègne. In front of the Hôtel de Ville stands an equestrian statue of Joan of Arc, who was handed over to the English at the siege of Compiègne. On the pedestal are these simple old words, said to have been her own, "*Je yray voir mes bons amis de Compienge* (1430)." I too made some friends in the town, and when I took leave of these *my "bons amis de Compienge,"* the evening shadows were lengthening. Anxious to get on another fourteen miles to the next town, Noyon, I asked, at a divergence of the road, which way to take, of a man in cobbler attire, who was placidly sitting on his doorstep, enjoying his evening pipe.

In the course of conversation he told me he had worked in Paris in a shop where there were English workmen, who had taught him English. At the word English, his wife, who had been standing with a group of neighbours beside the window, came forward with them to listen to her lord's learned talk, who no doubt had a mighty reputation as an English scholar. He rattled off the cardinal numbers in a mutilated state up to twenty, and then flung at me a string of the foulest words ever used in Billingsgate. After which this inexhaustible well of English undefiled was dry! Of course I complimented him on the elegance, purity, and extent of his English attainments.

CHAPTER III.

SLEEPING IN THE FIELDS.

WHEN complete darkness fell it saw me toiling on with bended back and anxious face, looking ahead for the light of some house or village where to rest my wearied limbs. But no light cheered me that night, for almost senseless with exhaustion and sleep, I was fain to creep under a rick of wheat-sheaves in a field, and there make my couch. The shouts and songs of the reapers greeted my ear when consciousness returned to me after I had slept ten hours' unbroken sleep. The spot where I had halted was not far from the third kilometric mark (less than two miles) from Noyon. Noyon is a place of great antiquity, having been a residence of Charlemagne and the place where Hugo Capet was crowned. The knowledge, too, that the great French divine, Jean Calvin, was born and spent his boyhood here made me tread its streets with greater interest and veneration. Just to show that I was not indifferent to the good that Calvin had done to the character of my countrymen, I halted and had breakfast, wondering—as much as the garrulity of my hostess would permit—how few have made a pilgrimage like mine to this shrine of the great Reformer.

The next place of note was Ham, famous for its old fortress, with huge towers and massive walls (thirty-nine feet thick), where so many men of fame have been prisoners. The late Emperor escaped hence in the guise of a workman, after he had spent five years within its walls. Hungry as I was on entering Ham, I could not help smacking my lips at the thought of the savoury viand denoted by the name in English. But, vain hope, the lieges there show no predilection for it, so that not a bit was obtainable. The wonder ceases when one finds that "Ham" is pronounced like *awng;* and remembers that it is the same word as is seen in Buckin*gham,* in *home,* and the Scotch *hame.*

Water is very scarce along this route ; there are few brooks, and these few had become broken chains of stagnant pools. But mild beer, called *bière du Nord,* is cheap and plentiful. At wayside houses I got a quart jug of it full for a penny.

As I lay reclining on a hill overlooking the town of St. Quentin, something in the landscape recalled my native place ; and overcome by emotion and the rush of associations, my mind sought relief in sleep. It was a sensation easier to be conceived than described which possessed me when with a confused idea of where I was, I opened my eyes, an hour later, on that ancient historic place lying in the valley before me, bathed in the gorgeous gold of the setting sun, and heard the evening breeze rustling among the leaves overhead. The rays of sunset have ever in them something sad yet soothing, something full of unrest yet prophetic of that perfect rest which the soul longs for, and when one is alone and far from home, this sentiment is intensified.

The number of tombstones in odd places in the outskirts of the town were suggestive of stern fights, the strong fortifications visible giving colour to the picture. My own countrymen had once, long ago (in 1551), scaled the walls where now these stand, shedding their blood at the caprice of a despotic queen. Here too were enacted two important scenes in the drama of the Franco-Prussian War : on October 1st, 1870, a struggle between the citizens and the Prussians, and on January 25th, 1871, a stiff battle between the Garde Nationale and the invaders. Besides the tombstones, however, no outward appearance of disaster is now apparent ; the busy streets are enlivened by streams of workmen quitting their day's labour in the factories and other public works in this handsome thriving place. At the northern extremity of the town I spent fully half an hour conversing with a young *douanier* whose friends had all been killed while defending their town. " Those who have all they once held dear lying in a bloody grave," he said, " will not lightly forget who sent them there, nor be slow to respond to the call, when that comes, to strike a blow in revenge for murdered kin and blasted home." I was surprised and pleased to find how sensible and well-informed he was, and how moderate and favourable his opinion of the English was. Our brief communion ended, as we grasped each other's hand, the *douanier* said, with tears in his eyes, "*Adieu, mon ami.*" We had spoken of the brotherhood of all nations, of that happier world where war and the need of war exist not.

Twenty-six miles had already been left behind me since morning; yet, on being told that Bohain—the nearest place where lodgings could be got—was twelve miles on, nothing daunted, but rather made reckless by the previous night's experience, I did not hesitate to push on.

Darkness fell soon and deep that night, and with it a thick, penetrating mist, which made it difficult to see a few yards in front.

It soon became evident that enthusiasm had vanquished discretion in my venturing to reach Bohain, for now the previous night's bivouac and the long distance already traversed began to tell on my strength. My pace slackened so much that when I thought I should have been at Bohain, in reality I was a mile or two from it. With an effort I bore up as far as the kilometric stone about equivalent to the twelfth milestone from St. Quentin (this being thirty-eight miles accomplished that day). Seeing neither light nor house, and concluding that (as often happened) I had been misinformed as to the distance, I crawled over a ditch into a field, where in a corner, covering myself with newly-cut grain (some of which came very acceptable as food), I was soon oblivious to the toils and the terrors of walking by night. A dull thudding and a sensation of cold and wet awoke me in a fright when it was still early morning. The mist was thick, excluding from view every object beyond two or three yards. The dew covered the ground as if it had rained heavily, having completely saturated me. To warm myself I rose, put on my knapsack above my topcoat, and went in the direction of the thudding. It was the farmer driving in some stakes. When he saw me, he let fall his hammer, from surprise at seeing a stranger on his ground so early. Imagine my chagrin when told that I had slept not 300 yards from the heart of the town.

CHAPTER IV.

SCENES BY THE WAY—A STRANGE LODGING.

BY nine o'clock I had covered ten miles, when I was lured asleep on the roadside by the sun's generous heat. Much refreshed, about noon I renewed my northward course and soon reached Le Cateau, through which the Iron Duke passed in his triumphal march to Paris from Waterloo. Here I was at a loss how to proceed, no one appearing to know the proper way to the frontier—I had come off the direct route for the sake of a short cut. In my dilemma I was referred to a lawyer who was. at his door taking leave of a client. He took me into his study and put a large detailed map before me from which I took a sketch of my route. He expressed great admiration for England and the English, and acknowledged them to be the best travellers in the world, unequalled in point of pluck and perseverance, their character and institutions admirable for their solidity and consistency. He knew no English himself, but made his little son tell me a few words to show that he was receiving a good education in English. He introduced me to his family, who were much interested in me and would have put me up for the night had I not been anxious to get nearer the frontier before nightfall.

I was trudging heavily along under the weight of knapsack and coat, as I entered at sunset a village called Englefontaine. An old lady was passing down the road, and seeing me, exclaimed in a voice full of sympathy, " *Vous souffrez, pauvre enfant!* " Looking up with a smile, I replied that I was suffering, but through my own choice. On learning I was English she straightway launched into a gushing stream of praise of my countrymen, dwelling long on the great kindness her son was receiving from families in England, where he was on business. There seems, also, to be a traditional feeling of respect and love in this district for the English, probably dating from Wellington's passage through it, when his humanity in protecting the inhabitants from plunder was so conspicuous.

As everyone made mention of a great forest right ahead, not feeling equal to encountering new uncertainties, I left the direct road and made towards Le Quesnoy, whose towers were visible in the distance from the top of the hill above the village.

The people in the French provinces are very ingenuous, in marked contrast to those of the capital. They seem greatly superior to them also in physique and common sense. Everyone along my route was most anxious to put me on the right road, telling me all they knew of its nature. The last dwelling in this village was a neat cottage embowered in vine and other climbing plants, with pretty flower-borders in front. Underneath the leafy porch sat a well-dressed man of middle age and his buxom dame. So charmed was I with their company that it was almost dark before we bade each other a regretful good-bye, the good lady reiterating that if ever my wanderings led me that way again, I should not mind if "no one was at the door," but go inside, where I should be doubly welcome. The happy, ruddy-faced children had gathered round us to look at me with wondering gaze, and listen with open mouth to my discourse.

Then followed the weariest part of all my walk. In front were the tantalizing towers, seeming only a mile when they were miles away; the weary watching for and counting of landmark after landmark cost me more loss of mental force than hours of mathematical study would have done. Quite wild with impatience and exhaustion, I canvassed all the houses in a hamlet to get lodging for the night, but to no avail. Nobody took in *voyageurs* there, *malheureusement pour moi*, as a young man sympathetically said to me. When at last the walls of Le Quesnoy were close at hand, I was forced to follow the road half round them, before finding a way over the entrenchments, which again were triple, three trenches and three ramparts. Even when over these my troubles were not ended, for it turned out that the town proper was half a mile farther in. When I got through the last gate into the town, not a soul was visible through the whole length of the street, and all was as quiet as if I had entered a city of the dead. I must get a bed, however, by hook or by crook. So at the first likely place I knocked loudly until a head appeared in the second storey demanding what was wanted. "Lodging," I said. "For how many?" "For one." "Very well." After a long while the bolts were withdrawn, and the most villainous-looking countenance I ever saw looked out. When the door was closed upon us, he asked in a suspicious way what I had in my knapsack, a question which greatly added to my impression that I had fallen into a thieves' den. Not to be cowed so, I made him draw me a pot of the *bière du Nord* and show me upstairs. He thereupon opened a half-concealed door and led me up a narrow spiral wooden stair, which creaked and groaned pitifully the while, past a loft, where the candlelight revealed an endless confusion of articles, such as coils of ropes, ladders, old shovels, and pans piled promiscuously on boxes and barrels, tables, chairs, and other furniture in grotesque assortment. My room contained two beds and two chairs, but otherwise was bare. Much to my fear, the door had no lock. As a precaution, therefore, I put my clothes in a bundle under my pillow, strapped my knapsack round one arm, and with the other hand clutching my stout umbrella, was soon sleeping the sleep of the weary. I could not have been asleep very long when something awoke me. For a moment I had the notion that my body had left the world for a more restful region, so great was the change from lying on the ground under the wheat-sheaves, as I had done on the two previous nights; but at the same moment a sound from below struck my ear as of a heavy resisting body being jerked upstairs. Step after step it was dragged up, amid a low murmur of voices. My fears, then, were not fanciful, and I was in a house of robbers and murderers! Now the noise was on the landing beside my door; a streak of light shot through the seams, and for a while all was silent. Then gently and noiselessly the door opened and a man's head was thrust in, which seemed to look and listen for an instant. My hand closed convulsively round my umbrella, while the rest of me was stiff and motionless through fear.

The door opened wide and a man entered with a bit of a candle stuck in a bottle. Some one helped him in with a large sack, which they placed softly in a corner. Then he brought in a hatchet, closed the door, and came towards me. Determined to have a struggle for my life, I started up with the bedclothes in my arms, intending to throw them over him if he came nearer and so hamper his movements till I could get the hatchet from him. "*He donc! vous ne dormez pas?*" (Hallo! then you are not asleep?) "No," I said; "but what's the hatchet for?" "Oh, I have just come in from mending fences." So the sack contained not a murdered body, but some pieces of wood left over from the fencing; and the imagined robber undressed and went into the other bed, leaving the end of the candle flickering and spluttering in its socket.

CHAPTER V.

ACROSS THE BELGIAN BORDER.

FROM this point, the difference in the appearance and manners of the people becomes more rapidly marked. Their build becomes stronger, their features more massive, and their complexion fairer, indicating the admixture of Flemish blood. Their manners assimilate to our own.

The frontier is marked by a stone column between the French and Belgian *Douanes*. A young Belgian ransacked my knapsack, but also gave me good cheer. Chimneys belching out smoke in volumes, pits, and black faces soon made it manifest that I had come into a country very different from France. The landscape becomes more and more like our own as one goes north; the trees get more bushy, and less tall; there are more hedges, more cosy parks, more hills and streams and wells. But one thing still proclaims that it is not Britain—the frequent sight of crosses and figures of Christ in wooded enclosures, some of them highly tasteful. The Flemish are even better Roman Catholics than the French.

In the Barrack Square I stepped on to the threshold of an *estaminet*, and asked for lodging. But the landlady said, "No." Whereupon I referred to the notice outside. "Oh!" she said, "we don't admit *gentlemen with hats*." "If that's the only obstacle, then I'll take off mine, for I want to stay here." So without more ado, I was seated beside the stove, enjoying buttered rolls and coffee. All the customers spoke Flemish in their slow and heavy accents. The host was busy in a corner working at his shoemaking trade. He was French, and, of course, a wag and a cynic. "Belgium," said he, "is two centuries behind the rest of the world. All the women go *à la messe* (to mass) here, but really it is to see the priest So my wife says, and she is Belgian."

At Soignies next day I got entangled in a rush of people, a 'gymnastic club' which was going with trumpet and drum to celebrate the anniversary of Belgian Independence. In the square, which was gay with shows and people in holiday attire, they shot with bows taller than themselves at elevated targets —a sort of popinjay. For my part, the shouts and the gaiety were not so pleasing as the calmness found within the church of St. Vincent Maldegaire (dating from the ninth century). Within its heavy, time-laden walls, if my spirit did not join in the mass, it at least wandered back over the long centuries, and in silent communion with all those spirits that had worshipped here, found refreshing solace.

Passing by bypaths, through the miles of Soignies woods, interspersed with fields and clusters of cottages, and through the clean town of Nivelles, by nightfall I was approaching the place of my country's glory. On my asking a little boy, whom I helped with his parcel, where he lived, he pointed in front to the right, and said, "At Hougomont." It did sound strange to hear the little fellow speak so unconcernedly of Hougomont as his home, a place enshrined, from my childhood, in hallowed memory. The grass is growing green now and the apple-trees flourishing where so much British blood reddened the soil.

It was now pouring heavily with rain, and had become pitch dark, so that it was dangerous to carry out my intention of sleeping on the battle-field of Waterloo. It was Sunday, too; and on a Sunday, when rain had been pouring in torrents as now, and the 'red rain' from friend and foe had soaked the ground, my countrymen had lain on this very ground, heaps upon heaps, with their foes, 'in one red burial blent.' Imagination scattered the darkness, and peopled the battle-field with bristling battalions and fiery squadrons meeting in deadly shock.

In the early morning I trudged over the length of the battlefield, which presented just such an appearance as we are told it did on the morning of the great fight: the soil wet and heavy, the trees 'dewy with nature's tear-drops.' Then I went up the Mont de Lion, a great conical mound of earth, about 100 feet high, and surmounted by a huge iron lion whose right fore-paw rests on a large ball. On this spot the Prince of Orange was killed, and round it the battle raged fiercest. When the Iron Duke revisited the field (in 1821, with George IV.), he was displeased that the ground had been altered. But then there was the precedent of the mound at Marathon to sanction this.

It seemed to me strange that the natives here take the side of the French, as far as I could make out. Possibly that is because France is the nearest country, and French is used as the chief language of their own. For instance, the guide Pirson—son of Martin Pirson, Napoleon's guide, and the man who gave Victor Hugo much information for his '*Les Misérables*' during his stay here, where he finished that novel—in describing the field from the top of the Mont de Lion, detracted as much as possible from the victory, and, on my smiling incredulously, he turned to me, and referred me to Victor Hugo. Him, however, I would not accept as an unprejudiced authority, considering that he belonged to the beaten side, and considering the prejudiced source of his information.

Three young girls, one a grand-daughter of Martin Pirson, go about selling flowers and other mementoes of the battlefield. These all say how the French soldiers related that after the rout the Prussians "gave no quarter, but the English gave *bread and water*." There is a lively recollection in the peasants' minds of the kilted Scotch, whom they regard as strong, brave fellows and the best of soldiers.

In the walled orchard of Hougomont farm I fell asleep, and awoke to find I had been through the struggle in a dream. This quiet green spot but a moment before I had imagined red with blood and choked with bloody corpses, as once it was, and yonder wide courtyard, noisy with the cackling of poultry and the lazy grunt of pigs, had resounded with far other than such peaceful sounds.

Leaving the village of Mont St. Jean and of Waterloo, I took my way along the Brussels road. This road is in miserable repair, and if ever I cursed 'aught inanimate' it was that, for all the while the thunder rolled overhead, and the rain battered on me from clouds and trees, and now and then my toe would catch on the broken causeway and send me tottering and splashing among the mudholes. If our poor soldiers took this route to Quatre Bras, one could hardly have blamed them had they been defeated.

Before dark I had wandered from end to end of Brussels, and obtained a fair idea of how it lay and, of the people's appearance. By this time my money had dwindled down to 29*s*., and accordingly I went down to the canal to procure a passage down to Antwerp by working for it. This was arranged on a Swedish barque, sailing next morning. Leaving my knapsack on board, for hours I wandered aimlessly through the thronged streets—where perhaps more beer is drunk than in any other place in the world—until lights went out and pleasure-seekers had dispersed.

In a street beside the new Hôtel de Ville, when sleep weighed on my senses, I curled myself up in a lawyer's broad doorway, with my umbrella open to arrest the raindrops that fell from the roof. I might have dozed about an hour, when a heavy hand on my shoulder roused me. Its owner warned me that I was sleeping in a locality where a robbery had been committed the other night. I thanked him for his friendly warning, but judged from his unprepossessing exterior that, had I been unconscious, another robbery would have been perpetrated in that locality. Having moved on to another district, I was again snugly ensconced in one of those beloved wide doorways, inveigled, by the drowsy ticking of a hall-clock inside, into the dreamy notion that I was safe and warm in my own room at home, when an accidental loud kick from my foot against the door awakened me, and not only me, but also a child within the house; and it thereupon set up such a terrified squalling that perforce I again changed my quarters.

Have you ever, yourself outside in the dread darkness, heard at dead of night the loud wail of woe that proclaims too surely the flight of some loved soul from this mortal earth? If you have, then you have heard the wildest, weirdest, woefulest thing in all humanity. That was my experience at the next house I lay down by, as it had been twice before when tramping in Scotland and in Ireland.

Inside a wide gate on a wooden threshold I snatched two hours' more sleep; then making a rough toilet at a street pump, I began my morning's peregrinations. Scarcely a person was afoot; the marks of yesternight's riot and gaiety had not yet been swept off the long wide streets. Within an hour I had picked up from the streets as many two-centime small coins as would pay for my breakfast.

It was a sight, and a sound as well, to be in the early morning at the Bourse Square, where greengrocers', milkmen's, butchers', costermongers' carts are ranged in long noisy trains, where the ear is deafened by the braying of the donkeys and the emulous barking of the big ungainly dogs which pull or help to pull the carts.

When I had joined the Swedish vessel on the canal, they set me to do odds and ends, such as giving a hand at the ropes and the capstan. But when news came that one of the canal locks was broken and would take two days to mend, the captain and mate found I could be serviceable to them in other ways also. First we spent a day in Brussels buying material and provisions for the ship, I acting as interpreter, for neither of them knew French. Then I gave them constant lessons in English, by the help of German, which is liker Swedish than English is. Finally the mate was overjoyed at discovering that I could work out the problems in trigonometry over which he was puzzling for his pass as captain. It was well for me that the delay arose, for it gave rest to my badly blistered feet, which were being sadly pinched by holes and splits in my boots.

At length a tug came and towed us out of the docks, past a perfect flotilla of barges, which in their turn were attached to the towing-line; and the whole long procession moved smoothly down the canal. These barges are kept very clean, are gaily but tastefully painted; they are of ancient type, with prow and stern rising in a curve and terminated by some grotesque figure. The bargeman's whole family lives on board, cooking and eating food on the open deck. Their young children are tied by the waists with strings to prevent their falling overboard, just as Herodotus tells us the lake-dwellers did with theirs. As dozens of these picturesque barges followed one after the other in the wake of our tall-masted vessel, moving grandly and noiselessly down the water between continuous rows of lofty trees on each bank, they formed quite a brilliant pageant.

English is used universally here by sailors, bargemen, and sluicekeepers, as indeed it is used in all ports, except perhaps in

France, as a medium of communication for nautical terms, such as 'Hold on,' 'Make fast,' 'Slack rope,' 'Let go.' But let not the traveller be thereby deluded into the hope that they know any more English than that.

When we stopped for the night, we spent two happy hours in an improvised concert—the mate with his concertina, I with my vocal pipe, and the bargemen and the families for an audience.

Two mornings later we were lying off Antwerp, whose hoary Cathedral was glittering in the sun, and its rich musical peals ravishing the ear like voices from another world. It was with great ado I could get away from the ship. The mate would have me to come on with them to Goteborg : " You no more leetle cabin-boy ; you second mate. Comm vis me ! "

In the steamboat wharfs I found a steamer sailing next night for Leith. The captain would not let me go as a deck passenger, but took me cabin at a reduced fare. It was well he did so, for on board were two college friends of mine who had been staying in Germany. In their company, two happy days were spent on the sea, getting braced up for the exertion still before me. After paying the reduced fare, there were left in my pocket only a few centimes and one franc, which I had foolishly neglected to change in Antwerp. In English money I had *only three halfpence.*

With this miserable sum, I set out at 6.30, a.m. to walk the forty-six miles between Leith and Glasgow. On this last stage of my journey I therefore set out once more alone, going round by Calton Hill and along Princes Street, convinced that I have nowhere seen anything dearer and lovelier than 'Edina, Scotia's darling seat.' About noon I sank down exhausted on a heap of hay beside the twentieth milestone from Glasgow. There I slept for an hour, and then started again. My three halfpence were already spent, and my franc was of no use. Weak from want of food and from the long walk, I dragged my limbs into Airdrie, where a banker in sympathy changed my franc. Then wearily pursuing my way, I reached the heart of Glasgow city, as the Tron Clock measured out the hour of eight.

The walk from Paris to Brussels occupied only six days. The whole tour lasted six weeks, its cost was only six guineas.

Cricket Across the Sea;

OR, THE

WANDERINGS AND MATCHES

OF THE

GENTLEMEN OF CANADA.

1887.

I prize my peerless pastime for its freedom and its fun,
It revels in the grassy plain and glows beneath the sun,
I've heard of foreign pleasures that are very fair to see,
But cricket, glorious cricket, is quite fair enough for me,
And he that will not play, or pay to help the manly game,
May lie forgotten in the grave—an unremembered name.
—"*My Sires of Old were Cricketers.*"

BY TWO OF THE VAGRANTS.

TORONTO:
JAMES MURRAY & CO., PRINTERS AND BOOKBINDERS.
1887.

TO HIS EXCELLENCY
THE MOST HONORABLE THE MARQUESS OF
LANSDOWNE, G.C.M.G.
GOVERNOR-GENERAL OF CANADA,
WHO HAS DONE NOT A LITTLE FOR THE GAME OF CRICKET IN
THIS COUNTRY, AND WHO GAVE HIS SYMPATHY AND
ASSISTANCE TO OUR TOUR,
THIS LITTLE BOOK IS WITH HIS PERMISSION
RESPECTFULLY DEDICATED
BY
THE AUTHORS.

PREFACE.

The scribes who have endeavored to record the doings of the Cricket Team of the Gentlemen of Canada in Great Britain, in 1887, are conscious that these pages will contain much that is of little interest to the general public, and perhaps have no right to expect that they will be read by many who are not members of the great brotherhood of cricketers. But if among the general public we may be so fortunate as to find some who will follow this account of our doings across the sea, to them perhaps are due a few words of explanation.

It has not been our purpose that this little book should be in any sense a "literary production," and regarded in that light it could not but be disappointing. The description of our tour must be to a great extent a mere diary of events, and in a production of that nature there is not much scope for elegant diction or poetic phrasing, even were the propriety of such a style of writing unquestionable.

We anticipate the objection too, of some uncongenial reader that there is not a little "sameness" in the descriptions of the different matches, by the explanation that this, from the very nature of our subject, cannot be obviated.

To all we explain, that the book has been written: *Firstly*, as a permanent and convenient record of our doings in the cricket field, and a statement of the lessons we learnt there; and *Secondly*, as a short account of such of our experiences in England, outside the cricket field, as we have deemed to be worthy of mention.

Having these objects we feel that to our cricketing friends, who have so generously expressed themselves as to our doings, no apology is needed; the tour was in our opinion an event of such moment in the history of the game in Canada, as to be deserving of some permanent record, and we confidently hope that our efforts will meet with their approval.

To all our readers, cricketers or otherwise, we trust that what has been written may not be without interest; and if this little book should be the means of awakening—to even a slight degree—more public interest in the noblest of all games, it will not have been written in vain by

TWO OF THE VAGRANTS.

CONTENTS.

	PAGE.
THE FIRST OVER...	9

CHAPTER I.
THE START 14

CHAPTER II.
THE GAME AT SEABRIGHT AGAINST ALL NEW YORK 22

CHAPTER III.
BOWLING ALONG 33

CHAPTER IV.
THE EMERALD ISLE.. 47

CHAPTER V.
SCOTLAND AND THE TROSSACHS.. 73

CHAPTER VI.
THE NORTHERN COUNTIES MATCHES 91

CHAPTER VII.
THE FIRST MATCH IN THE SOUTH............................ 109

CHAPTER VIII.
LORDS AND LONDON........................ 120

CONTENTS.

CHAPTER IX.
Portsmouth and the Oval 134

CHAPTER X.
Hampshire and the Home of Grace........................ 151

CHAPTER XI.
Staffordshire and the Hunting Counties 172

CHAPTER XII.
Liverpool 188

CHAPTER XIII.
West Cheshire and Norbury Park........................ 200

CHAPTER XIV.
What became of us...................................... 209

CHAPTER XV.
Valedictory 216

CHAPTER XVI.
Summary of Results...................................... 220

THE FIRST OVER.

The Why and Wherefore and the Wherewithal.

THE *why and wherefore* of our tour was an inspiration of the "Genial Manager"—the offspring of his own brilliant conception.

The *wherewithal*, too, was raised by a great financial scheme of which he was the original projector,—worked out upon the soundest benevolent principles. The stock subscribed was fully paid up, and consisted in the subscriptions of those who "took stock" in the manager's undertaking, and whose dividends will be paid in the benefits resulting to the game of cricket in this country; and if upon a financial statement being presented, the capital is found to have been swallowed up in the expenses, we are still confident that the subscribers, to whom no sordid motives of gain can be attributed, will yet feel that they have made a good investment.

When one wintry afternoon Mr. Lindsey first unburdened his bosom at a committee meeting of the Toronto Cricket Club of his idea of a tour through England by a cricket team of Canadian gentlemen, it was received very warmly by the representatives of that august body, as a dream, the accomplishment of which was much to be desired, but at the same time one which it would be well nigh impossible to carry out.

So many difficulties occurred to the minds of those present, which were voiced first in a general chorus, and then one at a time, that the ardour of any one else might have been dampened, and the necessity for these pages would never have arisen; but not so with the "Genial Manager." Like a thirsty throat, the more you try to damp his ardour the fiercer it burns; and when a dozen so thought insuperable objections had been categorically raised and satisfactorily answered, the aforesaid august body began to think that perhaps there was something in it after all, and that the G.M.'s head was still level.

The reasons he gave were something after this manner: Cricket has undoubtedly improved greatly in Canada in the last few years; considering the absence of so many of the advantages enjoyed in England, Australia, and the United States, we have been making rapid strides; we have learnt the rudiments but require finishing and polishing up; for the past three years Canada has won the International Match with the United States, and we may therefore, without undue conceit, consider ourselves to possess the material for a team not much inferior to the Philadelphia eleven who visited England in 1884; why then should we not make a similar venture? The probable benefit of such a tour to the game in Canada cannot be questioned; can we get the men and the money?

It was thought that both *might* be got, but that there would be many difficulties in the way. "The difficulties then must be overcome," said the G.M. oracularly. That settled it; no further objections were offered. The "august body" recognized a master hand, and left everything to its guidance.

The project being now no longer a secret, Mr. Lindsey in a letter to the Toronto press detailed his scheme, gave an outline of the proposed tour, and an approximate list of the eleven, and asked for the support of the press and the public.

The idea was kindly received and encouraged by both press and public, and to the press of Canada —and, indeed, of Great Britain as well—are the Canadian team greatly indebted for the hearty support accorded to their undertaking.

Difficulties were met as prognosticated, and were overcome as predicted. Difficulty No. 1; the men: The Manager consulted the leading cricketers of Toronto as to the selection of the team, and as men were enlisted one by one, their views, too, were considered in the choice of the remainder. Arthur Allan, Trinity College, Toronto; W. C. Little,

Ottawa, and W. A. Henry, Wanderers' club, Halifax, were the first to agree to go; then W. W. Vickers and W. W. Jones, Toronto C.C., and G. W. Jones, St. John, N. B., promised, and then E. R. Ogden, Toronto C.C. For a long time R. B. Ferrie and A. Gillespie, Hamilton, and D. W. Saunders, Toronto, were doubtful, but at length accepted definitely; and C. J. Annand, Halifax, and W. J. Fleury, Toronto, made up the twelve which it was decided to take.

Messrs. C. J. Logan, B. T. A. Bell, F. Harley, M. Boyd, and others among the best known cricketers had been asked, but for one reason or another could not accept; but the Manager was satisfied, and upon the whole it was felt that a fairly representative team had been got together. One feature of the selection was the subject of congratulation, that the men were all Canadians born, and in that respect were thoroughly representative.

Difficulty No. 2; the *wherewithal*: The idea of the Manager was that each man should pay half his expenses, and that the balance should be made up by subscriptions from supporters of the game throughout Canada, and from gate receipts in England. This idea was carried out, and to the liberality of the subscribers is due the successful issue of the enterprise. His Excellency the Governor-General, Sir Alexander Campbell, the Lieut.-

Governor of Ontario, Hon. Matthew Richie, the Lieut.-Governor of Nova Scotia, Hon. L. F. R. Masson, the Lieut.-Governor of Quebec, and a number of the prominent citizens of Canada, but particularly of Toronto—among whom may be especially mentioned Mr. George Gooderham and Hon. John Macdonald —by their patronage and liberality materially forwarded the project and ensured its success, as far as success could in that way be commanded.

Upon our success from a cricketer's standpoint, considering the objects of the tour and regarding it especially from an educational point of view, we have had very flattering assurances from the public and the press of Canada; and after a perusal of these pages, written when time has allowed us to calmly reflect upon the tour and judge of its results, untrammelled too by the exigencies sometimes pertaining to newspaper reports, we trust that the press and the public will find no reason to reconsider their verdict.

Chapter I.

The Start.

Everything must have a beginning, and our trip to England—for most of us, at least—began at the Union Station, Toronto. It is not always, or even often, that many persons turn out to say adieu to men leaving Toronto on a cricketing tour, but the difference between our ordinary cricket excursions and that we were then embarking on was wide, and the importance of the event was evidenced by the presence of nearly two hundred people at the station, to wish us a hearty God-speed.

W. C. Little, of Ottawa, had turned up in Toronto the day before, and that morning at the station; the old Trinity men, W. W. Jones and A. C. Allan, were there; W. W. Vickers and his reporter's note book were on hand; W. J. Fleury, who had been pressed into the service at the last moment, had his valise with him; R. C. Dickson, who started with a disreputable looking canvas satchel and came back with a tin uniform case, and C. N. Shanly, who left Canada's shores with an attenuated physique, and returned with one more resembling a Liverpool fish-wife's than his ordinary self, were ready to embark on their respective duties. George Lindsey, "The Manager," clad in his wonted seraphic smile, and holding firmly a leathern satchel which, when we learned its contents, was an object of much regard with the team, was as usual there or thereabouts, and Dyce Saunders, somewhat hot and not a little flurried, turned up in time, though not very much too soon. Rev. W. G. Aston, our chaplain who travelled *incog* was there, and last in making up his mind to go, and least in stature, was Lyon Lindsey, "Shrimps." There were also Henry Bethune, who was to take Ogden's place in the match against All New York, at Seabright; Capt. John Morrow, off for his summer vacation, which he purposed spending at the seaside, near New York—the first few days of which we trust he enjoyed with us at Seabright—and Mr. G. N. Reynolds, "the Sheriff," who was coming down to see that we got off safely.

Of course all our relatives within a convenient radius had come to say good-bye; a great many people, who had the best interests of cricket at heart, and were anxious to encourage, had come for a similar purpose. Then there were those whose presence could be justified on neither of the former grounds, and whose anxious faces and tearful eyes were but the outward and visible signs of inward and invisible feelings, that had perhaps shaped themselves in the form of words the night before, but which now perforce were only revealed by a soulful gaze, or perchance resolved themselves into the laconic but tender word, "farewell."

We had a vague future before us; each one it is true felt prepared to do his best, but in the distant New York, and in the still farther off England, who could predict what was to be our measure of success. Youth is naturally ambitious. We ascertained upon our way to New York that our average age was under twenty-three years, so it was perhaps the courage that is common to youth, stimulated by the approbation of friends and a sense of novelty in the situation, which put us in a different frame of mind from that in which a quiet contemplation of what we were really about to undertake would have left us.

Loud were the cheers that found their way to the roof of the old station, which we had often left before, and hearty and full of feeling were those which we sent up from the receding train, the last spoken words those we were leaving behind would hear us utter for some months to come.

We congratulated ourselves on having at last started, and Capt. John Morrow was strongly of the conviction that an event of such moment should be celebrated in wine and song, and further intimated that he was prepared to provide the wine if anyone else would undertake the task of warbling. It was agreed to accept the Captain's suggestion as far as his part of the task was concerned, and when President Townsend, who was going as far as Hamilton with us, rose to propose "Success to the English Tour," it was for the first time discovered, that in order to do the thing in the proper spirit, or rather in the spirits which Capt. Morrow had provided, it would be necessary for each in turn to borrow the President's glass; but a little matter of that kind did not stand in the way of our doing honour to the occasion.

The information that the train was at Hamilton had hardly been announced before the smiling face of Ferrie, and the herculean form of Gillespie made their appearance at the carriage door. Their friends and relatives too had come to say good-bye to them, and a jolly good cheer was the last report we had from the Ambitious City.

The day was warm, the assembly somewhat agitated; fortunately we had a special Pullman, and were not hampered by any of the restrictions which govern the ordinary travelling public, and our wonted upper garments soon gave place to our cooler cricket coats. Cigars were lighted, and while some contended for modest stakes at whist, others in the smoking compartment passed the time in telling stories, some of which resolved themselves after thrilling introductions into "catches" of the most exasperating sort. Upon one in particular was every man taken in, in turn, and after each new victim had sacrificed himself by admitting *that he had not heard it*, he was not satisfied until he had shifted some of the laughter created at his expense to the shoulders of another, *who had not heard it*, by entrapping him into listening to the story.

The last look at the beauties of Niagara was the last look at Canada, and ere long the delightful and soul-inspiring process of baggage examination was engaging the attention of the Manager, whose first official duty was successfully accomplished by the aid of a little of the blarney we were before long to become adepts in ; and the remnants of Capt. Morrow's hamper, and all the cigars, cigarettes and tobacco which were to last us for three months, became, for the time being, as much part of the legitimate assets of the United States as if Commercial Union had become an accomplished fact, in the early part of the season of 1887.

Perhaps there is no more wearisome occupation under ordinary circumstances than a half day's ride by daylight in a railway carriage ; but where there are twenty kindred spirits and a few packs of cards, there is no reason why a party of the kind should not enjoy themselves even under these circumstances. Every now and again, it would occur to some one that he had a little story to tell, which he might succeed in narrating to even more than one of his fellow-passengers, until each one grew so suspicious of the other's anecdotes, that even Wallace Jones' description of the ever-varying tints of the blue surface of Lake Geneva—had he been in a position then to have given it—would have immediately created a suspicion that there was some horrid "gag" lurking beneath the placid face of the deep. But the satiety of stories would not appease the ravishings of hunger and anxious enquiries as to the locus of the first feeding ground developed the fact that it was not far to Syracuse, where at the witching hour of ten o'clock we fed.

A pipe and then to bed, to dream of victory on the morrow, but not to sleep. The thermometer, like the fellows in the top berths, had climbed too high, which, with the everlasting clatter of the wheels, the swaying of the carriage as the train rounded the curves, the excitement of the situation, put sleep out of the question. When in the early dawn we hurried by the banks of the lovely Hudson, just awakening to the life of a new day, there were none too sound asleep to miss the view and before six o'clock the conversation, which at this early hour is usually confined to the porter and his reflections of himself in the boots he is cleaning, became general, and it was conceded that the night of unrest was but a poor preparation for the hard days' cricket which lay before us. However, it would take more than the loss of a night's rest to dishearten us, and the volume of repartee to which the baggage agent, who boarded the train a short distance out of New York, was treated, on his suggestion that he would take our seventy-eight pieces of baggage from Jay Street to Pier 8, at the modest sum of twenty-five cents per valise, showed that we were fully awake at least to the value of a quarter of a dollar. We do not think there is any one of us who will not admit that the average New York porter will do anything he can for you if you pay him what he asks, and you may depend upon it he never undervalues his services. The Manager at last struck a bargain with the porter, and we got all our effects transferred to the wharf, whence the steamer leaves for Seabright. We said all; the umpire's cricket bag may have gone to Africa, and his cricket trousers to have made "breech cloths" for the heathen of Timbuctoo, for all we know of their whereabouts, and yet the railway authorities have no doubt about it that the umpire has that cricket bag and those trousers somewhere concealed about his person yet.

Cyril Wilson, Pool and Sadleir, our old friends of Staten Island, were fellow-passengers on the steamer which was to take us to the yellow sands of New

Jersey, which, by the time we had reached, the ocean air and a natural process of starvation had given us such an appetite that we were more than ready to devour our breakfast. But before we could get a chance to sit down to host Pecani's succulent chops at Harmony Hall, which had been made ready as an hotel for us during our stay, we had the pleasure of shaking hands with our old friends from the Maritime Provinces, who were to share our successes and our defeats, George Jones and Henry; and here for the first time we wrung the hand of that "jolly little chap all round,"—C. J. Annand, *alias* " the Gunner," *alias* " and and," the "Etcetera." After breakfast to the ground.

Chapter II.

The Game at Seabright against all New York.

June 30.—Owing to our late arrival it was past noon before we reached the ground, which many of us remembered as the scene of the International victory of the year before. Our experience in that match had taught us the value of winning the toss, and we were disappointed that this luck did not fall to us now. Mr. Cyril Wilson, of course, took the innings and we went to the field. The ground we found had had a lot of work put on it, since our last visit, and was much improved; the wicket appeared fair, and the outfield being fast, it looked as though there might be some large scoring, particularly as after our long journey and sleepless night, our bowlers were not in very destructive form. No great stand was however made by our opponents; yet as the scoring was slow we did not get them all out till four o'clock for 98 runs, of which Mr. Cyril Wilson and Burrows contributed 15 and 31 respectively, the former by brilliant and the latter by patient cricket. Ferrie was too tired to be of much service with the ball, and the bowling honors fell to Annand, 5 for 27, and Allan, 2 for 0.

As we anticipated, the light was bad when we went in, and the sun behind Pool's arm made his bowling dangerous, while Tyers, the Manhattan professional, at the other end kept very straight, and at times bumped awkwardly. Our first three wickets fell for 7 runs and things looked rather blue for Canada, until the "right hand barrel of the Jones combination," G. W., and Henry improved the appearance of the score by putting on 30 runs, of which Jones was credited with 11, being cleaned bowled by Tyers, after refusing the previous ball which had upset his stumps. Gillespie then gave Henry some assistance, contributing himself a very useful 19, Henry in the meantime succumbing to Pool after making 17. Gillespie's wicket fell just before six o'clock, when stumps were drawn, leaving us with 74 runs for the loss of 7 wickets.

All day long, the match had been attentively watched by a number of spectators, whom the New York *Herald* described as the most fashionable ever seen at a cricket match in New York. Mrs. Herman Clarke and Miss Macdonald did the honours most acceptably, and by introducing us to their friends made our time, when not occupied with the game, pass most pleasantly. Gathered together under the shade of the capacious and handsome pavilion, were a large number of those who had come to the breezy Jersey coast, to spend a pleasant summer away from the heat of New York. The sympathies of these excellent people were as impartially divided between ourselves and their fellow-countrymen as they had been the year before, and since their friendship had been enlisted in our behalf we found no difficulty in feeling ourselves at home.

Before leaving Toronto, all the members of the team had received notification that they had been made honorary members of the Seabright Cricket and Lawn Tennis Club, and had also received an invitation from Miss Macdonald to a ball, to be given "in honour of the Canadian cricketers," at the pavilion of the club, on the evening of the first day of the match. An invitation had also come to dine with Mr. Herman Clarke, the club's popular mainstay, at Harmony Hall, on the evening of the following day. The Canadians surmised therefore, that they would be well looked after, and the events certainly justified their anticipations in this respect.

The day had been very hot, and at the conclusion of play, by common consent, a move was made for the sea, where among the huge rollers we disported ourselves as perhaps only those who are unaccustomed to the pleasures of sea bathing can, for a good half-hour. Then after a few foot races upon the sand, to get up the circulation, and having made away with an excellent dinner, we dressed for the ball.

When "Sheriff" Reynolds appeared in his war paint, it became evident at once that he was to be the belle of the ball. Dressed in a smile and an evening suit, he was the first to greet the hostesses. We had a preconceived notion that we would leave at an early hour, and perhaps a proper recognition of duty suggested this; but from whatever reason, this, like many another good resolution, was broken. If we ourselves were asked to say why we were not safely stowed away in bed by eleven, we could only answer that it was because we were but mortal and the temptations to remain were too strong for us. And who would wish himself in bed, when by remaining he could still listen to the charming music which constrained us to dance despite our tired limbs, claim in every succeeding dance the charming attention of some pretty girl, and ever and anon refresh himself from the spread at hand? And even when going became an absolute necessity, it was with great reluctance we said "good night."

The sun was up a good deal earlier the next morning than we were, though we did not miss our breakfast, the hour for which was a little postponed by another dip in the sea.

Punctually at the appointed time, Annand and

Wallace Jones, the two not-outs of the previous day, took their places at the wicket.

Every one was feeling in much better cricket form than upon the day before, except " the Gunner "—as we had come familiarly to term Annand—who, overcome by the heat, unfortunately had to retire of his own accord. Notwithstanding our improved condition the rest of the wickets fell quickly, and we were all out for 82, 16 runs less than the total of our opponents.

The New Yorkers commenced their second innings well, although Wilson was unfortunate. Tyers and Butler both played with great care and patience and defended their wickets against Ferrie and Gillespie for over after over, the score meanwhile mounting at a very slow rate. At one time these two batsmen played half-an-hour for only one run. The Hamiltonians would not have been known for the bowlers of the same name who trundled on the previous day, and each bowled in his very best form. Our fielding too, was declared admirable, and free from any mistakes. Ferrie at length bowled Tyers, as he had in the first innings, which was rather a feather in Bob's cap, as according to Tyers' own statement, he hadn't had his stumps rattled for two years. He had played a most careful innings of 14. It fell to Allan's lot to take the wickets of Butler and Burrows, the other two professionals, the latter being most brilliantly caught by Little at point, who took the ball almost off the bat. The rest of the team did not increase the score much, though Clarke tried for an hour to do so, but only got 7 runs.

This left us 98 runs to get to win, and on the now uncertain wicket, and in the dubious light, the result looked the matter of a toss up, though we had confidence in our ability to put on the required runs. The first wicket fell at 27, of which Saunders got 22, but this total was not increased at the fall of the second wicket. The two "Bluenoses," George Jones and Henry, put a complexion upon the game which relieved our minds and kept the scorers hard at work. Henry here first gave us an indication of what tremendous hitting powers he possessed, and to quote a New York paper, his innings was "the signal for the Seabrights to chase the bounding leather in adjoining gardens." His 31 was a dashing contribution, which was admirably seconded by George Jones' careful and well played 27. The third wicket fell at 69, and from this out the match was never in doubt, though in making the required runs we lost three more good wickets. Allan had the satisfaction of making the winning hit, which met with the applause and cheers from our fair spectators, for it was an exciting game and well won. With the result we were well pleased.

The policy of playing this match had been much criticised at home, and we all felt that upon its result depended a good deal more than the mere losing or winning of the game. The New York eleven was a strong combination and included the best professionals in the district, being pronounced by the New York *Herald* to be a better one than that which had played against the Gentlemen of Philadelphia, prior to their visit to England in 1884. We hoped that our victory here would be an earnest of our success in England.

ALL NEW YORK.

1st INNINGS.		3nd INNINGS.	
Mr. Cyril Wilson, ct. Allan, b. Gillespie	15	stpd. Saunders, b. Gillespie	2
Butler, b. Gillespie	6	ct. and b. Allan	21
Tyers, b. Ferrie	2	b. Ferrie	14
Mr. E. H. Outerbridge, ct. Saunders, b. Annand	4	b. Annand	0
Burrows, ct. and b. Annand	31	ct. Little, b. Allan	17
Mr. Herman Clarke b. Annand	4	stpd. Saunders, b. Gillespie	7
Mr. R. Mcagregor, b. Annand	0	b. Gillespie	6
Mr. J. L. Pool, ct. Jones, W. W., b. Annand	14	ct. Little, b. Gillespie	0
Mr. W. Shippen, l. b.w.b. Allan	12	b. Allan	2
Mr. M. Graham,ct. Little,b. Gillespie	4	ct. Henry, b. Gillespie	7
Mr. E. W. Sadleir, b. Allan	4	not out	0
Mr. E. W. Sadleir, not out	0	ct. Saunders, b. Allan	4
Leg byes, 1; no balls, 1	2	Leg byes, 1	1
Total	98	Total	81

RUNS AT THE FALL OF EACH WICKET.

	1.	2.	3.	4.	5.	6.	7.	8.	9.	10.	11.
1st Innings	17	22	26	43	59	59	70	79	90	97	98
2nd "	3	25	34	48	55	63	71	71	74	80	81

CRICKET ACROSS THE SEA.

BOWLING ANALYSIS.

	1st INNINGS.				2nd INNINGS.			
	Overs.	Runs.	Mdn's.	W's.	Overs.	Runs.	Mdn's.	W's.
Ferrie	16	23	5	1	15	15	9	1
Gillespie	23	46	5	3	21	18	10	5
Annand	12	27	3	5	9	26	2	1
Allan	1.1	0	1	2	14	21	7	4

Annand bowled one no ball.

GENTLEMEN OF CANADA.

1st INNINGS.

Mr. W. W. Vickers, l. b. w. b'd. Tyers 1
Mr. D. W. Saunders, b. Pool 3
Mr. G. W. Jones, b. Burrows 11
Mr. A. C. Allan, b. Pool 0
Mr. W. A. Henry, jr, b. Pool 17
Mr. W. C. Little, b. Pool 5
Mr. A. Gillespie, l. b. w., b. Tyers 19
Mr. W. W. Jones, l. b. w., b. Pool 10
Mr. C. J. Annand, not out 2
Mr. R. B. Ferrie, b. Pool 0
Mr. H. J. Bethune, b. Tyers 5
Mr. G. G. S. Lindsey, b. Tyers .. 0
Byes, 8; leg byes, 1 9

Total 82

2nd INNINGS.

b. Tyers 5
b. Burrows 22
ct. Outerbridge, b. Pool .. 27
not out 2
b. Tyers 31
hit wkt., b. Tyers 0
not out 8
run out 1
Byes, 1; leg byes, 2 3

Total 99

RUNS AT THE FALL OF EACH WICKET.

	1.	2.	3.	4.	5.	6.	7.	8.	9.	10.	11.
1st Innings	7	7	7	37	39	48	74	77	82	82	82
2nd "	27	27	69	73	76	94					

BOWLING ANALYSIS.

	1st INNINGS.				2nd INNINGS.			
	Overs.	Runs.	Mdn's.	W's.	Overs.	Runs.	Mdn's.	W's.
Pool	28	40	11	6	19	34	5	1
Tyers	19	19	14	4	21	34	8	3
Burrows	8	14	3	1	7	28	1	1

Fames optimum condimentum, the old Latin grammar says, and we incline to the belief that this is right, especially when the diners have acquired the *fames* by a two days' outing. We were in the best of spirits, and it is said that good digestion comes with merriment. Be these theories as they may, we had a keen appetite for the excellent dinner which Mr. Herman Clarke had so generously requested us to partake of. This gentleman had, from modesty, as he expressed it, installed Mr. Cyril Wilson, their captain, in the chair, and occupied the vice-chair himself; between them there were twenty cricketers on either side of the long table.

Cricketers' dinners have this great charm, that it never takes the conversation very long to become general, and on this occasion, before the second course was over, Annand from one end of the table, was recommending Outerbridge at the other, to try the fish balls, and the assembly in general were drinking to Herman Clark many happy *sauternes* of his birthday.

It must be remembered that it was Dominion Day, and we as Canadians were naturally filled with an extraordinary exuberance of patriotism, and a desire for fire-crackers, which latter of course we could not have, so had to content ourselves with the excellent substitute, the petulent pop of the Pommery bottle, which, every time one went off—as one very often did—heightened our enthusiasm, and we have no reason to think that it had not the same effect upon our friends.

After the *menu* had been disposed of, and the

health of the Queen of our fair Dominion and the President of the United States had been duly honoured, a song was called for. The dining room of Harmony Hall was once the theatre of a private house, and cries of " stage " sent the " Gunner" behind the footlights, whence he delighted us with his— now oh how familiar—song, "The Parson and the Clerk." Then Mr. Cyril Wilson rose and proposed the toast of the evening, expressing on behalf of the cricketers of America the kindest sympathy in our undertaking, applauding our just accomplished victory, and saying that the eyes of New York would be upon us when we played our games across the water. This brought The Manager to his feet to extemporize one of those eloquent efforts replete with oratorical flourishes and rhetorical graces, rounded off with the most telling apothegms, and fairly reeking with poetic license. Then more songs and speeches, and an admirable piece of whistling by one of our American friends, before the whole assembly resolved itself by general consent into a concert, and mounted the stage just as the champagne punch came on the boards.

When the curtain went down on the evening's performance almost everyone had taken his part in providing for the general amusement, and when the performers left the stage, the verdict was, that it was about the most enjoyable evening we had ever spent or could ever hope to spend.

Late as was the hour for breaking up it was not too late for some of us to refresh ourselves by a midnight dip in the ocean, but at length all the men got to bed, Mr. Herman Clark undertook to see his eleven safely home, and peace and order once more reigned at Harmony Hall.

Chapter III.

Bowling Along.

JULY 2.—It was with some difficulty next morning that the Manager collected his dissipated forces, but he knew that time and tide wait for no man, and it was unlikely that the S. S. *Furnessia* would either. We got away at half past ten, but not without paying our bus man $18, and on arriving at New York made at once for Pier 41, and saw our luggage on board before we allowed ourselves to think of lunch. Most of us sustained our weakened frames with a chop and a glass of beer at a restaurant not far from the dock, but several of the men went off to lunch with some of our Seabright friends at the Racquet Club, much against the will of the Manager, who did not like to loose sight of his youthful charges in that large and reputedly wicked city, and their non-appearance as the hour for sailing approached caused him to indulge in sundry cursory remarks, which, had they been heard by the delinquents, might have made them wish they had turned up at the appointed time. However, all were "on deck" before two o'clock, and for more than an hour we stewed and perspired on board the *Furnessia*, for the day was terribly hot, watching our fellow passengers come on board and the boat being got ready for sea.

We sailed about 3.30 amidst the cheers from friends on the pier who had come to get a last look at us; and sorry as we were to leave them, we were more than pleased to get out of the terrible heat we had been subjected to for the past two hours, and to feel the refreshing breeze as we steamed down the harbour and out past Sandy Hook.

When we had time to look about us we found that the steamer was crowded, and upon consulting the list of passengers noticed there were 230 on board. After enjoying the lovely sail down the bay, each man went to look after his luggage and put his berth to rights, by the time we had done which we were well outside of Sandy Hook, had said good bye to the pilot, and the bell had rung for dinner.

We all put in an appearance at table, except Wallace Jones, who from the moment of sailing earned his title of "the left hand barrel of the Jones combination," the right hand barrel not shewing signs of going off till after dinner. This meal was felt to be flat, stale and unprofitable as compared with the sumptuous repast which we had enjoyed the previous night. It was perhaps by comparison that it was not enjoyed as it might have been, but from whatever cause, at all events the men didn't care for it, and one by one, headed by the G.M., left the table just to glance over the ship's side and commune with the deep. Dickson, Shanly, Fleury, Henry, and Vickers, must have been hungry, for they stayed and finished their grub.

Next morning we were all at breakfast, with the exception of Wallace Jones, this exception being the rule throughout the voyage. Sunday morning on shipboard, if the weather is fine, gives one an opportunity of seeing the passengers when assembled in the saloon for service. In the afternoon you get time to think for yourself, to soliloquize or sleep. There is very little to do, and the only option left you is to take as much fun as possible out of your fellow passengers. But as fun on Sunday wont do, you have to wait till Monday to begin this, though it is possible to pave the way by getting to know the people. This is an easy thing to accomplish at sea, as the passengers always seem glad of any prospect of diversion. That night we made a good many acquaintances, and before we landed came to know the rest.

Next day we introduced cricket on deck, and like the rest of the people we played quoits, shuffle board and whist. The first ball produced went down one of the ventilators, the second to the bottom of the deep blue sea, the third, well—the third wasn't produced at all. In the evening we got up races which were a huge success, and created much merriment. Fat men of sixty shook the boat from stern to stern as they thundered down the deck; then fat men of forty took their turn, and the parsons, of whom there were ten, had their race. Other contests were keen and quicker, and Shanly, George Jones and Henry seemed to be about equally matched for fifty yards. The trophies presented to the victors were, for the most part, galvanized iron pails from the life-boats, and steamer chairs belonging to somebody else than the donor, both of which unfortunately had to be returned.

Pool selling on the run of the ship, which had commenced on the first day's log, increased as the days wore on in proportion as we wearied of all other amusements; the ladies especially exhibiting a marked avidity for this mild form of gambling. We won our share of the pools, but it was our constant regret that a young lady from New Jersey, "The Sky Lark," who had been placed in the charge of our party by her brother-in-law, whom we had met at Seabright, was never successful in drawing the lucky number. It was only by inducing the "Parson" to become a party to a fraud, that she was able on the last night to say, like the rest of us, that she had won once. It is only fair to Aston to say that he alone suffered by the fraud.

This young lady monopolized the attentions of one half of us; a fair actress from New York commanded those of the other, and between them they added much to the enjoyment of the trip. Whether it was the innocence of Artie's youth, or his handsome face or fascinating manner which attracted most, we cannot say—who can tell the subtle influences which sway the feminine mind—but some charm which he alone possessed made him *facile princeps* in one quarter. It must have been the sea air, which we are told works miracles sometimes, that changed the modest youth we had known upon land into a most accomplished "lady killer"; —but upon his doings we draw the curtain. Upon the way Henry achieved his success we leave the curtain up, because the stage is accustomed to the criticism of public opinion.

"Juliet," as we christened the devotee of the Muse of tragedy, captivated by her charming manner and ready anecdotes, and it was hard to say for some time which of the actors in her scene would be triumphant at the climax, but "the Villain," Henry, contrary to the usual *dénoûment* was the lucky man. The night Melpomine made us up for the negro minstrel show, with her cosmetics, after the barber had applied the burnt cork, more than one as he got the finishing touch and the flattering recommendation that he looked "just cute," thought he was a lap ahead, but as before explained, only to find that this was not the case.

Considering the short time we had for preparation and the limited supply of appliances necessary for such a performance, these minstrels were a success. We took some little trouble with them, and with the valuable assistance of some Harvard and Yale students, capital fellows, managed to keep the audience in good humour for an hour. The stewards put up a stage for us. "The Gunner" in G. W. Jones' py-jamas, with four bones from the cornbeef of the evening's dinner, occupied one end, the Manager, in a regulation plantation suit, borrowed from the *cuisinier*, and using a tin pan as a tambourine, the other; and the rest of our fellows with our Harvard and Yale friends made up the circle. The jokes and songs took well, and the inability of one of our most prominent soloists to strike the key note in "Some day," was taken by the audience as part of the performance, and was regarded as quite the funniest thing of the evening.

It was remarkable how we all slept on board, night and day; lying, sitting, or standing, we would drop off to sleep. Some influence seemed to have a particularly soporific effect upon "the Gunner," who, when rallied upon his drowsiness, complained that he was never able to rest comfortably at night, as Wallace Jones, his saloon companion, with his collection of "expectoratoons," took up enough room for two. When it was suggested to "the Gunner" that he should occupy the "*Palais Royal*," as Henry's commodious berth, freshened at will by the air from a port-hole had been christened, he concluded to do so and to leave "the Villain" to the entertaining society of sea-sick Wally. He slept well; Henry did not, and in the time for reflection that a sleepless night gives, determined to "get even" with the robber and his rest. Suspecting that the plot was not of Annand's own designing, and that others had been concerned in the conspiracy, he wisely said nothing the next morning, but determined to wreak vengeance on the offender by a deep laid scheme, in which finally all of us took a hand, to entrap the "Gunner." With cunning wiles the victim was induced to take possession of the "*Palais Royal*" the next night. A little loathe at first to do so he was at length persuaded, and retiring early, disrobed, donned his *robe de nuit*, and after locking the door, lay down in the luxurious bed, chuckling as he pictured to himself "the Villain's" wrath on finding himself again barred out. Whether through the perfidy of the other inmate of the *Palais* or not, has never been admitted, but when Henry came to the state-room door, he found the bolt had been drawn. It was a case of summary eviction; the recumbent "Gunner" was bundled out neck and crop into the passage and the door bolted; and, unfortunately for the evicted one, when he came to try the door of his own state-room, he found that locked too. Then he tried to climb into a cricket bag, but this, though of sufficient length, was not of large enough circumference to hold him. Then arose "a sound of revelry by night," and as it was nearly midnight, the people about, awakened from their sleep, thought we must have collided with an iceberg or were being attacked by pirates. Threats of smashing in a door brought a score of heads out of adjoining rooms to see who this brawler was. Those belonging to the gentler sex drew back when they saw the angelic form of the "Gunner" "clad in a robe of dazzling whiteness" and a cricket bat as if he meant to make mincemeat of somebody or anybody; others began to jeer at him, and for some minutes there was an interchange of compliments which, luckily for the reputation of the team, was put a stop to by the riotor being a length admitted as a companion to the cheery home of Jones.

It was not because the "Gunner" had recourse to the law for vengeance, that we had a trial by jury the next night; it was by "special request." The dining saloon was the court room, and a trunk upon two chairs was the bench, whereon Saunders attired in a white necktie, a waterproof and a wig, sat as judge to try, with the assistance of a jury, what damages, if any, Lydia E. Pinkham should secure for her lacerated affections from her alleged jilter, Jake Sharp.

Judge Bayley's son, of Illinois, after the barber had curled his hair, and the fair actress had again given the benefit of her experience in the "making up" line, was transformed into a not unattractive plaintiff, winning, by a judicious display of handkerchief and feminine grief, and by a modest hesitation in her manner of giving evidence, the approval of the audience, and the sympathy of the jury. So excellent was young Bayley's disguise that a great number of the passengers were loud in their denunciations of *her* boldness in "allowing her counsel to kiss her before all those people."

The defendant placed his case in the hands of Henry, his counsel, and as the six jurors were all over fifty years of age, he had nothing to fear from their susceptibility. The "Manager," arrayed like Henry, and the judge opened the case for the plaintiff, by whom he had been retained, and found his most amusing witness in the wife of the Rev. R. S. Barrett, of Atlanta, Georgia.

Though strenuous efforts were made on both sides, and able addresses by the counsel left the jury in doubt as to which was telling the truth or whether either was, the compromising letters written to and *by* the defendant by the ladies on the boat, were too much for Sharp; the judge summed up the evidence in favor of both, and before sending out the jury to consider their verdict, took the opportunity of tendering the congratulations of the passengers to the *Furnessia's* Captain on the anniversary of his birthday.

When the jury returned they found that the measure of damages for the damsel's blighted hopes and shattered affections was $50,000; but reserved to the defendant the option of marrying the once idol of his heart. Not having the money about him he adopted the latter course, and "the Gunner," who acted as parson, having asked "him" if he wanted "her," and received an affirmative reply, said: "Take her, you're married."

But by the time that a week has passed by at sea everything becomes monotonous, and you long for land with an increasing yearning as the sun rises on each succeeding day. When on the ninth day out we saw Tory light loom up in the distance, and Vickers come on deck in a starched collar and stiff felt hat, feelings of indescribable joy at the prospect of "land ho!" came over us, and we began to formulate tender adieux.

As there was fog, the rate of speed had to be reduced, and it was not till four o'clock the next morning that we were taken off by tender at Moville and sailed up Lough Foyle to Derry. Despite the rain and the cheerless sky, the sight of the clouds rolling off the hills to the west of Lough Foyle, revealing the lovely green fields and neat little cottages, and the picturesqueness of Green Castle were most refreshing after the monotonous sea-view with which our eyes had been wearied for the past ten days.

A great many people stayed up all night, though most of the passengers were going to land at Glasgow ; and many more appeared on deck in the early twilight to say good-bye to friends. Some of the farewells that were taken under the cover of night were not repeated in the morning light, some were.

We had little or no trouble with the customs authorities at Derry, and very soon our multitudinous *impedimenta* had been placed by two sons of Erin on a capacious cart which the small donkey between the shafts walked off with quite unconcernedly to the station. Before we set out for the hotel, the "Manager" received the thanks of many an old Irish woman from the steerage for the assistance given in passing their trunks through the customs as luggage of the Canadian Cricket Team. A kindly word of mention is due to the genial official who was satisfied when he found neither cigars nor dynamite in our hat boxes that there could be none of these in our larger pieces, and chalked them through without opening them. Perhaps this is an instance of Irish credulity, perhaps of Irish hospitality, at any rate the official knew that we were the " byes as was goin' to bate Dublin to-morre."

It didn't take us very long to find an hotel, and a good one Jury's proved to be. We had but two ambitions in life just then, and those were to get a wash and a good breakfast. What a comfort it was to be able to use both hands in laving ones face and not have to cling with one of them to the ubiquitous railing to insure oneself against being landed out into the passage by a sudden lurch. Thank heaven, no more lurching for two months at least! After thorough ablutions we sat down to— oh, what a breakfast!

Nearly everyone has read of the prandial meals of the gods, and many have eaten and paid for a breakfast at Delmonico's, but to us alone it was permitted to enjoy that one feed. Like Cleopatra's charms to Anthony, it made us "hungry where most it seemed to satisfy," and we were only stopped when the larder ran out. None of those who were there will ever forget either that breakfast or Wallace's vain endeavor to pile in at one sitting the thirty meals he was behind.

After this we all assembled in the smoking room, where the "Manager" read the team a moral lecture on Christian virtues, reminding us that we were not men very far advanced in life, that we had the reputation of Canadian cricket in our hands, to return it sullied or not as we did ill or well, and that throughout the task we had set ourselves, it would be always well to remember, that the effect of over-indulgence in hospitality would more than anything else stand in the way of our doing our best: whereupon every man promised to be strictly temperate, in the proper sense of the word, and we need hardly say the promises were faithfully kept.

The jaunting car is a grand institution. In groups of four we set off on cars to see what historic Derry looked like on the anniversary of the memorable 12th of July. Governor Walker's monument was decked in orange from base to capitol, and the female population of the town in the same color from head to foot, set off by an occasional ribbon of blue. The good-natured people did not look as if they would need the assistance of the Royal Irish Constabulary or of the local militia, which had been turned out for the occasion, to keep them from breaking the peace. We passed under one of the gates of the walled town, then back through another, and stopped at the Cathedral of St. Colomb, where are the beautifully carved organ built of the black oak of an old Armada ship, and the old tattered flags captured two centuries before from the besieging army of King James, and many other relics which had an unusual interest for us, perhaps because they were the first of the historic treasures of the old land which we were privileged to see.

Our carman then took us for a drive through the outskirts of the beautiful old town where we saw much to amuse us. Passing down a dirty back street we came across a very diminutive costermonger's donkey in a loaded cart, standing at the door of a hovel. As we jaunted by, the moke set up a terrific he-hawing, and the sight and sound new to us evoked some laughter from the party, which merriment called from our "kyar" driver the remark: "Begorra, gintlemen, but he's givin yes a royal accipshin."

Chapter IV.

The Emerald Isle.

JULY 12.—By two o'clock we were travelling by saloon carriage—a toy compared with a Pullman, but cosier, because we were closer together and could enjoy a common conversation—down through the green fields of Tyrone, Armagh, and Meath, to the sea. Nature can nowhere have been kinder to mankind than she has been among the fertile hills and valleys of North-Eastern Ireland, and neater dwellings than the little whitewashed houses of the cottars one could not wish to see. Then we crossed the Boyne, and in an hour were swinging around Dublin Bay to the capital of the Emerald Isle But we had not come all this way alone. Mr. McCarthy, of the *Freeman's Journal*, had come up to welcome us at Derry, and we were very fortunate in having so entertaining a guide to point out the different places of interest on our journey down to Dublin.

Mr. McCarthy's description of his interview with us, which appeared in print the next morning, was very humorous and fraught with poetic license; it, among other things, represented us as having spent the spring in practising on cocoa-nut matting wickets until the beginning of June, when the ice and snow of winter left us.

Arriving in Dublin about half-past six, we were met at the station by one or two friends and by Britten, our professional and factotum, then off we drove to the Shelbourne Hotel in Stephen's Green, passing on the way some buildings well known to us by name, among them Trinity College, the Bank of Ireland and the office of *United Ireland.*

At the Shelbourne we were glad to shake hands once more with "Teddie" Ogden, under whose leadership we were to play, and most of us had the pleasure of meeting for the first time Mrs. Ogden, who proved so agreeable a companion and so faithful a scorer throughout our trip. Awaiting us at the hotel were letters informing us that we had been made honorary members of the Phœnix and Leinster Cricket Clubs, and others inviting us to make use of the privileges of the University and Sheridan Clubs during our stay in Dublin.

Fagged by our journey after the long sea voyage and tired out from want of rest, none of us having had any sleep the night before, and anticipating a hard day's practice on the morrow, we resolved to retire very soon after dinner; but this was not to be. First, Mr. Hurford, the veteran secretary of the Phœnix Cricket Club, called and told us that their

Serene Highnesses the Prince and Princess of Saxe-Weimar had intimated that they would be present on the first day of our match, and that the Lord Lieutenant of Ireland had desired to have expressed his regret that his absence would preclude him from the pleasure of having us play an eleven of his own at the Vice-Regal Lodge. Then shortly after dinner came a note from Mr. Barrington, saying that an unfortunate mistake as to the time of the arrival of our train had taken a reception party to the station at a wrong hour, and conveying an invitation to spend the evening with him at the Sheridan Club. To the Sheridan we went, and there spent two or three very pleasant hours with our host and some of his genial friends, who thought ten o'clock altogether too early an hour for bed; but a moment's reflection and our weary limbs told us it was not too soon for us to seek our virtuous couches, although it was with not a little reluctance that we said good night to Mr. Barrington, who would have had us to remain till two " at any rate."

That gentleman in the course of the evening recalled many pleasant experiences of his visit in Canada, where he took the Gentlemen of Ireland's cricket team in 1879, and was kind enough to say that he would feel it a privilege to return to us in practical form some of the hospitality he had received when in our own land. Mr. Barrington did everything in his power to make us happy and feel at home in a new land, and his uniform kindness is one of the things that will ever be uppermost in our minds when we recall the incidents of our trip. We need not say we slept well that night. There was no longer the everlasting thump of the engines, the monotonous twirling of the screw or the up and down motion of the rocking ship, nor was the air reeking with a nauseating compound odour of bilge water and fresh paint.

Next morning we were like giants refreshed. Invitations came from the Phœnix Club to a dinner, to be given in our honor at the Sheridan Club on Friday, and from the Royal Irish Yacht Club to their regatta at Kingstown next day, after answering which we set out for the Phœnix Ground for practice.

Our coats, caps and sashes had been ordered in advance and were awaiting us at the Phœnix Clubhouse. They were of one color, maroon, and on the peak of the cap and pocket of the coat maple leaves in white silk had been worked, and a white silk cord binding the coat completed a toggery in which we rather fancied ourselves. The umpire, who from a proper sense of chivalry had the day before gone on to Glasgow with the fair actress to see her safely landed on British soil, turned up that morning on the Phœnix Ground.

It was not long before we discovered how stiff we were, and how much out of form and condition the sea voyage had left us, and our practice, perhaps because we indulged in too much of it, seemed to do us more harm than good. Then, too, Ogden got his finger damaged by a bumpy ball, as did also one or two others. That evening we went with Mr. Barrington, whom we had now come to term familiarly "C. B.," and a jolly friend of his, jocularly known as the "Nosey man," to Hengler's circus. In council of the whole the resolution was carried unanimously, that we were in mighty bad form to meet any eleven, much less the strong eleven to be pitted against us next day. Trinity College had the month before been beaten by an All England team by only one wicket, and they sent a contribution of five men, including Hynes, their captain, who at the last moment replaced T. C. O'Brien; and when one considers that it was possible to strengthen such an eleven as that by men from the Leinster and Phœnix clubs and from the army, and by an old Oxonian and an old Cambridge man, it will be readily admitted that the press was right, and the Irish Gentlemen not immodest when they said Ireland had never before put such an eleven in the field.

Next day, however (July 14), we were ready and

eager for the fray, and, having lost our first toss, took the field amidst applause at the Leinster Cricket Ground at Rathmines precisely at noon, to begin before a large assembly of people our first match on the old sod. Ferrie was deputed to bowl the first over, and the men took the following places in the field: Ogden, short slip; Saunders at the wicket; Little, at point; Vickers, (a position in the field soon disputed with) long stop; Henry, long slip; W. Jones, mid on; and Geo. Jones, mid off. Gillespie at cover, and Annand and Allan at long off and long leg respectively. Britten who is a Leinster professional stood as one of the arbiters of justice.

The wicket was very hard, the country having suffered a drought of six weeks, a thing almost unprecedented in the Emerald Isle. Emerson and Trotter went out first on behalf of Ireland, the former taking Ferrie's first ball. Even at the commencement we were visited with hard luck, for in bowling his fifth over Ferrie strained himself, and was rendered useless, as far as bowling was concerned, for the rest of the match; and indeed it was not till the tour was more than half over that he got back into something like his old form. Gillespie took Ferrie's place, and in his usual style commenced with three or four successive maidens, while Ogden who had been bowling from the start, continued to send them down from the other wicket.

The first impression that the batting of the Irishmen produced was one of admiration at its remarkable steadiness; they took no chances, and seemed to have had firmly inculcated in them the well-established principle, that runs will come if you will only wait for them. The runs came surely enough, and the "jubilee" had gone up before the first wicket fell. It was Trotter's, he being well caught and bowled by Annand, who had taken Ogden's place a few minutes before—One for 46.

We now saw that the making of a long score here was not the same wearying occupation it is in Canada, for there was a "boundary" on each side of the field to which if a ball rolled it counted four, and on the fast wicket if a ball escaped a fielder, it went for four to a moral certainty. In a long innings, boundary hits relieved the batsman of a great deal of hard work, and it astonished us, before we got used to it, to see how fast the runs were telegraphed where boundaries existed.

Blacker followed, but did not stay long, being caught by Gillespie at mid on; meanwhile Emerson had been batting very well, his cutting in particular exciting the admiration of us all. Cronin filled Blacker's place, and some very fine cricket was shown, before Gillespie clean bowled Emerson at 94. He had been in an hour and thirty minutes while making his 36 runs, and his patient innings was a fair sample of the kind of batting we were to have the pleasure of witnessing throughout our tour. E. Fitzgerald, a young Australian studying with his brother at Trinity, joined Cronin, and in a few minutes the century went up, which was the signal for the captain to try Allan in Annand's stead. None of our bowling had been good, the men were all stiff after our hard practice of the day before, and Allan was no exception to the rule. We were having a long spell of fielding, and were much relieved when the luncheon bell rang, previous to which, however, Wallace Jones had taken Gillespie's place, but without affecting the desired separation.

After a most substantial lunch both teams were photographed, an operation which, as the tour progressed, came to have a sameness about it which made it lose all its attractions. The intermission seemed to work some little improvement in us, for on attempting a run on a stroke from the first ball delivered after luncheon, Fitzgerald was run out— Four for 131. Dunn, an officer of the Eighth Liverpool Regiment, who made seventeen centuries last year, filled the vacancy and exhibited a freer style than any of his predecessors. With Cronin as an able coadjutor he rattled up the runs in short order, till at 155 the latter was caught by Vickers off Annand for a well made 45. The appearance of the Irish captain, Mr. Dunn, brought out a round of applause, but he did not stay long, being well caught at the wicket. Then J. P., the other Fitzgerald, came in, and the score was taken to 223 before he was caught by George Jones off Gillespie.

Of this large increase the retiring batsman had put on only 9 runs, the scoring being nearly altogether on Dunn's part. Then Hynes came, but before another run was added, Dunn was bowled by Allan—Eight for 223. Hamilton appeared, and the stand that was thereupon made showed how on occasions the tail can wag the team, for these two batsmen carried the score to 317, an increase, compiled by brilliant hitting on the part of Hamilton, and steady careful play on that of Hynes. Hamilton's wicket was the first of the two to fall, he being caught off a miss-hit by Ogden, off Wallace Jones, after having contributed 62 to the total. The same bowler was also responsible for Tobin's wicket, and Hynes was left not out for a well played 31. Total 319, of which the odd 19 were extras. Our fielding throughout the innings had been decidedly under the mark, and though there were several noteworthy exceptions, the work of the team on the whole in this respect was disappointing. The returns from the field were poor, and indeed in that feature of the game, as in all others, we found that we had a good deal to learn from the cricketers of the old land.

To our deficient fielding and to the want of condition of the bowlers, is to be attributed the long score made by the Irishmen, though they were undoubtedly a very strong batting team.

During the interval between the innings, Dr. and Mrs. Ogden and Lindsey had the honor of being presented to the Prince and Princess of Saxe-Weimar, who had shortly before come on the ground to the accompaniment of God Save the Queen, by the Liverpool Regiment band, which played at intervals during the afternoon. Their serene Highnesses were very gracious, and expressed themselves as much interested in our tour.

Canada's first innings was commenced at 5.40 by Allan and Vickers. Hynes (medium) commenced the attack for the Irishmen, and oh, horror! the last ball of his first over scattered Allan's stumps. Gillespie followed, and with Vicker's played out time, 20 runs being telegraphed at six o'clock.

At soon as we could change we mounted cars and made for Westland Row Station, where Mr. Barrington and a party of ladies were waiting to accompany us to Bray, to enjoy the cool air of that fashionable watering place. As we rolled past Kingstown in the train we caught a glimpse of the festivities going on there. About the club house numerous yachts, with all their bunting flying, danced up and down, while far off on the horizon could be seen the competing boats with their white wings spread for the homeward run. On arriving at Bray, we had a stroll on the parade before sitting down to dinner. Ere long corks were flying and we found ourselves doing two things at once, sustaining the inner man and listening to good Irish stories told in the most inimitable fashion, both of which made us feel decidedly happy. After dinner, as it was raining, and we could not go to the parade again, we were invited to the drawing room of a lady spending the summer at Bray, where we had songs, and the opportunity long to be remembered, of hearing Miss Barrington's excellent voice. By eleven o'clock we were homeward bound once more, and by midnight fast asleep.

The gentle rain which ever keeps the hills and dales of Ireland as green as the ivy that covers her churches or the emeralds which represent her in the British Crown, had fallen moderately over night, but affected not the wicket. Another fine day dispelled the clouds and our ideas of the incessant wet to be met with in the land of Erin. The two not outs of the night before faced the onslaughts of Hynes and the Leinster man. After a few runs J. P. Fitzgerald took the ball from Tobin, and scattered Vickers' stumps. Saunders came in, ran three runs and lost Gillespie, who had put one up off Fitzgerald, but not before he had put together a meritorious 28. He had played with great steadiness, though occasionally hitting hard, particularly to square leg. Emerson now became companion trundler to Fitzgerald, and between them soon disposed of the rest of the eleven, though Little and George Jones did the Derry act for a time. Saunders, Henry, Ogden and Annand only increased the total by eight runs, the telegraph showing seven for 50 when the last of them retired. Little began to score off each bowler, getting them to the boundary several times. Just after seventy had gone up Wallace Jones was clean bowled on a half volley by Emerson, who proved himself the most dangerous bowler we met in Ireland. His delivery was high, his pace inclined to fast, his length good, and he occasionally got on a good deal of work from the off. While the last man, Ferrie made three, Little had time to make fifteen, eight of which he secured from two successive fours off Emerson, who finally caught and bowled him. All out for 88, and off went the carrier pigeons to the different newspaper offices to tell that Canada had to follow on.

These birds are much used by reporters to carry hourly messages from the cricket field to head-quarters. The writing is fastened by an elastic band round the bird's ankle, then it is released. The first course is upwards, then it circles around once or oftener to get its bearings, mounts higher and goes direct to its destination. When several birds bound for different points are released at the same time, their airy circlings high above the field, their looking for home, and then their starts upon their different routes are beautiful to behold, and seem to impress you with the idea that there is something almost human about the movements of the winged messengers.

The Irish fielding was extremely good, and the bowling on the whole was good, though with the exception of Emerson's there was nothing particularly dangerous about it. It was that style to which we had been accustomed, and it is hard to say why we had made such a poor showing. Viewed calmly, and comparing this match with our subsequent ones we see no explanation for our failure in all the departments of the game here, except that we lacked practice, were stiff after our long voyage, and were generally out of condition, though we must not forget that the wicket was unusually quick, and that it took us some time to get accustomed to this—to us—novelty.

At the appointed hour Ferrie, the not out, and Saunders commenced the follow on. After a maiden over from J. P. Fitzgerald, Emerson bowled Ferrie on his second ball. The other Hamiltonian filled the breach manfully. At 23 an adjournment was made for lunch, after which the inevitable camera was again turned on, shooting Gillespie just at the moment when his face was lighted with a seraphic smile at the thought of how he would make the balance of his 51. Posterity now has the portrait. Very soon after resuming Saunders was bowled by Emerson for 16. Allan and Henry did not mend matters much, but George Jones helped Gillespie to take the score from 41 to the century. Just before the three figures had been telegraphed Gillespie had completed his jubilee, but he had not much longer to live, for with the total at 105 he was unfortunately run out. The band of the Welsh regiment, which had shortly before taken a rest, struck up "The girl I left behind me," as he strode to the pavilion. The *girl* left was George Jones, whose old school nick-name Biddy was resurrected, and when that name appears in these pages it will stand for the fickle Gillespie's first girl; his second he was not to meet till he got to London.

Gillespie's splendid innings of 54 had been carefully made, yet he had punished the bowling when it could be safely done by driving it and hitting it hard. The "girl left behind" did not long survive his partner. After hitting Hynes for 4 the bowler had his revenge, and Jones had to retire with 21 prettily made runs to his credit. The other men did nothing, the extras, 19, helping to swell the total to 129, which left us 102 runs behind and an innings to the bad.

Emerson's analysis speaks for itself. In the first innings it reads :—15 overs, 16 runs, 9 maidens and 5 wickets; in the second, 24 overs, 36 runs, 10 maidens and 4 wickets.

GENTLEMEN OF IRELAND.

1st Innings.

D. N. Trotter	ct. and b. Annand	20
D. N. Emerson	b. Gillespie	36
W. Blacker	ct. Gillespie. b. Ferrie	8
D. Cronin	ct. Vickers, b. Annand	45
E. Fitzgerald	run out	14
J. Dunn	b. Allan	67
J. H. Nunn	ct. Saunders, b. Ogden	8
J. P. Fitzgerald	ct. G. W. Jones, b. Gillespie	9
J. W. Hynes	not out	31
W. D. Hamilton	ct. Ogden, b. W. W. Jones	62
T. Tobin	b. W. W. Jones	0
Byes, 13; leg byes, 5; wides, 1		19
Total		319

RUNS AT THE FALL OF EACH WICKET.

	1.	2.	3.	4.	5.	6.	7.	8.	9.	10.
1st Innings	46	57	94	131	155	172	223	223	319	319

BOWLING ANALYSIS.

	Overs.	Runs.	Mdn's.	Wkts.
Ferrie	13	28	2	1
Ogden	36	94	8	1
Gillespie	46	88	13	2
Annand	27	39	9	2
Allan	7	22	1	1
W. W. Jones	14.1	25	3	2

Annand bowled 4 no balls.
Allan bowled 1 wide.

GENTLEMEN OF CANADA.

1st innings.		2nd innings.	
A. C. Allan, b. Hynes	0	b. Emerson	0
W. W. Vickers, b. J. P. Fitzgerald	4	b. Hynes	7
A. Gillespie, ct. Cronin, b. J. P. Fitzgerald	28	run out	54
D. W. Saunders, c. and b. J. P. Fitzgerald	3	b. Emerson	16
W. A. Henry, jr., b. Emerson	5	b. Emerson	0
E. R. Ogden, b. P. Fitzgerald	0	run out	0
G. W. Jones, b. Emerson	9	b. Hynes	21
C. J. Annand, b. Emerson	0	not out	4
W. C. Little, ct. and b. Emerson	21	b. J. P. Fitzgerald	4
W. W. Jones, b. Emerson	9	b. Hynes	4
R. B. Ferrie, not out	3	b. Emerson	0
Byes, 5; leg byes, 1	6	Byes, 12; leg byes, 6; wides, 1	19
Total	88	Total	129

RUNS AT THE FALL OF EACH WICKET.

	1.	2.	3.	4.	5.	6.	7.	8.	9.	10.
1st Innings	0	37	40	44	45	46	50	55	72	88
2nd Innings	0	35	39	41	105	109	111	120	124	129

BOWLING ANALYSIS.

	1st Innings.				2nd Innings.			
	Ovrs.	Mdns.	Runs.	Wkt.	Overs.	Mdns.	Runs.	Wkts.
Hynes	11	16	3	1	10	22	1	3
Tobin	11	12	6	0	6	8	3	0
J. P. Fitzgerald	15	28	1	4	19	34	5	1
Emerson	15	16	9	5	24	36	10	4
Nunn	0	0	0	0	6	10	2	0

Hynes bowled 1 wide.

We were now left with an hour and a half of this afternoon and all Saturday, so it was proposed to play a return match, to which, after consulting the wishes of the team, Ogden consented. It would hardly have done for us to have batted for the third time that day, so although the captain won the toss he could not turn his good fortune to advantage. The Irish team, which was changed in three cases,

S. G. Smith, T. P. Maxwell, and St. G. Considine taking the places of Blacker, Tobin and Trotter, was sent to bat. Hynes and Cronin commenced the batting and Ferrie and Gillespie the bowling. Both men scored rapidly, particularly off Ferrie, whose place Ogden took; but this change was not efficacious, and Wallace Jones tried his hand *vice* the captain. The telegraph showed 55 before Cronin was caught in the slips by Gillespie off Jones for a well put together 37. Hamilton came next and signalized his advent by lifting Jones over the ropes for 4, and making in all 9 off that bowler's over. He indeed hit savagely, putting on the runs at a great pace. Gillespie gave place to Annand, who in turn was supplemented by Ogden. In the meantime 90 had gone up, but just after, off Ogden's first ball, Hamilton was caught by Henry for a hard-hit 31. Dunn received a good deal of applause as he went to join Hynes. A 3 by him off Ogden sent up the century, which came out with Hynes, he being neatly stumped by Saunders. He had played very carefully for his 28 and had hard lines in getting out. He was about to refuse the ball off which he was stumped on account of the noisy applause of the spectators on seeing the century telegraphed. Emerson was the next man, and with Dunn played till stumps were drawn, when the score stood 124 for 3 wickets.

After such a drubbing as we had experienced at the hands of our Irish friends, and with every prospect of a repetition of it, it was only natural that we were easily disposed to drown care in mellow wine at the banquet that night.

As we sat around the festive board at the Sheridan Club we very soon perceived that it was no ordinary gathering. Mr. Hone, who was in Canada with the Gentlemen of Ireland in 1879, had come all the way from London to be present, while his brother had come from Cork. Mr. Hurford, too, was there, and in the course of the evening was presented with some handsome gold plate, in recognition of his long and able services for the Phœnix Club. We joined heartily in the feeling evinced toward Mr. Hurford, for he in no small way contributed to our comfort in Ireland.

We had seen the men of the Black Watch with their tartans, dirks and pouches about the streets of Dublin, and our hearts had gone out to them as we thought, with Rattray, how a list of the engagements in which their noble regiment had taken part would be "a military history of England in symbol." Several of the officers of this regiment, quartered just then at Dublin, officers of the Dragoons, too, were with us that night to do us honor. Mr. Arthur Palmer, son of the late Archdeacon Palmer, Mr. Matcherin, an admirable comic songster who accompanies himself on the banjo, Mr. Armstrong, who delighted us more than once with his fine tenor voice, were partaking of the excellent *menu.*

Mr. Charles Barrington presided, and after we had honored the toast of the Queen called upon us to drink the health of the Governor-General of Canada, which was done with a right good will, our fellows remembering the attitude of His Excellency towards their venture, cheered the toast the louder for it, but not louder than His Excellency's fellow-countrymen, who hold him in high esteem. Then Mr. Barrington rose at once to his feet and to a high degree of eloquence. In language which he alone can use he paid us no little compliment, at times growing so humorous in his remarks as to make the very glasses of the table shake with laughter. This gentleman, who, by the way, is a Home Ruler, would in the House of Commons lend brilliancy to the constellation of orators who there uphold the Irish cause.

The captain responded in fitting terms; the Manager excused himself from more than a heartfelt sentence of thanks to one and all, and especially Mr. Barrington, on the ground that when he came to the land of the Sheridans, the Burkes and the Barringtons, he ought to be permitted to listen rather than to speak. Saunders, whose restless eye had been scanning the horizon of the Leinster ground too often, where in the inviting shade of Irish oaks sat the pretty Irish girls, and who had lent his ear too much to silvery sounds, tuned to the prettiest brogue in the world, of the voice of these Irish sirens, unbosomed himself and told how he had seen the prettiest girls here that he had ever seen in his life, and that he didn't think that even the charm of the music of Orpheus excelled the beauty of their voices. We need hardly say that the enthusiasm with which we drunk the health of the Irish team could not have been greater, certainly not more genuine.

Mr. Matcherin sang "Two bally black eyes," a song, the poetry and sentiment of which so much impressed us that we determined upon mastering it, and it hereafter formed the brilliant nucleus of our European collection of comic songs. Now the "Baby," Fleury sings it. The evening about this time grew frolicsome, music and dancing, of the jig kind, filled up the far too quickly fleeting hours till stern duty impelled the majority of us to our hotel.

Those who were not playing in the match did not feel the necessity for returning so early, and remained at the club to tempt fortune with the cards, learning that Irishmen play whist, as they do everything else, well. When Aurora dawned in the east and shed her rosy tints through the windows of the club over the convivial battlefield, where bottles and men had struggled for the mastery only a few hours before, the last Canadian stepped out into Stephen's Green. The jaunting car drivers complained to him on his homeward route of the hard times they were experiencing. Not being able to employ them all to drive him the few yards to his hotel, the brilliant idea occurred to him to start the eight of them down Stephen's Green for a half sovereign.

Drawn up in line, the charioteers started at the word "Go!" Tearing down the street they came, raising a racket on the rubble road that might have awakened the dead, and probably did awake a majority of the guests at the Shelbourne Hotel. First past the post took the prize to the disgust of his competitors. The man who came last to the winning post was of the opinion that he was better on his feet than his horse was, and offered to run the seven other drivers a hundred yards for another donated half sovereign, to which proposition the belated Canuck acceded; and as the hurricane swept down the pavement past him, it was quite evident that Paddy knew what he was about, for he distanced the others and took the prize. Just then the proprietor of the hotel and two officers of the law put in an appearance, so while Canada retired to bed amid the "God bless yer honor" of the charioteers, Ireland adjourned to a neighboring hostelry to take a pull at the national beverage.

It was remarkable how the aspect of the game, which up till the time of the drawing of stumps over night had appeared to be going in favor of the home team, changed next morning; and it may here be noticed as a remarkable thing, which by its constant recurrence came to be almost proverbial, that we were always much more successful on the day after a banquet than our opponents. At twenty minutes after twelve Dunn and Emerson, the not outs of the night before, continued their innings to the bowling of Annand and Ogden. Off Annand's third ball Little snapped up the military man at point, and E. Fitzgerald came in. Both batsmen commenced to score freely and soon brought up the 140, though in a few minutes Annand succeeded in levelling Emerson's wicket. Telegraph 149, 5, 2. Then commenced an extraordinary procession, J. P. Fitzgerald, the next man, in trying to hit to leg, stepped on his wicket; Dunn, who followed, skied one close the wicket which Saunders held; Considine played Ogden on to his wicket, then Smith for a very short time held the bowlers in check. Gillespie took Ogden's place and in his second over got Smith caught off him in the slips. Maxwell, last man, when two runs had been added was clean bowled by Annand, at a quarter past one, the innings closing for 166. The last five batsmen, it may be noted, had only put on five runs between them.

Annand was in great form with the ball, his analysis being five wickets for 17 runs.

Very little time was lost, before Vickers and Saunders went in to face two successful Irish bowlers of the day before. Both batsmen started cautiously, then Vickers was caught by Nunn off H. Emerson for 4, and made way for Ogden, who now began his brilliant innings.

Upon Saunders' dismissal, the telegraph stood 34. 2. 15. We were in the hope that Gillespie, who had batted so well hitherto, and Ogden would not be separated before they had very materially increased the score; nor were we disappointed, for both set about making runs rapidly, the threes and fours which they put on keeping the scorers busy, who before the adjournment for luncheon had signalled 50.

Once more the deadly camera. But, alas, the "Duke" was not there. When all eyes turned to see the scorer "pose," he had gone. Lesson number three in Græco-Roman art nipped to the bud.

After lunch the 60 and 70 went up without a change, Ogden scoring most noticeably by driving, while Gillespie made some pretty half drives and smote, as was his wont, to leg. At 78 he was smartly taken at the wickets by E. Fitzgerald for a well made 30. Henry followed and did his first hitting. He knocked up 25 runs in short order, and saw the century go up before he was bowled by J. P. Fitzgerald. George Jones came and went, but Allan gave Ogden very valuable assistance, and by his contribution of 38 gave evidence of batting powers which augured well for further successes on the tour. Ogden's was the fifth wicket, he being run out after getting well set and giving signs of an intention to stay there the rest of the afternoon. The score stood at 192, to which Odgen had contributed 60 runs by excellent cricket. His hitting was clean, hard and popular. This leap from "ducks" to fame tickled the Captain immensely. Two runs later Allan fell a victim to Nunn after a fine performance. The rest of the eleven did not materially increase the score, *as they said*, because they didn't need to, for we were just 36 in advance of our friends. This was tit for tat, and games being equal, we agreed if possible, to return and try conclusions again at the end of our prescribed tour.

GENTLEMEN OF IRELAND.

J. W. Hynes, stpd. Saunders, b. Ogden	28
D. Cronin, ct. Gillespie, b. W. W. Jones	37
W. D. Hamilton, ct. Henry, b. Ogden	31
J. Dunn, ct. Little, b. Annand	20
D. N. Emerson, b. Annand	22
E. Fitzgerald, not out	18
J. P. Fitzgerald, hit wkt. b. Annand	0
J. H. Nunn, ct. Saunders, b. Annand	1
H. J. Considine, b. Ogden	1
S. C. Smith, ct. Annand, b. Gillespie	0
J. P. Maxwell, b. Annand	2
Byes, 4 ; leg byes, 2	6
Total	166

RUNS AT THE FALL OF EACH WICKET.

1.	2.	3.	4.	5.	6.	7.	8.	9.	10.
55	97	100	126	149	149	151	155	161	166

BOWLING ANALYSIS.

	Overs.	Runs.	M'dns.	W's.
Ferrie	5	19	1	0
Gillespie	23	28	8	1
Ogden	21	41	5	3
W. W. Jones	13	37	2	1
Annand	22	35	7	5

GENTLEMEN OF CANADA.

Vickers, ct. Nunn, b. Emerson	4
Saunders, b. J. P. Fitzgerald	15
Ogden, run out	60
Gillespie, ct. E. Fitzgerald, b. Nunn	30
Henry, b. J. P. Fitzgerald	25
G. W. Jones, ct. Smith, b. J. P. Fitzgerald	4
Allan, b. Nunn	38
W. W. Jones, ct. Nunn, b. Hynes	2
Little, b. Hynes	2
Annand, stpd. Fitzgerald, b. Hynes	0
Ferrie, not out	2
Byes, 16; leg byes, 4	20
Total	202

RUNS AT THE FALL OF EACH WICKET.

1.	2.	3.	4.	5.	6.	7.	8.	9.	10.
16	34	78	122	132	192	194	198	198	202

BOWLING ANALYSIS.

	Overs.	Runs.	Maidens.	W's.
J. P. Fitzgerald	23	52	6	3
Emerson	22	37	9	1
Hynes	22	44	7	3
Nunn	14.3	26	4	2
Dunn	4	15	0	0
Considine	4	8	0	0

Early that morning we had been on a tour of inspection and seen how the green water of the Liffey is made into brown porter by the Guinesses, had traced this performance through its various stages and partaken of the result, judging by which we pronounced the performance good. Right in the centre of Dublin stands Trinity College, the buildings of which are arranged very much in the same way as those of the Louvre. Hynes took us for a hurried run through these grand halls ; would that we had had time to tarry longer there. Close at hand is the Bank of Ireland, formerly the House of Parliament, whose plain Ionic architecture is noble in its simplicity. There the House of Lords remains in its original condition, just as it was before the Union.

Setting out one morning for Phœnix Park we called at the tavern from where the conspirators left to commit the Phœnix Park murders, and where they were overheard by a man sitting at an open window on the first flat. Later on we came to the little holes cut in the sod of the Park, just opposite the Vice-Regal Lodge, which mark the spot on which the Irish martyrs fell. So we saw a good deal of Dublin and learned to like it well.

After the conclusion of the game we had no more than time to change and get to our hotel for a moment, on the way to the station, before the train started and we were off to Kingstown, sorry, very sorry indeed, to take, what we did not then think would be our last look at Ireland, for we, as we said, had arranged, if possible, to return and play again with these generous gentlemen at the end of August. But this was not to be.

Chapter V.

Scotland.

JULY 18.—Arrived at Kingstown, we said goodbye to "C. B.," the "Nosey man" and Ireland, with the assurance that though we were leaving them we were "wid them," and after a parting pull at Guinness, took the fast packet boat for Holyhead. When the Manager came to count heads, exclusive of Holyhead, and found that "Papa Dyce" and the professor Britten were not of the number, he waxed wrathy. The story, as related by the wicket keeper, was, that lingering over his parting pull at Guinness, which he had taken from the hands of a pretty Dublin bar-maid, whose childhood had been spent among the Welsh hills, he forgot about the train and stayed yet longer to take his daily quota from her hands, and was astonished to find when he got through that the train had gone. That night he took a later train and got as far as Chester, where he and Britten were perforce to spend Sunday. He says he spent the day at church, nobody believed that, but on Monday he was in Edinboro' in time to go behind the sticks.

No sooner had the boat left Kingstown than the

"left hand barrel of the Jones combination" went below, nor did he show himself again till a delightful sail, of four hours' duration, across the Irish Sea we touched Holyhead, when he appeared "sickled o'er with the pale cast of thought." He said himself he'd been thinking.

Here our saloon carriage awaited us. Cosy little home, in which were were to jog all over England. What memories does not the mention of your number "147" recall? Have we not told to you the story of our last match when jogging on to the next? Have you not seen the fallacy of the platitude that all men are equal—at whist? Have you not felt the pliable form of the "Gunner" when used as a football? Have you not heard all our songs? And have you not heard many things that the authors of these pages have not heard? At any rate, you remember that Fitzgerald left Holyhead with us, but did not go to Edinburgh as we all did, though most of us deserted you for sleepers the very first night you carried us. But then it was a long way from Holyhead to Edinburgh, and took all night to do it in. Next morning, however, shortly after daybreak you brought us all into the capital of "Auld Scotia."

Soon we were driving with our seventy-eight pieces of luggage, now on the increase, past the monument of Walter Scott, who sits protected by lesser statues of the fictitious characters he has created, to the Waterloo Hotel.

Sunday was spent in driving about the Athens of modern Europe. First we climbed Calton Hill and saw the Nelson monument, then we drove around Arthur's seat, then to what is left of Holyrood Chapel and the Palace, where the stain on the spot where Rizzio was murdered is pointed out to you. Next we climbed to the Castle on the hill, which, at first sight, looked almost inaccessible, visited the University of Edinburgh, then drove through the parks and fine streets, past rows of substantial houses, past St. Giles, past columns and monuments, the one to the Prince Consort claiming most attention, home to an early dinner, after which we attended divine service at St. Mary's Cathedral. The evening was pleasantly spent with Mr. W. L. MacKenzie, who had been our guide during the day, before we turned in early to bed.

Our match with the Gentlemen of Scotland was to initiate the Scottish week in Edinburgh, the last three days of the week being devoted to a match between Yorkshire and Scotland. We reached the Grange Ground at Raeburn Place shortly before noon, and Ogden having again lost the toss took the field. L. M. Balfour, of the Grange club, the Captain and R. J. Pope, a member of the last Australian team in England, but who is now attending

Edinburgh University, commenced the innings at a quarter after noon, on a good fast wicket. The Scotch team was composed principally of Edinburgh men, and although disappointed of Lord George Scott, A. G. G. Asher and J. S. Carrick, the team was still a fairly representative one.

The Hamilton trundlers commenced the bowling for us, and though Ferrie was still suffering from the effects of his strain he bowled very well and had to do a lot of work. Runs came slowly till the score reached 20, when Balfour was clean bowled by Ferrie. Stevenson, the new comer, had only added 3 when he was served in the like manner by Gillespie, then came J. G. Walker, of Lasswade and Middlesex County. The two batsmen made a stand till at 51, Pope was got rid of by his playing Ferrie on. Marshall, of the Grange, joined Walker and another stand was made. Ogden had relieved Gillespie in the meanwhile and had been in turn replaced by Annand, but all these bowlers were more or less severely punished, though Ferrie had been bowling steadily and had sent down a lot of maidens. At 83, Marshall was well caught by Allan at mid-on after having made a well hit 27. A. O. MacKenzie, a left hander, took his place, a few overs later losing Walker who had succumbed to Ferrie. Five for 114. The last batsman had played a very steady innings and had been in upwards of an hour for his 34 runs. Johnston went in, and stayed until the bell tingled for lunch, when the Scotchmen had 142.

Almost immediately after lunch Johnston was caught at coverpoint by George Jones. Six for 124. Le Messurier joined MacKenzie and commenced by cutting Ferrie for 4, but Allan, who now changed with Ogden, found his way to his stumps with his second ball, a ripper. Don Wauchope gave MacKenzie lots of running, and these two batsmen brought up the total to 180, when the last comer also fell to Allan after having made a good 20. Macnair and Thornton did well themselves, and helped MacKenzie who had been making the most of his opportunities to bring out a respectable total. MacKenzie treated all the bowling with little respect till he fell to a good catch by Allan after having made 67. His was the last wicket and the innings closed for 253.

The Canadian fielding had been highly complimented, the two Merchistonians deserving special mention as having done good work under the shadow of their old school. During the morning a bad shy-in took Saunders on the foot and severely hurt him, and, though he fielded out the rest of the innings, he was unable to bat next day. The captain had, unfortunately as it turned out, agreed to play on until seven o'clock. As it was not yet five, we had still two hours to play, and as the evening advanced the light got by degrees beautifully less.

Vickers and George Jones began for Canada, the former being given out l. b. w. to Thornton when he had made 4. Ogden followed, and soon fell a victim to the same bowler for the same number of runs. George Jones played prettily, as usual, and Gillespie and he brought up the total to 33. At that stage of the game Gillespie was bowled by Le Messurier just before George Jones unfortunately ran himself out after making 19. Four for 43. Henry and Allan came in, but the latter retired without scoring. Henry soon got to work and sent the ball flying in all directions. He got most of the bowling and hit all the trundlers furiously, increasing the score principally by threes and fours. His strokes were vociferously cheered by some of the boys from Merchiston College, who had been given a half-holiday in honor of the visit of George Jones and Henry, old Merchistonian boys, and they evidently thought that the causes of this unexpected event, as well as the event itself, should receive an expression of their approval. But Henry's hitting certainly deserved applause, and at the drawing of stumps our score had been, mainly through his prowess, taken to 138 for the loss of seven wickets. Little, although not making many runs, had rendered Henry a great deal of assistance by holding up his wicket. He batted most patiently for three-quarters of an hour for 4 runs, and while in saw 62 runs added to the score. He had just come to the pavilion and been replaced by Wallace Jones, when stumps were drawn. Henry had then 76, and was not out.

By eight o'clock we were shaking hands with the Scotchmen and their friends in the drawing room of the Waterloo Hotel, for before we had left Ireland an invitation had come for a banquet to be given in our honor at the conclusion of the first day's play. The two pipers, adorned in plaid and kilt, who preceded us to dinner, and who made the corridors of the hotel ring with the martial music of the pibroch, as the procession wended its way to the dining room, claimed most of our attention and appreciation. The strains of music did not die away until we were all seated. A glance up and down the table revealed the fact that there were some sixty diners about Mr. J. W. Todd, who occupied the chair. The pipers were not the only warriors there. The gentlemen who were kind enough to join the opposing eleven in entertaining us were as delightful as could be found in great Edinburgh.

The early stages of a Scotch dinner are as formal as the proceedings in a court of justice, but by the time the *menu* has been half disposed of the frigidity, thaws out, and the conversation which begins in little babbling streams soon grows to a torrent.

If you want to hear a really good joke, you should get a Scotchman to tell it to you. Some of the anecdotes that we heard over our *pâtisserie à la Française* we enjoyed hugely. One most amusing incident happened at the table. A celebrated Scotch officer and an ardent Tory, sitting next to one of our fellows, was located just opposite another celebrated gentleman, Mr. Gladstone's political agent. The warrior evidently was uneasy, and longed for blood, which yearning increased as a conversation opposite on the merits of Mr. Gladstone grew eloquent. This was too much for the General, who had *sotto voce* confided to his neighbor that he didn't like "that fellow opposite," so he declared war by announcing it in very much the same tone of voice as that in which he would command a regiment to form a column of route, that he thought Gladstone was the worst scamp alive. The party attacked, "bided a wee," which passive line of action led the attacker to believe he had carried the day, and he accordingly relapsed into a smile and a better humor.

Later on the Canadians were toasted with Highland honors, a ceremony which requires one foot on the table and one on the chair. The aged General got fixed that way in time, but not for long. The castors on his chair rolled it from under him and he was forced to capitulate. Just here is where the "fellow opposite" got in his little *coup*. "I thought," said he, just as the warrior and the chair made up friends again, "the old gentleman wasn't quite sure of his base of supply when he got the information that Mr. Gladstone was a scamp." General plans another attack for another occasion.

After the Queen and Royal Family had been duly honored the chairman proposed the health of the visitors in very kindly terms.

That the Scotch will always extend their best hospitality, even to their opponents, we learned when we read how the Douglas entertained the Knight of Snowdoun, James FitzJames on Ellen's Isle, the night before his mortal combat with Rhoderick Dhu, at Coilantogle Ford. That we did not stand in any such hostile position as this to the cricketers of Edinburgh goes without saying, yet we wish to dwell upon the remarkable feeling of good-will for us and for our undertaking which existed that night in the hearts of our hospitable entertainers, and which was expressed by various speakers.

After the Captain had responded in fitting terms, and we had given three times three and a "tiger" for the Gentlemen of Scotland, the Honorable H. J. Moncreiff, in one of the ablest speeches we ever had the pleasure of listening to, proposed the toast "Scottish Cricket." The honorable gentleman carried us away back to the times of the Percys and the Douglasses, gave us a graphic picture of the genealogical tree, of which these redoubtable warriors were the root and of which the Moncreiffs were the trunk, told us how all the little Moncreiffs, branches of that great family, had done their part to bring the noble game of cricket to the high position it occupies among the favorite pastimes of Scotland, and further recalled how he and the chairman, in days gone by, had played the game among the hills of Perthshire and on the greens of Stirling, often times sending the ball in its parabolic flight clean over the "castle broad and deep."

Many a good old song made the welkin ring that night, and more than once the pipers squeezed music from the bags, till at last legs began to grow uneasy and then the reel began. The reel, the Highland fling, as only Scotchmen to the pipers' music and the power of wine can give it. Innes and Surgeon Foreman "whooped her up" in fine style and left no figure in that graceful and noisy dance undone, in order, as they said, that we might pick it up. One might as well expect to master the Indian war-dance; even Terpsichore, we'll wager, couldn't manage it; we tried but failed. Innes we were to fall across again in many pleasant ways, but he never showed us the Highland fling again. It's likely all slept well that night, certainly we did after the *finale* of our most delightful banquet.

The game was resumed the following morning at eleven o'clock. When 8 runs had been hit up Henry was caught in the slips off Le Messurier, after he had increased his overnight score by 2. Of his 78 runs 52 were made from 13 hits, a five with several threes making up nearly the whole balance. At the same total Wallace Jones was caught, also in the slips, off Thornton, and as Saunders was unable to bat, owing to his injury, the innings closed for 146; this necessitating a follow on.

Vickers and George Jones again commenced for Canada. The former was bowled by Thornton after making 6, but Jones, with Gillespie's assistance, brought the score to 32 before the Merchistonian was bowled by Le Messurier. He was soon followed to the pavilion by Gillespie who only contributed 8. But when Henry and Allan became associated, they commenced putting on the runs as fast as the former had done on the previous day, 30 being added in half as many minutes. Allan made a splendid drive to the on, putting Le Messurier clean over the grand stand, and during his partnership with Henry 50 runs were put on in 23 minutes. With a total of 82, Henry was disposed of by a splendid one-handed catch at mid-on by Macnair off MacKenzie. He had made 29 runs in the same dashing style as he had scored the day before, he getting but one single.

On Ogden's joining Allan the rare spectacle was witnessed of two left-handed batsmen playing two left-handed bowlers, Macnair and Thornton. The Captain, who commenced to score freely off Macnair, lost Allan at 98. Little followed, and Ogden brought up the hundred by driving Le Messurier, who had gone on in place of Macnair. The cricket got slow. Little played a long time without scoring and was at length taken at the wickets. Six for 103. With only 1 added Annand was stumped, then Wallace Jones, after making a single, was caught in the slips, the fate of most of our men, who now found the wicket bumping a good deal, Le Messurier's high deliveries being accordingly hard to keep down. At the same total Ogden was bowled by Thornton. This left us with 2 runs still wanting to save the innings defeat, so Saunders was pressed into the the service, and Ferrie and he managed to put on 12 runs, leaving the Scotchmen 6 to make to win, which Pope and MacKenzie did for them without the loss of a wicket. The match with the Gentlemen of Scotland thus ended in the defeat of Canada by 10 wickets.

GENTLEMEN OF SCOTLAND.

1st INNINGS.		2nd INNINGS.	
L. M. Balfour, b. Ferrie	13		
R. J. Pope, b. Ferrie	25	not out	7
H. J. Stevenson, b. Gillespie	3		
J. G. Walker, b. Ferrie	34		
T. R. Marshall, ct. Allan, b. Ferrie	27		
A. O. Mackenzie, ct. Allan, b. Annand	67	not out	1
R. H. Johnston, ct. G. W. Jones, b. Ferrie	6		
J. H. Le Mesurier, b. Allan	13		
A. R. Don Wauchope, b. Allan	20		
R. Macnair, ct. Little, b. Gillespie	19		
G. Thornton, not out	14		
Byes, 7; leg byes, 5	12		
Total	253	Total	8

RUNS AT THE FALL OF EACH WICKET.

	1.	2.	3.	4.	5.	6.	7.	8.	9.	10.
1st Innings	20	23	51	83	114	124	146	180	226	253
2nd "										

BOWLING ANALYSIS.

	1st INNINGS.				2nd INNINGS.			
	Overs.	Runs.	Md'ns.	W's.	Overs.	Runs.	Mdn's.	W's.
Ferrie	50	100	20	5	2	4	0	0
Gillespie	21	40	9	2				
Ogden	15	26	6	0	1.1	4	1	0
Annand	8.1	31	0	1				
Allan	19	44	6	2				

GENTLEMEN OF CANADA.

1st INNINGS.		2nd INNINGS.	
Vickers, l. b. w. bd. Thornton	4	b. Thornton	6
G. W. Jones, run out	19	b. LeMesurier	17
Ogden, b. Thornton	4	b. Thornton	16
Gillespie, b. LeMesurier	11	ct. Walker, b. Thornton	8
Henry, ct. Stevenson, b. LeMesurier	76	ct. Mackenzie, b. Macnair	29
Allan, b. Thornton	0	b. Thornton	24
Carried forward	114	Carried forward	100

GENTLEMEN OF CANADA.

1st INNINGS.		2nd INNINGS.	
Brought forward ..	114	Brought forward	100
Annand, ct. & b. LeMesurier....	5	stpd. Balfour, b. Thornton	0
Little, ct. Macnair, b. LeMesurier	8	ct. Balfour, b. LeMesurier	0
W. W. Jones, ct. Marshall, b. Thornton.....	5	ct. Macnair, b. LeMesurier	1
Ferrie, not out	0	b. Thornton	3
Saunders, did not bat (injured) ..	0	not out................ ...	4
Byes, 10; leg byes, 4	14	Byes, 1; leg byes, 3....	4
Total 146		Total 112	

RUNS AT THE FALL OF EACH WICKET.

	1.	2.	3.	4.	5.	6.	7.	8	9.	10.
1st Innings	18	26	33	43	46	71	133	146	146	146
2nd "	10	32	32	82	98	103	104	105	105	112

BOWLING ANALYSIS.

	1st INNINGS.				2nd INNINGS.			
	Overs.	Runs.	Mdns.	W's.	Overs.	Runs.	Mdns.	W's.
Thornton....	35.2	60	18	4	33.1	43	15	6
LeMesurier..	29	34	15	4	26	50	12	3
Macnair.....	9	25	2	0	7	15	3	1
Stevenson ...	3	13	1	0				

When, as Canadians, we were entertained at the hands of the gentlemen of any country or county with whom we had the good fortune to contend at cricket, we, perhaps not improperly gauged their generosity as a welcome to men who owed allegiance to the same Queen and flag as they themselves did and attributed their generosity to a desire that we should feel that what they termed our sportsmenlike venture, should receive some recognition from them as cricketers. But to Mr. Rogerson's kindness we had to attribute a different motive. He was head master of Merchiston Castle, a school where boys are taught the best precepts to guide them in the career of manhood, and from what we know of that gentleman himself, we feel sure that he takes a deep personal interest in the welfare of the pupils who pass under his hands. It was to show what kind reminiscences he had of the once captain, not only of his cricket eleven but of his school, as well as of his old football captain, Henry, that he invited them and their fellow willow-wielders to dine with him, as much, we think, as for any other reason.

When Mr. Rogerson rose in a fatherly way to greet us to the old school, where he had come in contact with so many Canadian boys, it was with no little emotion that he told how, not many years ago, when frightened parents and timorous authorities thought it best that the pupils should go to their homes away from the ravages of diphtheria, which had got a grip upon the school, Jones had volunteered to stay and nurse those of his school-fellows already stricken down, and fight with him the dread disease within the walls where George had learned to be a man.

A goodly number of the college boys were at the feast, which later resolved itself into a smoking concert, and interspersed between the songs that told of school boy love for college halls, many were the traditions related of bloodless battles fought in days of Jones and Henry. So in the smoke of pipes, in song and story, the evening slipped most pleasantly away and bed time came around. Before we broke up, Mr. Rogerson invited us to a practice on the Castle Green.

The next day was to be a holiday, and in the spirit of a holiday we put it in.

Soon after daylight we were jaunting away to Calendar, past the frowning castle of Stirling and the historic battlefield where Scotland's independence was secured and the royal standard of the Bruces floated on the breeze. A party of children had come to spend the day at Bannockburn, and as Saunders' head emerged from the window of number "147" to get a glimpse of the "bore stone," a Celtic urchin hollered to him "I say, mun, the last time ye washit ye're hair ye didna' dry it and its turned a' rusty." Could Papa Dyce have reached that youngster the field of carnage would have again been flooded with Scotch gore. At Calendar our party, including Dean Jones, of Trinity College, after purchasing copies of Scott's "Lady of the Lake," mounted a coach, piloted by a son of the soil in gaudy uniform, and drawn by four spanking bays, and started for Loch Katrine, famed in song. "The Duke's" recollections of the poet's lay precluded the necessity for reference to our books and "ere the Brig of Turk was won," he had told us in metre all about the run of the hounds, whose course we were following. By the "wild heaths of Uamvar," along the wooded road "where rose Ben Ledi's ridge in air," beside the lake of Vennachar we smoked, chatted, laughed and warbled such melodies that

> "To many a mingled sound at once,
> The awaken'd mountain gave response."

When the Teith had been crossed, we dismounted and walked from the Brig o' Turk to the Trossach's Hotel, where we had luncheon; after which we mounted again, and it was not long before we passed the little mountain, Ben Venue, and hauled up at the shores of famous Loch Katrine. For the first time we saw the heather, which on the bank opposite the landing stage was all a-fire, but the conflagration did not daunt the pibroch blower, whose advent from the far-off mountain side could be distinctly heard. Like Nero, he made music while his country was burning.

After just enough time to gather a few bunches of heather, we set sail out past Ellen's Isle, skimmed across the little lake, locked in on all sides by the flower-covered hills, and found ourselves all too soon at Stronachlacher. But there was much of interest in store for us yet, and the coaching stage to Inversnaid through the most rugged part of the Trossach scenery was charming; so was the long sail past big Ben Lomond down Ben Lomond's lake, at a time when the dogs were bringing in the sheep to fold upon the mountain side, behind which the sun was going to rest for the night. Then rail from Balloch Pier to Edinburgh.

But we had lost a comrade on the journey, for Little, in an ecstacy of admiration of Rob Roy's cave, fell to cogitating how that red-headed robber had here avoided every effort of the English garrison at Inversnaid to bring him to justice, and forgot that the steamboat, whose poetic movement amidst those enchanting scenes was run on base time, so was left amidst the grandeur of his surroundings and the afflictions of poverty, for he had left his purse at home. But he turned up safely next day.

After visiting Merchiston Castle next morning, we boarded "147" for smoky Newcastle. where by the coaly Tyne we hoped to give a better account of ourselves.

Chapter VI.

The Northern Counties Matches.

NORTHUMBERLAND.

Our first match in England commenced on the 22nd of July against the County of Northumberland on the South Northumberland club ground, at Gosforth Park, Newcastle. Ogden again lost the toss, and the Northumbrians commenced batting in the presence of rather a meagre number of spectators. Our team was the same as that at Edinburgh, except that Fleury was playing *vice* Saunders, whose sprained foot did not admit of his exerting himself without the assistance of a walking stick. Ferrie and Gillespie commenced the bowling for us, opening to Phillipson, Oxford's wicket-keeper, and C. R. Toomer. Neither of these batsmen did much, but the next two men, Farmer and Dawson, made a long stand and necessitated all the changes of our bowling being rung. They were still batting at luncheon, and eventually took the score to 163 before being separated shortly after resuming; but the remaining six wickets only added

46 runs, thanks to Ogden, who was well on the spot. Ferrie, whose sprain had been getting worse from over-exertion, dropped out after lunch and Lindsey took his place.

We commenced our innings shortly after four, and though Little, Allan and Ogden did nothing, George Jones and Gillespie made a long stand. The former played a good innings of 25, while the latter hit with more vigor than usual for his 44 and was dismissed on a catch at long leg near the boundary. Of the rest Henry, 14, and Annand, 10, alone got doubles, and the innings closed for 132, of which 23 were extras. There was half an hour left for play, and 20 runs were put on by Northumberland without the loss of a wicket.

Next morning Park and Dawson, the not outs, faced Allan and Ogden, and the first ball of the former's first over disposed of Park. Toomer and Dawson brought up the score to 56, and on the latter's retiring Ogilvie and his partner raised it to 71. Then Phillipson and Toomer made a heartbreaking stand, and the Captain was kept busy " in exercising of his brain" as to how to work the bowling which, notwithstanding his many changes, got unmercifully hammered. Even Henry was tried for a couple of overs. At length Phillipson was caught at the wickets by George Jones; and it may here be noticed that Phillipson, their wicket-keeper, got even with Jones by taking him at the wickets in both innings. The last batsman's 40 had been quickly put together and included no less than 8 fours. Farmer saw 189 go up as he went to the pavilion, and on Fenwick's supplanting him, Gillespie bowled Toomer for a splendid 78. Of the doings of the rest, Sample's 37, compiled in excellent style, need alone be noticed. Ogden, in this innings as in the other, was our most successful bowler, getting 7 for 110.

The Northumbrians having made 253, we wanted 331 to win and had three hours left to make them in. There was not much chance of our winning, but it was possible to make it a draw. We failed signally to do this, and the commencement of our innings was lamentable, the first five wickets falling for 18 runs. Henry, however, by some brilliant hitting, improved the look of the score sheet and contributed of the total of 118 no less than 57 runs, Annand again getting 10 and Fleury 14. This left us in the minority by 212. Our fielding in this match was hardly up to the standard, although the extras allowed to our opponents were only 14 as against 39 which they gave us.

The result was rather depressing, and it may have been our dejected looks which prompted a gentleman to invite us to his home, which adjoined the ground, to partake of his cheer, and where the health of the team was proposed in "extra dry." We were not very apprehensive about our health, but we drank to our success and better luck in bumpers. In a flight of surpassing and surprising eloquence the Manager gratefully acknowledged the compliment and thanked our entertainer for his hospitality.

GENTLEMEN OF NORTHUMBERLAND.

1st Innings.		2nd Innings.	
H. Phillipson, b. Gillespie	10	ct. G. W. Jones, b. Ogden	40
C. R. Toomer, ct. Gillespie, b. Ferrie	7	b. Gillespie	78
W. H. Farmer, ct. W.W. Jones, b. Ogden	68	ct. W. W. Jones, b. Ogden	18
J. W. Dawson, ct. Vickers, b. Ogden	69	ct. and b. Ogden	31
M. Fenwick, run out	14	ct. W. W. Jones, b. Ogden	9
J. F. Ogilvie, ct. Little, b. Ogden	8	ct. Fleury, b. Ogden	14
C. H. Sample, b. Gillespie	1	ct. Little, b. Gillespie	27
S. Brutton, ct. Lindsey, b. Ogden	5	ct. Fleury, b. Ogden	15
Rev. E. W. R. Walters, ct. Annand, b. Ogden	17	ct. G. W. Jones, b. Ogden	1
R. Phillipson, b. Ogden	0	not out	4
F. Park, not out	0	b. Allan	11
Byes, 8; leg byes, 2	10	Byes, 5	5
Total	209	Total	253

RUNS AT THE FALL OF EACH WICKET.

	1.	2.	3.	4.	5.	6.	7.	8.	9.	10.
1st Innings	8	24	140	163	183	186	189	194	209	209
2nd "	24	56	71	151	189	194	215	247	248	253

BOWLING ANALYSIS.

	1st Innings.				2nd Innings.			
	Overs.	Runs.	Mdn's.	W's.	Overs.	Runs.	Mdn's.	W's.
Ferrie	16	29	8	1	..	..	..	..
Gillespie	32	56	12	2	27	66	5	2
Allan	9	14	4	0	16	24	6	1
Ogden	27	49	9	6	45	110	16	7
Annand	16	43	5	0	3	13	1	0
W. W. Jones	7	9	3	0	7	17	2	0
Henry	..	..	..	..	7	18	3	0

GENTLEMEN OF CANADA.

1st Innings.		2nd Innings.	
G. W. Jones, ct. H. Phillipson, b. Walters	25	ct. H. Phillipson, b. Toomer.	3
Little, b. Toomer	0	b. Park	0
Allan, b. Walters	4	b. Park	4
Ogden, ct. Farmer, b. Toomer	5	ct. Fenwick, b. Toomer	3
Gillespie, ct. Dawson, b. R. Phillipson	44	b. Park	8
Henry, ct. Park, b. R. Phillipson	14	ct. Farmer, b. R. Phillipson	57
Vickers, b. R. Phillipson	0	ct. Ogilvie, b. Toomer	0
Annand, b Park	10	ct. Brutton, b. Toomer	10
W. W. Jones, b. Park	8	ct. Dawson, b. Walters	2
Fleury, not out	0	ct. Park, b. R. Phillipson	14
Lindsey, b. Park	0	not out	0
Byes, 8; leg byes, 14	22	Byes, 13; leg byes, 3; wides, 1	17
Total	132	Total	118

RUNS AT THE FALL OF EACH WICKET.

	1.	2.	3.	4.	5.	6.	7.	8.	9.	10.
1st Innings	0	14	35	43	89	105	111	132	132	132
2nd "	2	2	15	15	18	31	54	73	93	118

BOWLING ANALYSIS.

	1st Innings.				2nd Innings.			
	Overs.	Runs.	Mdn's.	W's.	Overs.	Runs.	Mdn's.	W's.
Toomer	13	46	3	2	14	37	5	4
Walters	20	42	9	2	9	21	2	1
R. Phillipson	10	21	3	3	7	14	4	2
Park	2.2	1	1	3	11	29	3	3

Walters bowled 1 wide.

DURHAM.

We left smoky Newcastle behind us at nine o'clock on Saturday night, and after an hour's ride reached Sunderland, where we found very comfortable quarters at the Queen's Hotel. After a stroll about the crowded streets full of workingmen, their wives and daughters, making purchases for the Sunday, and after gorging ourselves with several " fine lines" of cherries, we got to bed early, intending to have a good night's sleep and a good rest on the morrow, and we carried out our intentions in both particulars. From this time a legend was current among us of "Annie and her boots;" the only man who can tell the truth, the whole truth, and nothing but the truth about this story, which undoubtedly dates from this Saturday night at Sunderland, is Billy Vickers.

The next day, Sunday, was put in by us principally in letter-writing and in posting up our diaries which had been suffered to get in arrears since we had jotted down our reflections upon seasickness on board the *Furnessia*. A few of us went in the evening to St. Peter's Church, Monkweirmouth, a peculiar old structure, the original portion of which seemed to have been added to by building by its side at a later date another nave with a row of pillars between the two, a style of church architecture quite new to us. The church, we were told, was originally a monastery, and the old building, of which but a small part is now left, dates back to a very early period.

Monday, July 25th, was another fine day. The Ashbrooke Ground, where we played, is splendidly situated, and considering that this is its first year, the wicket played very well. At one end the rising ground has been terraced and forms an elevated vantage ground from which to enjoy the play. On the Durham team as chosen to play against us were several professionals, and as this was contrary to our arrangement we objected, but it appearing that their selection was an oversight on the part of the Durham committee and that it would be most inconvenient at that late date to make any change, we rested content with having made the protest, and played the team as chosen.

Again the lucky (?) coin came down wrong side up, and again we went to the field. T. Hutton, who went in first with Thompson, contributed 43 and was ably seconded by several members of the team; but it was towards the end of the innings that most of the runs were made by Mr. A. A. Mewburn, who made a creditable 87, in which he hit with great freedom, and at the same time played thoroughly sound cricket. He was not out, but had been missed once before he had scored and a second time at 50. Mr. Hurst who made 50, and Mr. Crossley who scored 31, both lent Mr. Mewburn valuable assistance in bringing the total to 281. Our bowling throughout had been very fair, Ogden with 5 for 67 having done best. We should particularly notice a catch by George Jones at mid-on, and a left-hander at point by Little. Wallace Jones, too, caught Mr. Crossley on a very hot one at cover. Our fielding up to the adjournment for lunch was conceded to be brilliant, but afterwards for some unaccountable reason, fell off lamentably.

George Jones and Saunders opened the ball for us, the latter having Wallace Jones to run for him as he had not quite recovered from his injury. These two batsmen ran the score up to 56 and called on several changes in the bowling, before Jones, in attempting to hit a full pitch, put it up to point. His 25 were very carefully and prettily made, and included several drives to the ropes. Gillespie and Henry were no sooner in than they were out, but Ogden with Saunders took the score to 86, before the former failed to stop a straight one, and a few runs later Saunders was bowled off his pads for a steady 46, in the making of which he was in for over an hour and a half. Allan played for a long time without scoring, and then knocked up 14 runs in short order. Annand made the third zero on our side, and Little and Vickers brought the score to 134 before the call of time, and came in with the fielders, with 16 and 10 respectively to their credit.

"The Gunner's" failure to score, we knew would cause his angry passions to arise, and when he was seen returning from the wicket with the fatal "duck" and an ominous pout, those of the team who inclined to a quiet life, were observed to sidle away from the " Gunner's " objective point, the pavilion ; while others of us who did not weep with those who wept, but rather made such a lachrymose occasion the season for getting in a little fun, waited for developments. The developments soon came—the first indication being a monosyllable uttered "not loud but deep." But monosyllables were inadequate to express the irate Haligonian's opinions of things in general, and of his hard luck in particular, and polysyllables, and involved sentences and curious figures of speech were rolled forth in torrents. After exhausting all known vocabularies "the Gunner" sunk into a state of hopeless despondency, whence however he was aroused, and his equanimity restored, almost as quickly as it had disappeared, by the temerity of Little, who offered odds to no takers that the "Etcetera" would make 100 at least in the second innings.

We had all been made members of the Sunderland Club (social), and spent a pleasant hour or two there that evening.

The next morning Vickers and Little put on 23 runs before the latter was caught and bowled. His 28 was a very useful innings, consisting of 6 fours and 2 twos. Wallace Jones and Vickers tried hard to avert the follow on but failed, the former getting 13 before he was bowled, when trying to pull a ball on his off wicket to leg. Another favorite stroke of the "Parsees" was a cut off the leg stump from a guard, a foot inside the inner wicket.

Neither of them ever came off. Fleury was given out l. b. w. by Shanly, leaving Vickers not out for an admirable 30, and the eleven 97 runs behind and obliged to follow on.

In our next venture Vickers, Saunders, George Jones and Gillespie put on but 20 runs, and it looked as if we might not suceed in saving an inning's defeat. Henry and Ogden, however, completely changed the appearance of the game. They both commenced to score with great freedom, and fours were the order of the day, varied by an occasional 3 or 2 from Ogden, but Henry did not spoil the similarity of his hits until he had made 44, which he accomplished in 11 strokes. They took the telegraph from 35 to 150 in 58 minutes, and, as may be imagined, kept the fielders hard at work and spoiled a good many bowlers' analyses. Henry at length succumbed to Mr. Crossby, after a splendid display of hard hitting, his 77 being made up of 16 fours, 2 threes and 7 singles. Little and Wallace Jones only contributed 15 between them, but Annand remained for some time and put several away to leg very nicely, in his contribution of 13, before Fleury took his place. Meanwhile Ogden continued to score freely and Fleury, too, after a little commenced to hit. When Ogden had made 77 he gave a chance at the wicket, his only mistake, and when he had increased his score to 90 we were all eager to see him complete his century, but, alas, when only 2 short of the coveted three figures, he was bowled, leaving Fleury not out for an excellent and patient 23. Ogden was batting over two hours and a half for his runs and throughout hit freely and with great judgment. The innings closed for 293, which gave us a lead of 196 and made a very even draw of the match. As there were only a few minutes left for play no decisive result could be looked for. Going in again T. Hutton was bowled by Gillespie for 8, and Mr. Pease left not out with 4. One wicket for 12, Durham requiring 184 to win, and having 9 wickets to fall.

COUNTY OF DURHAM.

1st INNINGS.		2nd INNINGS.	
T. Hutton, ct. Annand, b. Gillespie	43		
H. Hutton, ct. G. W. Jones, b. Ogden	15	b. Gillespie	8
T. Thompson, ct. Little, b. Annand	8		
Mr. T. Ward, b. Gillespie	6		
Mr. W. T. Whitwell, ct. Vickers, b. Gillespie	15		
Mr. H. S. Crossby, ct. W. W. Jones, b. Ogden	31		
Mr. A. A. Mewburn, not out	87		
Mr. J. A. Pease, ct. Allan, b. Ogden	2	not out	4
Mr. W. Hirst, b. Allan	50		
Mr. A. K. Williams, ct. Vickers, b. Ogden	12		
J. Harding, ct. Henry, b. Ogden	1		
Byes, 6; leg byes, 5	11		
Total	281	Total	12

RUNS AT THE FALL OF EACH WICKET.

1.	2.	3.	4.	5.	6.	7.	8.	9.	10.
19	45	62	87	92	148	152	233	268	281

BOWLING ANALYSIS.

	1st INNINGS.				2nd INNINGS.			
	Overs.	Runs.	Mdn's.	W's.	Overs.	Runs.	Mdn's.	W's.
Mr. Ogden......	29.2	67	8	5				
Mr. Gillespie...	38	90	9	3	5.3	10	2	1
Mr. Annand....	18	65	2	1	5	2	3	0
Mr. W.W. Jones	5	11	2	0				
Mr. Allan	14	37	4	1				

GENTLEMEN OF CANADA.

1st INNINGS.		2nd INNINGS.	
Saunders, b. Hirst	46	ct. Pease, b. Thompson	6
G. W. Jones, ct. and b. Hirst	25	b. Whitwell	6
Gillespie, ct. Williams, b. Mewburn	0	l.b.w., b. Whitwell	0
Henry, b. Hirst	0	b. Crosby	77
Ogden, b. Mewburn	16	b. Williams	98
Allan, ct. Thompson, b. Harding	15	run out	5
Annand, b. Hirst	0	l.b.w., b. Thompson	13
Little, ct. and b. Whitwell	32	b. Mewburn	1
Vickers, not out	30	ct. Harding, b. Thompson	9
W. W. Jones, b. Thompson	13	ct. Pease, b. Mewburn	9
Fleury, l.b.w. b. Thompson	0	not out	27
Byes, 2; leg byes, 5	7	byes, 31; leg byes, 11	42
Total	184	Total	293

RUNS AT THE FALL OF EACH WICKET.

	1.	2.	3.	4.	5.	6.	7.	8.	9.	10.
1st Innings.....	56	56	56	85	95	97	113	157	178	184
2nd Innings....	11	17	18	35	150	157	169	181	211	293

BOWLING ANALYSIS.

	1st INNINGS.				2nd INNINGS.			
	Overs.	Runs.	Mdn's.	W's.	Overs.	Runs.	Mdn's.	W's.
Thompson	13.3	31	2	2	15	35	6	3
Harding	19	31	9	1	8	20	3	0
Mr. Whitwell ..	16	25	8	1	21	58	8	2
Mr. Hirst	30	61	11	4	9	38	1	0
Mr. Mewburn...	25	22	12	2	13	43	1	2
Mr. Williams...	3	7	1	0	3.2	5	1	1
H. Hutton	..	..	..	..	10	32	0	0
Mr. Crosby.....	..	..	..	..	10	19	3	1
Mr. Ward......	..	..	..	..	1	1	0	0

Here we give a little scene enacted in the corridor of the hotel, just as it appears in the diary of one of our fellows.

The Lay of Saunders' Girl.

> "'Give me a kiss my charming gal'?
>   The cricketer said to a blue-eyed gal,
> 'I won't,' said she, 'you lazy elf
>   Just go ahead and help yourself."

Witness: And he did.
W. J. Fleury.   The Author.

DERBYSHIRE.

When we left Sunderland and crossed the Weir, we might have been said, to use the words of a well-known contributor to the Canadian press on cricket, "to have crossed the Rubicon," for we were in Buxton to wear, for the first time in England, the laurels of victory.

Unable to reach Buxton that night, we were obliged to make Manchester our headquarters till the morning, which we found a difficult task, for on application at midnight, under a drenching rain, for admission to six successive hostleries, we were met with the same unpleasant reminder that it was "hexhibition time," and that the hotels were "hall full hup." By one o'clock, however, we had been admitted into "The Brunswick," an edifice, no doubt, once the resting-place of the earliest nobles of this historic house, and, judging from our short acquaintance, we should not hesitate to declare that its foundation was co-eval with that of the noble line whose name it bears.

By seven we were astir, and at ten, in a shower of rain, we reached Buxton, a pretty little place much frequented by invalids for the virtues supposed to lie in the mineral waters everywhere prevalent. Just opposite our hotel was a picturesque little fountain fabled to have been erected by Mary Queen of Scots, who made yearly pilgrimages here for her health.

Adjoining the hotel are fine, large baths in which we had more than one genuine swim, though we were obliged to curtail the length of our plunges for the reason, that more than a few minutes' stay in the water necessitates the inhaling of too much of the gas which continually bubbles through it, and which has often proved injurious, and even fatal consquences have been known to follow a protracted bath.

"It never rains but it pours"—we won the toss, the game, and had what we had been looking for in vain ever since our arrival—a wet wicket. That we won the toss was the favor of fortune. That we won the game was mainly due to the scoring of Saunders, Henry and Allan, and to the bowling of Gillespie and Ogden.

Our first innings brought us 150 runs, of which Saunders made 46 after two hours of patient batting, and Henry 28 in a fewer number of minutes. Allan's 21 and the general contribution of the rest put our score where not even two essays of the Derbyshire Gentlemen could reach it. At four o'clock they began their innings, and in an hour and a quarter had all come and gone—taking with them in the aggregate but 42 runs.

At half-past five they were obliged to follow on, and lost three of their best wickets for 32 runs, Lindsey getting 2 of them for 6.

All day the wind had been blowing half a gale from the west which materially assisted Ogden in getting the ball across, but then by far the larger part of their bowling had the same advantage, for it was slow too.

Though the tree-tops almost kissed the ground and the bails refused to keep their places, "Butcher Bob," as the corpulent Shanly had been christened because of his resemblance to Virginius the cleaver, stood his ground, in his long, white umpire's coat, quite as unmoved by the fury of the gale, as in olden times were the Senators in long, flowing toga, by the applause of the Forum, which we are told resembled the wind among the oaks on Mount Garganus, and he was just as proud of his appearance as they were.

That evening some explored the pretty environs of Buxton, and enjoyed a quiet walk along the lovely roads and lanes. One charming spot called the "Lovers' Leap" seemed to take the fancy of several of the more romantic, whether by reason of the charming scenery of the spot, or of the tragic story whence the place derives its name, we are not able to say. Others accepted an invitation to the club and had no difficulty in passing an enjoyable evening.

Next morning the wind had somewhat abated, but Gillespie and Ogden were still "on the spot," and our fellows fielded like cats, so that soon after the sun had crossed the meridian the match had terminated in our favor by an innings and 40 runs.

We then adjourned, as we had done the day before, to Athelstone Terrace to lunch, when the Hon. L. K. Jarvis, who presided, welcomed us with hearty goodwill and begged for a renewal of hostilities if we should ever come to England again. That gentleman may rest assured that we will not forget his invitation if we ever do.

A grand lawn tennis tournament was being held in the beautiful Buxton Gardens, and the management had sent word to say that they hoped we would pay them a visit before our departure, and this we were delighted to do, and we had the pleasure of seeing Miss Lottie Dod, the championess of England, trying for supremacy in the single court with an almost equal foe, Miss Langrishe, and of witnessing

Campion, last year's Irish champion, striving for the laurels with Hamilton, who had played cricket against us in Ireland; but before we had the pleasure of witnessing the finish of either set we had to strike tent and make for "London by the sea."

GENTLEMEN OF CANADA.

1st Innings.

Saunders, ct. H. Shipton, b. Parke	46
G. W. Jones, ct. McLachlan, b. W. L. Shipton	5
Gillespie, b. H. Shipton	0
Henry, b. McLachlan	28
Ogden, b. H. Shipton	12
Vickers, b. H. Shipton	0
Allan, ct. Woodruff, b. Parke	21
Little, b. Parke	4
Annaud, l. b. w. b. H. Shipton	6
W. W. Jones, not out	13
Lindsey, b. Parke	4
Byes, 8; Leg Byes, 2; Wides, 1	11
Total	150

RUNS AT THE FALL OF EACH WICKET.

1.	2.	3.	4.	5.	6.	7.	8.	9.	10.
16	19	53	77	77	117	123	130	146	150

BOWLING ANALYSIS.

	Overs.	Runs.	Mdn's.	Wk'ts.
H. Shipton	29	58	6	4
W. L. Shipton	9	6	5	1
McLachlan	8	20	0	1
Finney	8	9	3	0
Grist	7	17	2	0
Parke	13	27	3	4

Parke bowled 1 wide.

GENTLEMEN OF DERBYSHIRE.

1st Innings.		2nd Innings.	
J. McLachlan, ct. Gillespie, b. Ogden	5	b. Lindsey	14
T. J. Warhurst, b. Ogden	3	ct. Little, b. Ogden	12
T. H. Parke, b. Gillespie	3	b. Gillespie	0
Carried forward	11	Carried forward	26

GENTLEMEN OF DERBYSHIRE.

1st INNINGS.		2nd INNINGS.	
Brought forward	11	Brought forward	26
R. G. Hawke, ct. and b. Gillespie	8	b. Gillespie	0
W. L. Shipton, b. Gillespie	8	ct. and b. Gillespie	3
H. Shipton, run out	1	ct. G.W Jones, b. Annand	8
J. L. Grist, ct. Allan, b. Gillespie	0	ct. and b. Ogden	1
T. G. Dickson, ct. Gillespie, b. Ogden	0	b. Annand	14
C. Finney, not out	4	b. Lindsey	5
L. F. Ward, ct. W. W. Jones, b. Ogden	4	not out	8
J. Woodruff, ct. Gillespie, b. Ogden	0	ct. Ogden, b. Annand	0
Byes, 5; Leg byes, 1	6	Byes, 3	3
Total	42	Total	68

RUNS AT THE FALL OF EACH WICKET.

	1.	2.	3.	4.	5.	6.	7.	8.	9.	10.
1st Innings	3	8	16	23	28	30	30	30	42	42
2nd Innings	25	31	32	35	35	39	39	55	68	68

BOWLING ANALYSIS.

	1st INNINGS.				2nd INNINGS.			
	Overs.	Runs.	Mdn's.	W's.	Overs.	Runs.	Mdn's.	W's.
Ogden	23.3	25	11	5	27	25	13	2
Gillespie	23	11	16	4	23	20	14	3
Lindsey	..	..	..	..	6	12	2	2
Annand	..	..	..	..	2.1	8	0	3

Chapter VII.

The first match in the South.

JULY 29 AND 30.—From Buxton to Brighton is a long run so we broke the journey at London, leaving at five and dining on the road at Rugby. It was nearly midnight when we reached the Euston Hotel, but before retiring we supped with our old friend "Juliet," at her rooms.

By ten o'clock the next morning we were whirling out of mighty London, which, from its magnitude, it seemed almost impossible to leave behind, then through the long tunnels under the South Downs till the sea, dancing in the merry sunlight, burst once more upon the view. A good whiff of the sea air is as bracing as a "cock-tail," and our spirits ran high at seeing it again. Out upon the ocean the fishing smacks were plying to and fro, with their woven wings nicely filled with the gentle breeze, while along the parade, the people who had just come over from Goodwood, and the last Jubilee sightseers were taking their morning outing. Princes from the Indies and Chinese diplomats saluted English nobles, and goodness only knows who else.

As soon as we could change to our maroon and

flannels we mounted a four-in-hand and were soon galloping, with more noise from the horn than the surf could drown, "along the shore of the loud resounding sea." We reached the grounds late, a breach of cricketing etiquette very unpardonable in England; but it was the train's fault, not ours. Who should be awaiting us but our "Parson," Aston, to whom we hollered a salutation from the top of the drag. This Anglo-Saxon form of greeting dumbfounded a duchess-dowager spectator, who evidently thought that that sort of thing was done by us by rubbing noses in Ojibway, for she ejaculated in blank astonishment and in an audible voice "why, I declare, they speak English!" This caused "the Baby," Fleury, to laugh so immoderately that the venerable lady formed a mental estimate that even if we had learned to speak English we had not yet learned how to be polite, and relapsed into her seat, quite satisfied that she really knew all about the ways of the aborigines of the great North American Continent.

The Sussex County ground at Hove, is one of the largest and best appointed in England, and if the wicket which they gave to us is no better than those they prepare for all who play there, it would, indeed, be a fastidious cricketer who could find fault with them. Dr. Grace says it is the best wicket in England.

We had hardly taken the field, where we had been sent, before it commenced to rain, and as there was no immediate prospect of Jupiter-pluvius shutting up his watering can, we defied him by going to lunch. Shortly after feeding we were able to resume, and very soon had three wickets for 20 runs, when rain again interfered with the match for five minutes.

Going on again Dudney and Smith pulled the score to 77 before the latter was run out by Saunders, who had already taken Lucas at the wickets. Heasman, who plays hard and accurately, succeeded in shewing some fine cricket, and saw Dudney nicely bowled by Allan, after a patient stand of 31, and Blackman stumped by Saunders, before he himself was sent to the pavilion by a piece of sharp fielding by Ogden.

The last comer, Clements, was the fourth man Saunders disposed of at the wickets that innings. It was no unfair estimate of the wicket-keeper's doings that day, to describe them, as our friends and the press did, as being quite equal to the work of the best English amateurs behind the sticks. Our fielding which had been improving from the day we left Ireland, was now so good as to be fairly termed excellent. Wallace Jones bowled most successfully getting four for 36, and also took Pilcox well on a sharp return. Gillespie held F. M. Lucas on a very hot one sent back to him by that player.

Being 206 behind, Saunders and George Jones started to catch up for Canada, but neither they nor Gillespie did anything, three wickets falling for 27 runs in the seventeen minutes before drawing, during which time we had to bat in a wretched light.

One might spend an evening at Brighton in a hundred ways; most of us spent it listening to a strolling band of negro ministrels, with a very Cockney accent, peculiar to the English negro, warbling the latest comic songs from London. Others strolled to the pier and listened to the bands of music, but all retired early to bed, feeling that we had our work cut out for us next day. And so we had, for after Henry had made 30 and Ogden 12, the rest of the team did so little that we had to follow on, being 133 runs to the bad.

Ferrie, whom we had hoped would have been able to have played here, was still so used up that Lindsey had to take his place. C. A. Smith, the best fast bowler we met in England, and one who will be before our eyes for some time to come as the Captain in Australia of Shaw and Shrewsbury's English team, was mainly responsible for our collaspe. His analysis gave him 8 wickets for 19 runs.

About noon we began our second venture well. Saunders and George Jones made a most determined stand, and had both got into the twenties before the

New Brunswicker fell a victim to Blackman, who was the destructive bowler of this innings. Not long afterwards Saunders succumbed to Pearson. Henry did not stay, but Ogden and Gillespie took the score past 70. Allan was the man destined to be the star of the innings and played carefully till the close for 34 without losing his wicket, the others assisting him to bring the total to 155.

Before the fall of the last wicket we lacked 2 of the Sussex total, and as the Manager strode to the wicket our hopes of getting them were not too sanguine. After he had driven a ball to the off for a single, run 4 more on it as the shy-in passed the wicket-keeper and travelled to the boundary, and then 1 more on another overthrow, making up the only 6 hit that was made so far on the tour, confidence was restored.

Major Edwards laid a shilling that he would not last the next over, this was promptly taken, and he did; and after the Manager had got to the other end the Major laid another "bob" on the same terms only to lose it, and it cost this military gentleman just one half sovereign for his want of confidence in the G. M., for the last wicket put on 24 runs.

With 23 to make to win, Sussex sent the two Lucases to the wicket, C. J. falling a victim to Saunders behind the stumps after scoring 3, but Heasman helped the brother, F. M. to win the match without the loss of any further wickets.

Thus ended the Brighton match in a victory for the Gentlemen of Sussex by 9 wickets. F. M. Lucas, who was not out then has since retired from the cricket field forever. Far from his home and the green fields he loved so well, fever has laid him all alone under the yellow sod scorched by an Indian sun. He was a noble fellow, one of a family, an eleven of which has kept a good team in the field for a whole day, and he was one of the best cricketers in this wonderful family. We can but weep for him for friendship's sake, now Sussex mourns him as a brother lost, and England will miss him when, to play for her, she calls upon her ablest sons.

GENTLEMEN OF SUSSEX.

1st INNINGS.		2nd INNINGS.	
Rev. F. F. J. Greenfield, ct. Allan, b. Gillespie	4		
C. J. Lucas, ct. Saunders, b. Ogden	7	ct. Saunders, b. Gillespie.	3
F. M. Lucas, ct. and b. Gillespie	8	not out	8
C. A. Smith, run out	44		
W. H. Dudney, b. Allan	31		
W. G. Heasman, run out	46	not out	12
A. Blackman, st. Saunders, b. W. W. Jones	18		
E. H. Stevens, not out	23		
C. Philcox, ct. and b. W. W. Jones	7		
F. T. Pearson, l. b. w., b. W. W. Jones	3		
F. Clements, b. W. W. Jones	5		
Byes, 4; leg byes, 5; no balls, 1.	10		
Total	206	Total	23

CRICKET ACROSS THE SEA. 115

RUNS AT THE FALL OF EACH WICKET.

	1.	2.	3.	4.	5.	6.	7.	8.	9.	10.
1st Innings	11	19	20	77	128	160	170	194	198	206
2nd "	8									

BOWLING ANALYSIS.

	1st INNINGS.				2nd INNINGS.			
	Overs.	Runs.	Mdn's.	W's.	Overs.	Runs.	Mdn's.	W's.
Ogden	27	38	10	1	2	7	0	0
Gillespie	37	59	12	2	4	4	2	1
Annand	12	18	4	0				
Lindsey	2	14	0	0				
Allan	20	34	5	1				
W. W. Jones	28.2	33	13	4	2	12	1	0

Annand bowled 1 no ball.

GENTLEMEN OF CANADA.

1st INNINGS.		2nd INNINGS.	
Saunders, ct. Philcox, b. Clements	2	b. Pearson	22
G. W. Jones, ct. Dudney, b. Smith	0	b. Blackman	21
Gillespie, b. Smith	11	b. Blackman	18
Henry, ct. Pearson, b. Smith	30	b. Blackman	3
Ogden, b. Smith	12	ct. Heasman, b. Clements	11
Allan, ct. Dudney, b. Smith	0	not out	34
Little, ct. Dudney, b. Smith	5	st. Dudney, b. Clements	7
Vickers, b. Smith	1	b. Clements	1
W. W. Jones, b. Smith	5	b. Smith	1
Annand, not out	4	ct. Dudney, b. Pearson	11
Lindsey, b. Smith	1	b. Smith	11
Leg-byes, 2	2	Byes, 8; leg byes, 5	13
		Wides, 1; no balls, 1	2
Total	73	Total	155

RUNS AT THE FALL OF EACH WICKET.

	1.	2.	3.	4.	5.	6.	7.	8.	9.	10.
1st Innings	0	4	22	46	46	59	60	68	70	73
2nd "	35	70	78	78	96	103	122	130	135	155

BOWLING ANALYSIS.

	1st INNINGS.				2nd INNINGS.			
	Overs.	Runs.	Mdn's.	W's.	Overs.	Runs.	Mdn's.	W's.
Clements	19	41	4	2	26	34	11	3
Smith	22.2	19	14	8	28.1	56	10	2
Philcox	4	11	0	0	4	8	0	0
Blackman					11	13	6	3
Pearson					9	29	1	2

Philcox bowled 1 no ball.   Pearson bowled 1 wide.

As it was but three o'clock, it was decided that Sussex should play on, and by five, thanks to the successful bowling of Wallace Jones, we had disposed of eight of them for just 100 runs. The improvement of this score on the last, from our point of view, justifies our publishing it.

GENTLEMEN OF SUSSEX.
CONTINUED INNINGS.

F. M. Lucas, b. W. W. Jones	8
W. G. Heasman, b. W. W. Jones	0
C. A. Smith, ct. Saunders, b. Allan	22
E. H. Stevens, ct. Little, b. W. W. Jones	5
W. H. Dudney, ct. Gillespie, b. Allan	12
A. Blackman, ct. and b. W. W. Jones	26
C. Philcox, b. Ogden	8
F. T. Pearson, b. Lindsey	11
F. F. J. Greenfield, not out	4
C. J. Lucas, to bat	0
F. Clements, to bat	0
Byes, 4	4
Total	100

RUNS AT THE FALL OF EACH WICKET.

1.	2.	3.	4.	5.	6.	7.	8.	9.	10.
6	14	31	47	47	70	96	100	—	—

BOWLING ANALYSIS.

	Overs.	Runs.	Mdn's.	W's.
W. W. Jones	19.1	36	4	4
Gillespie	4	21	1	0
Allan	6	15	2	2
Ogden	7	20	3	1
Lindsey	2	4	1	1

Smith and Henry were sprinters, it transpired, so Major Edwards, who is fond of a bit of sport, suggested a dash. After the proper officers had been appointed, the first heat was run, the men coming to the tape abreast; but in the second heat Henry had to acknowledge his antagonist's supremacy. The judges, who had both bet " a small decoction " upon the result of the race, retired with the competitors, the time-keeper, the starter and the referee to the pavilion to pay up. It was then that Major Edwards suggested our adjourning to Preston Park to see the International bicycle races, which we did, and had no sooner reached the Park ground, a magnificent gift of a benevolent gentleman to the public of Brighton, than we were invited to the enclosure ; whence we got the best view of the best bicycle contests we are ever likely to witness. Woodside, the American champion, carried off the prize in the ten mile contest, a clinking race.

Then our host took us to the old palace of the Georges, in the garden surrounding which music, bell ringing, concert and a score of different diversions were going on in the soft light of myriads of lanterns hung among the trees.

After supper and a pipe we turned in, but not before Major Edwards had invited some of us to see his coursing hounds next morning, and to lunch afterwards with him and Mrs. Edwards.

Those who did not go to the Pavilion spent the evening at the New Club, of which we had been made members, and went to London the same night. Those who stayed over were abroad early, wakened by the cheery shout of the fish-wife advertising her fresh mackerel, and were well repaid for their loss of sleep by a grand plunge in the sea and a stroll along the shore, listening to the sailors enticing pleasure seekers to their yachts by the cheery query, " Oos for the next jolly sail ?" Annand had started at daybreak for London in his cricket clothes, his valise, which some one always packed for him, having preceded him the night before, and "the Gunner" confidently assures us that he was not taken for one of Buffalo Bill's Wild West men when he arrived in the metropolis, although he admits he excited a good deal of unenviable attention.

After a visit to the Major's kennels and a look at his coursing hounds, we took a stroll on the Parade, where myriads of gaily clad people had congregated for an airing, and to enjoy the view of the sea as seen beyond the streaming bunting of the hundreds of craft drawn up along the shore.

Having added an appetizer at the club to the one brought on by the invigorating sea breeze, we made our way to headquarters, where we were introduced to Mrs. Edwards, who gave us a hearty welcome. There we spent one of the pleasantest afternoons we enjoyed while we were away, and so long as we have any recollections of the trip we will not fail to couple the kindliest of them with the names of Major and Mrs. Edwards, and we will ever consider it our privilege to have been present with and to have drunk the health of this estimable couple on the anniversary of their wedding day.

We had an hour left for a visit to the Aquarium before we left for London, where we found ourselves once more gathered together, this time at the famous Hotel Victoria, London's newest and jubilee travellers' resort.

We had been photographed by Hawkins at Brighton in what turned out to be an excellent group, and the Gentlemen of Sussex were kind enough to present each of us with a copy of the picture later on. These now hang framed in our collection, and as from time to time we look upon them they will recall the pleasant game we played at "London by the sea."

Chapter VIII.

Lords and London.

August 1 and 2.—The Hotel Victoria is conveniently situated and well appointed, and is beyond question the place to stay at in London. It is not a minute from Charing Cross.

When we rose on bank holiday morning in August, and met at breakfast, it was evident that any feeling of funk which might have existed among us at an earlier stage of our tour had quite disappeared, for on reading in the morning papers the name of the powerful team which was to play against us, only one gentleman on which had not at some time played for the Gentlemen of England against the players, we were not at all dismayed. Let us hasten to explain, it was not because we were confident of making even a respectable showing against them, but because we felt that we would do our best, and from experience gained and continued practice, we were now in a position to put our best foot foremost.

Over at the Oval the great Notts and Surrey match was soon to begin before thirty thousand spectators, a contest which was virtually to determine the supremacy of the winning club, for both were on their previous records, equally in advance of the other first-class counties in England.

When we had been transported in two breaks to the magnificent ground of the Marylebone Cricket Club, the famous "Lords," we found a large number of people waiting our appearance. A look at the ground revealed to us its great size, and its excellent appointments at once impressed us. On inquiry we learned that there was seating accommodation under cover for sixteen thousand people. It is, perhaps, needless to say that the pavilion and dining hall far surpass anything of the kind in England, and they have certainly been designed, not only with a view to convenience but to luxurious ease. Racket and tennis courts exist for those fond of good hard exercise.

The scoring apparatus is a most ingenious piece of mechanism, and enables a spectator at a glance to learn, after any run has been made, not only the total number of runs, the wickets down, and the last man's score, but also the individual scores of the two batsmen, which are increased run by run till a wicket falls.

The field looked level as a billiard table, and here, under as bright a sun as ever shone on old England, we were to play the most important match of our tour.

Ogden being again unsuccessful with the Duke's "certain" coin we were sent to the field, I. D. Walker and A. J. Webbe making their appearance at the wickets at twenty minutes to twelve. Ferrie and the captain, who began the bowling, made way for other trundlers, before at 50 Saunders took the veteran neatly behind the stumps. Ogden then came on again and was successful in disposing of the next three men, but not before 141 had been telegraphed, to which Webbe, Stoddart and Thornton had contributed 43, 36 and 20. The last named made his runs by much freer hitting than either of his more careful companions. O'Brien and Robertson who followed, each contributed 39, Farmer, meanwhile having been retired by Little, who took him at point on a really magnificent catch. The ball had been skyed where it was, perhaps, possible for the wicket keeper, short leg or the bowler to have got to it, but as none of them attempted it, Little, with excellent judgment, jumped in from point and got it almost on the ground.

Welman was destined to make the score of his side that day, but was badly let off by Gillespie in the long field on a drive, which, while the ball was coming, we would have laid heavy odds that fielder would have held; but he didn't and the last wicket was thus enabled to add 76 runs. Not but that Vernon, who is now captaining, we are pleased to note with success, one of the English teams in Australia, was quite worth his score and more too, but he was handicapped by a felon on his finger, which made his playing painful, and his chance of a slip much more probable than if he had been quite sound.

Our fielding was described by the London press as brilliant, and it was mainly due to our proficiency in this department of the game that the score was kept down to 309, for our bowling was on the whole poor. The wicket-keeper again distinguished himself behind the wickets, his work eliciting a lot of decidedly favorable comment.

At four o'clock Saunders and George Jones started for Canada and stayed together till 31, when the New Brunswicker was caught by Thornton in the slips. We had rather feared Robertson's bowling from his reputation, thinking him to be a fast edition of the Brighton demon, but were glad to find that we were able to handle him more successfully than we had managed Smith. Even Alcock who has most enviable record had a poor analysis in this match. Gillespie succumbed to Horner without scoring and Henry got but 12, nor was it till Ogden joined Saunders, who was playing patiently and in capital form, that the score began to assume reasonable proportions. The captain hit about merrily for 22 and when Allan took his place the telegraph showed 135. Runs came freely till at 153 Robertson found his way to Saunders' stumps, that batsman having by a 6 (4 from an overthrow) 4 fours, 2 threes, 8 twos and singles contributed a capital 62. Little's wicket fell that night at 161, leaving the remaining three wickets, including Allan not out with 29, to get 69 on the morrow to save the follow on.

But before we were to accomplish this we were to have the pleasure of dining in the pavilion as guests of the M. C. C. We were asked to sit down in mufti as it was a long way from the ground to the hotel and back. The Hon. E. Chandos Leigh, the President of the Marylebone Cricket Club in its centenary year, presided, supported on the left by Dr. Ogden and on the right by Lindsey, on whose right sat Sir Henry Ponsonby Fane, the Lord Chamberlain. The Club's Secretary, Mr. Perkins, occupied the vice-chair and on his left sat Mr. Thomas Collins, the father of our own "Dook."

The Chairman welcomed us to England as Canadians and as cricketers, and was kind enough to refer to our presence as an event of no small moment in the annals of the centenary year of the Marylebone Club. Our orators, the Captain and Manager, responded in fitting terms to the toast which some fifty gentlemen had done us the honor to drink. We then toasted our hosts and the opposing eleven, and accentuated the spirit of it by three rousing Canadian cheers.

After a response by Mr. I. D. Walker, the captain of the M. C. C., some of the gentlemen retired, wherupon the evening grew frolicsome and songs and stories enlivened the proceedings until nearly midnight, when after a processional hymn to the tune of "Marching back to Georgia," in which the Secretary took a leading part, we said good-night. It was particularly noticeable that our fellows who had attended St. Paul's and Westminster Abbey the day before were in great form for this valedictory chant.

When another fine day broke over Lords, and we were still abed, we little dreamed that before the sun set, we would achieve anything like the success we met with that day. Thanks to Allan, Annand and Wallace Jones, we not only saved the follow on but came within 55 of the 309 which the Gentlemen of the M.C.C. had amassed the day before. Annand for once had the luck to make a stand, and Allan added 49 runs by good, sound free cricket to his 29 of the night before. He was unfortunately the last man but one to get out. His 78 included 1 five, 6 fours, 6 threes and 8 twos.

Precisely at one o'clock Thornton and Walker strolled out to the wickets and stayed there, not only until lunch time, when they had piled up 91 runs in 50 minutes, but afterwards till the telegraph shewed 112, when Thornton was well caught as third man by Wallace Jones off Ogden, who was destined in this innings to make a brilliant bowling record for himself. Thornton's 58 was the first score of over the half century which he had ever succeeded in making at Lords, though by his free hitting he has made many a century elsewhere. Stoddart, who had an average of 300 runs,—having made 900 for three times out,—the week before retired with a single. Two for 114. Just then Webbe tossed up an easy one to Little at point and went to the pavilion with 36 to his credit. Three for 117.

On reference to the runs at the fall of each wicket it will be seen that the rest of the eleven fared badly, hardly averaging 6 runs apiece after Walker, like Stoddart, had been taken by Saunders at the wickets.

Ogden's analysis 9 for 83 runs speaks for itself, but George Jones' two rattling catches at mid-off need to be mentioned. Henry took Farmer just by the pavilion on the best catch that was made on the tour, and was loudly applauded for his brilliant bit of fielding. Saunders again kept wickets in first class style and thereby sent up his cricketing stock immensely.

In our second innings we had two hours to play, and wanted 248 runs to win. Of these we had made at the call of time 139 or just 109 short, for the loss of 6 wickets. George Jones and Allan were the main contributors to our second total and in this his best score so far, the "Blue nose" shewed to great advantage, making his 53 runs by faultless cricket. Allan did not lose his wicket, and to him falls the proud distinction of having made 113 runs at Lords, for once out. We need hardly say we were thoroughly satisfied with the result of our game, which may be fairly said to have ended in a respectable draw. In the two days no less than 894 runs were scored for the loss of 36 wickets, figures which shew at once the perfection and quickness of the wicket.

GENTLEMEN OF M. C. C.

1st Innings.		2nd Innings.	
A. J. Webbe, b. Ogden	43	ct. Little, b. Ferrie	36
I. D. Walker, ct. Saunders, b. W. W. Jones	14	ct. Saunders, b. Ogden	43
A. E. Stoddart, st'pd. Saunders, b. Ogden	36	ct. Saunders, b. Ogden	1
C. J. Thornton, ct. G. W. Jones, b. Ogden	20	ct. W.W. Jones, b. Ogden	58
T. C. O'Brien, b. Allan	38	ct. Gillespie, b. Ogden	6
J. Robertson, ct. Henry, b. Annand	37	ct. and b. Ogden	6
J. H. Farmer, ct. Little, b. Annand	2	ct. Henry, b. Ogden	0
C. H. Allcock, run out	10	b. Ogden	1
F. T. Welman, not out	50	ct. G. W. Jones, b. Ogden	9
C. E. Horner, b. Ferrie	0	ct. G. W. Jones, b. Ogden	6
G. F. Vernon, b. Gillespie	29	not out	0
Byes, 17 ; leg byes, 10	27	Byes, 22 ; leg byes, 3	25
Total	306	Total	191

RUNS AT THE FALL OF EACH WICKET.

	1.	2.	3.	4.	5.	6.	7.	8.	9.	10.
1st Innings	50	73	115	141	195	208	211	233	233	306
2nd "	112	114	118	130	147	149	179	185	185	191

BOWLING ANALYSIS.

	1st Innings.				2nd Innings.			
	Overs.	Runs.	Mdn's.	W's.	Overs.	Runs.	Mdn's.	W's
Ferrie	30	49	6	1	16	23	7	1
Ogden	37	80	12	3	32	83	7	9
Gillespie	25	71	4	1	11	18	4	0
W.W.Jones	7	24	1	1				
Allan	11	28	0	1	5	12	0	0
Annand	14	29	4	2	16	30	4	0

GENTLEMEN OF CANADA.

1st Innings.		2nd Innings.	
Saunders, b. Robertson	62	ct. Webbe, b. Horner	2
G. W. Jones, ct. Thornton, b. Horner	11	b. Robertson	53
A. Gillespie, b. Horner	0	l. b. w., b. O'Brien	10
Henry, ct. Robertson, b. Allcock	12	ct. sub., b. Allcock	14
Ogden, b. Allcock	22	ct. Webbe, b. Allcock	2
Allan, ct. Welman, b. Webbe	78	not out	35
Little, ct. and b. Stoddart	8		
Vickers, b. Stoddart	3		
Annand, b. Robertson	21		
Jones, W. W., not out	14	ct. and b. Robertson	4
Ferrie, b. O'Brien	0		
Byes, 20; leg byes, 2; wides, 1	23	Byes, 18; leg byes, 1.	19
Total	254	Total	139

RUNS AT THE FALL OF EACH WICKET.

	1.	2.	3.	4.	5.	6.	7.	8.	9.	10.
1st Innings	31	31	49	88	135	153	161	208	253	254
2nd "	13	16	40	62	129	139				

BOWLING ANALYSIS.

	1st Innings.				2nd Innings.			
	Overs.	Runs.	Mdn's.	W's.	Overs.	Runs.	Mdn's.	W's.
Webbe	20	27	11	1				
Robertson	29	50	12	2	16.2	28	9	1
Horner	24	30	12	2	20	40	7	1
Allcock	34	60	14	2	23	50	8	2
Walker	11	37	2	0				
Stoddart	7	14	1	2				
O'Brien	3	7	0	1	8	2	6	1

Allcock bowled 1 wide.

We were delighted to see that day, among those who had come to watch us play, the familiar faces of at least a "jubilee" of Canadian acquaintances, of whom we cannot refrain from mentioning by name the Rev. Head Master of Trinity College School, Port Hope, Dean Jones of Trinity University, who had more that once paid us the compliment of visiting us, Mr. and Mrs. Reynold Gamble, Mr. and Mrs. Harcourt Vernon, D'Arcy Boulton and George Brunel. "The Parson" and Fred. Jones, Biddy's brother, had been with us some days ere we concluded at Lords, but we are sorry to say left us there.

All these fellow countrymen, clothed and in their right minds, bore evidence to the fact that Canadians are not, as the chambermaid at the hotel had expected to find us, Indians after the manner of those who, in a suburb of London, had been chasing the stage coach in "Buffalo Bill's" wild west show day after day, to the terror of its occupants, usually some venturesome London notables.

Through the kindness of the committee of the St. George's Club, of which we were made honorary members, we had the privilege of meeting other Canadians in London, at that hospitable resort in Hanover Square. We received, too, invitations to play the Royal Engineers at Woolwich, and the Royal Artillery at Shoeburyness, at which latter place the officers expressed a desire to entertain us, and nothing but inability to find time for these matches prevented us from heartily accepting.

We had two days left in London, for a rest, before we were to join issue with the United Services at Portsmouth, and we were not at a loss for plenty of amusement to fill up the time at our disposal.

Our old friend Innes, who had been with us off and on ever since we left Scotland, dined us all at the Café Royal on Tuesday night, and later took us to his boxes at the Alhambra to see the Nadia ballet. After such a successful day, we were just in the humor for the free and easy spread which that gentleman had provided, and we think he will do us the credit to say that we did his hospitality justice. It was as pleasant a little event as we fell across on our trip, and the name of the gallant lieutenant will long be remembered by us; especially by Gillespie, for if "Mr. Gilloosby's" tender farewell to Lady Jane was not the beginning of what may ultimately ripen into a lasting affection, then we don't know anything about matrimony.

After "Mr. Gilloosby" had retired to rest, the Manager, who had arrived later at the hotel, knocked at his door and queried, in Cockney accent:

"Kan I 'ave yer butes, sir?"

"Oh! confound it, yes, I forgot to put them out," responded "Gilloosby" in a dreamy voice, which betokened his having been awakened out of a sound sleep. Getting up to repair his mistake, and on opening the door to get a streak of light to assist him in finding his errant "cowhides," he came face to face with the "G. M.," radiant in smiles, who congratulated him upon his success with Lady Jane. Just what "Mr. Gilloosby" said will not be repeated, and whether or not, after he had bolted the door, he again got up to put out his boots, which had been shied back through the fanlight, we don't know.

Next morning, after a late breakfast and a purchase of nearly half the dry goods of mighty London, we adjourned to see the concluding day's play of the great Notts-Surrey game. After lunching with Mr. Alcock and several of the gentlemen playing in the match at the Oval, we went on a tour of inspection with Lord Oxenbridge through the House of Lords and the House of Commons.

In the Lower House, the representatives of England's great people were discussing one of the crucial clauses of the land bill, and we had the pleasure of hearing many of the Irish members state their views as to the instructions which should be given to the commissioners, when fixing the rents of Irish farms, and of listening to the Irish Secretary and the leader of the Government in reply.

That evening we spent with friends, and next morning were journeying to Windsor Castle, where, through the kindness of Sir Henry Ponsonby Fane, we were admitted to the private as well as the State apartments of the Queen's residence. We were unable to take advantage of a drive through the park to Virginia Water, which had been arranged for us, as time would not permit. Having been thoroughly shown the chapels, towers, armouries and galleries of that grand old castle, lingering longest in the Waterloo chamber, where hang Sir Thomas Lawrence's portraits of the reigning sovereigns of Europe and of the leading statesmen and warriors conspicuous in the stirring events of 1812, and beside the tomb in the Albert Memorial Hall, where lie all that remains of the late Prince Leopold, we felt it a great privilege to be allowed to wander at will among the drawing-rooms and *salons*, where our beloved Queen lives the domestic life of which her people are so proud. The principal pictures which hang upon the walls of the long, private gallery are representations of events in the life of the Queen and her family, and there is a home appearance about the whole place, which shews that even Kings and Queens are human and love best, like every man and woman, what is natural and of their own kin. There were there many things upon which we dwelt with reverence, such as the Bible of the gallant

Chinese Gordon; others which excited our curiosity as Hadyn's harpsichord did; others at which we marvelled, as we did at the huge gold punch bowl of the last of the Georges. The presents from other monarchs were very numerous and beautiful, and made us feel how high our noble Queen stands in the estimation of the world. The spit in the kitchen, upon which the oxen are roasted at Christmas, bore testimony to the fact that amidst all this wealth and grandeur of the Royal Palace the poor are not forgotten.

Chapter IX.

Portsmouth and the Oval.

On Thursday evening, August 5th, we left the great metropolis and accompained by Mr. Lyndhurst Ogden who had joined us there, steamed down to Portsmouth, arriving about ten o'clock. We regretted to learn that we were too late to take advantage of an invitation from the General commanding the district, to a grand Military Musical Festival which was given in our honor by the massed bands of the garrison at Governor's Green.

Our headquarters at the Pier Hotel, South Sea, were very comfortable. The breeze blowing over from the sea which was but a quarter of a mile away, across the open common in front of us, was most welcome in the heat, which had become quite Canadian in its intensity.

The United Service Recreation ground was not far distant from the Hotel, and being "tooled" there in our brake next morning, we saw at a glance that there would be a lot of runs made. At all times the ground is a fast one, and on this occasion, by reason of the exceptionally dry weather, it was a little more so. Having the good fortune to win the toss, we expected to give our opponents a long field day, but our score of 159 was barely a "respectable total," and considering the favorable conditions of the wicket for scoring we ought to have done better.

We commenced badly. When our military opponents had been thrown out in skirmishing order, George Jones and Saunders paraded to the wickets, but the former soon got the right-about face and marched back again to the pavilion, being bowled for 4 by Adam, who also got Gillespie for 0 and Henry for 1. Three down for 23. On Ogden going in a stand was made, his wicket putting on 25 before he was bowled for a good 22 ; and shortly after Allan had filled the breach Saunders was bowled for a patient 33. Five for 76. At the same total Fleury was bowled, but Annand who followed helped Allan to take the score to 94, when the latter was retired for a meritorious 24. Vickers played well for his 20 and was then unfortunately run out, Of the others, Little (15) alone got into "doubles."

At four o'clock the United Services commenced their innings, the vanguard, Wyld and Bethune, making a long stand and putting on 84 runs before Wyld was caught at the wickets for 27. Our opponents were a very strong batting team, and with two exceptions got into double figures, Major Bethune making the first century which was made against us, 105, which he put together in about two hours by good cricket. Of the rest of the team, Barnes with 49 played perhaps the best innings, though we were very much taken with Major Wynyard's vigorous and pretty style. Col. Wallace, too, who was the officer in command of the United Service's eleven batted admirably for his 30, as also did Caunter, who was not out, for his 32. The total of the innings was the respectable figure 351. Our fielding at the start was good, but in the course of this long innings, as might be expected, the men got a little slack. Ferrie with 4 wickets for 96 was our most successful trundler.

It was not till one o'clock on the Saturday that we commenced our second innings in a minority of 191, and it looked quite as if we might be beaten in an innings, but the men played splendidly considering what an uphill game was before them, and succeeded after all in making a draw. This was mainly due to the invaluable contributions of Henry and Allan, the former of whom, though missed early in his innings, put together 66 runs by some tall hitting. Allan at first played most carefully and patiently, but when he got set knocked up his runs and "formed fours" at a good rate. His innings, we think, the best he played on the tour, and when he was stumped by Temple off a lob from Major Bethune, he had contributed 86. This total was made up of 6 fours, 7 threes, 7 twos and singles, but its value to us cannot be estimated merely by the number of notches it contained. On his retirement the telegraph showed 206 and before stumps were drawn at a quarter to seven, 61 more runs had been added. Some idea of the dogged way in which the men played to keep their wickets up and make a draw, may be gathered from the fact that we were batting exactly five hours for 267 runs. Gillespie and Fleury played very patiently for their 25 and 22, and Wallace Jones contributed a good 16. Besides this useful contribution, Fleury proved of much service in scoring leg-byes by performing a peculiar *flank movement* in which he became a great adept. Our total of 267 we had got for the loss of 10 wickets; we were playing 12 a side, and were therefore 75 runs on and had still a wicket to fall.

GENTLEMEN OF CANADA.

1st INNINGS.		2nd INNINGS.	
Saunders, b. Barnes	33	b. Adam	9
G. W. Jones, b. Adam	4	b. Adam	2
Gillespie, b. Adam	0	b. Hornby	25
Henry, b. Adam	1	ct. Westmoreland, b. Barnes	66
Ogden, b. Rice	22	b. Hornby	9
Allan, ct. Westmoreland, b. Rice	24	stp'd. Templar, b. Bethune	86
Fleury, b. Barnes	0	ct. Bethune, b. Barnes	22
Annand, ct. Wynyard, b. Caunter	22	b. Adam	1
Vickers, run out	20	b. Caunter	9
Little, b. Adam	15	not out	5
W. W. Jones, ct. Wallace, b. Wyld	8	b. Bethune	16
Ferrie, not out	3	to bat	
Byes, 2; leg byes, 4; no balls, 1	7	Byes, 12; leg byes, 5	17
Total	159	Total	267

RUNS AT THE FALL OF EACH WICKET.

	1.	2.	3.	4.	5.	6.	7.	8.	9.	10.
1st Innings.....	15	15	23	58	76	76	94	119	135	153
2nd Innings....	11	32	132	134	153	206	211	226	232	267

BOWLING ANALYSIS.

	1st INNINGS.				2nd INNINGS.			
	Overs.	Runs.	Mdn's.	W's.	Overs.	Runs.	Mdn's.	W's.
Adam	18.3	41	3	4	37	57	13	3
Hornby..........	5	14	0	0	26	38	14	2
Rice	34	51	13	2	22	47	6	0
Barnes	8	21	0	2	13.3	34	6	2
Caunter	15	22	4	1	25	39	11	1
Wyld	2	3	0	1	4	14	2	0
Bethune.........	..	..	..	..	12	21	1	2

Rice bowled 1 no ball.

UNITED SERVICES.

Major Bethune (late Hants Regt.), ct. Little, b. Ogden..........103
W. G. Wyld (Hants Regt.), ct. Saunders, b. Allan 27
E. G. Wynyard (King's Regt.), l.b.w., b. Ogden 20
G. Barnes (R.M.A.), l.b.w., b. Ferrie 49
H. A. Hornby (South Lancashire Regt.), ct. Saunders, b. W.
  W. Jones... 10
Captain Rice (Com. & Trans. Corps), ct. Ferrie, b. Gillespie.... 3
Lieut. Maurice (Royal Fusiliers), b. Ferrie..................... 27
Lt.-Col. N. W. Wallace (late K.R.R.), ct. Ogden, b. Allan 30
H. G. Westmoreland (Hants Regt.), b. Ferrie 21
J. E. Caunter (Welsh Regt.), not out 32
Lieut. Adam (South Lancashire Regt.), b. Ogden 13
Lieut. Templar (R.M.A.), b. Ferrie............................. 4
  Byes, 6; leg byes, 6....................................... 12

  Total 351

RUNS AT THE FALL OF EACH WICKET.

1.	2.	3.	4.	5.	6.	7.	8.	9.	10.	11.
84	127	178	204	209	226	271	279	299	320	351

BOWLING ANALYSIS.

	Overs.	Runs.	Mdn's.	W's.
Ogden	43	106	14	3
Ferrie ,...................	34	96	8	4
Gillespie	20	39	8	1
W. W. Jones...............	14	37	3	1
Allan	13	27	6	2
Annand	12	34	1	0

At the excellent lunch provided for us on the second day, Col. Wallace proposed, in very kind terms, the health of the team, and wished us success in our other matches, which sentiments were duly acknowledged by the Captain and the Manager. Before having done with the United Service Ground, we must not fail to record our appreciation of the efforts made to secure our comfort there, and in this, particularly recognize the kindness of Major Lambart, the Secretary.

On both days the play was watched by a large gathering, the most fashionable we had played before; however, we are perhaps not warranted in thinking that our maroon coats were the attraction,— it is the scarlet jacket, in England as the world over, that draws the ladies. The pleasure of the spectators, if not of the players, was enhanced by the performance each afternoon of selections by regimental bands; that of the Royal Marine Artillery played on Friday, and the Royal Marine Light Infantry on Saturday.

Corney Grain, who is so much in demand for afternoons in England, happened to be playing at Portsmouth, and Col. Wallace kindly secured the front row of seats for us at Portland Hall, Saturday night. Mr. Grain's best touches are his running hits at some of the absurdities of English social life, and he tickled us immensely by a vivid description of a visit of a school boy and his friend to his uncle, who took them to luncheon at his club on the afternoon of their arrival. The youngsters' feelings in the novel situation got the better of them, and the uncle rebuked Smoucher, his nephew, by admonishing him that while he was a boy he must behave as a gentleman, but when he grew up he could do as other men did; to which the only reply vouchsafed was a stentorian Haw! Haw! And so on in the same vein, occasionally breaking in with some charming little fragment on the piano.

So soon as the performance was over Mr. Grain accompanied us to sup with Colonel and Mrs. Wallace at "Eastern Villa." After doing justice to a very *recherché* supper, we adjourned to the smoking-room, where Lyndhurst Ogden amused the Englishmen with his description of "How we raised the wind" for Cricket in Canada ; and the iron tongue of midnight had tolled twelve long before we reluctantly left our bowls and cigars and strolled out into the fresh night air.

Arrangements had been made for our spending a busy Sunday, and through the kindness of Col. Wallace and Major Lambart, we were enabled to visit the strongest of the Spithead forts, built out in the sea, and which, having their fresh water supplied by means of a pipe connected with a spring in the rock under the forts, are almost independent of the mainland. The fleet having come into the harbour over night, we were taken by our steam launch down one line of iron-clads and up the other, passing the "Minotaur," "Bellerophon," "Monarch," and "Collingwood," as well as many others.

Col. Wallace, who, in spite of the extreme heat, was most indefatigable in his attentions, called at our hotel in the afternoon, and took us to the dockyards. The first thing which attracted our attention was a huge mass of steel, pointed at both ends, which turned out to be the "Camperdown," just launched. After inspecting the hydraulic apparatus for loading her turret guns, and being much astonished at finding her sides to be six feet in thickness, our guide led the way to the torpedo boats, passing on the way the "Shah," one of the old style of wooden war-ships. Safe on board one of the torpedo boats, the officer in command was kind enough to have one of the projectiles taken from its shell, and explained to us its mechanism, and demonstrated pratically the way it was propelled.

Having seen these deadly engines of war, the next thing in order was to witness their effectiveness, which was fully evidenced by the hole in the cove bunkers of the iron-clad "Resistance," then undergoing repairs in dry dock. Thence, passing the "Excellent" and the world famed "Victory" of mighty Nelson, we came to the dock where the "Trafalgar," then on the stocks, but since launched as the largest man-of-war afloat, was in course of construction.

After going over the "Euphrates," a troopship, we returned to our hotel, having spent a most enjoyable, and probably the most interesting day we experienced while away.

SURREY.

August 8th.—Eleven o'clock on Monday saw us all at the world-famed and now almost historic Oval.

Before commencing, we had a little practice at the nets from some of the ground bowlers, which, punctually at 11.25, was put a stop to by the ringing of the first bell. The Captain called "heads," the penny came down with the Royal image uppermost, and of course we went in. The pitch proved very fiery, not to say dangerous, and when George Jones and Saunders, who went in first, had put on 33 runs it "bumped" so badly, that Trollope, the Surrey Captain, after a consultation with his men, suggested a change of wicket, to which proposal the batsmen were not loath to accede. This stopped the play for a time, but almost immediately upon resuming George Jones was caught at point for 16, and a few overs later Saunders was out l. b. w. for 18. Allan and Henry made a stand, and the latter was just getting set when he was unluckily run out. Three for 81. Ogden and Gillespie added nothing, and when Allan was caught for a carefully made 30, six wickets had fallen for 88. Vickers and Annand while in together added 22, both batting in good form Little played patiently for his 13 not out, but none of the others did much, the last three wickets only adding 31, and we were all out at a quarter-past three for 141. The bowling on the whole was good, though no one shone particularly.

Wyld, who had played against us at Portsmouth, and Bush, commenced for Surrey; Ogden and Gillespie bowling first, but full many a time and oft had changes to be made before at length Bush was well caught by Gillespie in the long field off Ogden for a freely made 65. One for 131. Meanwhile, Wyld had played steadily, and when "coopered" by Ogden had made 57. His innings was a fine exhibition of batting. These were, however, the only two wickets we succeeded in getting that day and at half-past six Surrey had 203 runs, Trouncer and L. A. Shuter being the not outs, with 31 and 23 respectively.

Our fielding had not been good and several chances were missed. Early in the game Saunders, who had up to this time kept wickets in all the matches he had played in, had to retire from his post owing to a badly bruised hand.

While we were having our pleasant (?) little outing under the fierce afternoon sun, and when not engaged in tearing frantically after the ball to "save the boundary," we were offering up fervent prayers that the batsmen might inadvertently knock over their wickets, or handle the ball, or do anything else contrary to the rules of the game which would procure their dismissal; for we seemed incapable of effecting that result. All at once we were surprised and pleased to see both batsmen walk off together, as if by arrangement, towards the pavilion. The idea that they had had enough of it and were going to let some other men come in and amuse themselves by hammering the bowling for the rest of the afternoon flashed across our minds, which were by this time so addled by the combined influence of the heat and the monotony of leather hunting, that even such a circumstance as this would hardly astonish us; but we were scarcely less gratified to find that the retirement, though only a temporary one, was to meet halfway the celebrated "Oval Cup," brought on the field in the old silver bowl, on its mission to reinvigorate the batsmen and to revive the weary field. Though the first draught hissed and sizzled in our burning throats, the grateful nectar inspired us to renewed efforts, and made us no longer regret the hard work which created in us a double capacity for enjoying the refreshing cup. Only those who have roasted and then tasted can appreciate the sensation which once experienced can never be forgotten.

That evening we were entertained at a most excellent dinner by the Surrey Club at the Oval Pavilion. The President, Lord Oxenbridge, occupied the chair, and Mr. Alcock, who by his well-timed counsel and active services generously given, had done so much for us ever since the project of our tour was broached, filled the vice-chair. Several of the well known Surrey veterans were present, among them Dr. Jones and Mr. "Billy" Burrup, and we had also the pleasure of meeting here, for the first time, Mr. H. J. H. Scott, the Captain of the Australian team of 1886. After the toast of the Queen, which, it is needless to say, was here as everywhere drunk with the greatest enthusiasm, the chairman proposed the toast of " Our Royal Landlord, the Prince of Wales," and then " Our Guests," the Canadian team, of whom he spoke in the heartiest and kindliest way. Ogden, being unavoidably absent Lindsey responded, and before sitting down, in a few well-chosen remarks, thanked Mr. Alcock for the many services he had rendered the team in the arrangement of our tour, and for the great kindnesses received at his hands in other ways, and asked him to accept from us as a small memento of our visit and of our appreciation of what he had done for us, a silver cigar case and match box, which had been suitably inscribed. Other toasts followed, and some excellent speeches, one by Dr. Jones was really a masterpiece of oratory, in which the speaker dwelt upon the grandeur of the game and the manly qualities it called forth, and pictured an ideal match so eloquently as to quite carry away his audience. Some good songs, too, were sung, and after a very jolly evening we broke up about half-past eleven.

Next day, Trouncer had added but two to his overnight score when he was bowled by Gillespie, but it took a very long time to get rid of Shuter. He saw several wickets go down before he was at length dismissed for 102, a very good innings, albeit marred by several chances; several times, too, had he been clean beaten by the bowling. His score comprised 8 fours, 5 threes and 12 twos. He was well taken by Wallace Jones on a running catch at the Pavilion off Ogden, when the telegraph showed 384. Trollope played a good innings of 69 and Horner contributed a useful 25 (not out), the innings closing for 432.

Of our bowlers, Ogden was by far the most successful, taking 6 for 129. Gillespie, the only other to get more than one wicket captured two at a cost of 75.

With 291 runs to make to save a single innings defeat, we commenced our second venture at about four o'clock. There was only the prospect of a defeat or a draw, and on the cut up wicket and in the face of such a tremendous lead, it looked as if we might neither stay there till the call of time nor avert a defeat by an innings at least. Little and Saunders, however, commenced to play with a steady determination of securing a draw, and put on 61 runs before the former, after a careful and patient innings, was bowled by Horner for 23. Henry's innings, if it had not the merit of patience was none the less valuable, for he scored at a great rate, and seemed to be particularly strong in his half-drives, by which strokes he made several boundaries near the scoring booth. The total was taken to 127 before he was caught at the wicket by Bambridge off Bowden, who had discarded the gloves to try his hand with the ball. Allan partnered Saunders and at six o'clock, when stumps were drawn, both were still at it, Saunders being not out for an excellent innings of 71, the best of the match, as the English papers said, made up of 4 fours, 5 threes, 11 twos and singles, and Allan not out with 9. Total for two wickets 149, leaving us in a minority of 142 with 8 wickets to fall.

GENTLEMEN OF CANADA.

1st INNINGS.		2nd INNINGS.	
Saunders, l.b.w., b. Bush	18	not out	71
G. W. Jones, ct. Trollope, b. Horner	16		
Allan, ct. Bambridge, b. Harvey	30	not out	9
Henry, run out	16	ct. Bambridge, b. Bowden	40
Ogden, b. Bambridge	0		
Gillespie, b. Bambridge	0		
Vickers, l.b.w., b. Harvey	16		
Annand, ct. Trollope, b. Bush	12		
W. W. Jones, b. Bush	6		
Little, not out	13	b. Horner	23
Ferrie, ct. Langton, b. Horner	8		
Byes, 5; leg byes, 1	6	Byes, 6	6
Total	141	Total	149

RUNS AT THE FALL OF EACH WICKET.

	1.	2.	3.	4.	5.	6.	7.	8.	9.	10.
1st Innings	33	47	81	86	86	88	110	120	124	141
2nd Innings	60	129	..	..	..	..	..	..	..	..

BOWLING ANALYSIS.

	1st INNINGS.				2nd INNINGS.			
	Overs.	Runs.	Mdn's.	W's.	Overs.	Runs.	Mdn's.	W's.
Horner	24	41	12	2	25	45	7	1
Bush	33	51	12	3	14	23	4	0
Harvey	20	27	12	2	12	13	9	0
Bambridge	9	16	6	2	8	20	2	0
Trollope	1	0	1	0	4	16	0	0
Trouncer	..	..	..	..	7	12	4	0
Bowden	..	..	..	..	4	14	0	1

GENTLEMEN OF SURREY.

F. W. Bush, ct. Gillespie, b. Ogden	65
W. G. Wyld, b. Ogden	57
C. A. Trouncer, b. Gillespie	33
L. A. Shuter, ct. W. W. Jones, b. Ogden	102
E. C. Bambridge, ct. Vickers, b. Ogden	3
M. P. Bowden, ct. Ogden, b. Allan	5
T. P. Harvey, b. Ogden	16
W. S. Trollope, b. Annand	69
R. N. Douglas, ct. Little, b. Ogden	3
R. Langton, ct. Ferrie, b. Gillespie	10
C. E. Horner, not out	25
Byes, 23; leg byes, 20; wides, 1	44
Total	432

RUNS AT THE FALL OF EACH WICKET.

1.	2.	3.	4.	5.	6.	7.	8.	9.	10.
130	150	206	211	236	281	384	389	391	432

BOWLING ANALYSIS.

Ogden	78	129	35	6
Gillespie	40.3	75	12	2
Allan	26	31	8	1
Ferrie	28	49	10	0
W. W. Jones	22	44	8	0
Annand	18	60	3	1

Ferrie bowled 1 wide.

Mr. "Billy" Burrup has the distinction of being one

of those who virtually made the Oval, and for years he has been one of the most prominent members of the Surrey club: his past deeds are engraven in cold marble set into the wall of the large hall of the pavilion, but his heart beats warm as ever. Knowing how pleased young men are to be shewn the sights of the great city, he very kindly volunteered to act as guide for a day upon our return to London. We were not slow to close with such an advantageous offer, and Mr. Burrup was ready for us when we turned up. First he took us through the Bank of England, where we saw each of the component parts of that wonderful institution performing its functions. The next move was to Guildhall, where the Lord Mayor's Court was assembled for the first time after vacation; thence to Newgate gaol where we were shewn a number of objects of interest, among them the gallows upon which all the criminals confined there for the last thirty years, who had merited the punishment of death, had been hanged. Hard by was the bag of sand which had been used to test the rope by which Lipski had been hanged, and the good-natured warden who was shewing us about, "swung it into eternity" just to let us see "how it was done." Not contented with being our "showman," Mr. Burrup very kindly invited our party to refresh themselves at a neighboring hotel; again we accepted, and after a thoroughly enjoyable day left, very sorry to part with the genial gentleman who remembers the Surrey ground as a cabbage garden, and who was, indeed, mainly instrumental in rescuing it from the encroachments of brick and mortar and transmuting it into the famous Oval.

Chapter X.

Hampshire and the Home of Grace.

HAMPSHIRE.

AUGUST 10th.—We had to bundle out of London on Tuesday night without any dinner, and had a long and tedious run to Southampton, which we reached an hour before midnight, and retired after polishing off a hearty supper at the Royal Hotel.

The absence of rain for so long a period had left the county ground like iron in hardness, and at times the ball, driven from the pavilion end, would roll as much as 250 yards if it happened to escape the fence posts, which alone form the southern boundary of the ground. Fortune favored us in the toss, Saunders had the first whack at the new ball, and the Captain the next; Currie and Armstrong trundled it. The field was level as a billiard table, the wicket an excellent fast-scoring one and sure to yield a lot of runs. Saunders went at 22 and when 30 more had been added, Allan who had succeeded him succumbed with 6 to his credit; but Henry retired without scoring. George Jones joined Ogden and the first stand was made, his wicket putting on 54 runs to which he contributed 22; meanwhile his partner had given a hard chance in the slips after he had made 42. Gillespie and Little played steady cricket, and gave Ogden a chance to increase his score to 133 before he was "yorked" by Lacey.

This splendid innings of the Captain's was the batting feature of the tour, and he and we were very justly proud of it. He was in for three hours and treated the seven bowlers who attacked his stumps remorselessly, getting them 17 times to the boundaries, 5 times away for 3 and 13 times for 2. He played faultlessly to all parts of the field, never giving the ghost of a chance except, as before mentioned, when he was let off in the slips at 42. The last 3 wickets added nothing and the score closed for 219.

Wynyard and Westmoreland, who had played against us for the United Services, turned up here, the former doing duty behind the stumps in good, quick style, and holding on to three men there. He plays in dashing form, much in the same way as Lacey does, and we thought as much of his innings of 63 as of almost any other that was played against us. The first three wickets were expensive, Steele's falling at 69, and Lacey's and Wynyard's at 114, but the next three fell to Annand in rapid succession—Six for 130. Currie, Cave and, Armstrong contributed enough to bring the score to within a few of the two centuries, and at the drawing of stumps the

Gentlemen of Hampshire were within two of our score for the loss 9 wickets.

The following morning Col. Fellowes took us, after an early breakfast, to the Ordinance Survey Department, to which all the engineering and geographical surveyors, in the service of the country, send the results of their labor. It would hardly do to allow alien enemies, or even Fenians, to enter there, for all the strategical points of the realm are exposed to view on paper.

The forts which command the approaches to the Kingdom would not be so invulnerable to one acquainted with their paper counterparts as to him whose occular information about them is a view taken through an atmosphere of grape and canister. We had but one regret, an often expressed lament while we were away, and that was that we had so little time to spend upon such interesting and instructive subjects. But our first duty was to the game, and ere long the Colonel, who had taken so much trouble to make or morning pleasant, was keeping us busy fielding his runs. We were all glad that he, the Captain, made a good stand, even if it was the means of bringing the score of his eleven 6 runs in advance of our own.

The fielding and bowling of our opponents were good, though no one was signally successful with the ball, while for Canada Annand was very fortunate, his bowling being exceedingly useful. He got 5 good wickets for 57 runs.

Our second innings opened more auspiciously than the first, Saunders and the Captain keeping together till 63, when Ogden retired with 27 to his credit and with an average of 80 runs for the match. In twenty minutes Henry added as many runs, and came in with the telegraph showing 90. George Jones failed to score, and Gillespie partnered Saunders, who had been playing in fine form, till the latter was caught by Currie at 122, after having played a first rate serviceable innings of 55. Then Little joined the Hamiltonian and another good stand was made till Gillespie, who had made 45, unfortunately got his leg in front at 177. He had been rather down on his luck of late, and we were all glad that he had again come to the front, as he had in Ireland. The remaining five wickets added 33 runs, Allan going in too late to have an opportunity of scoring much. The innings yielded 211. The bowling honors fell to Wood and Steele, who captured 3 for 14 and 5 for 36, respectively.

At a quarter to five, or an hour and three-quarters before the time for drawing, Steele and Lacey strolled out to the wicket. Wynyard and Steele, who had given so much trouble in the first innings, were safely in the pavilion by the time the scorers had telegraphed 21. At 44 Fleury took Lacey at the off boundary on a magnificent catch, which performance apparently tickled the large number of spectators who began to feel deeply interested in the now uncertain result of the game.

Gillespie was well on the spot and a victory for Canada was quite on the cards, more especially after he had caught and bowled Westmoreland when that batsman had made 36. The four best wickets had yielded but 53. Ere long 8 wickets were down for 112 runs, and hopes of another win for our side ran high, but Currie and Wood, by steady work, saved their eleven from defeat. When the pavilion bell tolled the hour for retiring, the Gentlemen of Hampshire were 60 runs behind and had two wickets to fall, the game thus resulting in a draw, perhaps in favor of Canada. Our relief wicket-keeper, George Jones, who always did well at that post, had nipped up Westmoreland on the first day, and had allowed our opponents only ten extras in the two innings of 370 runs. Gillespie mowed down 5 wickets for an average of but 8 runs each. This was our fifth drawn game.

GENTLEMEN OF CANADA.

1st INNINGS.		2nd INNINGS.	
Saunders, stpd. Wynyard, b. Currie	13	ct. Currie, b. Armstrong	55
Ogden, b. Lacey	133	b. Lacey	27
Allan, ct. Wynyard, b. Steele	6	not out	4
Henry. ct. Steele, b. Currie	0	b. Fellowes	20
G. W. Jones, ct. Wynyard, b. Fellowes	22	ct. Steele, b. Fellowes	2
Gillespie, ct. Fellowes, b. Currie	14	l. b. w., b. Steele	45
Carried forward	188	Carried forward	153

GENTLEMEN OF CANADA.

1ST INNINGS.		2ND INNINGS.	
Brought forward,	188	Brought forward	153
Little, ct. Currie, b. Wood	17	ct. Wynyard, b. Steele	16
Annand, stpd. Cane, b. Wood	7	b. Steele	0
Vickers, ct. and b. Lacey	0	b. Steele	9
Fleury, not out	0	b. Steele	7
Ferrie, stpd. Cane, b. Wood	0	stpd. Cane, b. Currie	2
Byes, 3; leg byes, 4	7	Byes, 20; leg byes, 3; wides, 1	24
Total	219	Total	211

RUNS AT THE FALL OF EACH WICKET.

	1.	2.	3.	4.	5.	6.	7.	8.	9.	10.
1st Innings	22	51	52	106	142	207	217	217	219	219
2nd "	63	90	108	122	177	178	188	204	204	211

BOWLING ANALYSIS.

	1st INNINGS.				2nd INNINGS.			
	Overs.	Runs.	Mdn's.	W's.	Overs.	Runs.	Mdn's.	W's.
Currie	35	70	10	3	21.2	32	5	1
Armstrong	13	27	5	0	13	36	4	1
Steele	21	38	9	1	26	36	14	5
Fellowes	14	42	2	1	12	24	42	2
Young	3	2	2	0	2	5	0	0
Lacey	8	19	1	2	19	31	11	1
Wood	5.2	14	1	3	5	23	0	0

Wood bowled 1 wide.

GENTLEMEN OF HANTS.

1st INNINGS.		2nd INNINGS.	
E. G. Wynyard, b. Annand	63	ct. Annand, b. Gillespie	9
D. A. Steele, ct. Little b. Ogden	25	ct. Saunders, b. Ogden	10
F. E. Lacey, b. Ferrie	32	ct. Fleury, b. Gillespie	17
H. G. Westmoreland, ct. G. W. Jones, b. Annand	0	ct. and b. Gillespie	36
P. A. Ch. de Crespigny, b. Annand	0	b. Gillespie	3
A. Young, ct. Saunders, b. Annand	8	b. Annand	10
C. E. Currie, ct. Little, b. Ogden	18	not out	31
B. S. Cane, ct. Allan, b. Ferrie	25	b. Ogden	7
H. Armstrong, b. Ogden	17	ct. Annand, b. Gillespie	1
A. H. Wood, ct. and b. Annand	8	not out	17
Lt.-Col. J. Fellowes, not out	23	to bat	
Byes, 4; leg byes, 2	6	Byes, 2; leg byes, 2	4
Total	225	Total	145

CRICKET ACROSS THE SEA.

RUNS AT THE FALL OF EACH WICKET.

	1.	2.	3.	4.	5.	6.	7.	8.	9.	10.
1st Innings.....	69	114	114	116	130	130	169	173	188	225
2nd "	19	21	44	53	78	100	109	112	—	—

BOWLING ANALYSIS.

	1st INNINGS.				2nd INNINGS.			
	Overs.	Runs.	Mdn's.	W's.	Overs.	Runs.	Mdn's.	W's.
Gillespie.....	4	14	0	0	32	52	13	5
Ferrie	19	61	1	2				
Allan........	16	39	4	0				
Ogden	15.2	48	4	3	25	68	3	2
Annand	16	57	3	5	7	21	0	1

GLOUCESTER.

The first four days of the week had been spent in hard work. We had to rush from the ground at Hampshire, and after a hurried meal travel until eleven o'clock at night before we reached Salisbury, where we made the Cathedral Hotel our half-way house on the road to Yatton.

We soon learned that the female custodian of the pewters and the "opped hale," like Potiphar's wife, was fair to look upon. Each man took his potation and ate his sandwich supper in the tap-room, the flowing bowl being filled and handed to him by the fair Goddess of the Wine Cup. There was very close running between the fellows for first place in the pretty bar maid's esteem, but it was conceded that "the Duke" was a lap ahead of the rest when time was called. As we had to be up by five we didn't linger so very long over our supper. Across the way in the rival hostelry, a belated tenor was invoking

Euterpe in song and drinking libations to the goddess of the lyre. Between the drinks, the melody of the lay was wafted through our open windows. All at once the strains of "Some day" fell upon our ears for the first time, and then we learned what we had missed, when Vickers told the audience on the *Furnessia*, after several ineffectual attempts to get "Some day" started, "Its no use boys, I can't do it."

"The Babies," Fleury and Lyon Lindsey, were bent on taking in all the sights and scenery within a convenient radius of the places we stopped at. Recollecting that they were in the city where the celebrated Salisbury Cathedral had been moved from forgotten Sarum, they concluded that it was not their policy to miss a view of it. Disregarding the trivial fact that the night was pitch dark, they wandered forth at midnight to behold the venerable structure with its architectural beauties of the time of Henry III. "Sable night had nearly driven his car half round on the starless heaven" ere they returned. Their views on the architecture of that ancient pile are obscured in oblivion; they never related what they saw.

Next morning without a bite to eat, we were all aboard the 6.05 train for Bristol, save and except the Captain and his wife who made their appearance in a four wheeler at 6.06. The horses, the driver and the occupants, bore evidence of fatigue, Teddie had apparently not been called in time, and with dishevelled hair and unbuttoned boots, turned up just at the last moment with his wife and his trunks in a cab, and his collar in his coat pocket, but he had left his good humour behind. They jumped aboard as the whistle sounded, and we were soon whirling past the remains of the old British encampments, whose fosses and mounds dot the hillsides for miles between Salisbury and Bristol. Cut out of the chalk cliff in the White Horse Vale, is a large animal, perhaps half-a-mile in length, known as the white steed of Alfred the Great. An altercation between "the Parsee" and "the Gunner" as to whether it was "bas-relief" or "hollow," put an end to the whist with which eight of us were trying to keep ourselves awake, and roused from the arms of Morpheus those who were trying to make up for a deficient night's rest. The question is still undecided.

When one has been travelling for three hours on an empty stomach there is, perhaps, nothing less calculated to put him right than a railway station breakfast.

At nine o'clock we trooped our weary way into Bristol's "first-class" refreshment room and waited a weary hour before the ham and eggs put in their appearance; would we had never tasted the coffee.

En route at 10.15 we reached Yatton at 11 o'clock.

There is no hotel at this place, so we made arrangements to have our seventy-eight pieces of luggage, minus our cricket bags, sent on to Weston-Super-*Mud.* As the fellows dived into their trunks for some of the wearing apparel that they needed, we were forcibly reminded of our arival at Derry, when the same "seventy-eight" ran the gauntlet of the Customs authorities. The "Genial Manager" who had charge of the luggage was more forcible than polite in his language when he found that our traps would have to be piled up at the station to await another train, ere they could go on to their point of destination.

As Mr. Chamberlayne was not aware of the hour at which we would arrive, we had to shoulder our knapsacks and march to the field of battle, at which we arrived tired out, dirty, and in the worst possible humor. The original arrangement had been to play the Gentlemen of Gloucester at Clifton, but this was subsequently altered to the match at Yatton. Mr. Tankerville Chamberlayne, Cricket's best patron in the famous County of Gloucester, had generously invited us to play his eleven of the same County, upon his private ground; a ground of which he may well be proud. Some eight acres had been enclosed by a high canvas wall, and a large luncheon and larger refreshment tents, had been hoisted within the enclosure. Behind the neat little pavilion, in front of which we were photographed with the contesting team, a large dancing tent had been put up, where the villagers tripped the light fantastic at the conclusion of each day's play, to the music of the band which whooped it up for us in the afternoon. As the bandsmen had assembled on the ground before we got there, and bunting was flying from every available post, the whole scene bore a holiday aspect which was refreshing.

Mr. O. G. Radcliffe later on welcomed us to Yatton, and told us how disappointed Mr. Chamberlayne was that family illness prevented him from greeting us personally, and expressed regret that his ignorance of the hour of our arrival had interfered with his sending his cart to the station for our traps.

After we had donned our maroon and were limbering up with a little practice, a hearty laugh in the direction of the entrance gate turned our attention to the arrival of the great Dr. W. G. Grace, a cricketer whose record entitles him to the admiration of all lovers of the game, and one whom we were delighted to have the pleasure of playing with. When as youngsters, some of us had watched Mr. Fitzgerald's Eleven, of which W. G. Grace was one, playing away back in 1872 on the old Toronto Cricket Ground, we little dreamed that in 1887 we would be bearding the lion in his den. Of that visit to Canada the Doctor has very kindly recollections and mentioned several incidents of the trip. He shook hands with us cordially, flipped up the coin which came down as Ogden said it would, and went off to make ready for the fray. There is perhaps no keener Gentleman cricketer in England than the man who stands out in bold relief as the ablest of them all.

When the County of Gloucester plays with the first-class counties of England, seldom, if ever, do more than two professional players appear upon the Eleven, it is therefore, perhaps, in a position to put the strongest amateur county Eleven in England in the field. But the choosing of the team was not confined to Gloucester, for as Yatton is in Somersetshire, F. A. Smith, who is reported to be the hardest hitter in South Western England made one of the team.

The Captain took Saunders with him to the wicket, but came back without him at 34. Henry, Allan and Gillespie fell before the telegraph had got much past the 60, and by the time 63 had been reported Saunders strode into the pavilion, having succumbed to Hale after making 29. This bowler and Page did all the damage up to this point. George Jones and Little set about following the example which Saunders had set, and played so steadily that they brought on Dr. E. M. Grace, whose brother caught Jones off one of his lobs, after he had made 23. Six for 116. Little, whose batting had steadily improved through the tour, did not lose his wicket, and saw all the rest out and 140 hoisted before he came in with 31 to his credit. Dr. W. G. Grace was not successful with the ball, getting but one wicket at a cost of 61 runs, but his brother's lobs got him 3 wickets for 20.

The luncheon table laden with the good things of this world, was graced by the presence of Mrs. Grace and young W. G. Mr. Chamberlayne had spared no pains to give us a good lunch and he succeeded admirably; we were only sorry that he himself could not be present. An itinerant wasp stung Page on the tongue, which circumstance frightened the orators and constrained them to silence.

At four o'clock the two Graces commenced the innings for Gloucester, and we expected almost any amount of leather hunting. They kept up a running conversation while in together, and some of their remarks were very humorous, and on this occasion, as always, they put the large concourse of spectators in a good humor, to the merriment of whom George Jones added not a little in an early stage of the innings, by going head first over the ropes and upsetting a bench in a frantic attempt to save a boundary hit. Dr. "E. M." retired at 49, just after his brother had given an impossible chance to Allan at the boundary. Henry who was keeping wickets had nipped up the retiring batsman. The next two wickets fell for next to nothing.

Page, the lion of the day, played the steadiest innings we had ever seen, but when he hits or cuts he does it with a will, and it was in this way he made his grand score. He had not a long partnership with Dr. Grace. Ferrie had never trundled better than he did that day and succeeded in clean bowling four men and rattling the stumps behind the famous " W. G.," whereupon his eye glistened as it only does when Bob is pleased. Four for 89. So the great hero of English cricket had made 59 runs against us. Page played a grand innings of 79 before Allan held him off Wallace Jones, who got 4 wickets in this innings for 35 runs. Smith hit up 24 in a few minutes and was the last victim that night, the telegraph reading 195, 7, 24, at the close of the day's play.

Dr. Wickstead is a jolly, generous, good natured Englishman, and after we had run down to Weston, and through the kindness of Mr. Cox, Ferrie's brother-in-law, been quartered, some of us at "Swiss Villa" his own beautiful place, others at "Glentworth" his brother's, Mr. Campbell Cox's residence, and others at the Club, and after we had donned our evening togs, we turned up for dinner on Dr. Wickstead's lawn. His beautiful gardens were lighted with Chinese lanterns hung among the trees and by fairy lamps set among the flower beds. Spread under the naked canopy of Heaven was the feast, which ere long, we were pitching into with a right good will. The Doctor made a neat little congratulatory speech, to which the "Manager" responded, expressing his inability to thank our host sufficiently for his great kindness and substantial hospitality. As soon as the last course had been cleared away, a band of strolling minstrels made its appearance on the lawn and kept us roaring with laughter till we were forced to say good night, stern duty requiring us for slumber.

Before one o'clock next day the rest of Mr. Tankerville Chamberlayne's Eleven of the Gentlemen of Gloucester had finished their innings for a total just a century in advance of ours.

Promptly Ogden and Saunders went out, and by 5.15, or in three hours and a half, excluding the time for lunch, we had scored 283 runs, an average of 70 an hour. The quickness of the fine wicket can be gathered from these figures. When the score stood at 49, Ogden was bowled by Dr. "E.M." for 20; then Henry went in and hit, 2 fours off the first two balls. Pullen's next over he hit for 15, and "W. G's" subsequent one for 12, making in all 27 off two consecutive overs. Saunders fell a victim at 74, having meanwhile punished the bowling to the tune of 32. Henry was in just 46 minutes during which time he hit one 6 clean out of the ground, and 13 fours, which strokes earned for him the title from Dr. Grace of the "Canadian Bonner." His score of 88 was the best he made on the tour. Three wickets for 176 runs. After Gillespie had succumbed for a single, all the rest of the team scored. Little again played a patient innings of 25, but to Vickers and Ferrie is to be attributed the merit of saving the match, by putting on between them 50 runs for the last wicket. Ferrie hit up 27 and Vickers 26, without losing his wicket.

The Canadians had thus put victory beyond the reach of their opponents, for they were 184 on, an hour and a half before the time for drawing.

The first two Gloucestershire wickets fell for 17, the third, Page's, for 56, and at half past six 113 runs had been scored without any further loss. Pullen was the hero of his side this time, with 47 not out, which he put together by free hard hitting. The remaining seven wickets would have required to have made 81 runs to have won.

The announcement of the sixth, and at the same time the fifth consecutive draw, called from the "right hand barrel of the Jones combination," the remark, that all Australia could not beat us in a two days' match if they would let us go in first. Dr. Grace was good enough to say that he was surprised at the immense improvement in our form on that which he had seen when visiting Canada in 1872, and he said he saw no reason why the success of cricket should not be as well assured from this out in Canada, as it had for some time been in the far-off sister Colony, Australia.

GENTLEMEN OF CANADA.

1st Innings.		2nd Innings.	
Saunders ct. Pullen, b. Hale	29	ct. Bush, b. Croome	32
Ogden b. Page	18	b. E. M. Grace	20
Henry ct. Croome, b. Page	0	ct. Pullen, b. E. M. Grace	88
Allan ct. Troop, b. Hale	9	b. W. G. Grace	17
Gillespie run out	2	ct. and b. E. M. Grace	1
G. W. Jones ct. W. G. Grace, b. E. M. Grace	23	ct. and b. W. G. Grace	16
Little, not out	31	ct. sub. b. W. G. Grace	25
Annand, run out	7	ct. Croome, b. E. M. Grace	15
Vickers. l.b.w., b. E. M. Grace	0	not out	26
W. W. Jones b. W. G. Grace	9	ct. E. M. Grace, b. W. G. Grace	5
Ferrie b. E. M. Grace	0	ct. Hale, b. W. G. Grace	27
Byes 9, Leg Byes 3	12	Byes 4, Leg Byes 6, Wides 1	11
Total	140	Total	283

RUNS AT THE FALL OF EACH WICKET.

	1.	2.	3.	4.	5.	6.	7.	8.	9.	10.
1st Innings..	34	34	59	63	63	116	125	126	139	140
2nd Innings..	36	67	176	178	181	207	210	215	233	283

BOWLING ANALYSIS.

	1st Innings.				2nd Innings.			
	Overs.	Runs.	Mdn's.	W's.	Overs.	Runs.	Mdn's.	W's.
W. G. Grace..	34	60	10	1	44.3	100	12	5
Page	27	18	16	2	14	48	3	0
Hale	12	22	2	2	7	12	3	0
Radcliffe	4	7	2	0				
E. M. Grace..	12.3	21	4	3	38	100	10	4
Croome.	..	..	..	..	7	12	3	1

(Croome bowled 1 wide.)

GENTLEMEN OF GLOUCESTERSHIRE.

1ST INNINGS.		2ND INNINGS.	
W. G. Grace b. Ferrie	59		
E. M. Grace ct. Henry b. Ogden	15	b. Ferrie	10
W. W. F. Pullen b. Ferrie	3	not out	47
O. G. Radcliffe ct. G. W. Jones b. Ogden	6	b. Ogden	4
H. V. Page ct. Allan, b. W.W. Jones	79	ct. Gillespie, b. Ferrie	23
W. Troup b. Ferrie	14		
F. A. Leeston-Smith ct. Gillespie, b. W. W. Jones	24		
A. C. Croome b. W. W. Jones	2	not out	15
E. L. Griffiths b. Ferrie	14		
H. Hale ct. Gillespie, b. W. W. Jones	17		
J. A. Bush, not out	2		
Byes 4	4	Byes 1, Leg Byes 3	4
Total	239	Total	103

RUNS AT THE FALL OF EACH WICKET.

	1.	2.	3.	4.	5.	6.	7.	8.	9.	10.
1st Innings	49	74	85	89	147	192	195	212	232	239
2nd Innings	15	17	56							

BOWLING ANALYSIS.

	1ST INNINGS.				2ND INNINGS.			
	Overs.	Runs.	Mdn's.	W's	Overs.	Runs.	Mdn's.	W's.
Ogden	19	66	2	2	9	31	2	1
Gillespie	17	50	5	0	2	6	1	0
Annand	6	12	1	0				
Ferrie	37	65	9	4	15	45	4	2
Allan	4	8	1	0				
W. W. Jones	16	34	5	4	6	17	1	0

There had been a tennis party at "Swiss Villa" in the afternoon, and there was to be a ball in the evening, and by the time those of us who were not quartered at Mr. Cox's had assembled there the first dance was over. Here was a chance! The girls of

England, of whose beauty and charms we had heard so much, we had hitherto met only in a casual way about the cricket fields, except at the evening at Mrs. Colonel Bowlby's at Portsmouth; but now we were to have a jolly good dance with them. Though the evening was warm we went right in for it, and the way we waltzed through the programme that night calls back the time when, as school-boys, we used to start at No. 1 and keep it going till all the other guests but ourselves had said good bye.

When the candles had burned low, and the approach of Sunday morning all too soon put an end to the festivities, the tender adieus showed what excellent use we had been making of our opportunities; and we sighed as we thought of the enviable time Bob Ferrie would have when he came, as he had arranged, to spend a month with his sister, Mrs. Cox, before sailing for home. We even believe some of us grew jealous in advance.

Just what went on in Weston when Bob got back there he has always kept dark, and we have had to get our light from signs. When he met us aboard boat we took copious notes. If possible, the brightness of his eye had increased; more labor was bestowed in placing the front hair just where it looked best; he had only one of the Birmingham dog-collars left; he insisted on having his shoes pipe-clayed three times a day; was for ever lamenting the fact that tennis was an impossibility on board boat, and at times he would stand gazing out to sea with a soulful expression of countenance quite foreign to his former vivacious manner. From all these indications, we inferred that he must have made up his mind to chuck up his position as sidesman in Christ's Church, Hamilton, and go into the church itself—with somebody else. Next afternoon Mrs. Cox lunched us all; and on the quiet Sunday at "Swiss Villa" we got a glimpse of home life, which, as we lay about the lawn, called up recollections of our own far-away nests, to which we were soon to sail back, and which made us feel that "Home is the sacred refuge of our life." Never can we forget the kindness of Mr. and Mrs. Cox; never can we sufficiently thank them for creating the brightest spot on the page of our English tour.

Little Regie Cox had a pony, which he had trained to the ways of the Indian beasts, which throw their riders in the great Wild West show. The "Parsee" did not quite tumble to the trick at once, but did after his first endeavor to sit the brute, also after his second and third ventures, after which he was willing to admit that the pony had learned its lesson well, but still he thought that with practice he might ride that animal yet; but, then, we all knew as well as he did that he wouldn't have another opportunity of trying and getting spilled again.

But where was "Butcher Bob"? He hadn't been heard of for two whole days. There was but a concession line between us and the hunting counties, and he had "taken the fence" and brought up in Warwickshire. Was it to "*pour* upon the brook that babelled by" a Canadian libation to the Avon bard? Was it to Kenilworth, lured by the sad tale of Amy Robsart's fate, that he went his way? No; the young lady's name was not Amy, nor did she dwell at Stratford on the stream.

From "Swiss Villa" to the train was from the sublime to the inevitable, and while the good people of Weston-super-Mare were wending their way to the evening service we were rattling over the iron road to the great centre of the manufacturing industries of England, the home of "the veritable descendants of Tubal Cain." After supper at the Queen's Hotel we put in a good night's rest, as near to Heaven as the proprietor could send us, which could not have been very far away, preparatory to leaving next morning for Stoke.

Chapter XI.

Staffordshire and the Hunting Counties.

STAFFORDSHIRE.

AUGUST 15TH.—After an early breakfast, a two hours' run brought us to Stoke, where we put up at the North Stafford Hotel, conveniently close both to the station and to the ground. We found ourselves surrounded by so few of the usual evidences of a town that we had some doubts as to where Stoke exactly lay, but on enquiry found that we were in the very centre of the place, which is indeed little else than a collection of pottery ovens.

The Staffordshire Captain won the toss, and went in upon what appeared a good wicket. The ground is not prettily situated, but has the merit of being large, and could be made a good one. The feature of the home innings was undoubtedly the batting of Heath, who played an almost faultless innings of 82, not out. Six other men got doubles; of these Cozens with 31 and Fishwick 21 were the most successful.

Saunders and Ogden, as had been their custom of late, began for Canada, and between them put on 40 without the loss of a wicket, when Ogden received a severe blow on the head, which compelled him to retire for a time, and he could not resume his innings that day. Allan failed to come off, but Henry soon knocked up 25. Gillespie again got his leg in front after scoring 4, and when stumps were drawn for the day we had 146 for the loss of four wickets; George Jones and Little being not out. Saunders had been batting almost till drawing of stumps, and played a good innings of 44.

The next day Ogden was able to continue his innings, and added a good 17 to his 20 of the night before. George Jones played an excellent innings, cutting and driving well for 44, and when Fleury joined Little a useful stand was made, both batsmen playing carefully, but punishing the bowling when the opportunity offered. This partnership was productive of 100 runs. Little at length was bowled by Heath, who had gone on with lobs, for a meritorious and carefully played 54. Fleury held up his wicket till the last, being not out for a very well played 56, for which he was presented with a cricket bag by the "G. M.," who had not expected him to make the half century, and, to his cost, had backed his opinion with a cricket bag. Our total of 313 runs was the largest score we made on the tour.

Staffordshire, in their second innings, commenced well, putting on 111 for the first 2 wickets, to which Heath, by another excellent display, contributed 47, and Bromfield, by scarcely less meritorious cricket, 36. None of the rest of the team, however, did much, the last 7 wickets contributing only 34, inclusive of 9 extras. Of this collapse, Gillespie was mainly the cause; bowling in fine form he took 6 wickets for 51 runs.

The wicket had worn badly, and we found did not play nearly as well as it had promised. Where the batsman stood, and in some spots on the pitch the gravel and refuse from the furnaces which formed the sub-soil began to come up through the turf; and at one end the batsman stood in a hole three or four inches deep.

With but 62 runs to get to win, it looked a certain victory for Canada if the fifty-five minutes left gave us sufficient time to win in. The policy was adopted of trying to hit up the runs quickly, and the event showed it be a false one. Ogden got a single off the first ball of the innings, and then Henry " the Slogger," in attempting to get in a boundary hit off the second, was stumped. Allan, after making 2, was taken on a rattling catch in the country. Two for 3, and Ogden, soon after, was captured at mid off. Three for 5. Fleury's first ball nearly hit him on the head, and going out to pat the treacherous spot he was stumped. Four for 5. Saunders too was stumped. Five for 7. Little and Gillespie each succumbed to the first ball they received. Seven for 8, Geo. Jones having made the other run, and he and Wallace Jones brought the score to 18 when George was bowled by Allcock, who was working wonderful execution, with the assistance of Capes behind the stumps. Eight for 18. Ferrie now, as he had shown us before he could, filled the lamentable gap, and with Wallace Jones, raised the total to 37 before the call of time, when, with two wickets to go down, we still wanted 25 of the coveted 62. It was a narrow squeak, and we have but our rashness to blame for the miserable *finale*, although we were, no doubt, handicapped by the wretched condition of the wicket and the bad light.

This apology does not, however, detract from the merit of Allcock's performance with the ball. His analysis reading 7 for 15, is wonderfully good, and we must not forget to mention Capes' agility behind the wickets. The end, though of course very disappointing, was very exciting, and the two thousand spectators enjoyed it immensely. This was our seventh draw.

On the morning of the second day, by the kindness of the Mayor of the town, Mr. Leeson, a number of us were shown the great potteries of the Mintons, and were much pleased and not a little instructed by the beautiful ware we saw there, and by the lucid explanations by our kind guide of the process of manufacture.

CRICKET ACROSS THE SEA.

GENTLEMEN OF STAFFORDSHIRE.

1st Innings.		2nd Innings.	
Rev. S. C. Voules, ct. Henry, b. Gillespie	12	ct. Little, b. W. W. Jones	0
H. J. Dixon, b. Ogden	14	b. Ogden	11
C. H. Allcock, b. W. W. Jones	15	ct. Saunders, b. Ogden	13
D. H. Brownfield, b. Allan	17	stpd. Saunders, b. Gillespie	36
A. H. Heath, not out	82	ct. Gillespie, b. W. W. Jones	47
J. H. Copestake, b. Gillespie	9	b. Gillespie	0
G. B. Capes, b. Ogden	7	b. Gillespie	5
F. L. Cozens, b. Ferrie	31	ct. Fleury, b. Gillespie	9
H. Fishwick, b. Ogden	21	not out	15
A. L. Thompson, hit wkt., b. Ogden	9	ct. Little, b. Gillespie	0
Rev. P. Mainwairing, b. Ferrie	3	b. Gillespie	0
Byes, 4; leg byes, 5	9	Byes, 7; leg byes, 2	9
Total	229	Total	145

RUNS AT THE FALL OF EACH WICKET.

	1.	2.	3.	4.	5.	6.	7.	8.	9.	10.
1st Innings	25	27	53	65	89	98	161	198	222	229
2nd "	22	58	111	111	112	118	123	132	143	145

BOWLING ANALYSIS

	1st Innings.				2nd Innings.			
	Overs.	Runs.	Md'ns.	W's.	Overs.	Runs.	Md'ns.	W's.
Ogden	33	58	15	4	20	32	7	2
Ferrie	20.3	60	2	2				
Gillespie	22	38	6	2	22.2	51	5	6
W. W. Jones	14	33	3	1	10	22	1	2
Allan	9	20	2	1	7	31	0	0
Lindsey	5	11	2	0				

GENTLEMEN OF CANADA.

1st Innings.		2nd Innings.	
Saunders, ct. and b. Allcock	44	stpd. Capes, b. Allcock	2
Ogden, ct. Capes, b. Heath	37	ct. Voules, b. Fishwick	3
Allan, b. Fishwick	0	ct. Copestake, b. Allcock	2
Henry, ct. Brownfield, b. Allcock	25	stpd. Capes, b. Allcock	0
G. W. Jones, ct. Brownfield, b. Allcock	44	b. Allcock	5
Gillespie, l. b. w., b. Allcock	4	b. Allcock	0
Little, b. Heath	54	ct. Voules, b. Allcock	0
Carried forward	208	Carried forward	12

GENTLEMEN OF CANADA.

1st INNINGS.		2nd INNINGS.	
Brought forward	208	Brought forward	12
Fleury, not out	56	stpd. Capes, b. Allcock	0
W. W. Jones, b. Heath	6	not out	7
Lindsey, ct. Voules, b. Heath	3		
Ferrie, stpd. Capes, b. Heath	11	not out	14
Byes, 21; leg byes, 7; wides, 1.	29	Byes, 4	4
Total	313	Total	37

RUNS AT THE FALL OF EACH WICKET.

	1.	2.	3.	4.	5.	6.	7.	8.	9.	10.
1st Innings	40	69	125	135	160	206	276	289	297	313
2nd "	1	3	3	5	5	5	8	18		

BOWLING ANALYSIS.

	1st INNINGS.				2nd INNINGS.			
	Overs.	Runs.	Md'ns.	W's.	Overs.	Runs.	Md'ns.	W's.
Allcock	54	98	18	4	12	15	4	7
Fishwick	30	63	8	1	9	9	4	1
Cozens	9	25	1	0				
Voules	25	33	12	0				
Dixon	3	6	1	0				
Heath	17	46	2	5	3	9	0	0
Mainwairing	5	13	1	0				

Voules bowled 1 wide.

WARWICKSHIRE.

AUGUST 17TH.—When we left Stoke on Tuesday, rain had begun to fall, and our journey to Birmingham was made to the accompaniment of thunder and lightning. It was midnight before we reached our hotel, where it would seem we had not been expected, for it took some time to rouse up anybody who could show us our rooms. Early next morning, some of the fellows strolled out for a look about the great manufacturing city, and at breafast the last of the exploring party, Bob Ferrie, dropped in, remarking that it was a splendid place for shopping. " Why ! what have you bought ?" was the general chorus, in answer to which, Bob produced two dog collars from his trousers' pocket. On being cross-examined, he reluctantly admitted that he didn't own any dogs, but he thought the collars pretty, and they certainly were cheap, and so he invested, and intended on returning to Canada to buy two dogs to fit the collars.

During breakfast "The Duke," who had been staying at another hotel, in order to pick up part of his wardrobe, which he had ordered "my tailor" to send there, announced that a lady we would all be glad to see, was in the reception room, and whom we were astonished to find to be the "Skylark," whom we had last seen on the "*Furnessia*," waving her handkerchief as a farewell to us, as we steamed up Lough Foyle on the tender.

The county ground is situated on the Edgbaston Road, in the suburbs of Birmingham. The Gentlemen of Warwickshire took the innings, Bainbridge having won the toss, and at 12.30 the bell called out the players, when Ogden and Gillespie commenced the attack against Cox and Bainbridge. The wicket had been greatly soddened by the previous night's rain. This was certainly Gillespie's day on, for he proved quite unplayable, first bowling Bainbridge for 2, then the Rev. F. G. Page for 0.

Cox was caught off him by Geo. Jones, and then he rattled Wheeler's stumps. Four for 7 was a good beginning, but Johnson and Docker made a stand, and the fifth wicket did not fall till at 65, the former was bowled by Allan for 30. Soon after Docker, who ought to have been held in the long field early in his innings, retired with an equal number to his credit. The next three men did little, the ninth wicket falling for 81, when we were stopped by rain. A regular thunderstorm broke over the ground, the "gentle" came down in torrents, and the field was so "waterlogged," and such pools of water were left on the pitch that it became evident no more cricket could be played there that day.

Most of us spent the afternoon shopping, and in seeing, in the short time at our disposal, what we could of the city. The evening being chilly, we had a fire lighted in our private sitting-room and improvised a little free and easy concert, at which each one in turn contributed to the general harmony or discord in proportion as he sang in or out of tune. Saunders here made his first and last appearance in public as a vocalist.

Next morning saw all the Warwickshire men out for 106, no one offering much resistance to Gillespie, whose bowling was wonderfully good, his analysis for the innings reading 41 overs, 26 maidens, 27 runs, 5 wickets. We must not forget to mention three fine catches by George Jones in the long field.

Ogden and Saunders commenced our innings and were not separated till at 32 the latter was bowled by Cox's first ball, (underarm), having contributed but 7. Allan lent Ogden valuable assistance, and they took the score to 93 before the Captain was caught and bowled by Hill for a capital innings of 56, in which he hit with more than ordinary vigor. Allan had played in his prettiest style for 39 before he was well stumped by Page. Henry did nothing, George Jones got 14, Gillespie 12, and then Fleury and Wallace Jones made a useful stand, and after the latter had been got l. b. w. for a good 20, his late partner, with Vickers, took the score to within 1 of the double century. Fleury contributed a good 30, and Vickers played steadily for his 10. The total was raised to 204, a lead of 98. There were but two hours left to finish in.

Hill was far and away the most successful Warwickshire bowler, his analysis of seven wickets for 59 sufficiently evidences the good work he did.

The second innings of Warwickshire was to them even more unsatisfactory than the first. Bainbridge, who made his 17 well, and Docker who put together a good 24, not out, alone could do anything with Ogden, and at 6 o'clock nine wickets were down for 64 runs. Bainbridge most courteously offered a half hour's extension of time, but only half of this was required to get the last wicket, which fell at 73, Canada winning by an innings and 25 runs. Ogden was mainly answerable for this happy termination, his analysis of 36 overs, 28 maidens, 27 runs and 8 wickets, all clean bowled, needs no commendation from us. Gillespie and Allan, though less fortunate, also bowled very well.

Here we had the pleasure of again shaking hands with the Hon. E. Chandos Leigh, the President of the M. C C., whose country seat is in Warwickshire, and who was a spectator during the first day's play; and of meeting Whitby, who was in Canada in 1885, and who, having hurt his hand, could not play against us.

We think, perhaps, the ground had something to do with our easy victory, for the English cricketer's bane, a wet wicket, was our opportunity. It more nearly resembled our wickets in Canada, which seldom attain the fastness which characterized those upon which we had played hitherto, except at Buxton, where we had also won easily. This was our fourth victory.

We made a rush for the train, but on arrival at the station found it would not be made up for some minutes, and while waiting we ran across our old friend Stewart, who came to Canada with the West Indian Eleven, and whom we had seen before at the Oval.

GENTLEMEN OF WARWICKSHIRE.

1st Innings.		2nd Innings.	
H. W. Bainbridge, b. Gillespie	2	b. Ogden	17
F. T. Cox, ct. G. W. Jones, b. Gillespie	5	b. Ogden	3
Rev. F. G. Page, b. Gillespie	0	b. Ogden	9
P. Johnson, b. Allan	30	b. Ogden	0
E. Wheeler, b. Gillespie	0	b. Ogden	0
D. Docker, b. Gillespie	30	not out	24
Hon. G. Verney, ct. G. W. Jones, b. W. W. Jones	2	b. Ogden	0
E. J. Jobson, ct. G. W. Jones, b. Ogden	8	b. Ogden	5
H. G. Hill, run out	7	ct. Saunders, b. Allans	2
J. S. Flavel, not out	14	b. Ogden	1
V. Schofield, b. Ogden	7	b. Gillespie	5
No balls, 1	1	Byes, 4; leg byes, 3	7
Total	106	Total	73

RUNS AT THE FALL OF EACH WICKET.

	1.	2.	3.	4.	5.	6.	7.	8.	9.	10.
1st Innings	4	7	7	7	65	70	70	80	86	106
2nd "	12	12	28	32	35	46	48	57	64	73

BOWLING ANALYSIS.

	1st INNINGS.				2nd INNINGS.			
	Overs.	Runs.	Mdn's.	W's.	Overs.	Runs.	Mdn's.	W's.
Ogden	27	31	13	2	36	27	28	8
Gillespie	41	27	26	5	25.2	31	9	1
Annand	9	19	1	0				
Allan	3	9	0	1	11	8	7	1
W. W. Jones	9	19	2	1				

Annand bowled 1 no ball.

GENTLEMEN OF CANADA.

Saunders, b. Cox	7
Ogden, ct. & b. Hill	56
Allan, stpd. Page, b. Johnson	39
Henry, ct. Flavel, b. Hill	2
G. W. Jones, ct. Jobson, b. Verney	14
Gillespie, ct. Verney, b. Hill	12
Little, b. Hill	6
Fleury, ct. Wheeler, b. Hill	30
W. W. Jones, l. b. w., b. Hill	20
Vickers, stpd. Page, b. Hill	10
Annand, not out	2
Byes, 3; leg byes, 3	6
Total	204

RUNS AT THE FALL OF EACH WICKET.

1.	2.	3.	4.	5.	6.	7.	8.	9.	10.
32	93	95	116	129	139	146	181	199	204

BOWLING ANALYSIS.

	Overs.	Runs.	Mdn's.	W's.
Hill	44.2	59	17	7
Johnson	25	60	6	1
Cox	13	30	4	1
Bainbridge	3	17	0	0
Jobson	2	8	0	0
Verney	9	24	1	1

LEICESTERSHIRE.

AUGUST 19TH.—Arrived at Leicester, we drove to the Bell Hotel, an old fashioned hostelry built for the accommodation of the sparser travelling public in the good old coaching days, where we were driven through an archway into the court-yard. The large influx of visitors rather upset the calculations of "mine host," and at least one of the team had to put in his night's rest on something made up of four chairs and a table.

We had a three mile drive in the morning to the County ground, on the Aylestone Road, and found there that the wicket had suffered somewhat from the late rain.

The Leicester Captain, Arnall-Thompson, won the toss, but elected to take the field. Saunders and Ogden again went in first, but did not remain together long, the former being soon caught in the slips, nor did Allan, who supplanted him, make a long stay. Two for 15. George Jones, however with Ogden made a grand stand. Both batsmen getting set, hit about right merrily, and the latter had contributed an excellent 54 before F. Wright smashed his off wicket. George Jones drove and cut beautifully, and the score had been taken to 103 for 4 wickets before he succumbed. His 59 was put together in pretty and fine free style.

All the other batsmen scored, five of them getting double figures. Henry hit four boundaries and a single for his 17, and Gillespie, for a like score, played carefully; Annand, too, made his runs well. Our innings realized 228. Arnall-Thompson, for Leicestershire, bowled admirably, his analysis reading 6 for 86.

A. Wright and de Trafford commenced for the home team, the former being the steadiest batsman and the slowest scorer we met anywhere; he was a wonderful "stayer," and gave us a lot of trouble. His partner had but 3 when he was beautifully bowled by Ogden. Townsend, next man, helped the score not a little, but he and two others were dismissed that evening in a bad light for a total of 67.

Next day Wood, one of the not outs, increased his score to 45, and the score was taken to 209 before the last wicket fell.

For this W. E. Arnall, who got 27, and A. E. Wright, who carried his bat through the innings, and was not out for 63, which he had taken three hours and twenty minutes to make, were mainly responsible. Our loose fielding contributed not a little to the score, but it must be remembered that these were the last two days of another week's hard cricket. George Jones and Vickers, however, each made a good catch near the ropes.

We commenced our second innings fairly, but the total of 141 was mainly acquired by the fine batting of Allan and George Jones, who made 37 and 44 respectively, in excellent style. After their dismissal the rest did little, and at 5.15 Leicester was left with 158 to get to win, and but an hour to make the runs in; an impossible task. The match was, of course, a draw, the eighth of the tour, but we had captured three wickets for 40 at the call of time.

An old Canadian "pal," N. P. Tod, whom we were all glad to meet again, turned up here, and afterwards in Liverpool.

GENTLEMEN OF CANADA.

1st INNINGS.		2nd INNINGS.	
Saunders, ct. de Trafford, b. Arnall-Thompson	2	b. F. Wright	13
Ogden, b. F. Wright	54	b. F. Wright	10
Allan, b. S. R. Wright	0	ct. Arnall-Thompson, b. Arnall	37
G. W. Jones, ct. Stainton, b. F. Wright	59	b. Arnall	44
Henry, ct. Parsons, b. Arnall-Thompson	17	b. F. Wright	13
Gillespie, b. Arnall-Thompson	17	run out	2
Little, b. Arnall-Thompson	14	ct. Stainton, b. Arnall	2
Carried forward	163	Carried forward	121

GENTLEMEN OF CANADA.

1st Innings.		2nd Innings.	
Brought forward	163	Brought forward	121
Annand, ct. Stainton, b. Arnall-Thompson	24	ct. Wood, b. Arnall-Thompson	0
Ferrie, ct. de Trafford, b. Arnall-Thompson	7	stp'd. Stainton, b. Arnall-Thompson	0
W. W. Jones, not out	11	not out	6
Vickers, ct. Stainton, b. F. Wright	9	ct. Stainton, b. Arnall	3
Byes, 7; leg byes, 7	14	Byes, 9; leg byes, 2	11
Total	228	Total	141

RUNS AT THE FALL OF EACH WICKET.

	1.	2.	3.	4.	5.	6.	7.	8.	9.	10.
1st Innings	2	15	80	103	157	157	183	200	213	228
2nd Innings	25	30	49	106	117	129	130	130	132	141

BOWLING ANALYSIS.

	1st Innings.				2nd Innings.			
	Overs.	Runs.	Mdn's.	W's.	Overs.	Runs.	Mdn's.	W's.
Arnall-Thompson	54	86	21	6	33	45	14	2
S. R. Wright	18	34	9	1	9	12	5	0
F. Wright	47.3	53	27	3	21	41	9	3
Arnall	8	25	3	0	21.2	32	9	4
Parsons	4	16	0	0	..	..	..	..

GENTLEMEN OF LEICESTERSHIRE.

1st Innings.		2nd Innings.	
A. E. Wright, not out	63	not out	1
C. E. de Trafford, b. Ogden	3	b. Gillespie	10
Rev. W. Townshend, ct. Little, b. W. W. Jones	22	not out	8
C. Marriott, b. W. W. Jones	7	ct. Little, b. Gillespie	2
J. Parsons, ct. Saunders, b. Allan	2		
W. C. Wood, b. Ferrie	45		
R. W. G. Stainton, b. Ogden	4		
H. T. Arnall-Thompson, b. Ferrie	10		
F. Wright, ct. Vickers, b. Ogden	10	ct. Vickers, b. Gillespie	14
S. R. Wright, ct. Ogden, b. Ferrie	0		
W. E. Arnall, ct. G. W. Jones, b. Ogden	27		
Byes, 16	16	Byes, 4; leg byes, 1	5
Total	209	Total	40

CRICKET ACROSS THE SEA.

RUNS AT THE FALL OF EACH WICKET.

	1.	2.	3.	4.	5.	6.	7.	8.	9.	10.
1st Innings.....	4	40	50	55	145	150	161	174	174	209
2nd Innings....	16	25	27	..	..	..	..	..	..	..

BOWLING ANALYSIS.

	1st INNINGS.				2nd INNINGS.			
	Overs.	Runs.	Mdn's.	W's.	Overs.	Runs.	Mdn's.	W's.
Ogden	49.2	69	22	4	14	23	6	0
Gillespie	24	30	11	0	15	11	9	3
Ferrie	26	56	7	3	..	..	..	..
W. W. Jones..	16	22	9	2	..	..	..	..
Allan	10	16	3	1	..	..	..	..
Annand	..	..	..	..	1	1	0	0

Chapter XII.

Liverpool.

August 22.—A few of the men left Leicester on Saturday night to stay with friends, but the majority remained over until the Sunday morning. There was not much energy left in the party, and the Lord's day was spent very lazily, none even venturing a stroll about mighty Liverpool. The truth of the matter was we were beginning to get stale, and it is a matter almost of surprise that no one succumbed to the hard work during the whole tour.

The Aigburth ground, which is several miles out of Liverpool and is reached in a few minutes by rail, lies a little farther up the Mersey and is the prettiest ground we saw, and perhaps the largest, but the trees, which add much to its beauty from an artistic point of view, are a drawback to it from a cricketer's standpoint, as they seriously interfere at times with the line of sight in catches. No money has been spared by the cricketers of Liverpool to make it everything that a cricket ground should be, and in time it may come to rival the Old Trafford ground at Manchester, one of England's most famous cricket-fields.

We lost the toss and were sent to the field. Lancashire, it is well known, is one of the strongest of the first-class counties, and boasts, amongst its cricketing families, the Hornbys and the Steels, who have turned out some of the best players in the country. We found, as we expected, that a very formidable eleven had been chosen to represent the Gentlemen of Liverpool and District. The district about Liverpool abounds in clubs, and these had been freely drawn upon.

C. L. Jones and Cecil Holden began with some very steady play, against which Ogden and Ferrie were unable to do anything. When Allan was tried, however, Jones gave a catch to Little at point with the score at 57. Then another heart-breaking stand was made. At luncheon time there were 87 runs for but one wicket down, and on resuming play it was not till 120 had been telegraphed that Saunders neatly stumped Holden, whose patient batting had yielded him 64 runs. Steel, his partner, is a fine, free hitter, and was not very long in making his 54, though he saw Ravenscroft and Hornby come and go before he went himself. Roper, the Captain, was caught and bowled by our Captain without scoring. Radcliffe and Kemble, when together, prolonged the innings while they contributed 62 between them; the rest, however, did little, and at twenty minutes past five the last wicket had fallen for 233.

The light had grown wretched and considerably handicapped our chances of doing much that night, besides the bowlers were very difficult and succeeded in disposing of seven of us within the hour for 61 runs. Henry managed to get his eye on the ball, notwithstanding the poor light, and "milled" the deliveries of all the trundlers indiscriminately before Evans rattled his stumps. He had gone in third wicket down and his was the sixth wicket to fall with the total at 61, of which he himself had contributed 48.

This unfortunate start had, however, no apparent effect upon our spirits at the dinner tendered to us that night. In the absence of the Earl of Sefton, President of the club, Mr. Charles Langton occupied the chair, and made a most eloquent speech in proposing the toast of the " Guests of the evening." Roper, the Captain, is the best comic vocalist we listened to, and we took good care to secure selections from his *repertoire* to add to our's. The Captain and the Manager acknowledged the courtesy of our hosts for the Canadians and we did our share of the singing. Several gentlemen, who had not been playing, by their joviality and good fellowship, added much to the enjoyment of an evening, which, while rattling back to Liverpool shortly after eleven, we agreed was one of the jolliest we had spent.

The first sixteen minutes of the next day's play

were taken up by our last three batsmen in making 17 runs, the innings closing for the small total of 78. Of course a follow on was necessary, we being 155 behind.

As we had so often done before, we played our better innings on the second day, and had we made anything worth calling a score over night, we might have made a draw of the game. As it was we very nearly did so, the necessary runs required to win the match being hit up just eight minutes before the time for drawing stumps.

To our total of 229 there were six good contributions—a steady beginning of 34 from Saunders, a patient 32 from Little, 16 from the Captain, a lively 69 from Henry and two useful scores of 23 and 24 from George Jones and Gillespie respectively. Henry here established his right to be classed as a first rate, hard-hitting batsman, for he hammered first-class bowling to the tune of 117 runs. One of his tremendous drives narrowly escaped landing on the top of the big drum which belonged to a Charity school occupying one end of the grand stand. About sixty of these youngsters, who could hardly have averaged thirteen years of age, marched on to the ground in the early part of the morning to the music of their own band, and it was a comical sight to see these young shavers blowing through trombones and bass-horns almost as large as themselves. They played wonderfully well and formed a pretty picture as they marched.

There were a hundred minutes left when Jones and Holden commenced to make the necessasy 76 for Liverpool. At 2 Ferrie bowled Holden; Steele came in and stayed till 42, when Henry caught him magnificently in the slips; Ravenscroft fell at 46 and Roper at 55; Hornby and Jones, at 22 minutes past six, had made enough to win the match, Canada thus suffering defeat for the fifth time, by six wickets.

Notwithstanding our severe drubbing, it was a good match, and plenty of good cricket was shown and duly applauded by the spectators, of whom a goodly number were present both days. Though our fielding was at times anything but good, except in the way of "muffing," some fine catches were made, one especially by Wallace Jones at deep square leg, is deserving of being recorded.

The Liverpool bowling was very good, Evans being particularly successful, his analysis reading for the two innings—54 overs, 94 runs, 27 maidens and 13 wickets—a remarkably good performance.

GENTLEMEN OF LIVERPOOL AND DISTRICT.

1st Innings.	2nd Innings.
C. L. Jones, ct. Little, b. Allan.. 23	not out................. 29
C. Holden, ct. Saunders, b. Ogden 64	b. Ferrie 1
H. B. Steel, ct. Little, b. Gillespie 54	ct. Henry, b. Ferrie..... 27
Carried forward......141	Carried forward......57

GENTLEMEN OF LIVERPOOL AND DISTRICT.

1st Innings.		2nd Innings.	
Brought forward	141	Brought forward	57
J. Ravenscroft, ct. Henry, b. W. W. Jones	4	run out	0
E. C. Hornby, ct. W. W. Jones, b. Ogden	9	not out	8
E. Roper, ct. and b. Ogden	0	st'pd. Saunders, b. Gillespie	2
H. Ratcliffe, b. Ferrie	32		
A. T. Kemble, b. Ferrie	30		
G. Nicholson, b. W. W. Jones	5		
T. Evans, ct. Fleury, b. W. W. Jones	0		
F. Jones, not out	2		
Byes, 6; leg byes, 4	10	Byes, 3; l. b., 5; w'ds., 1	8
Total	233	Total	76

RUNS AT THE FALL OF EACH WICKET.

	1.	2.	3.	4.	5.	6.	7.	8.	9.	10.
1st Innings	57	131	144	154	154	175	214	227	227	233
2nd "	2	42	46	55						

BOWLING ANALYSIS.

	1st Innings.				2nd Innings.			
	Overs.	Runs.	Mdn's.	W's.	Overs.	Runs.	Mdn's.	W's.
Ogden	40	71	18	3	15	21	5	0
Gillespie	12.2	32	2	2	11.1	11	6	1
Ferrie	33	40	12	1	18	35	8	2
W. W. Jones	19	44	4	3	Ferrie bowled 1 wide.			
Allan	9	24	2	1				
Annand	4	12	0	0				

GENTLEMEN OF CANADA.

1st Innings.		2nd Innings.	
Saunders, b. F. Jones	2	stp'd. Kemble, b. Evans	34
Little, b. Evans	3	ct. C. L. Jones, b. Evans	32
Ogden, b. Evans	0	b. Evans	16
Henry, b. Evans	48	ct. and b. Hornby	69
Allan, b. F. Jones	4	b. Evans	0
G. W. Jones, ct. and b. Evans	0	b. Holden	23
Gillespie, ct. and b. Hornby	5	ct. Evans, b. Hornby	24
Fleury, b. Evans	0	ct. Steel, b. Evans	4
W. W. Jones, run out	11	ct. Ratcliffe, b. Evans	4
Annand, ct. Holden, b. Hornby	1	b. Hornby	3
Ferrie, not out	0	not out	0
Byes, 1; wides, 3	4	Byes, 13; l. b., 6; wides, 1	20
	78		229

RUNS AT THE FALL OF EACH WICKET.

	1.	2.	3.	4.	5.	6.	7.	8.	9.	10.
1st Innings	5	5	5	42	48	61	61	73	78	78
2nd "	26	26	121	147	163	203	213	222	229	229

BOWLING ANALYSIS.

	1ST INNINGS.				2ND INNINGS.			
	Overs.	Runs.	Mdn's.	W's.	Overs.	Runs.	Mdn's	W's.
Evans	19	36	9	5	35.1	58	18	6
F. Jones	15	33	6	2				
Hornby	3.1	5	1	2	36	81	10	3
Nicholson	..	..	..	..	11	32	2	0
Holden	..	..	..	..	10	22	2	1
Roper	..	..	..	..	3	14	0	0
Steel	..	..	..	..	3	2	1	0

F. Jones bowled 3 wides. Hornby bowled 1 wide.

This was the last night we were to be together; the time had at length come when we who had lived together for as many weeks, linked in a common interest, were soon to separate. We had grown accustomed to meeting new friends, and after an all too short a period of intercourse bidding them a regretful adieu; but then we, that is seventeen of us, found companionship amongst ourselves which could atone for the loss of newly made acquaintances, and there always existed a feeling of security against *ennui* in the knowledge of the numerical strength and genial temperament of the party. But the feeling that a dissolution of ourselves, so to speak, was about to take place had a most depressing effect. We had that night, at any rate, left together, and we resolved to make good use of it.

A farewell dinner was ordered in one of the private dining rooms of our hotel, the London and

North-Western, and to do that institution credit it was a good one. We soon polished it off, lighted our cigars, and agreed to interchange opinions on the merits of the tour. What might have been a cheerless evening turned out to be a most enjoyable one. The way of it was this. The fellows thought that "the Manager's" enterprise in conceiving, working-up, and successfully carrying through the tour, deserved some permanent recognition at their hands in addition to their often expressed heart-felt thanks. They had procured a handsome gold monogram locket, on the reverse side of which they had had inscribed " *From the Gentlemen of Canada in commemoration of their tour and as a token of their gratitude.*"

When the Captain rose to present it on behalf of the team, and in a neat little speech conveyed to the " G. M." the good-will and gratitude of the eleven, he brought that individual from far away down in in the depths of grief and sent him to the seventh heaven of delight at this graceful appreciation of his services. In reply, besides saying how much he would ever prize this evidence of his compatriots' regard for him, " the Manager " made a brief retrospect of the principal events of the tour, and suggested that each " county " should be heard from in turn, and by way of a start gave the toast of the " Maritime Contingent," which was drunk with an enthusiasm which showed how much the rest of us valued their services and had learned to like them.

"The Villain," who led in the averages, waxed eloquent in response. He apologised for his beard and volunteered to present it to some charitable institution if "Gilhooley" would do likewise with his. He pledged himself to eschew teetotalism and to leave his earthly gains to found a distillery, when time did for him what he proposed to do with his beard. The "Gunner" made a brilliant oratorical effort, the most luminous scintillation of genius in which was, that he was, as he had so often said before, "the handsomest man on the team." "Biddy' spoke for an hour and three-quarters; began by painting a graphic word-picture of the rustic simplicity of his Acadian home; dwelt at length on the charms of the beautiful "Evangeline" as typical of the girls of his native hamlet; explained the philology of the name of the village of St. John, and how it came to be called, not after the Baptist, but after the St. John who subsequently became Lord Bolingbroke; entered at length into the superior mineral wealth and commerical ascendancy of the eastern end of North American continent, of which his home was the capital and his uncle the defeated candidate at the last election, and wound up with a eulogy on the architectural, though phœnix-like, supremacy over the rest of Canada, of the place where he was born. By the time he got through we were willing to believe anything, even that New Brunswick's proudest boast was the finest place in all this mundane sphere. And yet there was not one word about cricket in the whole story which was longer than the shorter catechism.

Then we got the Hamilton contingent on their feet. " Mr. Gilloosby's " speech took one second to deliver and consisted of six words, which won't bear repeating, but was quite free from the sancity usually pertaining to orations given at Presbyterian "bun struggles," or even at ordinary " tea fights." It was sad to thus behold him, " the wreck of a once happy home." When Bob Ferrie got on his pins it was noticed that his locks were dishevelled, but when he recalled how he had clean bowled both the Graces, the few hairs on the top of his head erected themselves with pride, though later a tear glistened in his usually merry eye, when he lamented the fact that for nearly half the tour his painful strain had made him useless as a bed-ridden monk, while others were fighting the battle at his hands.

The burden of Artie's speech was that he had taken more good wickets on more bad balls than any man on the team; after which the " Parsee " gave a disertation on "sea sickness and one thousand and one remedies—as prescribed for himself by three hundred and thirty-seven kind souls on a transatlantic voyage, all warranted to cure,"—and he guaranteed from practical experience, that every one of them can be tried by one patient in nine days without their laying him out, though it may sometimes come to be a question of holding out between the patient and the last dose.

Teddie, our own Captain, learned that night how delighted we were with his generalship. He had come out best in the bowling, stood well up in the batting averages, and had captained the eleven with complete satisfaction to all and without getting one bit thinner. It was often a marvel to us how, fragile as he appeared to be, he could use his hands, his bat and his head so much and so well, and "come up after each occasion smiling from below." He earned the good opinion expressed of him that night, and he said he believed he was the proudest man among us.

We quote "the Duke's" eloquence just as it flowed from his lips. "It is kind of you," he said, "to laud my strict adherence to my work, true, I have never shunned it, but it is as impossible for a Dickson to neglect what he has undertaken as it is for him to wear his hat straight, and it is perhaps in my particular case the less probable that I should omit to do my duty, for am I not a scholar of the military school, do I not even now hold a commission in the Denison horse?"

Then "Shrimps," as "Juliet" had christened Lyon Lindsey, made the speech of the evening. "Gentlemen," he said, "I shall never regret coming on this tour." "Why?" said somebody. "Because," said "Shrimps," "Because, Why?" demanded everybody. "Because," said "Shrimps" again. "But you haven't told us why," said the assembled multitude. "Because why," ejaculated the embarrassed "Shrimps," whereupon Ferrie rolled on the floor in fit of laughter, the chairman moved that the meeting adjourn, and we never learned because why?

Next morning Saunders left for home, Gillespie went to Scotland, Ferrie to Weston, and the rest of us to Oxton Park to play the Cheshire match.

CHAPTER XIII.

West Cheshire and Norbury Park.

AUGUST 24TH.—To get to Birkenhead across the Mersey, always full of ocean-going craft, we took a steamer that morning: next day we went under the river. Carriages were waiting for us at the landing stage, and soon we were driving along the beautiful road through Birkenhead Park, passing the cricket ground of the same name to the Oxton ground, the field of battle. This pretty field nestles at the foot of the green Cheshire Hills, which rise tier on tier like Pelion, Ossa and Olympus, till they lose themselves in far-off Snowdon, which, too, might make a lovely home for gods.

The Cestrians made the respectable total of 210 runs, among which were many commendable scores. Several of the men who had played against us at Liverpool joined issue with us again here, and were the main contributors to the score of their side. Ere the sun set that night we had lost five wickets for 134 runs, Little being the last man to go, after making a patient and well-played 51.

The day had been hot, so we were delighted at the prospect of a drive to New Brighton, a distance of five miles, in the cool of the evening. We dined at this breezy refuge of overheated millionaires and home of the English oyster, and sailed leisurely up the river later on to Liverpool.

Next morning we only increased our score to 162. In Cheshire's second innings they got but 138, to which Holden contributed a prettily-made 63. The wicket was getting somewhat treacherous, so Little came off, as he always did under those circumstances, and held four men at point. Vickers made a magnificent catch at the boundary, which the wind made difficult to judge.

We were 186 behind at half-past four, but did not get anywhere near that number of runs by six o'clock. In fact we lost nine wickets in making 90, and as Mr. T. Harris Hodgson—not long ago President of the Montreal Cricket Club—was playing for us, we had two wickets more to lose at the call of time.

We had an excellent double group photograph taken at Oxton, copies of which we procured later on. A good number of spectators graced the grounds both days, and were very liberal in their applause. Next day, Friday, we said good-bye to the Captain and his wife and to Vickers, and started for London in our saloon carriage, with which, like with everything else, we had to part. Good-bye, "147."

GENTLEMEN OF WEST CHESHIRE.

1st Innings.		2nd Innings.	
C. Holden, ct. Shanly, b. Lindsey.	8	ct. Little, b. Allan.	63
J. Ravenscroft, b. Allan.	62	ct. Little, b. Ogden	2
W. T. Davies, ct. Henry, b. Shanly	21	b. Ogden	9
K. Monteath, b. Allan.	32	ct. Ogden, b. Lindsey.	1
J. Curwen, ct. and b. Ogden	3	ct. Henry, b. Ogden	5
F. Aspinwall, ct. Henry, b. Ogden	41	b. Ogden	8
G. C. Paton, ct. Allan, b. Ogden.	5	ct. Little, b. W.W. Jones	7
G. W. Wild, b. Allan	5	ct. Little, b. Allan	6
A. C. Bamford, b. Allan	0	b. Allan	7
J. Bretherton, ct. Vickers, b. W. Jones	10	ct. Lindsey, b. Ogden.	16
W. Brooke-Stevens, not out.	7	not out	1
C. E. Steen, ct. and b. Allan.	1	b. Ogden.	0
Byes, 7; leg byes, 7; wides, 1.	15	Byes, 9; leg byes, 4...	13
Total	210	Total	138

RUNS AT THE FALL OF EACH WICKET.

	1.	2.	3.	4.	5.	6.	7.	8.	9.	10.	11.
1st Innings..	25	84	109	130	136	151	167	167	192	206	210
2nd Innings..	6	18	21	30	66	100	110	119	124	138	138

BOWLING ANALYSIS.

	1st Innings.				2nd Innings.			
	Overs.	Runs.	Mdn's.	W's.	Overs.	Runs.	Mdn's.	W's.
Ogden	31	67	7	3	39	31	24	6
Allan	32.2	55	12	5	14	24	5	3
Lindsey	10	26	2	1	17	36	4	1
Annand	11	20	7	0	14	22	4	0
Shanly	6	21	1	1				
W. W. Jones	7	12	4	1	6	12	2	1

Allan bowled 1 wide.

GENTLEMEN OF CANADA.

1st Innings.		2nd Innings.	
Ogden, l. b. w., b. Bretherton	9	c. Monteath, b. Brooke-Stevens.	26
Little, b. Monteath	51	b. Monteath	2
Allan, b. Bretherton.	26	b. Monteath	1
Henry, b. Brooke-Stevens	17	b. Monteath	8
G. W. Jones, ct. Brooke-Stevens, b. Monteath.	19	b. Bretherton.	3
Carried forward	122	Carried forward	40

GENTLEMEN OF CANADA.

1st Innings.		2nd Innings.	
Brought forward	122	Brought forward	40
Fleury, b. Monteath	3	ct. Ravenscroft, b. Bretherton	20
W. W. Jones, b. Bretherton	2	b. Steen	1
Annand, b. Bretherton	10	not out	17
Vickers, ct. Brooke-Stevens, b. Bretherton	8	ct. Ravenscroft, b. Bretherton	0
T. H. Hodgson, b. Monteath	0	ct. Ravenscroft, b. Brooke-Stevens	2
Lindsey, b. Bretherton	6	to bat	
C. N. Shanly, not out	0	to bat	
Byes, 2; leg byes, 9	11	Byes, 4; l. b., 5; n. b., 1	10
Total	162	Total	90

RUNS AT THE FALL OF EACH WICKET.

	1.	2.	3.	4.	5.	6.	7.	8.	9.	10.	11.
1st Innings	14	60	93	128	134	135	143	148	151	157	162
2nd Innings	9	13	27	30	64	65	65	74	90		

BOWLING ANALYSIS.

	1st Innings.				2nd Innings.			
	Overs.	Runs.	Mdn's.	W's.	Overs.	Runs.	Mdn's.	W's.
Bretherton	33.1	44	15	6	16	28	9	3
Monteath	23	52	5	4	15	35	3	3
Steen	8	27	2	0	5	4	3	1
Brooke-Stevens	8	16	2	1	4.3	13	0	2
Holden	1	12	0	0				

Brooke-Stevens b. 1 n. ball

NORBURY PARK.

When we were at Lord's, Mr. C. I. Thornton had said that Mr. J. W. Hobbs would be glad if we would meet an eleven of his at Norbury Park before leaving for home, an invitation which we had accepted. On the way down to London from Liverpool we saw the names of Mr. Thornton's eleven advertised in *Cricket* as follows: H. R. H. Prince Christian Victor,

Lord Throwley, C. I. Thornton (captain), H. J. H. Scott, C. P. de Paravicini, C. W. Burles, C. E. Cottrell, F. Fielding and W. W. Read, with Bowley and Mills. Weakened as we had been by the loss of nearly all our bowling, we were in a mortal funk, till we learned that the unfinished Surrey-Sussex match would keep the last three mentioned men busy the next day, and our minds grew easier.

Mr. Hobbs' beautiful ground lies in his private park on the left of an artificial lake, and is as level as a billiard table, with the greenest turf we saw in all England; and the wicket, too, is excellent. This gentleman is an enthusiastic supporter of the Surrey County Club, and does much towards securing the professional talent for that eleven.

Lyndhurst Ogden, who had long before promised to play in this match, turned up in time; but we were a man short, and pressed young Aston, the "Parson's" brother into our service, and the game began before a large number of spectators, which, as the day wore on, increased to over a thousand.

Lindsey won the toss, and, of course, took the innings, the most surprising circumstance about which was the uniformity of the scoring. Nearly every man made 20, or thereabouts. Each of the first four wickets got the two decades. Henry got three of them, and the sixth wicket fell at 140. Lindsey and Wallace Jones pulled the score to 160 before we retired to lunch.

A most regal spread awaited us in the dining-room, and we did it ample justice. Mr. Hobbs presided, and on his right sat the Prince and on his left the "Manager." After the health of the Queen, Mr. Thornton called on his eleven to toast us, which they did in bumpers. The "Manager" thanked our host, on behalf of the Gentlemen of Canada, for the pleasurable treat he had given us in asking us to play this match, and proposed his health, which was enthusiastically drank by everyone, and also the health of the opposing eleven, which we drank alone, but none the less cheerfully.

When play was renewed, the rest of our side brought the score to 191, Lindsey being not out, 26.

In ten minutes Thornton and Burls were at the wickets, then hit up 40 in short order. The policy we adopted was to spread our field and wait for catches, which came in every instance but one. The first two wickets Wallace Jones got on hot returns. Scott, the captain of last year's Australian eleven, who we will always remember with pleasure, and in whom as a brother colonial we felt quite an interest, made things lively for some time, but after getting 41, sent one to Aston, who held on to it. Kemp's was the only wicket clean bowled. Prince Christian Victor, after playing steadily for a time, drove one to Lindsey in the long field, and retired. Brown did not stay long, though Cotterell had been doing admirably, till, after making 46, he gave Annand a catch, which was accepted. This, the seventh, wicket fell for 173, or 18 short of our total, and excitement began to run high.

Paravicini joined Partridge, and they added five runs; then Partridge skied one to Fleury in the long field. Eight for 178. Hornsby came in, and was at once caught by Henry at cover, off Allan. The excitement was considerable when Fielding came to the wicket. He played Allan's next ball, but tipped the succeeding one, and George Jones, behind the stumps, accepted the proffered opportunity, and we were left winners by 13 runs.

A spontaneous cheer went up from the large crowd of spectators, and hundreds grouped about the pavilion, blocking our entry, and shouting, "Well done, Canada!" It was largely due to Wallace Jones' bowling that we won the match, he getting five wickets for 52 runs.

It wanted half an hour of time, and, though it was a one-day match, we continued. Allan and George Jones went in again, and made a record in the line of fast scoring, and did it, too, without either of them succumbing. Off twelve overs they made between them 78 runs in 24 minutes, which rapid work the scorers, Lord George Pratt and "Shrimps," said was too fast for them to conveniently tally. Thus ended the tour of The Gentlemen of Canada in England, after one of the pleasantest matches we had played, and one with the result of which we need hardly say we were entirely satisfied.

GENTLEMEN OF CANADA.

1ST INNINGS.		2ND INNINGS.	
Little, b. Scott	25		
G. W. Jones, ct. Prince Christian Victor, b. de Paravicini	20	not out	33
Allan, b. Cotterell	24	not out	44
Fleury, run out	23		
Henry, b. Cotterell	31		
L. Ogden, ct. Burls, b. Paravicini	7		
Annand, ct. and b. Cotterell	4		
W. Aston, b. Brown	1		
W. W. Jones, b. Cotterell	14		
Lindsey, not out	26		
C. N. Shanly, b. Cotterell	0		
Byes, 12; leg byes, 3; wides, 1	16	Byes, 1	1
Total	191	Total	78

RUNS AT THE FALL OF EACH WICKET.

1.	2.	3.	4.	5.	6.	7.	8.	9.	10.	11.
31	68	70	114	122	144	147	147	187	191	191

BOWLING ANALYSIS.

	1ST INNINGS.				2ND INNINGS.			
	Overs.	Runs.	Mdn's.	W's.	Overs.	Runs.	Mdn's.	W's.
Cotterell	25.1	65	6	5	2	14	0	0
Hornsby	6	28	1	0	..	..	..	..
de Paravicini	11	33	3	2	..	..	..	..
Scott	10	26	3	1	5	18	2	0
Brown	15	23	7	1	..	..	..	..
Prince Christian	..	..	..	..	4	29	0	0
Kemp	..	..	..	..	1	16	0	0

Brown bowled 1 wide,

MR. C. I. THORNTON'S ELEVEN.

C. I. Thornton, ct. and b. W. W. Jones	24
C. W. Burls, ct. and b. W. W. Jones	19
H. J. H. Scott, ct. Aston, b. Allan	41
A. F. Kemp, b. Annand	16
C. E. Cotterell, ct. Annand, b. W. W. Jones	46
H. R. H. Prince Christian Victor, ct. Lindsey, b. W. W. Jones	13
Carried forward	159

MR. C. I. THORNTON'S ELEVEN.

Brought forward	159
C. A. Brown, ct. G. W. Jones, b. Annand	4
J. C. Partridge, ct. Fleury, b. W. W. Jones	8
P. de Paravicini, not out	2
H. J. Hornsby, ct. Henry, b. Allan	0
F. Fielding, ct. G. W. Jones, b. Allan	0
Byes, 2; leg byes, 2; wides, 1	5
Total	178

RUNS AT THE FALL OF EACH WICKET.

1.	2.	3.	4.	5.	6.	7.	8.	9.	10.
33	53	84	116	147	153	173	178	178	178

BOWLING ANALYSIS.

	Overs.	Runs.	Mdn's.	W's.
Annand	21	57	2	2
W. W. Jones	19	52	4	5
Allan	8.4	31	1	3
Lindsey	2	21	0	0
Shanly	2	12	0	0

Allan bowled 1 wide.

Chapter XIV.

What became of us.

AFTER our return to London that night, Henry started off for Liverpool where he joined Ogden and Vickers, who, with him played for the local eleven at Hawarden, on Monday, in sight of Mr. Gladstone's home.

Next day we disbanded, and here properly ends the account of the doings of the men. From this time we were no longer the Canadian Cricket team, but mere individuals, and as such our separate histories, though doubtless some incidents in them might be worth recording, are not public property. Still a few words may be necessary to bring our book to a legitimate conclusion, so that our readers who have followed us thus far may not be left in the dark as to whether we ever did get back safely to our native soil, or whether some of us may not still be standing, open-mouthed on Westminster Bridge, endeavouring to solve by mental arithmetic the often submitted problem, "how much is the annual revenue to the Corporation of the City of London from the sale of street sweepings." It requires but a few words to dispose of each with.

Uncle Dyce was already on the sea full of disappointment at having so hastily to return, and well-nigh reduced to utter despair by having a young lady and a couple of fox hounds placed in his charge for the voyage out. On arriving at New York, his relative position to his wards was just reversed, for there he found himself almost in the charge of the fair enslaver, and actually in charge of a United States customs official, by reason of the "dorgs" not having been duly entered before leaving. Our Captain and his good wife, who had become very popular amongst us, sailed a few days later by the *City of Rome*, having, we believe, come to the conclusion that there are many worse ways of spending the last six weeks of a wedding tour than by converting it into a cricket tour through England.

Tannie Gillespie as we said before left us at Liverpool and made for Scotland, where he spent three weeks in trying to climb the genealogical tree, and in endeavoring to discover an infallible formula for testing the remoteness of any individual member of the clan "Gilloosby" from the original "propositus," when given his height and fighting weight. We need not follow Little down to Gloucestershire, nor recount his prowess with the tennis racquet. We blush rather that the mighty should have so greatly fallen as to take to "sister sports." But then as the member from Ottawa explained, he had no one to play cricket with, and when it was insinuated that even a tennis player required an opponent to make a game, he did not altogether concur, at least, he said he didn't call her " an opponent." Nor will we sail with Bob Shanly across the channel to Jersey, and tell how he fairly mowed down the " lilies " there, or flirted under the shade of the native cabbage at the " five o'clocks." Nor yet will we let out the amount in current coin of the realm spent by him on anti-fat when he found his corpulence becoming incompatible with his dignity.

We will not say what Vickers did among the Cheshire hills, nor will we say who walked with him along the old Roman roads where he took his daily stroll. We only know how, after his return, he gave every evidence of having done justice to the dairy products of this wonderful little county. Suffice it to relate that these last four fellows sailed by the *Ethiopia* from Glasgow, on the 15th of September, and arrived home safely after a pleasant voyage.

Bob Ferrie, too, had left the team at Liverpool and returned to Weston, the envied of those of us to whom the jolly dance at " Swiss Villa" and the image of the sweet English face of some fair partner were most pleasant memories. The ruthless " masher," however, seems to have had things all his own way and has embittered our several cups of happiness with gall, by announcing that not one of us stands the ghost of a chance, and that he alone ranks first with them all. But we know better than that.

"Cashmere" had gone to Scotland with his cricket bag and tin uniform case, but we cannot stop even to tell how the "Duke" was accorded a fitting reception by the Highland clans, nor how owing to his military box and stride, he was mistaken for one of Her Majesty's A.D.C's, engaged on the business of Crown, and accordingly saluted with due formalty by a sergeant's guard at York.

Artie Allan left with his spiritual adviser, our "Parson," for a tour through the English lake country, and the latest advices from "his Reverence" lead us to hope that his refractory charge has again settled down to the ways of an average nineteenth century Christian. He will, lucky dog, spend the winter in Italy.

We keep secret what happened to the "Gunner" after he left Norbury Park. His subsequent history is, indeed, to some extent shrouded in mystery. He was heard of as having made some runs for his old club, Penge, about the time that he was expected to join the "Remnant" in their ascent of the Rigi, but the "Gunner" did not come to the scratch, and it was afterwards learned that Surrey contained attractions, or rather an attraction, compared with whom the beauties of Switzerland were to him common place. He even found it impossible to tear himself away in time to come out with the last of the team in the *City of Rome*, and eventually had to "go it alone" by another boat.

Henry's movements after the game at Hawarden are somewhat mysterious, however we are not going to tell tales on "the Villain." He found the metropolis full of interest and can tell more about it than any of us, but he is versatile and easily took a deep concern in New Zealand on the passage home. Born and brought up in the "Village of Halifax," the aboriginal simplicity of the Maoris no doubt raised a fellow feeling in his breast.

We had no special correspondent with the "Remnant," consisting of the two Lindseys, both "barrels of the Jones combination," and the "Rustic," Fleury, on their tour through France, Switzerland, Germany, Belgium and Holland, so cannot give the particulars of the mishap which befel "Biddy" and the "Manager," who found themselves locked out of house and home one night, "quite early, you know," and had to sleep in the *Jardin des Tuilleries*; nor tell how the "G. M." desecrated the shrine of St. Perrier Jouet, or some such Saint, held deservedly high in the estimation of the German people, by purloining from one of their venerable shrines the sacred candle of the day; nor vouch for the circumstance that the "Parsee" and "Shrimps" nearly broke the bank at the *Kursaal de Geneve* one night, and were the next night themselves "dead broke" at the same innocent game of *but*. Nor does our information allow us to describe the *bal des Etudiants*, or how "Shrimps" broke a record there; or how "the Remnant," all but the "Rustic," got strapped in Holland and pleaded for advances in vain, "Biddy" even going so far as to offer his bronze *Milo* as collateral; but the miser was inexorable, and lived like a fighting cock, while the rest starved; or why the "G. M." was taken into custody by a German customs officer because the ace of hearts of the party's whist pack did not bear the official stamp. After some perilous escapes, these tourists all turned up safely in England, and eventually were joined by Ferrie, Henry and Dickson, and sailed together on the *City of Rome* from Liverpool on the 28th of September.

New acquaintances were made by them with some of their fellow passengers, and several touching little incidents occurred on the way out, but these, too, were of a personal nature, so we refrain from giving details. At New York the parting with the "Maritime contingent" was a sad affair, and all hands "blew noses" with unfeigned regret. Many were the expressions of sorrow as the last Canadians shook hands and divided, some setting out for the rising, others in the direction of the setting sun.

The western bound contingent came on to the

Bridge together, where Bob Ferrie, who "knew the ropes" and a custom house officer, said he would manipulate the trunks and save unnecessary bother, and he kept his word as far as his companions were concerned, but, unfortunately for himself, he was taken in hand by a different official, who spotted the Birmingham dog collar and a few more pairs of gloves than any one person would wear in a few years, and promptly marked his luggage "Bond," with a big B, and sent it through to Hamilton in charge of two detectives and a dog.

Ere long all were at their destinations, back to the old station whence not so very long since, though it seemed an age, we had left, cheered by the crowd and followed by the good wishes of our country; back to our own homes, the dearest spots in all this big world, be the others what they may.

Chapter XV.

Valedictory.

To any who have enjoyed the pleasures of the tour of the Gentlemen of Canada, the singing its funeral dirge is a sad task. That it is "over," we have reluctantly to admit, yet we believe that the good it has done is not interred with its bones, but will, phœnix like, rise from the ashes of the past and inaugurate a new era in Canadian Cricket.

That the tour has stimulated the feeling in this country in favor of the game, we have been assured; that it has done much for those who took part in it, a comparison of our scores in sequence will prove, and another season will we trust demonstrate; that it will bring about a more frequent interchange of visits between the old land and the new, there can be no doubt, for it is expected that no less than three elevens, one from each part of the United Kingdom, will visit Canada next year, and again in the following season, the Gentlemen of the North of England are to come.

It was to learn upon the English cricket fields by the lesson of experience the best features of the good

CRICKET ACROSS THE SEA. 217

old game that we went away, and we believe that we have to some extent mastered our task. That we have been immensely benefited by the experience we think there is no doubt; the constant playing could not fail to develop whatever latent talent might exist, while the coming in contact with the finished players of the game at its own home, must of itself have had a general educating effect.

Quite contrary to our expectations we did least in bowling. The wickets did not suit us, though Ogden has a very creditable analysis, one entitling him to high praise. On the other hand our batting which we regarded as our weakest point, turned out to be quite otherwise. Our average of runs is a good one and hardly less than that of our opponents. The leading batting averages are good, and the top scorers well abreast in the race for first place. The great difficulty we had to face was the fastness of the wickets, to which we were altogether unaccustomed, and with which it took us sometime to become familiar. Our fielding was at all times favorably commented on, and was that department of the game in which perhaps we excelled.

We won as many games as we lost, and there were nine unfinished matches. We have no reason to be dissatisfied with our record, and are conscious that we did our best. We suffered from fatigue caused by overwork; too many matches were
14

crowded into too short a time, and we were in no form at all for the earliest of them. They were but preparatory practices to us; for an ocean voyage left us quite unprepared to undertake such games as these without a good week's licking into shape. But as we said we are not dissatisfied, and will know better again, should any of us have the good fortune to have a hand in making the arrangements for the next eleven to visit the mother land.

Cricket is part of the national life of England, and it is only fair to attribute a large measure of our welcome to the desire that the game may someday make the pulse in the colony beat with the same vigorous throb as that which cricket sends to the heart of the English sportsman. To us, as Canadians, too, as part of the English people, much good fellowship was extended. The little bannerettes marked "50 not out," float in this jubilee year on the breeze in every English town as evidence of the loyalty of those who play the game. We believe we were not wanting in enthusiasm on this fiftieth anniversary of the coronation year, and from our hearts sent up to the mast head our jubilee bannerette in honor of our Queen. We wish we could but make the good folk of the mother land know of the depth and breath of our gratitude for their kindness to us. At all times these generous people would rather have had us win than claim victory for themselves, and on all occasions we were most hospitably entertained. We trust we have left impressions behind us which will lead those we were among to think kindly of us.

Working together so long in a common cause brought us closer together in spirit; the far-off Bluenose joined heart as well as hand with his Ontario brother in fighting the same battle, and this welding together of the different cricket communities of the country cannot but have an influence for good. Friendships have been formed which we for our part value as we value life, and when around the winter fire stories are told of all we did "across the sea," those who are there will always have a fond spot in their hearts for absent friends.

CHAPTER XVI.

Summary of Results.

FROM the tables given below a good deal of interesting information can be gleaned. They have been compiled by Mr. R. C. Dickson, the official scorer from his books, with the usual accuracy with which he does matters of this sort, and can be relied on as being quite correct.

RESULTS OF MATCHES.

June 30th and 1st July.—Vs. All New York and Ground—won by 5 wickets (12 aside).
July 14th and 15th.—Vs. Gentlemen of Ireland—lost by an innings and 102 runs.
July 16th.—Vs. Gentlemen of Ireland—won by 5 wickets (on 1st innings).
July 18th and 19th.—Vs. Gentlemen of Scotland—lost by 10 wickets.
July 22nd and 23rd.—Vs. Gentlemen of Northumberland—lost by 211 runs.
July 25th and 26th.—Vs. Gentlemen of Durham—drawn: Durham 281 and 12 for 1 wicket; Canada 184 and 293.
July 27th and 28th.—Vs. Gentlemen of Derbyshire—won by an innings and 40 runs.
July 29th and 30th.—Vs. Gentlemen of Sussex—lost by 9 wickets.
August 1st and 2nd.—Vs. Gentlemen M. C. C.—drawn; M. C. C. 306 and 189; Canada 254 and 139 for 6 wickets.
August 5th and 6th.—Vs. Gentlemen of United Services—drawn; Canada 159 and 267 for 10 wickets; U. S. 351 (12 aside).
August 8th and 9th.—Vs. Gentlemen of Surrey—drawn; Canada 141 and 149 for 2 wickets; Surrey 432.
August 10th and 11th.—Vs. Gentlemen of Hants—drawn; Canada 219 and 211; Hants 225 and 145 for 8 wickets.
August 12th and 13th.—Vs. Gentlemen of Gloucestershire—drawn; Canada 140 and 283; Gloucestershire 239 and 103 for 3 wickets.

CRICKET ACROSS THE SEA. 221

August 15th and 16th.—Vs. Gentlemen of Staffordshire—drawn;
Staffordshire 229 and 145; Canada 313 and 37 for 8 wickets.
August 17th and 18th.—Vs. Gentlemen of Warwickshire –won by
an innings and 25 runs.
August 19th and 20th.—Vs. Gentlemen of Leicestershire—drawn;
Canada 228 and 141; Leicestershire 209 and 40 for 3 wickets.
August 22nd and 23rd.—Vs. Gentlemen of Liverpool and District—
lost by 6 wickets.
August 24th and 25th.—Vs. Gentlemen of Cheshire—drawn; Cheshire
210 and 138; Canada 162 and 90 for 9 wickets (12 aside).
August 27th.—Vs. Mr. C. I. Thornton's Eleven—won by 13 runs (on
1st innings).

BATTING AVERAGES OF THE TEAM.

	No of Matches.	No. of Innings.	Times Not Out.	Runs.	Highest in Innings.	Highest in Match.	Average.
1. W. A. Henry..	19	34	0	879	88	117	25.85
2. D. W. Saunders	16	28	2	613	71*	89	23.58
3. Dr. E. R. Ogden	17	30	0	701	133	160	23.37
4. A. C. Allan....	19	35	6	622	86	113	21.45
5. G. W. Jones...	19	34	1	606	59	103	18.36
6. W. J. Fleury..	9	16	4	206	56*	56	17.17
7. W. C. Little...	19	32	3	431	54	56	14.86
8. A. Gillespie....	17	30	0	392	54	82	13.07
9. W. W. Jones..	18	31	6	234	20	24	9.36
10. C. J. Annand..	18	30	5	212	24	27	8.48
11. W. W. Vickers	16	27	2	185	30*	39	7.4
12. G.G. S. Lindsey	7	9	2	51	26*	26	7.29
13. R. B. Ferrie...	12	19	7	80	27	27	6.67

* Signifies not out.

HOW PUT OUT.

	Times Bowled.	Times Caught.	Times Stumped.	Times Run Out.	Times l.b.w.	Times Hit Wicket.	Times Dismissed for 0.
1. W. A. Henry.	16	16	1	1	0	0	5
✓2. D. W. Saunders	12	10	3	0	1	0	0
3. Dr. E. R. Ogden	19	8	0	2	1	0	4
4. A. C. Allan....	16	10	2	1	0	0	8
5. G. W. Jones...	13	19	0	1	0	0	2
6. W. J. Fleury..	4	5	1	1	1	0	5
7. W. C. Little...	19	9	1	0	0	0	4
8. A. Gillespie. ..	11	10	0	3	5	1	8
9. W. W. Jones...	15	7	0	1	2	0	0
10. C. J. Annand..	9	9	3	2	2	0	6
11. W. W. Vickers.	11	8	1	1	4	0	6
✓12. G. G. S. Lindsey	6	1	0	0	0	0	2
13. R. B. Ferrie...	5	3	4	0	0	0	7

BOWLING ANALYSIS.

	Overs.	Maidens.	Runs.	Wickets.	Average.
Dr. E. R. Ogden.....	817.3	311	1520	91	16.70
A. C. Allan	279.3	84	559	32	17.47
W. W. Jones.........	241.3	78	516	29	17.79
A. Gillespie	669.3	248	1100	59	18.65
C. J. Annand	287.2	66	679	29	23.41
R. B. Ferrie..........	373.1	109	789	32	24.66
✓G. G. S. Lindsey	40.	10	106	4	26.50

CRICKET ACROSS THE SEA.

HOW OPPONENTS WERE OUT.

	Caught.	Bowled.	Caught and Bowled.	Stumped.	Leg before Wicket.
Ogden	53	30	5	2	1
Allan	14	15	2	0	1
Jones, W. W.	19	5	3	1	1
Gillespie	25	27	4	3	0
Annand	14	12	3	0	0
Ferrie	9	22	0	0	1
Lindsey	2	2	0	0	0

Wides—Allan, 3; Ferrie 2.
No balls—Annand, 7.

TOTAL CATCHES MADE BY EACH.

Allan, 11; Annand, 9; Ferrie, 2; Fleury, 8; Gillespie, 16; Henry, 9; Jones, G. W., 17; Jones, W. W., 12; Little, 25; Lindsey, 2; Ogden, 11; Saunders, 18; Vickers, 8. Wicket-keeping—Saunders caught 16 and stumped 7, G. W. Jones caught 6; Henry caught 2.

COMPARATIVE TABLE.

	Gentlemen of Canada.	Opponents.
Completed Innings	26	29
Total wickets lost	318	285
Total Runs made	5676	5656
Average runs per wicket	17.85	19.85
Number of duck eggs	57	34
Extras received	449	312

www.ingramcontent.com/pod-product-compliance
Lightning Source LLC
Chambersburg PA
CBHW020536300426
44111CB00008B/692